GEMS OF CHINESE
LITERATURE

EDITED BY

HERBERT A. GILES

Late Professor of Chinese in the University of Cambridge

IN TWO VOLUMES BOUND AS ONE

VOLUME I—PROSE   VOLUME II—VERSE

PARAGON BOOK REPRINT CORP., NEW YORK

DOVER PUBLICATIONS, INC., NEW YORK

This edition, first published in 1965, is an unabridged republication of the two-volume second
revised and enlarged edition published by Kelly &
Walsh, Inc., in 1923. This edition is a joint publication of Paragon Book Reprint Corp. and Dover
Publications, Inc.

Library of Congress Catalog Card Number: 64–18450

Manufactured in the United States of America

Paragon Book Reprint Corp.   Dover Publications, Inc.
140 East 59th Street   180 Varick Street
New York, N.Y. 10022   New York, N.Y. 10014

TABLE OF CONTENTS

VOLUME ONE.

CHOU AND CH'IN DYNASTIES (6th to 2nd Century B.C.)

CH'ING DYNASTY (A.D. 1644 TO A.D. 1912).

VOLUME TWO.

INDICES.

GEMS OF CHINESE
LITERATURE

EDITED BY

HERBERT A. GILES

Late Professor of Chinese in the University of Cambridge

Volume I — Prose

What work nobler than transplanting foreign thought?
                                                —CARLYLE.

PREFACE TO SECOND EDITION

A SECOND edition of this book has been long overdue, blocked, like many other enterprises, by the war. Its aim will be found fully set forth in the extract, given below, from the preface to the first edition. That edition has been carefully revised, and by many additional translations has been doubled in size and brought down to the present day. Short biographical notices will now be found with all the authors quoted, whose names have further been given in an English-Chinese index, as a means of easy identification by students. Poems have been omitted; they are to appear in a companion volume.

HERBERT A. GILES

December, 1922

EXTRACT FROM PREFACE TO FIRST EDITION

THE present volume is a venture in a new direction. English readers will search in vain for any work leading to an acquaintanceship, however slight, with the general literature of China. Dr. Legge's colossal labours have indeed placed the canonical books of Confucianism within easy reach of the curious; but the immense bulk of Chinese authorship is still virgin soil and remains to be efficiently explored.

I have therefore ventured to offer an instalment of short extracts from the works of the most famous writers of all ages, upon which time has set an approving seal. These are chronologically arranged, and cover a period extending from 550 B.C. to A.D. 1650—two thousand two hundred years. Short biographical and dynastic notices will be found scattered through the volume in their proper places; also such brief foot-notes as seemed to me necessary to the occasion.

"Untold treasures," says Professor G. VON DER GABELENTZ, "lie hidden in the rich lodes of Chinese literature." Now without committing myself to exaggeration or misdirection as to the practical value of these treasures, I dare assert that the old pride, arrogance, and exclusiveness of the Chinese are readily intelligible to any one who has faithfully examined the literature of China and hung over the burning words of her great writers. I do not flatter myself that all the extracts given will be of equal interest to all readers. I have not catered for any particular taste, but have striven to supply a small handbook of Chinese literature, as complete as circumstances would permit.

In the process of translation I have kept verbal accuracy steadily in view, so that the work may be available to students of Chinese in one sense as a key. But with due regard to the requirements of a general public, impatient of long strings of unpronounceable names and of allusions which for the most part would be shorn of all meaning and point, I have eliminated these, wherever it was possible to do so without obscuring or otherwise interfering with the leading idea in the text. I have also been compelled sometimes to expand and sometimes to compress;—on the one hand, by an extreme grammatical terseness, intelligible enough in the original; on the other, by a redundancy of expression, which, while offering wide scope for literary *tours de force* (compare Psalm cxix.), contrasts strangely with the verbal condensation aforesaid. It must however always be borne in mind that translators are but traitors at the best, and that translations may be moonlight and water while the originals are sunlight and wine.

H. A. G.

16*th October*, 1883.

NOTE ON CHINESE LITERATURE

THE CHOU AND CH'IN DYNASTIES: 550–200 B.C.

THE texts of this period may be described as rude and rugged in style, but full of vigorous expression, and unmatched in dramatic power. Many scenes in the *Tso Chuan* are brought as vividly before the mind of the reader as are the incidents of the *Iliad* and *Odyssey*. Unfortunately, such excellences depend upon something beyond the reach of a translator, who has to be content with a barely approximate result.

In poetry, excluding the *Odes*, we have the beautiful but in some cases terribly obscure *Rhapsodies*, chiefly from the pen of CH'Ü P'ING, who might not inaptly be compared with PINDAR in diction and wealth of words. In philosophy, the subtle speculations of MO TI, YANG CHU, and CHUANG TZŬ, the great exponent of the doctrines enunciated by LAO TZŬ, would beyond all doubt have commanded a hearing in the contemporary schools of Greece.

THE HAN DYNASTY: 200 B.C. TO A.D. 200.

The literature of the Hans reflects the stateliness of the age. It is further distinguished by a tone of practical common sense, strikingly and logically expressed. The meanings of words were still however by no means accurately fixed, neither had the written language reached that degree of stylistic polish it was ultimately destined to acquire. Consequently, the scrupulous translator often finds himself involved in a maze of impossible collocations, from which he has to extricate himself by the clue of logic alone. Yet it was under such conditions that SSŬ-MA CH'IEN—truly named the Herodotus of China—committed to writing his most splendid history, and CH'AO TS'O drew faithful conclusions from long and elaborately worded premises.

The poetry of the period may be dismissed as wanting in that essential which differentiates poetry from didactic verse. The philosophers of the day occupied themselves chiefly in editing and commenting upon the sacred books. Their interpretations were duly accepted for many centuries until at length doomed to pale in the flood of a brighter light. (See *Chu Hsi*). This was also the age of forgery on a grand scale, extending even to the end of the 3rd century A.D. To the labours of forgers of this time we are probably indebted for the bulk of the *Tao Tê Ching*, the work of LIEH TZŬ, many chapters of CHUANG TZŬ, etc.

THE SIX DYNASTIES: A.D. 200–600.

This period was virtually an interregnum, an age of literary stagnation.   Though covering no fewer than four centuries, it produced but one really great writer, in consequence, probably, of the disturbed and unsatisfactory state of public affairs, so unfavourable to the development of literary talent.   It was during these years that Buddhism took the firm grip upon the religious susceptibilities of the Chinese people which it holds at the present day.

THE T'ANG DYNASTY: A.D. 600–900.

With the final establishment of the above dynasty authorship rapidly revived.   It was the epoch of glittering poetry (untranslatable, alas!), of satire, of invective, of irony, and of opposition to the strange and fascinating creed of Buddha.   Imagination began to come more freely into play, and the language to flow more easily and more musically, as though responsive to the demands of art.

THE SUNG DYNASTY: A.D. 960–1200.

This was admittedly the Elizabethan age of Chinese literature. More great writers in all branches flourished under this than under any other dynasty before or since.   Their styles are massive and grand, without grammatical flaw, exquisitely cadenced, and thrilling the reader with an inexpressible thrill.   They exhibit to perfection what the Rev. ARTHUR SMITH, a most accurate writer on Chinese topics, calls "an indescribable loftiness of style, which resembles expression in music."

The poetry of the age is second only to that of the T'angs. The historians rank with, but after, their famous predecessor of the Han dynasty.   But CHU HSI swept away the existing interpretations of Confucianism, and established his own for ever.

THE YUAN AND MING DYNASTIES: A.D. 1260–1644.

Under the Yuan (Mongol) and Ming dynasties, literary execution remained stationary as regards accuracy of structure and balance of sentences.   Imaginative power became visibly weaker, to decline later on to a still lower level of rule-and-line mediocrity.   These two dynasties have been bracketed together; partly because it is impossible to say exactly when the Mongol dynasty either began or ended, and partly because the dates so far assigned have been more nominal than exact. Further, the Mongols, detested aliens, held sway for such a comparatively short period that they hardly left any characteristic mark on the face of Chinese literature.

THE CH'ING (MANCHU) DYNASTY: A.D. 1644–1912.

The first edition of this book ended with the collapse of the Ming dynasty and the establishment of Manchu rule. I then contented myself by saying that the literature of the present dynasty has hardly passed beyond the limits of essayism and artificial verse. The book-market is flooded with collections of essays and poems on themes chosen from the sacred books, logically worded and correctly constructed, but wanting in the chief feature of the work of genius —originality of thought. Still from a literary point of view, there have been not a few elegant composers both of poetry and of prose. Chief among these we may reckon LAN LU-CHOU, author of the *Whole Duty of Woman*, and of a vast number of essays on a variety of subjects; also TSENG KUO-FAN, the hero of the T'ai-p'ing rebellion, and father of the present Ambassador to Western Powers. As an actual specimen of the best style of modern composition, I may draw the reader's attention to the Chinese preface, in *cursiv-schrift*, which adorns the cover of the first edition of this book. It was very kindly written for me by a rising young graduate of Foochow, named NIEN YUN-TING, through the medium of my friend, Mr. KU HUNG-MING (M.A., Edinburgh), to whose wide acquaintance with the literatures and philosophies of China, England, France, Germany, and Ancient Greece and Rome, I am indebted for many luminous suggestions. This preface runs as follows:—

"For sixteen years past I have been a diligent student of the language and literature of the Chinese people. I have now attempted to render into the English tongue specimens of their standard authors of past ages, in the hope that my countrymen may thereby learn something of the literary achievements of a great empire, whose inhabitants held learning in high esteem when our own painted forefathers were running naked and houseless in the woods and living on berries and raw meat." [1]

In this second edition I have included extracts from the two writers mentioned above, as well as others from the pens of distinguished men of this dynasty, down to quite recent times, concluding with specimens of the matter and style of a brilliant Republican author

---

[1] "My poor friend, the young master of arts who indited the preface for your *Gems*, is dead, and has not left his peer."—*Letter of 12th August* 1883.

and statesman who is still working for his country's good. It is usual
to make light of Manchu scholarship; perhaps because of the ease
with which they were allowed to obtain the coveted degrees. I have
not been able to insert any specimen of Manchu style or imagination
in the following collection; it should always be remembered, however,
that the two Emperors, K'ANG HSI and CHIEN LUNG, by their
production of most important works of reference,—the standard
lexicon of the Chinese language, more than one huge encyclopædia,
an enormous dictionary of literary phraseology of all ages, new
editions of classical and historical works, etc., etc.—have placed
Chinese scholars, native and foreign, under a deeper obligation than
all the other Emperors of China put together.

GEMS
OF CHINESE LITERATURE

THE DUKE OF CHOU

DIED 1105 B.C.

[The following is not a translation; it is not even an ordinary paraphrase. It is an attempt to give the spirit of an ancient document by picking out the more interesting sentences and stringing them together, omitting such portions as would require long explanations and be wearisome to the general reader. Dr. Legge has given in his Chinese Classics, vol. III, p. 399, a full translation with copious notes. It only remains to add that the Duke of Chou was a younger son of King Wên, the founder and posthumously first ruler of China under the feudal system which lasted for eight hundred years; and that this edict was issued by order of the Duke's elder brother and second actual sovereign, reigning as King Ch'êng.]

AGAINST DRUNKENNESS

THUS saith the King:—"Make known these important commands in the State of Mei.

"When our great and good father, King Wên, laid the foundations of our empire in the west, daily and nightly he warned his officials, saying, 'For sacrifice you may use wine.' And whenever God has favoured the people, it has been because wine was in use only at the great sacrifices. But whenever God has sent down His terrors, and the people have become disorganized and have lost their moral balance, this has always been due to indulgence in wine. So too when States, small and great alike, have similarly suffered, misuse of wine has always been the cause of their downfall.

"Hearken, then, to these instructions, all you high officers and others! When you have done your duty in ministering to your parents and serving your sovereign, then you may drink and eat until you are tipsy and replete. Again, when after constant examination and a course of virtuous conduct you have ministered with sacrifices to the spirits, then you may proceed to indulge yourselves with festivity. Thus, you will be serving your sovereign, God will approve of your great virtue, and you will never be forgotten by the royal House.

"The drunkenness of the last ruler of the House of Yin, and of his creatures, caused the resentment of the people to be heard on high; and God sent down calamity on Yin, because of these excesses God is not cruel; people bring punishment on themselves.

"It is not a pleasure to me to issue these numerous commands. The ancients had a saying, 'A man should not seek to see himself in water, but as reflected in other people.' Ought we not then to look back to the House of Yin, which has now perished, in order to secure repose for our own times?

"If persons congregate together to drink, let them all be seized and sent to me at the capital; I will put them to death. Those officers of the House of Yin who have always been accustomed to drink may be exempted from this penalty. Let them be taught; and then, if they obey, they may be allowed to enjoy distinction. Otherwise, I will show no pity.

LAO TZŬ

7TH AND 6TH CENTURIES B.C.

[Lao Tzŭ was a great Teacher whose birth has been assigned to various ages, of which 604 B.C. has perhaps the best claim. Legend has gathered around his name, and it has even been stated that he was the son of a virgin. He is known to the Chinese as the author of a number of remarkable sayings which have been preserved in the writings of ancient philosophers and which were brought together and issued, with a large amount of absurd padding, in the form of a book—the so-called *Tao Tê Ching*—possibly as early as the Second Century B.C. He is regarded as the founder of Taoism, the doctrine of the WAY.]

THE goodness of *doing* good is not real goodness.

When merit has been achieved, do not take it to yourself; for if you do not take it to yourself, it shall never be taken from you.

By many words wit is exhausted; it is better to preserve a mean.

Keep behind, and you shall be put in front; keep out, and you shall be kept in.

He who grasps more than he can hold, would be better without any; he who strikes with a sharp point, will not himself be safe for long.

Good words shall gain you honour in the market-place; but good deeds shall gain you friends among men.

To see oneself is to be clear of sight.

He who knows how to shut, uses no bolts,—yet you cannot open; he who knows how to bind, uses no ropes,—yet you cannot undo.

He who does not desire power nor value wealth,—though his wisdom be as a fool's, shall he be esteemed among men.

He who, conscious of being strong, is content to be weak,—he shall be a cynosure of men.

A great principle cannot be divided.[1]

The empire is a divine trust; it may not be ruled. He who rules ruins; he who holds it by force, loses it.

Mighty is he who conquers himself.

If you would contract, you must first expand. If you would weaken, you must first strengthen. If you would take, you must first give.

Fishes cannot be taken from water; the instruments of government cannot be delegated to others.

If the WAY prevails on earth, horses will be used for agriculture; if not, war-horses will breed in camp.[2]

To the good I would be good. To the not-good I would also be good,—in order to make them good.

In governing men and in serving God, there is nothing like moderation.

Govern a great nation as you would cook a small fish.

Recompense injury with kindness.

Desire not to desire, and you will not value things difficult to obtain.

---

[1] You must not approbate and reprobate.
[2] No campaign will ever end.

K'UNG FU-TZŬ

(*Latinized into* CONFUCIUS.)

B.C. 551–479.

[Confucius was the Socrates of China. He taught virtue for its own sake, unsupported by reference to the supernatural, any reliance upon which he steadily, though indirectly, condemned. He seems, however, to have thoroughly believed in a God; but whether as a force moral, or a force moral, or both, it is quite impossible to decide. Under no circumstances can he be regarded as the founder of a "religion" in the ordinary sense of the term, with a priesthood, sacraments, dogmas, etc.; though what is now called "Confucianism" was actually based in pre-Confucian days on revelation.

Confucius held several official appointments, and finally rose to be chief Minister of Justice in his native State. He "became the idol of the people, and flew in songs through their mouths." But by the intrigues of a neighbouring prince, he found himself compelled to resign office, and went into voluntary exile, wandering from place to place, and employing himself in literary pursuits, until at length he returned home, where death came upon him in the seventy-third year of his age.

He was an editor rather than an author. He collected and edited the ancient national songs now known as the *Odes*. He arranged and edited those old records which form the *Canon of History*. It is claimed by Mencius that he compiled the annals of his own State (but see *Yüan Mei*), dating from some 200 years previous to the times in which he lived. His discourses were treasured up in the hearts of his disciples, and were committed to writing in later years.]

EXTRACTS FROM THE DISCOURSES

THE Master said—

A plausible tongue and a fascinating expression are seldom associated with true virtue.

A youth should be filial at home, respectful abroad. He should be earnest and truthful. He should overflow in love to all, but cultivate the friendship of the good. Then, whatsoever of energy may be left to him, he should devote to the improvement of his mind.

Let loyalty and truth be paramount with you. Have no friends not equal to yourself. If you have faults, shrink not from correcting them.

Learning without thought is labour lost. Thought without learning is intellectual death.

The study of the supernatural is injurious indeed.

Yu! shall I teach you in what true knowledge consists? To know what you do know, and to know what you do not know—that is true knowledge.

A man without truthfulness!—I know not how that can be.

In mourning, it is better to be sincere than to be punctilious.

He who offends against God[1] has none to whom he can pray.

Riches and honours are what men desire; yet except in accordance with right these should not be enjoyed. Poverty and degradation are what men dread; yet except in accordance with right these should not be avoided.

The faults of men are characteristic of themselves. By observing a man's faults you may infer what his virtues are.

If a man hear the Truth in the morning, he may die in the evening without regret.

Chi Wên thought thrice and then acted. The Master said, Twice will do.

Man is born to be upright. If he be not so, and yet live, he is lucky to have escaped.

Those who know the Truth are not equal to those who love it; nor those who love it to those who delight in it.

A disciple having asked for a definition of charity,[2] the Master said LOVE ONE ANOTHER! Having further asked for a definition of knowledge, the Master said, KNOW ONE ANOTHER!

The Master said—

Rare are they who prefer virtue to the pleasures of sex.

The commander-in-chief of an army may be carried captive, but the convictions even of the meanest man cannot be taken from him.

A disciple having enquired about serving the spirits of the dead, the Master said, You are not even able to serve living men. How then should you serve spirits? Having further enquired about death, the Master said, You do not even understand life. How then should you understand death?

---

[1] Understood down to A.D. 1200 by the masses as an anthropomorphic Being, resident in the sky and in control of the four elements; but subsequently explained by Chu Hsi, the most famous of all commentators, as "abstract Right."

[2] In its theological sense. *See* I Corinthians, xiii, Authorized Version. Since this volume was first published, the Revised Version has substituted "love" in all cases.

The Master said—

In hearing litigations, I am like any one else.   I differ, in wishing to prevent these litigations.

Some one asked Confucius, saying, Master, what think you concerning the principle that good should be returned for evil?   The Master replied, What then will you return for good?   No: RETURN GOOD FOR GOOD; FOR EVIL, JUSTICE.

A disciple having asked for a rule of life in a word, the Master said, Is not *Reciprocity* that word?   WHAT YOU WOULD NOT OTHERS SHOULD DO UNTO YOU, DO NOT UNTO THEM! [1]

When his stable was burnt down, Confucius left the Court and said, "Has any man been hurt?"   He did not ask about the horses.

A feudal noble said to Confucius, "The villagers of my State are upright men.   If a father steals a sheep, his son will give evidence against him."   Confucius replied, "The uprightness of the villagers in my State is different from that.   A father will shield his son, and a son will shield his father.   This is what I call uprightness." [2]

---

[1] An attempt has been made to show that this is after all only a negative (and therefore comparatively worthless) enunciation of the Golden Rule as expressed positively by Christ.   The worthlessness, if any, lies in the terms of such an argument. For instance, you would not that others should abstain from helping you in trouble. Therefore you do not abstain from helping them in trouble.   Consequently, you help them ; thus doing unto others what you would they should do unto you.

[2] It may be interesting to compare a recent case, in London, of a man accused of harbouring his son, a deserter from the army.

The man said that his son had been in the house only a week, and he could not drive him out.

Mr. Boyd.—You should have informed the police.

The accused.—I should never have heard the last of it from my family.

Mr. Boyd.—I appreciate that you were in a difficult position, but it is a serious offence.   You must pay £10 or go to prison for six weeks.

TSO-CH'IU MING

PROBABLY 4TH AND 5TH CENTURIES B.C.

[Very little is known of this writer, whose very name is a matter of doubt. His important work, the *Tso Chuan*,[1] was a so-called commentary on the Annals of the Lu State, mentioned on p. 4. Those annals consisted of bald statements of the principal events which took place in the successive years of each prince's reign. Tso-ch'iu Ming supplemented these by detailed accounts of the various incidents alluded to; and thus we have a vivid panorama of the wars and treaties, the intrigues and dissensions, the loves and hates, of China's feudal age. The style of the work is grand in the extreme, and is a perfect repertory of Chinese proverbs and familiar household words.]

THE BATTLE OF CH'ANG-CHŎ

In the tenth year of his reign, in spring, in the first moon, Duke Chuang defeated the army of the Ch'i State at Ch'ang-Chŏ.—*Annals.*

THE State of Ch'i having declared war against us, our duke was about to give battle, when a man named Kuei begged for an audience. Kuei's clansmen had said to him, "The authorities will decide upon the proper strategy; what place will there be in their counsels for you?" To which Kuei had replied, "They are but a poor lot, and have no idea whatever of deep-laid plans."

Accordingly, Kuei was admitted to see the duke, and at once enquired, saying, "On the strength of what is your Highness about to fight?" "I have never monopolized the comforts of food and raiment," replied the duke; "I have always shared with others." "That," said Kuei, "is a small favour, extending only to a few. The people will not rally round you on that account alone." "Then," continued the duke, "in the sacrifices to the Gods I have trusted more to earnestness of heart than to costly displays." "That again," objected Kuei, "is an insufficient basis. The Gods will not bless your arms on that account alone." "And in all judicial investigations," added the duke, "though oft-times unable to ascertain the precise truth, I have always given my decision in accordance with the evidence before me." "Ha!" cried Kuei; "so far you have done your duty to the people, and you may risk a battle on that. I myself pray to be allowed to accompany your Highness." To this the duke acceded, and took Kuei with him in his own chariot.

---

[1] This title has been taken by some to mean literally "Helping Commentary," and the work has been attributed to Confucius himself.

The battle was fought at Ch'ang-chŏ; and on sighting
the enemy our duke would have forthwith given orders to
beat an attack, but Kuei said "Not yet!" Only when the
enemy's drums had sounded thrice did Kuei shout out,
"Now!"

Our victory was complete; and the duke would
promptly have given orders to pursue, had not Kuei again
said, "Not yet!" The latter then alighted and examined
the tracks of the enemy's chariot-wheels; after which he
got up on the hand-rail in front, and following the flying
foe with his eye, cried out, "Now!" Thereupon the order
was given to pursue.

When the battle had been gained, our duke asked Kuei
for an explanation of his tactics. "A battle," replied Kuei,
"depends wholly upon the martial ardour of the combatants.
At the first roll of the drum, that ardour is violently excited;
with the second, it begins to flag; with the third, it is
exhausted. Now, when the enemy's ardour was at this
last stage, ours was at its highest pitch: therefore we
conquered them. Still, against a formidable foe, one should
be prepared for anything. I feared an ambuscade; but I
found that their wheel-tracks were in evident disorder. I
then looked at their standards, and saw that these also were
in confusion. Therefore I gave the word to pursue."[1]

BURNING A WIZARD

[Twenty-first year of Duke Hsi :—In summer there was a great drought.—*Annals.*]

Thereupon the duke wished to burn a wizard; but his
chief minister said to him, "That will avail nothing against
the drought. Rather mend the city walls; diminish
consumption; be economical; and devote every energy to

[1] My first acquaintance with the sacred books of China was through the medium
of Dr. Legge's translations ; and when I subsequently came to make free use of native
commentaries, I could not but be impressed by the strict verbal accuracy of his
renderings, especially in regard to the *Tso Chuan.* To this rule there are necessarily
exceptions, of a more or less serious character ; but their grand total would be wholly
insufficient to cast a shadow upon that which is truly a monument more lasting than
brass. Sir Thomas Wade, whose scholarship was of a vastly inferior order, characterized
Legge's work as "wooden." His own rendering of "The *Lun Yü*, being Utterances of
Kung (*sic.!*) Tzŭ," is beneath contempt.

gathering in the harvest. This is the proper course to take: what can a wizard do for you? If God now desires his death, he might as well have never been born. And if he can cause a drought, to burn him would only make it worse."

The duke followed this advice; and in the ensuing season, although there was distress, it was not very bad.

HOW YEN-TZŬ WOULD NOT DIE WITH HIS PRINCE

[Twenty-fifth year of Duke Hsiang:—In the fifth moon, in summer, Ts'ui of the Ch'i State, slew his prince.—*Annals.*]

Duke Chuang committed adultery with Ts'ui-tzŭ's wife, and Ts'ui-tzŭ slew him. Thereupon Yen-tzŭ planted himself at the door of the latter's house.

"Are you going to die with your prince," cried his attendants. "Was he my prince only?" asked Yen-tzŭ, "that I alone should die." "Will you flee the country?" said the attendants. "Was his death my crime, that I should flee?" asked Yen-tzŭ. "Will you then go home?" enquired the attendants. "Where," said Yen-tzŭ, "is there a home for him whose master is dead? It is not enough for a prince to be merely above the people; the commonwealth is in his hands. It is not enough for a minister merely to draw his pay; the commonwealth is his trust. Therefore, when the prince dies for the commonwealth, his minister dies with him; when the prince flees, his minister flees also. But if a prince dies or flees in consequence of matters which concern only himself, who, save his own private associates, can be expected to share his fate? Besides, if some one else, under obligations similar to my own, slays the prince, why should I die, why flee, why go home?"

By-and-by, the door was opened and Yen-tzŭ went in; and, pillowing the corpse upon his lap gave vent to tears. He then arose, and striking the ground three times with his heel, went out. People advised Ts'ui-tzŭ to put him to death; but Ts'ui-tzŭ replied, "He is a popular man, and to leave him in peace will be to win over the people."

Ts'ui now placed another duke upon the throne, and became his chief minister, Ch'ing Fêng being appointed minister of the Left. And when the people were taking the oaths of allegiance in the State temple, beginning, "May those who are not true to Ts'ui and Ch'ing——," Yen-tzŭ, looking up to heaven, sighed and said, "May I, in whatsoever I do not submit to those who are loyal to the prince and true to the commonwealth, be answerable to God!" He then smeared his lips with the blood.

A TUNNEL

[In 721 B.C., the mother of Duke Chuang of the Ch'ing State conspired against him, with a view to put her younger son on the throne. The plot failed.]

Then the Duke placed his mother under restraint, swearing to her the following oath:—"Until we meet in the Underworld, I will not look upon you again,"—an oath of which he shortly repented. Later on, one of the frontier officials, who had heard the story, came to pay his respects. The Duke entertained him with a meal, and noticed that he put aside a portion of the meat served to him. On the Duke asking him why he did so, the official replied, "Your servant has a mother, who always shares his food; she has never tasted your Grace's meat, and I beg to be allowed to keep some for her." The Duke said, "Ah, you have a mother to whom you can give things; alas! I have no mother." The official ventured to ask how this could be; and the Duke told him, adding that he now repented of his oath. "This need not trouble your Grace," said the official. It will be necessary only to dig down to the Underworld and form a tunnel in which the meeting can take place. Who shall say that this is not in accordance with your oath?" The Duke agreed, and entered the tunnel singing,

> Herein we find
> Our peace of mind,

while his mother came in singing,

> Without, no more
> Was joy in store,

and thus they became mother and son as before.

LIEH TZŬ

[An imaginary philosopher, said by Chuang Tzŭ (*q.v.*) to have been able to "ride upon the wind and dispense with walking," and generally regarded as a creature of Chuang Tzŭ's own brain. The small work from which the following extracts are taken, was written up some centuries later. It is in a pseudoarchaic style, and is not wanting in interest.]

REST

TZŬ KUNG said to Confucius, "Master, I am aweary, and would fain have rest."

"In life," replied the sage, "there is no rest."

"Shall I, then, never have rest?" asked the disciple.

"You will," said Confucius. "Behold the tombs which lie around; some magnificent, some mean. In one of these you will find rest."

"How wonderful is Death!" rejoined Tzŭ Kung. "The wise man rests, the worldly man is engulfed therein."

"My son," said Confucius, "I see that you understand. Other men know life only as a boon: they do not perceive that it is a bane. They know old age as a state of weakness: they do not perceive that it is a state of ease. They know death only as an abomination: they do not perceive that it is a state of rest.

"How grand," cried Yen Tzŭ, "is the old conception of Death! The virtuous find rest, the wicked are engulfed therein. In death, each reverts to that from which he came. The ancients regarded death as a return to, and life as an absence from, home. And he who forgets his home becomes an outcast and a by-word in his generation."

DREAM AND REALITY

A man of the State of Chêng was one day gathering fuel, when he came across a startled deer, which he pursued and killed. Fearing lest any one should see him, he hastily concealed the carcass in a ditch and covered it with plantain-leaves, rejoicing excessively at his good fortune.

By-and-by, he forgot the place where he had put it; and, thinking he must have been dreaming, he set off towards home, humming over the affair on his way.

Meanwhile, a man who had overheard his words, acted upon them, and went and got the deer. The latter, when he reached his house, told his wife, saying, "A woodman dreamt he had got a deer, but he did not know where it was. Now I have got the deer; so his dream was a reality." "It is you," replied his wife, "who have been dreaming you saw a woodman. Did he get the deer? and is there really such a person? It is you who have got the deer: how, then, can his dream be a reality?" "It is true," assented the husband, "that I have got the deer. It is therefore of little importance whether the woodman dreamt the deer or I dreamt the woodman."

Now when the woodman reached his home, he became much annoyed at the loss of the deer; and in the night he actually dreamt where the deer then was, and who had got it. So next morning he proceeded to the place indicated in his dream,—and there it was. He then took legal steps to recover possession; and when the case came on, the magistrate delivered the following judgment: — " The plaintiff began with a real deer and an alleged dream. He now comes forward with a real dream and an alleged deer. The defendant really got the deer which plaintiff said he dreamt, and is now trying to keep it; while, according to his wife, both the woodman and the deer are but the figments of a dream, so that no one got the deer at all. However, here is a deer, which you had better divide between you."

When the Prince of Chêng heard this story, he cried out, "The magistrate himself must have dreamt the case!" So he enquired of his prime minister, who replied, "Only the Yellow Emperor and Confucius could distinguish dream from reality, and they are unfortunately dead. I advise, therefore, that the magistrate's decision be confirmed."

WHY CONFUCIUS WAS SAD

Confucius was one day sitting at leisure, when Tzŭ Kung went in to attend upon him. The disciple noticed that his master wore a sorrowful air; but not venturing to ask the reason, went out and told Yen Hui. Thereupon Yen Hui seized his guitar and began to sing; at which Confucius called him in and said, "Hui, why are you alone glad?" "Master," retorted Hui, "why are you alone sorrowful?" "First answer my question," said Confucius. "I once heard you declare," explained Yen Hui, "that he who was contented with his lot and prepared for the appointments of destiny, could not be sorrowful. Accordingly, I am glad."

The master's expression for a moment changed. Then he answered, saying, "I did use those words. But you are misapplying them here. Such utterances are of the past. Rather adopt those which I deliver now. Alas! you know only the superficial principle that he who is contented with his lot and prepared for the appointments of destiny cannot be sorrowful. You do not perceive the deeper sorrow entailed by this very absence of sorrow. I will tell you all.

"You cultivate yourself. You accept success or failure as they may come. You see that life and death are independent of your efforts. You maintain your moral and mental equilibrium. And you consider that under such conditions of contentment and preparedness you are without sorrow.

"Now, I edited the *Odes* and the *Book of History*. I defined the functions of Music and Ceremonial. I did this in order to benefit the whole earth, and to be a guide for posterity. I did not do it merely for my own personal advantage, nor for that of my own individual State. But now, even in my own State, the obligations between prince and subject are forgotten; charity and duty to one's neighbour are passing away; and right feeling is all but gone. If then the truth cannot prevail for a brief space in a single State, how is it likely to prevail over the whole earth through all generations to come? I know now that all I have achieved is in vain; and I am utterly at a loss to discover the true remedy. Therefore I am sad."

MO TI

4TH AND 5TH CENTURIES B.C.

[A philosopher of the Sung State, who flourished in the days between Confucius and Mencius, and who propounded a doctrine of "universal love," in opposition to the "selfish" school of Yang Chu, as the proper foundation for organized society. He showed that under such a system all the calamities which men bring upon one another would altogether disappear, and that the peace and happiness of the Golden Age would be renewed. He was vigorously denounced by Mencius, who exhibited the unpractical side of an otherwise fascinating doctrine. See *Liang Ch'i-ch'ao*.]

LOVE ONE ANOTHER.—I

THERE are two men, one of whom discriminates in his love for his fellows; the other loves all men equally. The former argues, "I cannot feel for my friends so strongly as I feel for myself, neither can I feel for my friend's parents so strongly as I feel for my own parents." As a consequence of this, he may see his friend hungry, and will not feed him; he may see him cold, and will not clothe him; he may see him sick, and will not nurse him; he may see him dead, and will not bury him. Not so the latter; he will not argue thus nor will he act thus, but he will say, "He who wishes to attain distinction among men, will feel for his friend as he feels for himself, and for his friend's parents as for his own." Therefore, when he sees his friend hungry, he will feed him; cold, he will clothe him; sick, he will nurse him; and dead, he will bury him. Such will be the language of one who loves all men equally, and such will be his behaviour.

LOVE ONE ANOTHER.—II

Of old, Duke Wên liked his soldiers to wear coarse clothes; and therefore all his Ministers wore sheepskin robes, leather sword-belts, and caps of rough silk, both when having audience and when on duty at Court. Why did they do this?—The Duke liked it, and therefore his Ministers did it.

Of old, Duke Ling liked his soldiers to have small waists; and therefore his Ministers made it their rule to have only one meal a day. They drew in their breath before buckling on their belts; they held on to the wall to help themselves to get up; and by the end of a year they were all in danger of turning black from starvation. Why did they do this?— The Duke liked it, and therefore his Ministers did it.

Of old, Prince Kou Chien liked his soldiers to be brave, and instructed his Ministers to train them accordingly. When they had followed out these orders, the Prince set fire to a ship in order to test the soldiers, crying out, "All our State jewels are on board!" He then beat the Drum for advance; and when the soldiers heard its irregular rattle, they rushed headlong to trample out the fire, about a hundred men losing their lives in the attempt, whereupon the Prince beat the gong for retreat.

Now, to achieve fame by scanty food, or coarse clothes, or loss of life, is repugnant to the feelings of people in general; but if they are ready to face such trials merely to gratify their sovereign, how much more could they not achieve if stimulated by mutual love and by mutual interests?

DIVINE VENGEANCE

If we do not do that which God wishes us to do, but do that which God wishes us not to do, then God too will not do that which we wish Him to do, but will do that which we wish Him not to do. What are those things which men wish not to suffer?—disease, misfortune, and bewitchment. Now, if we do not do what God wishes us to do, but do that which He does not wish us to do, we shall drag the myriad people of the empire along with us into misfortune and bewitchment.

KUNG-YANG KAO

5TH AND 4TH CENTURIES B.C.

[A commentator on the Annals of the Lu State, said to have been compiled by Confucius. Nothing is known of his life. On the authorship of the Annals, see *Yüan Mei.*]

THE MARQUIS OF CHI MADE A GREAT EXODUS [1]

WHAT is meant by a Great Exodus?—Extinction.

Who extinguished?—The Ch'i State extinguished.

Then why not say Ch'i extinguished?—To avoid the name of Duke Hsiang of Ch'i. In such cases in the Annals, the name of a good man is always omitted.

What goodness was there in Duke Hsiang? He avenged an injury.

What injury?—Owing to slander by the then Marquis of Chi, a distant ancestor of his had been boiled alive at the suzerain's capital;[2] and what Duke Hsiang did on this occasion was actuated by an overwhelming sense of duty to the manes of this ancestor.

How many generations back was this ancestor?—Nine generations.

May an injury be avenged even after nine generations? —It may be avenged even after one hundred generations.[3]

---

[1] To save his people from the horrors of war. The commentator Ku-liang Ch'ih (*q.v.*) says "he did not leave a single man behind him," which can only mean that his partisans and retainers followed him, as he handed over the feudal throne to a brother. The State of Chi was ultimately absorbed by the victors.

[2] In 893 B.C. The present entry refers to 689 B.C.

[3] The principle of the blood-feud has been attributed to Confucius ; but the attribution has only been found in works—the Book of Rites and the Family Sayings—neither of which, certainly not the latter, as possessing the stamp of authenticity.

KU-LIANG CH'IH

4TH AND 5TH CENTURIES B.C.

[Author of another commentary upon the Annals said to have been compiled by Confucius. Nothing is known of his life except that he was a pupil of one of the disciples of Confucius, who was born 507 B.C. Even his personal name is differently given as Shu and Ch'ih.]

PRAYING FOR RAIN

PRAYERS for rain should be offered up in spring and summer only; not in autumn and winter. Why not in autumn and winter? Because the moisture of growing things is not then exhausted; neither has man reached the limit of his skill. Why in spring and summer? Because time is then pressing, and man's skill is of no further avail. How so? Because without rain just then nothing could be made to grow; the crops would fail, and famine ensue. But why wait until time is pressing, and man's skill of no further avail? Because prayers for rain are the same as asking a favour, and the ancients did not lightly ask favours. Why so? *Because they held it more blessed to give than to receive;* and as the latter excludes the former, the main object of man's life is taken away. How is praying for rain asking a favour? It is a request that God will do something for us. The divine men of old who had any request to make to God, were careful to prefer it in due season. At the head of all his high officers of State, the prince would proceed in person to offer up his prayer. He could not ask any one else to go as his proxy.[1]

---

[1] A commentator adds, "If we are not to ask favours of God, how much less may we ask them of one another. Persons who recklessly ask favours, should not be treated with the consideration to which they would otherwise be entitled."

YANG CHU

4TH CENTURY B.C.

[A heterodox thinker who taught the doctrine of *egoism*, as opposed to the *altruism* of Mo Tzŭ (*q.v.*), also a dissenter from Confucianism pure and undefiled. Yang Chu has left us no book. His views, as given below, are taken from chapter VII of the work ascribed to Lieh Tzŭ (*q.v.*), the authenticity of which has already been discussed under the name of its alleged author. These views are supposed to be stated in the actual words of Yang Chu, and at any rate may be held to represent adequately the opinions of the great egoist.]

IS LIFE WORTH LIVING?

A HUNDRED years are the extreme limit of human life,—an age which not one in a thousand attains.

Let us take the case of a man who does. His helpless infancy and his helpless old age will together occupy nearly half the time. Pain and sickness, sorrow and misfortune, actual losses and opportunities missed, anxieties and fears, —these will almost fill up the rest. He may possibly have some ten years or so to the good; but even then he will hardly enjoy a single hour of absolute serenity, undarkened by the gloom of care. What, then, can be the object of human existence? Wherein is happiness to be found?

In the appointments of wealth and luxury? Or in the enjoyment of the pleasures of sense? Alas! those will not always charm, and these may not always be enjoyed.

Then again there is the stimulus of good report, there is the restraint of law, in things we may do and in things we may not do. And thus we struggle on for a breath of fame, and scheme to be remembered after death; ever on our guard against the allurements of sense, ever on the watch over our hearts and actions. We miss whatever of real happiness is to be got out of life, never being able even for a single moment to relax the vigilance of our heed. In what do we differ, indeed, from the fettered captives of a gaol?

The men of old knew that with life they had come but for a while, and that with death they would shortly depart again. Therefore they followed the desires of their own hearts, and did not deny themselves pleasures to which they felt naturally inclined. Fame tempted them not; but led by their instincts alone, they took such enjoyments as lay in their path, not seeking for a name beyond the grave. They were thus out of the reach of censure; while as for precedence among men, or length or shortness of life, these gave them no concern whatever.

A disciple asked Yang Chu, saying, "Here is a man who values his life, and loves his body so that he may escape death; is that possible?" "We know," replied Yang Chu, "that there is no one who does not die." "So that he may obtain a very long life," said the enquirer; "is that possible?" "We know," replied Yang Chu, "that no one has a very long life. Life cannot be kept by being valued, nor can the body be strengthened by being loved. Moreover, what will long life do for you? The five passions, with love and hate, are still with us, as of old. Comfort and discomfort of our four limbs are still with us, as of old. The miseries and pleasures of this life are still with us, as of old. The changes of good government and rebellion are still with us, as of old. And since these things are actually heard and seen and do alternate, even a hundred years seem too many; how much more miserable would be a still further prolongation of life?" To this the enquirer rejoined, "If this is so, then a short life would be better than a long one, an end which could be reached by falling on a spear or a sword, by water or by fire." "Not so," answered Yang Chu; "once you are born, regard life as a disease, and bear it, following the desires of your heart until death comes; being about to die, regard death as a disease, and bear it, following its lead until there is an end of you. Life and death should both be regarded as diseases, and both should be borne as such; why worry about slowly or quickly in these matters?"

EGOISM v. ALTRUISM

Yang Chu said, A certain man would not part with a single hair in order to benefit any one. He turned his back on his country and went into retirement, occupying himself with agriculture. The Great Yü (*see* below), who did not employ himself for his own advantage, became paralysed on one side. The men of old, if by losing one hair they could advantage the empire, would not give it; but all would offer the whole body, which was not wanted. If no man ever lost a single hair, and no man ever advantaged the empire, the empire would enjoy good government. An enquirer then asked Yang Chu, saying, "If by sacrificing a single hair *you* could help the world, would you do it?" "The world," replied Yang Chu, "could most certainly not be helped by a single hair." "But if it could," urged the enquirer, "would you do it?" To this, Yang Chu returned no answer, and the enquirer took his leave.

SELF-SACRIFICE

Yang Chu said, The admiration of the empire is for Shun, Yü, Chou,[1] and Confucius; its detestation, for Chieh and Chou.[1]

Shun was engaged in ploughing and in making pottery. His four limbs never knew a moment's rest; his palate was never tickled and his belly never full; his parents ceased to love him, and his brothers and sisters ceased to care for him. He had lived for thirty years before he asked his parents' leave to be married; and when Yao resigned the throne to him (2255 B.C.[2]), he was already old, his mind was impaired, and his son was worthless, so he handed on the throne to Yü and dragged out a melancholy existence until the end. Here was a divine man who exhausted all the poisons of this life.

When K'un failed to reduce the waters of the flood[3] and was put to death, Yü (his son), ignoring the question of vengeance, took over the task and worked at it with great

---

[1] These two words are quite distinct in Chinese; in speech, they are differently toned; and in writing, the characters used are differently formed.

[2] Since the discovery of the inscribed bones and their interpretation by Lo Chên-yü and L. C. Hopkins, these early dates are no longer regarded as legendary.

[3] A more or less local catastrophe, which has been foolishly identified with Noah's flood.

energy. A son was born to him, but he had no time to care for it; he even passed his own door without going into the house. He was paralysed on one side; his hands and feet became hard and horny; when he received the throne from Shun (2205 B.C.), his palace was a humble cottage, though his State regalia was magnificent; and thus he dragged out a melancholy existence until the end. Here was a divine man whose life was sorrowful and wretched.

After the death of the Martial King, his heir being a child, Duke Chou became Regent (1122 B.C.). One of the feudal nobles was aggrieved, and mutterings were heard throughout the Four States. The Duke had to stay in the east; he killed his elder brother and banished his younger brother; [1] and then he dragged out a melancholy existence until the end. Here was a divine man whose life was full of dangers and alarms.

Confucius (551–479 B.C.) preached the doctrines of the rulers of old, and took service under the princes of his day. In the Sung State, the tree under which he was preaching was cut down; in the Wei State, his traces were obliterated; in the Shang and Chou States, he was reduced to want; in the Ch'ên and Ts'ai States, he was in danger of his life; he had to take rank below Chi, whose chief Minister insulted him; and thus he dragged out a melancholy existence until the end. Here was a divine man whose life was all hurry, without a moment's leisure.

All these four holy men failed to get a single day's enjoyment out of life. Dead, their fame will last for ten thousand generations; but they will get no reality out of that. Though praised, they do not know it; though rewarded, they do not know it—any more than if they were logs of wood or clods of clay.

Chieh (1818 B.C.) inherited vast wealth and enjoyed the dignity of the throne. He had wit enough to enable him to hold in check his officials, and power enough to make

---

[1] Out of loyalty to the reigning house.

himself feared within the empire. He gave himself over to the lusts of the ear and of the eye; he carried out to the uttermost every fanciful scheme, and had a glorious time until the end. Here was a divine[1] man whose life was all pleasure and dissipation.

Chou (1154 B.C.) likewise inherited great wealth, and enjoyed the dignity of the throne. His power enabled him to do anything, and he might have gratified any ambition. He indulged his passions with his concubines, spending long nights in such revelry. He did not bother about rites and ceremonies or his duties, and had a glorious time until he was slain.[2]

These two scoundrels had every pleasure in life that they wished to have. Dead, they will be branded as fools and tyrants; but they will get no reality out of that. Though reviled, they do not know it; though praised, they do not know it;—what difference is there between these two and logs of wood or clods of clay?

Those four holy men, although objects of admiration to all, suffered miseries throughout their lives and then died like everybody else. Those two scoundrels, although objects of detestation to all, enjoyed themselves throughout their lives and also died like everybody else.

---

[1] As being the vice regent of God. Defeated in battle, he was banished 1766 B.C. and died three years later.

[2] Defeated in battle, he perished in the flames of his own palace.

CHUANG TZŬ

4TH CENTURY B.C.

[A most original thinker, of whom the Chinese nation might well be proud. Yet his writings are tabooed as heterodox, and are very widely unread, more perhaps on account of the extreme obscurity of the text than because they are under the ban of the Confucianists. What little is known of Chuang Tzŭ's life may be gathered from some of the extracts given. He is generally regarded as an advanced exponent of the doctrines of Lao Tzŭ. So late as the 4th century A.D., the work of Chuang Tzŭ appears to have run to fifty-three chapters. Of these, only thirty-three now remain; and several of them are undoubtedly spurious, while into various other chapters, spurious passages have been inserted.]

LIFE, DEATH, AND IMMORTALITY

I.

FOUR men were conversing together, when the following resolution was suggested:—"Whosoever can make Inaction the head, Life the backbone, and Death the tail, of his existence,—that man shall be admitted to friendship with us." The four looked at each other and smiled; and tacitly accepting the conditions, became friends forthwith.

By-and-by, one of them, named Tzŭ-yü, fell ill, and another Tzŭ-ssŭ, went to see him. "Verily God is great!" said the sick man. "See how he has doubled me up. My back is so hunched that my viscera are at the top of my body. My cheeks are level with my navel. My shoulders are higher than my neck. My hair grows up towards the sky. The whole economy of my organism is deranged. Nevertheless, my mental equilibrium is not disturbed." So saying, he dragged himself painfully to a well, where he could see himself, and continued, "Alas, that God should have doubled me up like this!"

"Are you afraid?" asked Tzŭ-ssŭ. "I am not," replied Tzŭ-yü. "What have I to fear? Ere long I shall be decomposed. My left shoulder may become a cock, and I shall herald the approach of morn. My right shoulder will become a cross-bow, and I shall be able to get broiled duck. My buttocks will become wheels; and with my soul for a horse, I shall be able to ride in my own chariot. I obtained life because it was my time; I am now parting with it in accordance with the same law. Content with the natural sequence of these states, joy and sorrow touch me not. I am simply, as the ancients expressed it, hanging in the air, unable to cut myself down, bound with the trammels of material existence. But man has ever given way before God: why then, should I be afraid?"

By-and-by, another of the four, named Tzŭ-lai, fell ill, and lay gasping for breath, while his family stood weeping around. The fourth friend, Tzŭ-li, went to see him. "Chut!" cried he to the wife and children; "begone! you balk his decomposition." Then, leaning against the door, he said, "Verily God is great! I wonder what he will make of you now. I wonder whither you will be sent. Do you think he will make you into a rat's liver[1] or into the shoulders of a snake?"

"A son," answer Tzŭ-lai, "must go whithersoever his parents bid him. Nature is no other than a man's parents. If she bid me die quickly, and I demur, then I am an unfilial son. She can do me no wrong. She gives me form here on earth; she gives me toil in manhood; she gives me repose in old age; she gives me rest in death. And she who is so kind an arbiter of my life, is necessarily the best arbiter of my death.

"Suppose that the boiling metal in a smelting-pot were to bubble up and say, 'Make of me an Excalibur'; I think the caster would reject that metal as uncanny. And if a sinner like myself were to say to God, 'Make of me a man, make of me a man'; I think he too would reject me as uncanny. The universe is the smelting-pot, and God is the caster. I shall go whithersoever I am sent, to wake unconscious of the past, as a man wakes from a dreamless sleep."

II.

How do I know that love of life is not a delusion? How do I know that those who fear death are not mere lost lambs which cannot find their way back to the fold?

---

[1] The Chinese believe that a rat has no liver.

A daughter of the Governor of Ai, when first captured by the Chins, saturated her robe with tears; but afterwards, when she went into the prince's palace and lived with him on the fat of the land, she repented having wept. And how do I know that the dead do not now repent their former craving for life?

One man will dream of the banquet hour, but wake to lamentation and sorrow. Another will dream of lamentation and sorrow, but wake to enjoy himself in the hunting-field. While men are dreaming, they do not perceive that it is a dream. Some will even have a dream in a dream; and only when they awake do they know that it was all a dream. And so, only when the Great Awakening comes upon us, shall we know this life to be a great dream. Fools believe themselves to be awake now.[1]

III.

Chuang Tzŭ one day saw an empty skull, bleached, but still preserving its shape. Striking it with his riding-whip, he said, "Wert thou once some ambitious citizen whose inordinate yearnings brought him to this pass?—some statesman who plunged his country in ruin and perished in the fray?—some wretch who left behind him a legacy of shame?—some beggar who died in the pangs of hunger and cold? Or didst thou reach this state by the natural course of old age?"

When he had finished speaking, he took the skull, and placing it under his head as a pillow, went to sleep. In the night, he dreamt that the skull appeared to him and said, "You speak well, Sir; but all you say has reference to the life of mortals, and to mortal troubles. In death there are none of these. Would you like to hear about death?"

Chuang Tzŭ having replied in the affirmative, the skull began:—"In death, there is no sovereign above, and

---

[1] "To any one who objects that all we see, hear, feel and taste, think and do, during our whole being, is but the series and deluding appearances of a long dream, and therefore our knowledge of anything be questioned; I must desire him to consider that, if all be a dream, then he doth but dream that makes the question."—LOCKE.

no subject below. The workings of the four seasons are unknown. Our existences are bounded only by eternity. The happiness of a king among men cannot exceed that which we enjoy."

Chuang Tzŭ, however, was not convinced, and said, "Were I to prevail upon God to allow your body to be born again, and your bones and flesh to be renewed, so that you could return to your parents, to your wife, and to the friends of your youth,—would you be willing?"

At this, the skull opened its eyes wide and knitted its brows and said, "How should I cast aside happiness greater than that of a king, and mingle once again in the toils and troubles of mortality?"[1]

IV.

Life is a state which follows upon Death. Death is a state which precedes Life. Which of us understands the laws that govern their succession?

The life of man is the resultant of forces. The aggregation of those forces is life: their dispersion, death. If, then, Life and Death are but consecutive states of existence, what cause for sorrow have I?

And so it is that all things are but phases of unity. What men delight in is the spiritual essence of life. What they loathe is the material corruption of death. But this state of corruption gives place to that state of spirituality, and that state of spirituality gives place in turn to this state of corruption. Therefore, we may say that all in the universe is comprised in unity; and therefore the inspired among us have adopted unity as their criterion.

THE DEATH OF LAO TZŬ

When Lao Tzŭ died, and Ch'in Shih went to mourn,[2] the latter uttered three yells and departed.

---

[1] Reminding us strangely of *Hamlet*.
[2] Of course only in the Taoist sense—*i.e.*, more to take note of the death than for purposes of condolence, etc.

A disciple asked him, saying, "Were you not our Master's friend?" "I was," replied Ch'in Shih. "And if so, do you consider that was a fitting expression of grief at his loss?" added the disciple. "I do," said Ch'in Shih. "I had believed him to be the man (*par excellence*), but now I know he was not. When I went in to mourn, I found old persons weeping as if for their children, young ones wailing as if for their mothers. And for him to have gained the attachment of these people in this way, he too must have uttered words which should not have been spoken, and dropped tears which should not have been shed, thus violating eternal principles, increasing the sum of human emotion, and forgetting the source from which his own life was received. Such emotions are but the trammels of mortality. The Master came, because it was his time to be born; he went, because it was his time to die. For those who accept the phenomenon of birth and death in this sense, lamentation and sorrow have no place. Death is but the severance of a thread by which a man hangs suspended in life. Fuel can be consumed; but the fire endureth for ever."

THE DEATH OF CHUANG TZŬ'S WIFE

When Chuang Tzŭ's wife died, Hui Tzŭ went to condole. He found the widower sitting on the ground, singing, with his legs spread out at a right angle, and beating time on a bowl.

"To live with your wife," exclaimed Hui Tzŭ, "and see your eldest son grow to be a man, and then not to shed a tear over her corpse,—this would be bad enough. But to drum on a bowl, and sing; surely this is going too far."

"Not at all," replied Chuang Tzŭ. "When she died, I could not help being affected by her death. Soon, however, I remembered that she had already existed in a previous state before birth, without form, or even substance; that while in that unconditioned condition, substance was added to spirit; that this substance then assumed form; and that the next stage was birth. And now, by virtue of a further change, she is dead, passing from one phase to another like the sequence of spring, summer, autumn, and winter. And while she is thus lying asleep in Eternity, for me to go about weeping and wailing would be to proclaim myself ignorant of these natural laws. Therefore I refrain."

ON HIS OWN DEATH-BED

When Chuang Tzŭ was about to die, his disciples expressed a wish to give him a splendid funeral. But Chuang Tzŭ said, "With Heaven and Earth for my coffin and shell; with the sun, moon, and stars as my burial regalia; and with all creation to escort me to the grave,— are not my funeral paraphernalia ready to hand?" [1]

"We fear," argued the disciples, "less the carrion kite should eat the body of our Master;" to which Chuang Tzŭ replied, "Above ground, I shall be food for kites; below, I shall be food for molecrickets and ants. Why rob one to feed the other?

"If you adopt, as absolute, a standard of evenness which is so only relatively, your results will not be absolutely even. If you adopt, as absolute, a criterion of right which is so only relatively, your results will not be absolutely right. Those who trust to their senses become, as it were, slaves to objective existences. Those alone who are guided by their intuitions find the true standard. So far are the senses less reliable than the intuitions. Yet fools trust to their senses to know what is good for mankind, with alas! but external results.

---

[1] Compare the following lines by Mrs. ALEXANDER, from *The Burial of Moses :*—
And had he not high honour ?—
  The hillside for his pall ;
To lie in state while angels wait
  With stars for tapers tall ;
And the dark rock pines like nodding plumes
  Above his bier to wave,
And God's own hand in that lonely land
  To lay him in the grave.

HOW YAO WISHED TO ABDICATE

The great Yao begged Hsü-yu to become Emperor in his stead, saying, "If, when the sun and moon are shining brightly, you persist in lighting a torch, is not that misapplication of fire? If, when the rainy reason is at its height, you still continue to water the ground, is not that waste of labour? Now, sir, do you assume the reins of government, and the empire will be at peace. I am but a dead body, conscious of my own deficiency. I beg you will ascend the throne."

"Ever since you, sire, have directed the administration," replied Hsü-yu, "the empire has enjoyed tranquillity. Supposing, therefore, that I were to take your place now, should I gain any reputation thereby? Besides, reputation is but the shadow of reality; and should I trouble myself about the shadow? The tit builds its nest in the mighty forest, and occupies but a single twig. The tapir slakes its thirst from the river, but drinks enough only to fill its belly. To you, sire, belongs the reputation: the empire has no need for me. If a cook is unable to dress the sacrifices, the boy who impersonates the corpse may not step over the wines and meats and do it for him."

INFERENCE

Chuang Tzŭ and Hui Tzŭ had strolled on to the bridge over the Hao, when the former observed, ' 'See how the minnows are darting about! That is the pleasure of fishes."

"You not being yourself a fish," said Hui Tzŭ, "how can you possibly know in what the pleasure of fishes consists?"

"And you not being I," retorted Chuang Tzŭ, "how can you know that I do not know?"

"That I, not being you, do not know what you know," replied Hui Tzŭ, "is identical with my argument that you, not being a fish, cannot know in what the pleasure of fishes consists."

"Let us go back to your original question," said Chuang Tzŭ. "You ask me how I know in what consists the pleasure of fishes. Your very question shows that you knew I knew. I knew it from my own feelings on this bridge."

INDEPENDENCE

Chuang Tzŭ was one day fishing, when the Prince of Ch'u sent two high officials to interview him, saying that his Highness would be glad of Chuang Tzŭ's assistance in the administration of his government. The latter quietly fished on, and without looking round, replied, "I have heard that in the State of Ch'u there is a sacred tortoise, which has been dead three thousand years, and which the prince keeps packed up in a box on the altar in his ancestral shrine. Now do you think that tortoise would rather be dead and have its remains thus honoured, or be alive and wagging its tail in the mud?" The two officials answered that no doubt it would rather be alive and wagging its tail in the mud; whereupon Chuang Tzŭ cried out "Begone! I too elect to remain wagging my tail in the mud."

THE PERFECT MAN

The perfect man is like a spirit. Were the ocean to be scorched up, he would not be hot. Were the Milky Way to be fast frozen, he would not feel cold. Of thunder which rives mountains, of wind which lashes the sea, he is not afraid; and thus, charioted on the clouds of heaven, or riding on the sun and moon, he journeys beyond the limits of mortality. Exempt from the changes of life and death, how much more is he beyond the reach of physical injury. The perfect man can walk under water without difficulty; he can touch fire without being burnt.[1]

---

[1] Compare the foolish taunts of Reid and Beattie, who asked Bishop Berkeley why "he did not run his head against a post, walk over precipices, etc.; as, in accordance with his theory, no pain, no broken limbs could result."—LEWES' *Hist. of Philos.* II., p. 287.

DRUNKENNESS

A drunken man who falls out of a cart, though he may suffer, yet will not die. His bones are jointed like those of other people, but he meets the accident under different conditions. His mental equilibrium is undisturbed. Unconscious of riding in the cart, he is equally unconscious of falling out of it. The ordinary ideas of life, death, and fear, find no place in his breast; consequently, when thrown into collision with matter, he is not afraid. And if a man can thus get perfect mental equilibrium out of wine, how much more should he do so out of the resources of his own nature? It is there that the wise man takes refuge; and there no one can injure him. To those who would wreak vengeance upon him, he opposes neither spear nor shield; nor does he heed the brick which some spiteful enemy may hurl at his head.

ARCHERY

Lieh Yü-k'ou instructed Poh-hun Wu-jên in archery. Drawing the bow to its full, he [the teacher] placed a cup of water on his elbow and began to let fly. Hardly was one arrow out of sight ere another was on the string, the archer all the time standing like a statue. Poh-hun Wu-jên cried out, "This is shooting under ordinary conditions; it is not shooting under extraordinary conditions. Now I will ascend a high mountain with you, and stand on the edge of a precipice a thousand feet in depth, and see if you can shoot like this then." Thereupon Wu-jên went with his teacher up a high mountain, and stood on the edge of a precipice a thousand feet high, approaching it backwards until one-fifth of his feet overhung the chasm, when he beckoned Lieh Yü-k'ou to come on. But Yü-k'ou had fallen prostrate on the ground, with the sweat pouring down to his heels.

CAUSALITY

The Penumbra said to the Umbra, "At one moment you move: at another you are at rest. At one moment you sit down: at another you get up. Why this instability of purpose?"

"I depend," replied the Umbra, "upon something which causes me to do as I do; and that something depends upon something else which causes it to do as it does. My dependence is like that of a snake's scales or a cicada's wings (which do not move of their own accord). How can I tell why I do one thing or do not do another."

DREAM AND REALITY

Once upon a time I dreamt I was a butterfly, fluttering hither and thither, to all intents and purposes a butterfly. I was conscious only of following my fancies (as a butterfly), and was unconscious of my individuality as a man. Suddenly, I awaked; and there I lay, myself again. I do not know whether I was then dreaming I was a butterfly, or whether I am now a butterfly dreaming that it is a man. Between a man and a butterfly there is necessarily a barrier; and the transition is called *Metempsychosis*.

CH'Ü-P'ING

4TH CENTURY B.C.

[A famous poet and minister of one of the feudal princes. Being unjustly dismissed from favour, he committed suicide by drowning, and his death gave rise to an annual spring festival, known as the Dragonboat Festival, at which an imaginary search for his body is made in every available stream of water throughout the Eighteen Provinces.]

CONSULTING THE ORACLE

THREE years had elapsed since Ch'ü-p'ing [1] was dismissed from office, and still he was unable to obtain an audience of his prince. His fervent loyalty had been intercepted by the tongue of slander. He was broken in spirit and knew not whither to direct his steps. In his doubt he repaired to the Chief Augur and asked for a response. The Chief Augur thereupon arranged the divining-grass and wiped the tortoise-shell, saying, "What, sir, are the points on which you desire to be enlightened?"

"Tell me," cried Ch'ü-p'ing, "whether I should steadily pursue the path of truth and loyalty, or follow in the wake of a corrupt generation. Should I work in the fields with spade and hoe, or seek advancement in the retinue of a grandee? Should I court danger by outspoken words, or fawn in false tones upon the rich and great? Should I rest content in the cultivation of virtue, or practise the art of wheedling women in order to secure success? Should I be pure and clean-handed in my rectitude, or an oily-mouthed, slippery, time-serving sycophant? Should I hold on my course like an impetuous charger, or oscillate, with the indecision of a duck in a pool, to and fro as self-interest commands? Should I yoke myself a fellow in the shafts with Bucephalus, or shamble along by the side of Rozinante? Should I vie with the wild goose in soaring to heaven, or scramble for food on a dunghill with hens? Of these alternatives I would know which to choose. The age is muddy and will not be made clean. The wing of the cicada outweighs a thousand pounds. The priceless goblet is set aside

---

[1] This use of the third person is common in Chinese Literature.

for the delf cup.   Flatterers fill high places: men of worth
are ignored.   Alas! who is there that knows my worth?"

The Chief Augur gathered up his divining apparatus
and saluted Ch'ü-p'ing, saying, "A foot is oft-times too
short; an inch, too long.   The implements of my art are
not adequate to your requirements.   Think for yourself,
and translate your thoughts into action.   The divining-grass
and the tortoise-shell would avail you naught."

THE FISHERMAN'S REPLY

When Ch'ü-p'ing was dismissed, he wandered away to
the banks of a river, and there poured forth his soul in verse.
His colour changed.   His body wasted to a skeleton.

One day a fisherman accosted him, saying, "Are you
not his Excellency the Prime Minister?   What has brought
you to this pass?"

"The world," replied Ch'ü-p'ing, "is foul; and I alone
am clean.   There they are all drunk, while I alone am sober.
So I am dismissed."

"Ah!" said the fisherman, "the true sage does not
quarrel with his environment, but adapts himself to it.   If,
as you say, the world is foul, why not leap into the tide and
make it clean?   If all men are drunk, why not drink with
them, and teach them to avoid excess?   Of what avail
are these subtle thoughts, these lofty schemes, which end
only in disgrace?"

"I have heard," rejoined Ch'ü-p'ing, "that the bather
fresh from the bath will shake the dust from his hat and
clothes.   How should he allow his pure body to be soiled
with the corruption of earth?   I am willing to find a grave
in the bellies of the fishes that swim in this stream: I will
not let my purity be defiled by the filth and corruption of
the world."

The fisherman laughed, and keeping time with his oar,
sculled off, singing,—

My tassel I'll wash if the water is sweet;
If the water is muddy 'twill do for my feet.

THE GENIUS OF THE MOUNTAIN

Methinks there is a Genius of the hills, clad in wistaria, girdled with ivy, with smiling lips, of witching mien, riding on the pard, wild cats galloping in the rear, reclining in a chariot, with banners of cassia, cloaked with the orchid, girt with azalea, culling the perfume of sweet flowers to leave behind a memory in the heart.   But dark is the grove wherein I dwell.   No light of day reaches it ever.   The path thither is dangerous and difficult to climb.   Alone I stand on the hill top, while the clouds float beneath my feet, and all around is wrapped in gloom.

Gently blows the east wind: softly falls the rain.   In my joy I become oblivious of home; for who in my decline would honour me now?

I pluck the larkspur on the hillside, amid the chaos of rock and tangled vine.   I hate him who has made me an outcast, who has now no leisure to think of me.

I drink from the rocky spring.   I shade myself beneath the spreading pine.   Even though he were to recall me to him, I could not fall to the level of the world.

Now booms the thunder through the drizzling rain. The gibbons bowl around me all the long night.   The gale rushes fitfully through the whispering trees.   And I am thinking of my prince, but in vain; for I cannot lay my grief.[1]

---

[1] The above translation of what is more correctly a song has been versified and published without a word of acknowledgement by Mr. Cranmer-Byng in his "Lute of Jade" (which has been called a "Loot of Jade"), p. 32, as follows :—

Methinks there is a genius
Roams in the mountains,
Girdled with ivy
And robed in wisteria (sic), etc., etc.

SUNG YÜ

3RD AND 4TH CENTURIES B.C.

[Nephew of the famous Ch'ü P'ing, and like his uncle a statesman and a poet. His poems are included among the "Rhapsodies of Ch'u."]

WIND

KING Hsiang of the Ch'u State was strolling in the palace on the Epidendrum Terrace, with Sung Yü and Ching Ch'a in attendance. A breeze suddenly got up, causing the king to draw his robe across his breast as a protection. "The air bites shrewdly," he said; "do I, the sovereign and my people feel it alike?" Sung Yü replied, "This breeze belongs to your Majesty alone; how could the people share it?" "But wind," said the king, "is a vivifying principle of the universe; it is universally exhilarating, and it does not distinguish in its favours between those who are honoured and exalted and those who are humble and lowly. You, sir, just now spoke as if the breeze belonged personally to me, the sovereign. How is this so?" "I have learnt from my teacher," answered Sung Yü, "that forks in the mulberry-tree invite nests and that hollows and holes invite wind, the reason in each case being the different qualities of wind." "But where does wind come from?" asked the king. "Wind," replied Sung Yü, "is produced on the earth, and rises from the tips of the green duckweed leaves; it rushes wildly through ravines and valleys, and roars loudly in large holes. Climbing the slopes of Mt. T'ai, it dances beneath the pines and the cypresses, with streams of whirling water, with angry flashes of flying flames and peals of booming thunder. Now, back to the holes while blowing from every quarter, flinging about stones, breaking off the ends of branches and destroying the undergrowth of the forest.

"Then, when it begins to abate, after having scattered far and wide the beauty of foliage, it rushes into hollows and rattles door-bars, while a brightness is diffused around as now it calms down and now it comes again. Therefore this pure cool virile wind is wafted about, up and down; it mounts the lofty city walls and enters far into the palace; it touches flowers and leaves, and stimulates their vitality; it wanders among the cinnamon and pepper-trees, and soars round and round over the rolling waters; it strikes at the spirit of the hibiscus; it robs the orchid and scatters the asaram; it levels the magnolia and shrivels the poplar. Returning to its lair, it plays havoc with artemisia and other fragrant plants; it moves to and fro in the court-yard, or northwards to the Jade Hall, where it runs up the silk curtains and passes into the nuptial chamber. That is why it is called the sovereign's wind.

"The effect of this wind upon those who are in it, is to make them look sad, and chilled, even to sobbing. Pure and fresh, it cures disease and sobers the drunk; it sharpens one's sight and hearing; it gives repose to the body and comfort to the man; and thus it is called the virile wind of the sovereign."

"Well put, indeed," said the king. "Now can you tell me about the wind of the people." "The wind of the people," replied Sung Yü, "rises with a gust in the slums. It sweeps up clouds of dust from holes; suddenly roused, it brings troubles, piercing through crevices and attacking doors; it disturbs graves and blows about dead ashes; it throws everything into confusion, whirling along rotten flesh and other horrors, until at last it passes through the jar-mouth windows and so into the rooms of the cottage.

"The effect of this wind upon those who are in it, is to make them altogether dull and full of anxiety, driving out warmth and engendering dampness and distressful emotions. It breeds disease and produces fevers; affecting the lips, it causes sores; reaching the eyes, it makes them red; it harasses by a racking cough, so that people care nothing whether they live or die; and thus it is called the feminine wind of the people."

UNPOPULARITY

The Prince of Ch'u said to his prime minister,[1] "What have you done that should cause the officers and people of this State to abuse you so clamorously?"

"Abuse me indeed they do," replied the minister; "but pardon my boldness, and I will explain. A stranger was singing in one of our villages the other day, and this was the subject of his lay:—There is the music of the masses; there is the music of a narrower circle; that of a narrower circle still; and lastly, the classical music of the cultured few. This classical music is too lofty, and too difficult of comprehension, for the masses.[2]

"Among birds there is the phœnix: among fishes, the leviathan. The phœnix soars aloft, cleaving the red clouds, with the blue firmament above it, away into the uttermost realms of space. But what can the poor hedge-quail know of the grandeur of heaven and earth? The leviathan rises in the morning in one ocean to go to rest at night in another. But what can the minnow of a puddle know of the depth of the sea?

"And there are phœnixes and leviathans, not only among birds and fishes, but among men. There is the Sage, full of nervous thought and of unsullied fame, who dwells complacently alone.—What can the vulgar herd know of me?"

---

[1] *Sc.* to the writer.

[2] It is vulgarly believed that the Chinese have no music—worthy the name. That they had what they themselves were pleased to call music, a thousand years before Christ, is beyond all doubt; and an idea of its æsthetic value may be gathered from the following extracts from the *Tso Chuan* (see p. 7):—
They sang to him the Odes of Chou. "Admirable!" said he; "this is the expression of earnest endeavour, without any resentment."
They sang to him the Odes of P'ei. "Admirable!" said he; "here are those who sorrow, and yet are not distressed."
They sang to him the Odes of Pin. "Admirable!" said he; "they are expressive of enjoyment without license."
They sang to him the Odes of Wei. "Admirable!" said he; "what harmony! Here is grandeur with delicacy, like a defile, dangerous, yet easily traversed."
Their ancient music, however, disappeared, and with it the Canon of Music which was formerly included among the Six Classics (now Five), at some period subsequent to the campaign of Alexander the Great in Central Asia. The music of Greece took its place; "cette fille ailée," said Professor Chavannes, "du génie hellenique erra jusque chez les Chinois qui furent émerveillés de sa beauté, mais qui ne surent pas lui conserver sa pureté native."

T'AN KUNG

3RD AND 4TH CENTURIES B.C.

DIVORCE

WHEN Tzŭ-shang's mother died, he would not attend her funeral. A disciple asked his father, Tzŭ-ssŭ (grandson of Confucius), saying, " Did not your father attend his divorced mother's funeral?" "He did," replied Tzŭ-ssŭ. " Then why cannot you make Tzŭ-shang do likewise? " rejoined the disciple. " My grandfather," said Tzŭ-ssŭ, " was a man of complete virtue. With him, whatever was, was right. I cannot aspire to his level. As long as the deceased was my wife, she was my son's mother. When she ceased to be my wife, she ceased also to be his mother."

From that time forth, it became a rule among the descendants of Confucius not to attend the funeral of a divorced mother.

THE BURIAL OF CONFUCIUS

A certain man travelled from afar to witness the funeral obsequies of Confucius. He stayed at the house of Tzŭ-hsia, who observed, "A sage conducting a funeral is one thing: a sage's funeral is another thing. What did you expect to see? Do you not remember that our Master once said, 'Some persons pile up earth into square, others into long-shaped tumuli. Some build spacious mausolea, others content themselves with small axe-shaped heaps. I prefer the heaps.' He meant what we call *horse-neck* heaps. So we have given him only a few handfuls of earth, and he is buried. Is not this as he would have wished it himself?"

ON MOURNING

One day Yu-tzŭ and Tzŭ-yu saw a child weeping for the loss of its parents. Thereupon, the former observed, " I never could understand why mourners should necessarily jump about to show their grief, and would long ago have got rid of the custom. Now here you have an honest expression of feeling, and that is all there should ever be."

" My friend," replied Tzŭ-yu, "the mourning ceremonial, with all its material accompaniments, is at once a check upon undue emotion and a guarantee against any lack of proper respect. Simply to give vent to the feelings is the way of barbarians. That is not our way.

"Consider. A man who is pleased will show it in his face. He will sing. He will get excited. He will dance. So, too, a man who is vexed will look sad. He will sigh. He will beat his breast. He will jump about. The due regulation of these emotions is the function of a set ceremonial.

" Further. A man dies and becomes an object of loathing. A dead body is shunned. Therefore, a shroud is prepared, and other paraphernalia of burial, in order that the survivors may cease to loathe. At death, there is a sacrifice of wine and meat; when the funeral cortège is about to start, there is another; and after burial there is yet another. Yet no one ever saw the spirit of the departed come to taste of the food.

" These have been our customs from remote antiquity. They have not been discarded, because, in consequence, men no more shun the dead. What you may censure in those who perform the ceremonial is no blemish in the ceremonial itself."

BURYING ALIVE

When Tzŭ-chü died, his wife and secretary took counsel together as to who should be interred with him.[1] All was settled before the arrival of his brother, Tzŭ-k'ang; and then they informed him, saying, " The deceased requires

---

[1] The custom of burying living persons with the dead was first practised in China B.C. 580. It was said to have been suggested by an earlier and more harmless custom of placing straw and wooden effigies in the mausolea of the great.

some one to attend upon him in the nether world. We must ask you to go down with his body into the grave." "Burial of the living with the dead," replied Tzǔ-hêng, "is not in accordance with established rites. Still, as you say some one is wanted to attend upon the deceased, who better fitted than his wife and secretary? If this contingency can be avoided altogether, I am willing; if not, then the duty will devolve upon you two."

From that time forth the custom fell into desuetude.[1]

BAD GOVERNMENT

When Confucius was crossing the T'ai mountain, he overheard a woman weeping and wailing beside a grave. He thereupon sent one of his disciples to ask what was the matter; and the latter addressed the woman, saying, "Some great sorrow must have come upon you that you give way to grief like this?" "Indeed it is so," replied she. "My father-in-law was killed here by a tiger; after that, my husband; and now my son has perished by the same death." "But why, then," enquired Confucius, "do you not go away?" "The government is not harsh," answered the woman. "There!" cried the Master, turning to his disciples; "remember that. Bad government is worse than a tiger."

A STRANGE CONGRATULATION

When Chao Wu had completed his palace, all the great nobles went to offer their congratulations. One of them said, "How beautiful! how grand! how spacious! Here you will sing: there you will weep: and here the clans will gather together."

---

[1] In the 8th moon (B.C. 590) Duke Wên of Sung died. He was the first duke who had an elaborate funeral. Clam mortar was used for lining the grave. There were additional horses and carriages; and human beings were now for the first time interred alive with the dead.—*Tso Chuan.*

"Ah!" replied Chao Wu; "may it indeed come to pass that I shall sing here, and weep there, and that here the clans will gather together; for thus I should go down to the grave of my forefathers with my head safely on my shoulders." So saying, he bowed twice towards the north, striking his brow upon the ground.

"Well-timed," exclaims the superior man, "was the panegyric; and well-timed also was the prayer." [1]

THE SONG OF THE COFFIN

An old friend of Confucius having lost his mother, the Master went to assist in varnishing the coffin. "Ai-ya!" exclaimed the friend as he brought the coffin in, " 'tis long since I have had any music." Thereupon he began to sing—

Striped like the wild cat's head, Smooth as a maiden's hand Ai-yah! Ai-yah!

[alluding (1) to the grain of the wood and (2) to the varnish.] [2]

Confucius pretended not to hear, and moved away; but one of his disciples cried out, "Master, should you not have done with a fellow like this?"

"It is not right," replied Confucius, to disregard the duties we owe to our parents; neither is it right to disregard the duties we owe to our friends."

---

[1] The strange part of the congratulation was to allude, even indirectly, to the hateful contingency of death, as suggested by the word "weep." But the reply skilfully turned into a compliment what must otherwise have been taken as an affront.

[2] The music is not part of the text. These few bars are given merely as a sample of a Chinese popular air.

FROM THE HISTORY OF THE
CONTENDING STATES.—*ANONYMOUS*

THE ELIXIR OF DEATH

A certain person having forwarded some elixir of immortality to the Prince of Ching, it was received as usual by the door-keeper. " Is this to be swallowed? " enquired the Chief Warden of the palace. " It is," replied the door-keeper. Thereupon, the Chief Warden purloined and swallowed it. At this, the prince was exceedingly wroth, and ordered his immediate execution; but the Chief Warden sent a friend to plead for him, saying, " Your Highness' servant asked the door-keeper if the drug was to be swallowed; and as he replied in the affirmative, your servant accordingly swallowed it. The blame rests entirely with the door-keeper. Besides, if the elixir of life is presented to your Highness, and because your servant swallows it, your Highness slays him, that elixir is clearly the elixir of death; and for your Highness thus to put to death an innocent official is simply for your Highness to be made the sport of men."

The prince spared his life.

MÊNG TZŬ

(*Latinized into* MENCIUS.)

B.C. 372–289.

[Mencius is China's "second sage." He was to Confucius much what St. Paul was to Christ. The great principles which were henceforth to guide the nation had been already enunciated, and to these Mencius added nothing new. He lacked the inspiration which has placed Confucius in the front rank of the world's Prophets. But he did good work in expounding and disseminating the message which the Master had left behind him; especially in denouncing the theories of Mo Ti and Yang Chu (*qq. vv.*). His writings have been justly included in the Canon of Confucianism, and for more than twenty centuries his name has been a household word over the length and breadth of China.]

HALF MEASURES

KING HUI of Liang said to Mencius, "I exhaust my energies in the administration of government. If the harvest is bad on one side of the river, I transfer a number of the inhabitants to the other, and send supplies to those who remain. No ruler among the neighbouring States devotes himself as I do to the welfare of his people. Yet their populations do not decrease; neither does mine increase. How is this?"

Mencius replied, "Your Majesty loves war. Let us take an illustration from war:—

"The drums beat: blades cross: arms are flung aside: the vanquished seek safety in flight. Some will run a hundred yards and then stop; others, fifty only. Can those who run fifty laugh at those who run a hundred?"

"No, indeed," replied the king; "it was flight in both cases."

"And so," rejoined Mencius, "your Majesty, perceiving the application of what I have said, will not (under present conditions) expect your population to exceed the populations of neighbouring States.

"Let the times for agriculture be not neglected, and there will be more grain than can be eaten. Let no close-meshed nets sweep your streams, and there will be more fishes and turtles than can be eaten. Let forestry be carried on in due season, and there will be more wood than can be used. Thus, the people will be able to feed their living and bury their dead without repining; and this is the first step towards establishing a perfect system of government.

" Let the mulberry-tree be cultivated in accordance with regulation; then persons of fifty years old will be able to wear silk. Let due attention be paid to the breeding of poultry, and swine, and dogs; then persons of seventy years old will be able to eat meat. Let there be no interference with the labour of the husbandman; and there will be no mouths crying out for food. Let education of the people be reverently attended to;—above all, let them be taught their duties towards their parents and brethren;—and there will be no gray-headed burden-carriers to be seen along the high-way. For, where septuagenarians wear silk and eat meat, where the black-haired people are neither hungry nor cold, it has never been that perfect government did not prevail.

"Your dogs and swine are battening on the food of men, and you do not limit them. By the roadside there are people dying of hunger, and you do not succour them. If they die, you say, 'It was not I; it was the bad season.' What is this but to stab a man to death, and say, 'It was not I; it was the weapon?' O king, blame not the season for these things, and all men under the canopy of heaven will flock to you."

King Hui repiied, " I beg to receive your instructions."

Mencius continued, " Is there any difference between killing a man with a bludgeon and killing him with a sword! "

" There is none," answered the king.

" Or between killing him with a sword and killing him by misrule?" pursued Mencius.

" There is none," replied the king again.

" Yet in your kitchen," said Mencius, "there is fat meat, and in your stables there are sleek horses, while famine sits upon the faces of your people, and men die of hunger in the fields. This is to be a beast, and prey upon your fellow-man.

" Beasts prey upon one another, in a manner abhorrent to us. If, then, he who holds the place of father and mother to the people, preys upon them like a beast, wherein does his prerogative consist?

" Confucius said, ' Was he not without posterity who first buried images with the dead?'—meaning that these, being in the likeness of man, suggested the use of living men. What then of him who causes his people to die of hunger? "

BORN IN SIN

Kao Tzŭ said, " Human nature may be compared with a block of wood; duty towards one's neighbour, with a wooden bowl. To develop charity and duty towards one's neighbour out of human nature is like making a bowl out of a block of wood."

To this Mencius replied, " Can you without interfering with the natural constitution of the wood, make out of it a bowl? Surely you must do violence to that constitution in the process of making your bowl. And by parity of reasoning you would do violence to human nature in the process of developing charity and duty towards one's neighbour. From which it follows that all men would come to regard these rather as evils than otherwise."

Kao Tzŭ said, "Human nature is like rushing water, which flows east or west according as an outlet is made for it. For human nature makes indifferently for good or for evil, precisely as water makes indifferently for the east or for the west."

Mencius replied, " Water will indeed flow indifferently towards the east or west; but will it flow indifferently up or down? It will not; and the tendency of human nature towards good is like the tendency of water to flow down. Every man has this bias towards good, just as all water flows naturally downwards. By splashing water, you may indeed cause it to fly over your head; and by turning its course you may keep it for use on the hillside; but you would hardly speak of such results as the nature of water. They are the results, of course, of a *force majeure*. And so it is when the nature of man is diverted towards evil."

Kao Tzŭ said, " That which comes with life is nature."

Mencius replied, " Do you mean that there is such a thing as nature in the abstract, just as there is whiteness in the abstract? "

" I do," answered Kao Tzŭ.

" Just, for instance," continued Mencius, " as the whiteness of a feather is the same as the whiteness of snow, or the whiteness of snow as the whiteness of jade? "

" I do," answered Kao Tzŭ again.

" In that case," retorted Mencius, " the nature of a dog is the same as that of an ox, and the nature of an ox the same as that of a man."

Kao Tzŭ said, " Eating and reproduction of the species are natural instincts. Charity is subjective and innate; duty towards one's neighbour is objective and acquired. For instance, there is a man who is my senior, and I defer to him as such. Not because any abstract principle of seniority exists subjectively in me, but in the same way that if I see a white man I recognise him as such, because he is so objectively to me. Consequently, I say that that duty towards one's neighbour is objective or acquired."

Mencius replied, " The cases are not analogous. The whiteness of a white horse is undoubtedly the same as the whiteness of a white man; but the seniority of a horse is not the same as the seniority of a man. Does our duty to our senior begin and end with the fact of his seniority? Or does it not rather consist in the necessity of deferring to him as such? "

Kao Tzŭ said, " I love my own brother; but I do not love another man's brother. The distinction arises from within myself; therefore I call it subjective or innate. But I defer to a stranger who is my senior just as I defer to a senior among my own people. The distinction comes to me from without; therefore I call it objective or acquired."

Mencius retorted, " We enjoy food cooked by strangers just as much as food cooked by our own people. Yet extension of your principle lands us in the conclusion that our appreciation of cooked food is also objective and acquired."

ABDICATION OF THE EMPEROR YAO

A disciple asked, saying, "Is it true that Yao (2357 B.C.) gave the throne to Shun[1] (2255 B.C.)?" "It is not true," replied Mencius; "the Son of God[2] cannot take the throne and give it to any one." "Yes," said the disciple, "but Shun got it. Who gave it to him?" "God gave it to him." "Oh, God gave it to him, did He? Were there any particular commands as to what his duties would be." "No," replied Mencius; "God does not speak. God made manifest His will through Shun's own behaviour." "Oh," said the disciple, "through Shun's own behaviour, was it? How did He manage that?" "The Son of God," replied Mencius, "can recommend any one to God, but he cannot make God give that man the throne. Just so, the feudal nobles can recommend any one to the Son of God, but they cannot make the son of God appoint that man to be a feudal noble. Likewise, a Minister can recommend any one to his suzerain, but he cannot make his suzerain appoint that man to be a Minister. In those days of old, Yao recommended Shun to God, and God accepted him; he let the people see what sort of man Shun was, and the people accepted him. Therefore I said, God does not speak; He manifests his will through behaviour." "May I ask," said the disciple, "how this was managed." "Yao," replied Mencius, "caused Shun to preside over the sacrifices; and as the spirits were well pleased, God accepted him. Yao also caused him to preside over the conduct of affairs; and as affairs were well administered and a general well-being prevailed, the people accepted him. Thus, it was God and the people who gave Shun the throne; and therefore I said that the Son of God cannot give the throne to any one.

---

[1] For more about Shun, see *Yang Chu.* "On Self Sacrifice."

[2] More commonly called the "Son of Heaven"; but now that the word *t'ien* has been shown to mean an anthropomorphic Deity—to all intents and purposes *the* Deity, as universally recognized,—it seems only proper to use the term "God" without reserve. That *t'ien tzŭ* means the "Son of God" is also beyond the reach of argument. This phraseology may doubtless shock many who are more concerned with accidentals than with essentials. It must however be remembered that priority is on the side of the Chinese, who created the term and used it widely centuries before the Christian era.

CHARITY OF HEART

There are dignities of God, and there are dignities of man. Charity of heart, duty towards one's neighbour, loyalty, and truth—these are the dignities of God. To be a duke, a minister of State, or a high official—these are the dignities of man. The men of old cultivated the dignities of God, and the dignities of man followed. The men of to-day cultivate the dignities of God in order to secure the dignities of man; and when they have obtained the dignities of man, they cast aside all further thought of the dignities of God. In this they greatly err, and the probability is that they will lose their dignities of man as well.

Charity of heart is the noblest gift of God; it is a house, so to speak, in which a man may live in peace. No one can prevent us from possessing this gift; if we have it not, that is due to our own folly.

Charity of heart subdues uncharitableness just as water subdues fire. But people nowadays employ charity of heart much in the same way as if they were to try to put out a blazing cartload of firewood with a single cupful of water; and then when they fail to put out the flames, they turn round and blame the water.[1]

YANG CHU AND MO TI

"Master," said a disciple, "people all declare that you are fond of disputing; I venture to ask if this is so." "It is not," replied Mencius; "the fact is that I cannot do otherwise. Inspired rulers are no longer in power; the feudal barons have thrown off all restraint; and idle scholars are discussing unorthodox themes. The words of Yang Chu and Mo Ti fill the empire, and those who are not on the side of one will be found on the side of the other. Yang's doctrine is *Every man for himself*, which means that he

---

[1] It is plain that on this all important topic, much slurred over by many, the Chinese have nothing to learn from St. Paul.

recognizes no ruler. Mo's doctrine is *Love all equally,*
which means that he does not recognize the special claim
of a parent. But to recognize neither parent nor ruler is
to be a brute beast. If these doctrines are not checked, and
the doctrines of Confucius are not put forward, heterodox
teachings will delude the people, and charity of heart and
duty towards one's neighbour will cease to prevail. Then,
beasts will be led on to devour men, and men will soon be
devouring one another. I am alarmed by these things, and
address myself to the doctrines of the inspired men of old
in order to oppose Yang and Mo.[1]

SEPARATION OF SEXES

A philosopher asked Mencius, saying, "That men and
women, in giving and receiving, shall not touch hands,—is
such the rule of propriety?" "It is," replied Mencius.
"But supposing," said the philosopher, "that a sister-in-law
was drowning, should a man not give her a hand and pull
her out?" "A man," answered Mencius, "who could see
his sister-in-law drown and not give her his hand, would be
a wolfish brute. That men and women, in giving and
receiving, do not touch hands, is a rule of propriety; but
when a sister-in-law is drowning, to give her a hand and
pull her out comes under the head of exceptions to the rule."
"Just now," retorted the philosopher, "the empire is
drowning; why do you not pull it out?" "The drowning
empire," replied Mencius, "must be saved by the eternal
principles of Right; a drowning sister-in-law by the hand.
Would you have me save the empire by my hand?"

---

[1] For the views of these writers, see the extracts given under their names.

HSÜN TZŬ

3RD CENTURY B.C.

[Famous chiefly for having sustained the heterodox theory that the nature of man is evil in opposition to the Confucian doctrine that man is born good and becomes evil through his environment.]

BORN IN SIN

B Y nature, man is evil. If a man is good, that is an artificial result. For, his condition being what it is, he is influenced first of all by a desire for gain. Hence, he strives to get all he can without consideration for his neighbour. Secondly, he is liable to envy and hate. Hence, he seeks the ruin of others, and loyalty and truth are set aside. Thirdly, he is a slave to his animal passions. Hence, he commits excesses, and wanders from the path of duty and right.

Thus, conformity with man's natural disposition leads to all kinds of violence, disorder, and ultimate barbarism. Only under the restraint of law and of lofty moral influences does man eventually become fit to be a member of regularly organised society.

From these premises it seems quite clear that by nature man is evil; and that if a man is good, that is an artificial result.

LI SSŬ

3RD CENTURY B.C.

[Was for a long period prime minister and trusted adviser of the prince who finally annihilated the feudal system which prevailed under the Chou dynasty, and seated himself upon the throne as the First Emperor of China. It was then that Li Ssŭ suggested the entire destruction of existing literature, with a few trifling exceptions, in order to break off absolutely all connection with the past; a design which was rapidly carried into practical effect, though not to the extent which has been generally supposed, and from the operation of which the sacred books of Confucianism were saved only by the devotion of a few. Li Ssŭ was himself an accomplished scholar, and invented a form of writing which remained in vogue for several centuries, until superseded by the style now in use.]

ON THE EMPLOYMENT OF FOREIGNERS

THE high officers of State had combined to persuade the Prince of Ch'in to dismiss all foreign nobles and other strangers from the Court, urging that such persons were there only in the interests of their masters. This proscription would have included me. I therefore sent up the following Memorial:—

May it please your Majesty,

The present scheme for proscribing strangers is in every way a fatal step. Have we not innumerable examples in the past of the employment of foreigners, to the greater glory of the State and to the infinite advantage of the people?

From the mountains of Tibet your Majesty receives jade; from elsewhere, jewels. Bright pearls, good blades, fine horses, kingfisher banners, triton-skin drums,—of such rarities not one is produced at home, yet your Majesty delights in all. But if nothing is to be used in future save local produce, then will rich pearls shine no more at Court, then will the elephant and the rhinoceros contribute their ivory no more, nor the ladies of Chao throng the Imperial hareem, nor sleek palfreys stand in the Imperial stables, nor gold, nor pewter-ware, nor brilliant hues glow within the Imperial walls.

And if all, too, which adorns the seraglio, and ministers to the pleasure of eye and ear, must for the future be of local growth; then adieu to pearl-set pins, to jewelled eardrops, to silken skirts and embroidered hems;—welcome the humble and the plain, there where beauty no longer reigns supreme.

Take for instance our local music—shrill songs shrieked to earthen and wooden accompaniments—as compared with the magnificent harmonies of other States. Those we have rejected in favour of these, simply because the latter contributed most to the pleasure of sense.

In the choice of men, however, this principle is not to prevail. There is to be no question of capacity or of incapacity, of honesty or of dishonesty. If he be not a native, he must go: all foreigners are to be dismissed. Surely this is to measure men by a lower standard than music and gems! No method this for stretching the rod of empire over all within the boundary of the sea.

As broad acres yield large crops, so for a nation to be great there should be a great population; and for soldiers to be daring their generals should be brave. Not a single clod was added to T'ai-shan in vain: hence the huge mountain we now behold. The merest streamlet is received into the bosom of Ocean: hence the Ocean's unfathomable expanse. And wise and virtuous is the ruler who scorns not the masses below. For him, no boundaries of realm, no distinctions of nationality exist. The four seasons enrich him; the Gods bless him; and, like our rulers of old, no man's hand is against him.

But now it is proposed to deliver over the black-haired people into the power of the foe. For if strangers are expelled, they will rally round the feudal princes. The leaders of the age will retire, and none will step forth to fill the vacant place. It is as though one should furnish arms to a rebel, or set a premium upon theft.

Many things that are not produced here are nevertheless highly prized. Countless men who were not born here are nevertheless loyal of heart. Therefore to dismiss all foreigners will be to make our enemies strong; for those who suffer expulsion will go to swell the hostile ranks.

There will be but hollowness within and bitterness without; and danger will never cease to menace the State.

On reading the above, the Prince of Ch'in cancelled the edict respecting the proscription of foreigners, and I was restored to office.[1]

---

[1] "The iniquity of the writer," observes a commentator, "must not blind us to the beauty of his appeal."

HAN FEI

[Died 233 B.C. A student of criminal law and procedure, who rose to distinction but incurred the enmity of a rival and was thrown into prison where he committed suicide. Fifty-five of his essays, in a more or less corrupt state, are still extant, and are especially valuable as containing many of the sayings attributed to Lao Tzŭ, woven later on, sometimes with portions of his own commentary, into the spurious work known as the *Tao Tê Ching*.]

CIRCUMSTANCES ALTER CASES

OF old Mi Tzŭ-hsia was much attached to the Prince of the Wei State, where there was a law that any one who should furtively ride in one of the royal chariots would be punished by having his feet cut off. Now when Mi's mother was ill and her illness was reported to him, he went boldly off in one of the Prince's chariots to see her. On hearing of this, the Prince entirely approved, saying, "Filial piety! For the sake of his mother he risked the loss of his feet."

On another occasion, Mi was strolling with the Prince in a fruit-garden; and finding that a peach, of which he had partly eaten, was unusually sweet, he offered the remaining piece to the Prince. The Prince said, "Love for me! He forgets himself." Mi's face fell, and his attachment abated. The Prince added, "He furtively rode off in one of my chariots, and now he wants to feed me with the balance of his peach." Mi's second act was inconsistent with his first. By the first he showed himself to be a good man, and by the second he incurred punishment, thus illustrating the extreme difference between love and hate. Thus, when there is love for a ruler, wisdom steps in and familiarity is increased; but when there is hatred of a ruler, there comes cause for punishment and the result is alienation. So that when admonishing a ruler, it becomes necessary to consider the question of love or hatred before offering advice. A dragon is a deadly reptile which, however, can be trained to be fit for riding; but if a fishbone a foot long should stick in its throat and a man should try to remove it, there would be an end of the man. Now rulers, too, have fishbones sticking in their throats, and what is the fate of those who try but fail to remove them?

BRUTALITY *v.* HUMANITY

Yo Yang was a general in the army of the Wei State. When he attacked Chung-shan, his son was in the beleaguered city. The prince of Chung-shan boiled this son alive and sent some of the broth to his father, who received it sitting in his military headquarters and drank up a whole cupful. The marquis of Wei, speaking in commendation, said to an officer, "Yo Yang ate his son's flesh for my sake." "If he ate his own son," replied the officer, "who is there whom he would not eat?" When Yo Yang had captured Chung-shan, the marquis duly rewarded him, but became suspicious of his loyalty.

One day, when Mêng Sun was out hunting, a fawn was captured. Mêng Sun bade his huntsman put it on a cart and take it home; but the dam followed and bleated so piteously that the huntsman could not bear to be unkind to the animal, and let the fawn go. When they got home, Mêng Sun asked where the fawn was, and the huntsman said, "I could not bear to be so unkind, and I gave the fawn back to its dam." Mêng Sun was furious at this, and dismissed the man from his service; but three months later he recalled him, and appointed him to be tutor to his son. Upon this, an official of the Court said, "Not long ago, you punished this man, and now you appoint him to be tutor to your son; how is this?" Mêng Sun replied, "If he cannot bear to be unkind to an animal, how will he bear to be unkind to my son?"

Therefore it is said that clever trickery is not equal to stupid sincerity. Yo Yang was rewarded and became an object of suspicion; the huntsman was punished and became more trusted than ever.

LIU AN, HUAI-NAN TZŬ

[Died 122 B.C. Ruler of Huai-nan, and grandson of the founder of the Han dynasty. A student of Taoism under its grosser aspects, he directed his attention to alchemistic research and to the discovery of an elixir of immortality. Becoming mixed up in some treasonable conspiracy, he perished by his own hand.]

DOES GOD INTERVENE?

OF old, Shih K'uang played before the Court a piece entitled "White Snow," the action of which was rendered by a cast of supernatural beings.[1] Down came a storm of wind and rain; the Duke was stricken with old age, while afterwards his State became red with drought.

When a woman of the people cried aloud her wrongs to God, thunder and lightning came down and struck the palace of the Duke to ruins, crushing his Highness and breaking his limbs, followed by the sea flooding over the whole.[2]

A blind musician and his wife from the people occupied a very lowly position, below even that of the humblest official. Nevertheless, with great earnestness they put aside their personal occupations and devoted themselves to worshipping the saints, so that their devotion became known and received encouragement in heaven above.

Thus it is clear that no matter whether isolated in the wilds, or in concealment at a distance, or in a double-walled stone house, or separated by intervening obstacles and dangers, there is no place to which a man can escape from God.

When our Martial King (1122 B.C.) attacked the tyrant Shou, while crossing the river at the ford of Mêng, the spirit of the wicked Marquis (who had been drowned there) stirred up the waves to fury against him, with a bitter wind and so black a pall of darkness that men and horses could not see one another. Then the Martial King, grasping in his left hand a golden halberd and in his right hand a

---

[1] And therefore blasphemous.

[2] For misgovernment.

white-tasselled staff, shook them at the river, saying, "I am the ruler of all under the sky; who dares to cross my path?" Thereupon, the wind fell and the waves were stilled.

The Duke of the Lu State had become involved in trouble with the Han State, and a battle was raging fiercely when the sun began to set. The Duke seized his spear and shook it at the sun, which forthwith went back three zodiacal spaces in the heavens.

Thus, if we keep our physical nature complete, and preserve our spirituality, this will allow of no injury to the body. In the hour of danger or difficulty, such earnestness will appeal to God; and if there has been no departure from the great archetype,[1] what is there which cannot be accomplished?

ON THE NATURE OF TAO

Tao roofs over the sky and is the foundation of the earth; it extends north, south, east, and west, stretching to the eight extreme points in those directions. Its height is beyond reach and its depth is unfathomable; it enfolds both the sky and the earth, and produces things which had been formless. It is like the flow of a spring, which starts bubbling up from nothing but gradually forms a volume of rushing muddy water which again gradually becomes clear. Therefore, if set vertically, it will block all the space between the sky and the earth; if set laterally, it will touch the shores of the Four Seas; inexhaustible by use, it knows neither the fulness of morning nor the decay of night; dispersed, it fills space; compressed, it is scarce a handful; scant, it can be ample; dark, it can be light; weak, it can be strong; soft, it can be hard. Though open on all sides, it contains the two cosmogonical Principles; it binds up the universe, while making manifest the sun, moon, and stars;

---

[1] Tao. For this writer's conception of Tao, see the following extract, with which may be compared the views of Chuang Tzŭ, his predecessor.

it is thick as clay, and yet is watery; it is infinitesimally
fine, and yet it can be subdivided; it makes mountains rise
high and valleys sink low; it makes beasts to walk, birds
to fly, the sun and moon to shine, the stars to move, the
unicorn to come forth, and the phœnix to hover above us.

The first two Emperors of old (3rd millennium B.C.)
obtained control of Tao, and established themselves in the
centre of all things (China), and by their divine influence
brought about civilization and gave peace to the world.
Thus, the sky duly turned round, while the earth stood still,
and the wheel of human life revolved without ceasing.

SSŬ-MA CH'IEN

1ST AND 2ND CENTURIES B.C.

[Author of the first general *History of China*. The work begins with the reign of Huang Ti, the Yellow Emperor (2697 B.C.), and closes with the year 104 B.C., at about the period described in the subjoined extract. As a youth, Ssŭ-ma Ch'ien had travelled widely throughout the empire. He finally settled down as Grand Astrologer; but his spirited defence of Li Ling (*q.v.*) when overthrown and captured by the Huns, brought down upon him the wrath of the Emperor. He was subjected to the punishment of mutilation, and ended his days in disgrace. He reformed the calendar, and determined the chronology which still obtains in China.]

A CENTURY BEFORE CHRIST

(BY AN EYE-WITNESS)

Wealth, vice, corruption,—barbarism at last.
And history, with all her volumes vast,
Hath but *one* page.

WHEN the House of Han arose, the evils of their predecessors had not passed away. Husbands still went off to the wars. The old and the young were employed in transporting food. Production was almost at a standstill, and money became scarce. So much so, that even the Son of Heaven had not carriage horses of the same colour; the highest civil and military authorities rode in bullock-carts; and the people at large knew not where to lay their heads.

At this epoch, the coinage in use was so heavy and cumbersome that a new law was made, under which the people themselves cast money, the gold unit being equal to sixteen ounces. But the laws were too lax, and it was impossible to prevent grasping persons from coining largely, buying largely, and then holding against a rise in the market. The consequence was that prices went up enormously. Rice sold at 10,000 *cash*[1] per picul: a horse cost 100 ounces of silver. But by-and-by, when the empire was settling down to tranquility, His Majesty, Kao Tsu, gave orders that no trader should wear silk nor ride in a carriage; besides which, the imposts levied upon this class were greatly increased, in order to keep them down. Some years later, these restric-

---

[1] About 25 *cash* used to go to a penny. Now (1923) approximately 63 *cash* equal a penny. 1 *picul* = 133 1/3 lbs.

tions were withdrawn; still, however, the descendants of traders were disqualified from holding any office connected with the State.

Meanwhile, certain levies were made on a scale calculated to meet the exigencies of public expenditure; while the land-tax and customs' revenue were regarded by all officials, from the Emperor downwards, as their own personal emolument, and such revenue was not entered in the ordinary expenses of the empire. Grain was forwarded by water to the capital for the use of the officials there; but the quantity did not amount to more than a few hundred thousand piculs every year.

Gradually, the coinage began to deteriorate and light coins to circulate; whereupon another issue followed, each piece being marked "half an ounce." But at length the system of private issues led to serious abuses, resulting first of all in vast sums of money accumulating in the hands of individuals; finally, in rebellion; until the country was flooded with the coinage of the rebels, and it became necessary to enact laws against any such issue in the future.

At this period, the Huns were harassing our northern frontier, and soldiers were massed there in large bodies, in consequence of which food became so scarce that the authorities offered certain rank and titles of honour to those who would supply a given quantity of grain. Later on, a drought ensued in the west, and in order to meet necessities of the moment, official rank was again made a marketable commodity, while those who broke the law were allowed to commute their penalties by money payments. And now horses began to reappear in official stables; and in palace and hall, signs of an ampler luxury were visible once more.

Thus it was in the early days of the dynasty, until some seventy years after the accession of the House of Han. The empire was then at peace. But for such catastrophes as flood and drought, the people had been in the enjoyment of plenty. The public granaries were well stocked; the government treasuries were full. In the capital, strings of *cash* were piled in myriads, until the very strings rotted, and their tale could no longer be told. The grain in the Imperial storehouses grew mouldy year by year. It burst from the crammed granaries, and lay about until it became unfit for human food. The streets were thronged with horses belonging to the people, and on the high roads whole droves were to be seen, so that it became necessary to prohibit the public use of mares. Village elders ate of the best grain and also meat. Petty government clerkships and the like lapsed from father to son; the higher offices of State were adopted as surnames. For there had gone abroad a spirit of self-respect and of reverence for the law, while a sense of charity and of duty towards one's neighbour kept men aloof from disgrace and shame.

At length, under lax laws, the wealthy began to use their riches for evil purposes of pride and self-aggrandisement and oppression of the weak. Members of the Imperial family received grants of land, while from the highest to the lowest, every one vied with his neighbour in lavishing money on houses, and appointments, and apparel, altogether beyond the limit of his means. Such is the everlasting law of the sequence of prosperity and decay.[1]

Then followed extensive military preparations in various parts of the empire; the establishment of a tradal route with the barbarians of the south-west, for which purpose mountains were hewn through for many miles. The object was to open up the resources of those remote districts; but the result was to swamp the inhabitants in hopeless ruin. Then, again, there was the subjugation of Korea; its transformation into an Imperial dependency; with other troubles nearer home. The Huns violated their treaty and broke in upon our northern frontier, with great injury to the empire. Nothing in fact but wars and rumours of wars from day to day. Those who went to the war carried money with them; those who remained sent

---

[1] For further on this law, see *Fulness and Decay*, by Ou-yang Hsiu.

money after them. The financial stability of the empire was undermined, and its impoverished people were driven thereby into crime. Wealth had been frittered away, and its renewal was sought in corruption. Those who brought money in their hands received appointments under government. Those who could pay escaped the penalties of their guilt. Military merit opened the door to advancement. Shame and scruples of conscience were laid aside. Laws and punishments were administered with severer hand.

From this period must be dated the rise and growth of official venality.

ON CHANG LIANG

Educated people mostly deny the existence of a spiritual world. Yet they will concede supernatural attributes to things; as for instance in the story of Chang Liang's *rencontre* with the old man who gave him that wonderful book.[1]

Now, that the founder of the Han dynasty should find himself involved in difficulties was a mere matter of destiny. But that Chang Liang should so often come to his aid,— there we detect the hand of God.

His Majesty said, "In concocting stratagems in the tent for winning battles a thousand miles away, I cannot compare with Chang Liang." And I too had always entertained great respect for the genius of this remarkable man. But when I saw his portrait, lo and behold! his features were those of a woman. However, according to Confucius, "If we always chose men for their looks, we should have lost Tzŭ-yü." [2] And the same is true of Chang Liang.

---

[1] Chang Liang was the friend and adviser whose counsels contributed so much to the success of Kao Ti (*q.v.*), founder of the House of Han. Having had occasion, in his youth, to oblige an old man by picking up his sandal for him, the latter is said to have presented him with a book from which he drew the wisdom that distinguished him so much in after life.

[2] A disciple, chiefly remarkable for great ugliness combined with lofty mental characteristics.

CONFUCIUS

The *Odes* have it thus:—"We may gaze up to the mountain's brow: we may travel along the great road;" signifying that although we cannot hope to reach the goal, still we may push on thitherwards in spirit.

While reading the works of Confucius, I have always fancied I could see the man as he was in life; and when I went to Shantung I actually beheld his carriage, his robes, and the material parts of his ceremonial usages. There were his descendants practising the old rites in their ancestral home;—and I lingered on, unable to tear myself away. Many are the princes and prophets that the world has seen in its time; glorious in life, forgotten in death. But Confucius, though only a humble member of the cotton-clothed masses, remains among us after many generations. He is the model for such as would be wise. By all, from the Son of Heaven down to the meanest student, the supremacy of his principles is fully and freely admitted. He may indeed be pronounced the divinest of men.

COURAGE

He who will face death at the call of duty must necessarily be brave. There is no difficulty in merely dying: the difficulty lies in dying at fitting junctures only.

When Hsiang-ju carried in the jewel,[1] and with haughty gesture cursed right and left of the Prince of Ch'in, death was the worst he had to fear; yet few would have been bold enough to act as he did. His courageous attitude commanded the admiration even of an enemy; and when on his return he forbore to risk death in a wrong cause, he gained for himself a name which shall endure for ever.

Verily, wisdom and courage were well combined in that man!

---

[1] A remarkable stone in the possession of the Prince of Chao, from whom it had been demanded by the Prince of Ch'in, in exchange for fifteen cities, which however were never intended to be handed over. Hsiang-ju managed to out-manœuvre the enemy, and bore back the stone in triumph to his master.

KAO TI

REIGNED 202–195 B.C.

[This wonderful man, who founded the splendid House of Han, raised himself from the plough-tail to the throne. He was a simple peasant, named Liu Pang; but his genius soon placed him at the head of those malcontents who sought to shake the tyrannical yoke of the Ch'ins; and from that time until he was proclaimed Emperor, his career was one of uninterrupted success.]

PROCLAMATION

FELLOW-COUNTRYMEN!

You have long groaned under the despotic sway of the Ch'ins. To complain openly was to incur the penalty of extermination. Even casual words of objection were punished by decapitation of the individual.

Now, it was agreed between myself and the other nobles that whosoever first entered the territory of Ch'in should rule over it. Therefore I am come to rule over you. With you, I further agree upon three laws, viz:—

1. For murder, death.
2.. For injury to the person, proportionate punishment.
3. For theft, proportionate punishment.

The remainder of the Ch'in laws to be abrogated.

The officials and people will continue to attend to their respective duties as heretofore. My sole object in coming here is to eradicate wrong. I desire to do violence to no one. Fear not.

My camp is for the moment at Pa-shang. I await the arrival of my colleagues in order to ratify the terms of our agreement.

WÊN TI

REIGNED 179–157 B.C.

[Bastard son of Kao Ti. The tone of this letter is especially remarkable, as addressed by the Emperor to the captain of a barbarian horde. But the irresistible power of the Huns had already begun to make itself severely felt.]

TO THE CAPTAIN OF THE HUNS

WE respectfully trust that the great Captain is well. WE have respectfully received the two horses which the great Captain forwarded to Us.

The first Emperor of this dynasty adopted the following policy:—All to the north of the Long Wall, comprising the nations of the bow and arrow, to be subject to the great Captain: all within the Long Wall—namely, the families of the hat and girdle, to be subject to the House of Han. Thus, these peoples would each pursue their own avocations,—OURS, agriculture and manufacture of cloth; yours, archery and hunting,—in the acquisition of food and raiment. Father and son would not suffer separation; suzerain and vassal would rest in peace; and neither side would do violence to the other.

But of late WE hear that certain worthless persons have been incited by the hope of gain to shake off their natural allegiance. Breaches of moral obligation and of treaty have occurred. There has been forgetfulness of family ties; and the tranquility of suzerain and vassal is at an end. This, however, belongs to the past. Your letter says, " The two States had become friendly; their rulers friends. The tramp of armies had been stilled for more peaceful occupations, and great joy had come upon successive generations at the new order of things." WE truly rejoice over these words. Let us then tread together this path of wisdom in due compassion for the peoples committed to our charge. Let us make a fresh start. Let us secure quiet to the aged; and to the young, opportunity to grow up, and, without risk of harm, to complete their allotted span.

The Hans and the Huns are border nations. Your northern climate is early locked in deadly cold. Therefore WE have annually sent large presents of food and clothing and other useful things; and now the empire is at peace and the people prosperous. Of those people, WE and you are, as it were, the father and mother; and for trivial causes, such as an Envoy's error, we should not lightly sever the bonds of brotherly love. Heaven, it is said, covers no one in particular; and Earth is the common resting-place of all men. Let us then dismiss these trifling grievances, and tread the broader path. Let us forget bygone troubles in a sincere desire to cement an enduring friendship, that our peoples may live like the children of a single family, while the blessings of peace and immunity from evil extend even to the fishes of the sea, to the fowls of the air, and to all creeping things. Unresting for ever is the course of Truth. Therefore let us obliterate the past. WE will take no count of deserters or of injuries sustained. Do you take no count of those who have joined our banner.

The rulers of old never broke the faith of their treaties. O great Captain, remember this. And when peace shall prevail once more, rest assured that its first breach will not proceed from the House of Han.

CH'AO TS'O

DIED 155 B.C.

[An Imperial counsellor, chiefly known by his strenuous opposition to the system of vassal princes, which had been in part re-established under the Han dynasty after the total abolition of feudatory government by their predecessors, the Ch'ins. Ultimately, when a coalition of seven vassal princes threatened the very existence of the dynasty, Ch'ao Ts'o was shamefully sacrificed by the Emperor, with a view to appease the rebels and avert the impending disaster.]

ON WAR

MAY it please your Majesty,

Ever since the accession of the House of Han there have been constant irruptions of Tartar hordes, with more or less profit to the invaders. During one reign they twice fell upon Lung-hsi, besieging the city, slaughtering the people, and driving off cattle. On another occasion, they made a further raid, murdered the officials and garrison, and carried away everything upon which they could lay their hands.

Now, victory inspires men with additional courage: with defeat their *morale* disappears. And these three defeats at Lung-hsi have left the inhabitants utterly demoralised, with never a ray of hope for the future. The officials, acting under the protection of the Gods and armed with authority from the Throne, may strive to renew the *morale* and discipline of their soldiers, and to raise the courage of a beaten people to face the onset of Huns flushed with victory. They may struggle to oppose many with few, or to compass the rout of a host by the slaughter of its leader. The question, however, is not one of the bravery or cowardice of our people, but rather of the strategy of our generals. Thus it is said in the *Art of War*, "A good general is more indispensable to success than a good army." Therefore we should begin by careful selection of competent generals. Further, there are three points upon

which the fate of a battle depends.   These are (1) Position,
(2) Discipline, and (3) Arms.[1]

We read in the *Art of War*, "(1) A country intersected
by ditches and watercourses, or marshy, or woody, or
rocky, or overgrown with vegetation, is favourable to the
operations of infantry.   Two horsemen are there not equal
to one foot-soldier.

" Gentle slopes of soft earth, and level plains, are
adapted to the manœuvres of cavalry.   Ten foot-soldiers
are there not a match for one horseman.

" Where the route lies between high hills some distance
apart, or through defiles with steep precipices on each side,
the conditions are favourable to bowmen.   A hundred soldiers
with side-arms are there no match for a single archer.

" Where two armies meet at close quarters on a plain,
covered with short grass and giving plenty of room to
manœuvre, the conditions are favourable to lancers.   Three
men with sword and buckler are not equal to one of these.

" But in jungle and amid thick undergrowth, there is
nothing like the short spear.   Two lancers are there not
equal to one spearman.

" On the other hand, where the path is tortuous and
difficult, and the enemy is concealed from view, then swords-
men carry everything before them, one man thus equipped
being more than a match for three archers.

"(2) If soldiers are not carefully chosen and well
drilled to obey, their movements will be irregular.   They
will not act in concert.   They will miss success for want of
unanimity.   Their retreat will be disorderly, one half fighting while the other is running away.   They will not respond
to the call of the gong and drum.   One hundred such as these
will not hold their own against ten well-drilled men.

"(3) If their arms are not good, the soldiers might as
well have none.   If the cuirass is not stout and close set,

---

[1] These words were penned about two thousand years ago ; and yet Mr. DEMETRIUS
BOULGER (*horresco referens*), in the June number of the *Fortnightly* for 1883 treats
us to the following :—
    "China has yet to learn that arms alone will not make an efficient army."

the breast might as well be bare. Bows that will not carry, are no more use at long distances than swords and spears. Bad marksmen might as well have no arrows. Even good marksmen, unless able to make their arrows pierce, might as well shoot with headless shafts. These are the oversights of incompetent generals. Five such soldiers are no match for one."

Therefore, the *Art of War* says, "Bad weapons betray soldiers. Raw soldiers betray their general. Incompetent generals betray their sovereign. Injudicious sovereigns betray their country." The above four points are of vital importance in military matters.

May it please your Majesty. There is a difference in outline between great things and small ones. There is a difference in power between the strong and the weak. There is a difference in preparation between dangerous enterprises and easy ones. To truckle and cringe to the powerful,—this is the behaviour of a petty State. To mass small forces against one great force,—this is the attitude of a hostile State. To use barbarians as a weapon against barbarians,—this is what we do in the Central State.

The configuration of the Hun territory, and the particular skill there available, are not what we are accustomed to at home. In scaling mountains and fording rivers our horses do not excel; nor our horsemen in galloping wildly along precipitous mountain paths, shooting as they go; nor our soldiers in endurance of cold, hunger, and thirst. In all these respects the Huns are our superiors. On level ground we beat them out of the field. Our bows, our spears, are incomparably better than theirs. Our armour, our blades, and the manœuvres of our troops, are unmatched by anything the Huns can show. When our good archers discharge their arrows, the arrows strike the target all together, against which their cuirasses and wooden bucklers are of no avail. And when it comes to dismounting and hand-to-hand fighting with sword and spear in the supreme struggle, the victory is easily ours. In these respects we excel them.   Thus, the Huns may be compared with us in strength as three to five.   Besides which, to slaughter their myriads we can bring tens of myriads, and crush them by mere force of numbers.   But arms are a curse, and war is a dread thing.   For in the twinkling of an eye the mighty may be humbled, and the strong may be brought low.   The stake is great, and men's lives of no account.   For him who falls to rise no more, the hour of repentance is past.

Now the maxim of our ancient kings was this:—"The greatest safety of the greatest number."   And as we have among us several thousand barbarians who, in point of food and skill, are closely allied to the Huns, let us clothe them in stout armour and warm raiment, arm them with trusty bows and sharp blades, mount them on good horses, and set them to guard the frontier.   Let them be under the command of a competent general, familiar with their customs, and able to develop their *morale* according to the military traditions of this empire.   Then, in the event of arduous military operations, let these men go to the front, while we keep back our light war-chariots and horse-arches for work upon level ground.   We shall thus have, as it were, an outside and a lining; each division will be employed in the manner for which best adapted; our army will be increased, and the greatest safety of the greatest number will be achieved.

It is written, " The rash minister speaks, and the wise ruler decides."   I am that rash minister, and with my life in my hand I dare to utter these words, humbly awaiting the decision of your Majesty.

ON THE VALUE OF AGRICULTURE

"A bold peasantry, their country's pride."

When the people are prosperous under the sway of a wise ruler, familiar with the true principle of national wealth, it is not only the tiller of the soil who fills his belly, nor the weaver alone who has a suit of clothes to his back.

In the days of Yao [1] there was a nine years' flood: in the days of T'ang, a seven years' drought. Yet the State suffered not, because of the preparations which had been made to meet such emergencies. Now, all within the boundary of the sea is under one sceptre; and our country is wider and its inhabitants more numerous. For many years Heaven has sent upon us no visitation of flood or drought. Why then is our provision against emergency less? The fertility of the soil is not exhausted; and more labour is to be had. All cultivable land is not under tillage; neither have the hills and marshes reached their limit of production; neither has every available idler put his hand to the plough.

Crime begins in poverty; poverty in insufficiency of food; insufficiency of food in neglect of agriculture. Without agriculture, man has no tie to bind him to the soil. Without such tie, he readily leaves his birth-place and his home. He is like unto the birds of the air or the beasts of the field. Neither battlemented cities, nor deep moats, nor harsh laws, nor cruel punishments, can subdue this roving spirit that is strong within him.

He who is cold examines not the quality of cloth: he who is hungry tarries not for choice meats. When cold and hunger come upon men, honesty and shame depart. As man is constituted, he must eat twice daily, or hunger; he must wear clothes, or be cold. And if the stomach cannot get food and the body clothes, the love of the fondest mother cannot keep her children at her side. How then should a sovereign keep his subjects gathered round him?

The wise ruler knows this. Therefore he concentrates the energies of his people upon agriculture. He levies light taxes. He extends the system of grain storage, to provide for his subjects at times when their resources fail.

---

[1] 2356 B.C. An attempt has been made, as stated under *Yang Chu* (note) page 20, to identify this with Noah's flood. It was ultimately drained away by the engineering skill of an individual known in history as the Great Yü. "Ah!" says a character in the *Tso Chuan*, "if it had not been for Yü, we should all have been fishes."

Man makes for grain, just as water flows of necessity in the direction of a lower level. Gold, silver, and jewels, are powerless to allay the pangs of hunger or to ward off the bitterness of cold; yet the masses esteem these things because of the demand for them among their betters. Light and of limited bulk, a handful of such valuables will carry one through the world without fear either of cold or hunger. It is for these things that a minister plays false to his prince. It is for these things that a man lightly leaves his home:—a stimulus to theft, the godsend of fugitives!

Grain and cotton cloths come to us from the earth. They are produced in due season by the labour of man, and time is needed for their growth. A few hundred-weight of such stuffs is more than an ordinary man can carry. They offer no inducement to crime; yet to be without them for a single day is to suffer both hunger and cold. Therefore the wise ruler holds grain in high honour, but degrades gold and jewels.

Now in every family of five there is an average of at least two capable husbandmen, who have probably not more than a few roods of land, the yield of which would perhaps be not more than a hundred piculs. In spring they have to plough; in summer, to weed; in autumn, to reap; in winter, to store; besides cutting fuel, repairing official residences, and other public services. Exposed, in spring, to wind and dust; in summer, to scorching heat; in autumn, to fog and rain; in winter, to cold and frost,—from year's end to year's end they know not what leisure means. They have besides their own social obligations, visits of sympathy and condolence, the nourishment of orphans, of the aged, and of the young. Then, when flood and drought come upon them, already compassed round with toil and hardship, the government pressing harshly, collecting taxes at unsettled times, issuing orders in the morning to revoke them at night,—those who have grain sell at half value, while those who have not borrow at exorbitant usury. Then paternal acres change hands; sons and grandsons are sold to pay debts; merchants make vast profits, and even petty tradesmen realise unheard-of gains. These take advantage of the necessities of the hour. Their men do not till: their women do not spin. Yet they all wear fine clothes and live on the fat of the land. They share not the hardships of the husbandman. Their wealth pours in from the four quarters of the earth. Vying in riches with kings and princes, in power they out-do the authorities themselves. Their watchword is gain. When they go abroad they are followed by long retinues of carriages and servants. They ride in fine coaches and drive sleek horses. They are shod in silk and robed in satin. Thus do they strip the husbandman bare of his goods; and thus it is that the husbandman is an outcast on the face of the earth.

At present, the merchant is *de jure* an ignoble fellow; *de facto*, he is rich and great. The husbandman is, on the other hand, *de jure* an honourable man; *de facto*, a beggar. Theory and practice are at variance; and in the confusion which results, national prosperity is out of the question. Now there would be nothing more presently advantageous than to concentrate the energies of our people upon agriculture; and the way to do this is to enhance the value of grain by making it an instrument of reward and punishment. Let rank be bestowed in return for so much grain. Let penalties be commuted for so much. By these means, rich men will enjoy honours, husbandmen will make money, and grain be distributed over the face of the empire. Those who purchase rank in this way will purchase out of their surplus; and by handing this over to the Imperial exchequer, the burden of taxes may be lightened, one man's superfluity making up for the deficiency of another, to the infinite advantage of the people. The benefits of this plan may in fact be enumerated under the following heads:— (1) Sufficiency for Imperial purposes; (2) Light taxation; (3) Impetus given to agriculture.

Then again, at present a horse and cart are taken in lieu of three men under conscription for military service, on the ground that these are part of the equipment of war. But it was said of old, "An you have a stone rampart a hundred feet high, a moat a hundred feet broad, and a million of soldiers to guard the city, without food it shall be of no avail."

From the above it is clear that grain is the basis of all government. Rather then bid men gain rank and escape conscription by payments of grain: this would be better far than payment in horses and carts. Rank can be given at will by the mere fiat of the Emperor, and the supply is inexhaustible; grain can be produced from the earth by man in endless measure; and rank and exemption from penalty are what men above all things desire.

Therefore, I pray your Majesty, bestow rank and commute penalties for grain-payments; and within three years the empire will be amply supplied.

WU TI

[This Emperor is famous for his long and magnificent reign of fifty-four years; for his energetic patronage of scholars engaged in the resuscitation of Confucian literature; for the brilliant exploits of his generals in Central Asia against the Huns; for the establishment of universities and literary degrees, etc., etc. For a reply to the Proclamation annexed, see Tung-fang So.]

HEROES WANTED!—A PROCLAMATION

EXCEPTIONAL work demands exceptional men. A bolting or a kicking horse may eventually become a most valuable animal. A man who is the object of the world's detestation may live to accomplish great things. As with the untractable horse, so with the infatuated man;—it is simply a question of training.

WE therefore command the various district officials to search for men of brilliant and exceptional talents, to be OUR generals, OUR ministers, and OUR envoys to distant States.

TUNG-FANG SO

2ND CENTURY B.C.

[Popularly known as "The Wag." The following memorial was forwarded by him in response to the Proclamation of Wu Ti (*q.v.*), calling for heroes to assist in the government. Tung-fang So became at once an intimate friend and adviser of the young Emperor, continuing in favour until his death. On one occasion he drank off some elixir of immortality, which belonged to the Emperor, and the latter in a rage ordered him to be put to death. But Tung-fang So smiled and said, "If the elixir was genuine, your Majesty can do me no harm; if it was not, what harm have I done.]

SELF-RECOMMENDATION

I LOST my parents while still a child, and grew up in my elder brother's home. At twelve I learn to write, and within the year I was well advanced in history and composition. At fifteen, I learnt sword exercise; at sixteen, to repeat the *Odes* and the *Book of History*—220,000 words in all. At nineteen, I studied the tactics of Sun Wu,[1] the accoutrements of battle array, and the use of the gong and drum, also 220,000 words in all, making a grand total of 440,000 words. I also carefully laid to heart the sayings of the bold Tzŭ Lu.[2]

I am now twenty-two years of age. I am nine feet three inches in height.[3] My eyes are like swinging pearls, my teeth like a row of shells. I am as brave as Mêng Fên, as prompt as Ch'ing Chi, as pure as Pao Shu, and as devoted as Wei Shêng.[4] I consider myself fit to be a high officer of State; and with my life in my hand, I await your Majesty's reply.

---

[1] A skilful commander who flourished in the sixth century before Christ, and wrote a treatise on the art of war.

[2] One of Confucius's favourite disciples, specially remarkable for his courage. Whatever he said, he did. Of him, Mr. Watters said in his "Tablets in the Confucian Temple," p. 20, "It is very unfair of Dr. Legge to call him 'a kind of Peter,' meaning of course Simon Peter, a man who lacked faith, courage and fidelity, and moreover cursed and swore."

[3] We must understand a shorter foot-rule than that now in use.

[4] Hereby hangs a pretty tale. Wei Shêng was a young man who had an assignation with a young lady beneath a bridge. At the time appointed she did not come, but the tide did; and Wei Shêng, rather than quit his post, clung to a pillar and was drowned.

SSŬ-MA HSIANG-JU

DIED 117 B.C.

[A distinguished statesman, scholar, and poet, who flourished during the reigns of Ching Ti and Wu Ti of the Han dynasty. In his early days, he eloped with a young widow, and the two of them ran a wine-shop until her father came to the rescue with pecuniary assistance.]

AGAINST HUNTING

I HAD accompanied the Imperial hunt to Ch'ang-yang. At that time His Majesty (Wu Ti, 2nd century B.C.) was an ardent follower of the chase, and loved to slaughter bears and wild boars with his own hands. Therefore I handed in the following Memorial:—

May it please your Majesty,

I have heard that although the human race is comprised under one class, the capabilities of each individual are widely different. Thus we praise the strength of this man, the swiftness of that, and the courage of a third. And I venture to believe that what is true of us in this respect is equally true of the brute creation.

Now your Majesty enjoys laying low the fierce quarry in some close mountain pass. But one day there will come a beast, more terrible than the rest, driven from its lair; and then disaster will overtake the Imperial equipage. There will be no means of escape, no time to do anything, no scope for the utmost skill or strength, over the rotten branches and decaying trunks which help to complete the disorder. The Huns rising up under your Majesty's chariot-wheels, the barbarians of the west clinging on behind, would hardly be worse than this. And even if, in every case, actual injury is avoided, still this is not a fitting scene for the presence of the Son of Heaven. Besides, even on smooth ground and on a beaten track there is always risk of accident,—a broken rein or a loose pin; how much more so in the jungle or on the rough mountain-side, where, with the pleasure of the chase ahead and no thought of danger within, misfortune easily comes?

To neglect the affairs of a mighty empire and to find no peaceful occupation therein, but to seek for pleasure in the chase, never wholly without peril,—this is what in my opinion your Majesty should not do. The clear of vision discern coming events before they actually loom in sight: the wise in counsel avoid dangers before they definitely assume a shape. Misfortunes often lie concealed in trifles, and burst forth when least expected. Hence the vulgar saying, *He who has piled up a thousand ounces of gold, should not sit with chair overhanging the dais;* which proverb, though trivial in itself, may be used in illustration of great matters. I trust that your Majesty will deign to reflect hereon.

THE PRINCE OF CHUNG-SHAN

[An Emperor of the Han dynasty was feasting several of his vassal princes who had come to pay their respects at Court, when it was observed that one of them shed tears at the sound of the music.[1] His Majesty enquired the cause of his distress, and the following was the prince's reply. He had been a terrified witness of the unexpected fall of a number of his colleagues, apparently without other reason than the caprice of their Imperial master excited by the voice of secret slander, and was evidently afraid that his own turn might be at hand.]

MUSIC

MAY it please your Majesty!

There are moments when those who sorrow must weep, when those who are pensive cannot restrain their sighs. And so, when Kao Chien-li struck his lute, Ching K'o bowed his head and forgot to eat; when Yung Mên-tzŭ vented his sorrow in song, Mêng Ch'ang-chün uttered a responsive cry. Now, mine has been a grief pent up for many a day; and whenever music's plaintive strains reach my ear, I know not how it is, my tears begin to flow.

Enough spittle will float a mountain; enough mosquitoes will cause a roar like thunder; a band of confederates will catch a tiger; ten men will break an iron bar. Combination has ever prevailed even against the greatest of the great.

And I,—I live afar off. I have but few friends, and none to intercede on my behalf. Against enough calumny, the purest purity and the ties of kindred cannot prevail. Light things may be piled on a cart until the axle snaps: it is by abundance of feathers that birds can raise their bodies in the air. And when I see so many of my colleagues tangled in the meshes of treason, my tears are beyond control.

When the sun is glowing brightly in the sky, the darkest corners are illumined by its light. Beneath the beams of the clear moon, the eye discerns the insect on the wing. But when dark clouds hide the sky behind their

---

[1] See note to *Unpopularity*, by Sung Yü. (page 38).

murky veil; when storms of dust thicken the surrounding
air;—then even mighty mountains are lost to sight behind
the screen of intervening things.

Thus I am beyond the pale, while the lying tongues of
courtiers chatter behind my back. The way is long, and
none will speak on my behalf. Therefore I weep.

Rats are not flooded out of shrines: mice are not
smoked out of a house, lest the buildings suffer withal.
Now, I am but distantly related to your Majesty: still we
are as the calyx and the fruit of the persimmon. My rank
may be low: still I address your Majesty as my elder
brother. But the courtiers round the Throne: their claims
to relationship are thin as the pellicle of the rush, light as
the down of the wild goose. Yet they combine, and each
supports the other. They bring about separations in the
Imperial family, until the ties of blood vanish like melting
ice. It was this that drove Poh Ch'i into exile: it was this
that hurried Pi Kan to his grave.

It is said in the *Odes,* "Sorrow stabs my heart, and I
am overwhelmed with sad thoughts. Vainly trying to
sleep, I do naught but sight. My grief is aging me. My
heart throbs with it, like a throbbing head." And such,
may it please your Majesty, is my case now.

LI LING

1ST AND 2ND CENTURIES B.C.

[Su Wu, the friend to whom this letter was addressed, had been sent(100 B.C.) on a special mission to the court of the Huns, where, because he would not renounce his allegiance, he was thrown into prison and remained in captivity for nineteen years. He subsequently effected an escape, and returned to China, whence he wrote to Li Ling (who had meanwhile surrendered to the Huns) in a sense that will be gathered from a perusal of the latter's reply.]

A REPLY

O TZŬ-CH'ING,[1] O my friend, happy in the enjoyment of a glorious reputation, happy in the prospect of an imperishable name,—there is no misery like exile in a far-off foreign land, the heart brimful of longing thoughts of home! I have thy kindly letter, bidding me be of good cheer, kinder than a brother's words; for which my soul thanks thee.

Ever since the hour of my surrender until now, destitute of all resource, I have sat alone with the bitterness of my grief. All day long I see none but barbarians around me. Skins and felt protect me from wind and rain. With mutton and whey I satisfy my hunger and slake my thirst. Companions with whom to while time away, I have none. The whole country is stiff with black ice. I hear nought but the moaning of the bitter autumn blast, beneath which all vegetation has disappeared. I cannot sleep at night. I turn and listen to the distant sound of Tartar pipes, to the whinnying of Tartar steeds. In the morning I sit up and listen still, while tears course down my cheeks. O Tzŭ-ch'ing, of what stuff am I, that should do aught but grieve? The day of thy departure left me disconsolate indeed. I thought of my aged mother butchered upon the threshold of the grave. I thought of my innocent wife and child, condemned to the same cruel fate. Deserving as I might have been of Imperial censure, I am now an object of pity to all. Thy return was to honour and renown, while I remained behind with infamy and disgrace. Such is the divergence of man's destiny.

---

[1] Su Wu's literary name or style.

Born within the domain of refinement and justice, I passed into an environment of vulgar ignorance. I left behind me obligations to sovereign and family for life amid barbarian hordes; and now barbarian children will carry on the line of my forefathers.[1] And yet my merit was great, my guilt of small account. I had no fair hearing; and when I pause to think of these things, I ask to what end I have lived. With a thrust I could have cleared myself of all blame: my severed throat would have borne witness to my resolution; and between me and my country all would have been over for aye. But to kill myself would have been of no avail: I should only have added to my shame. I therefore steeled myself to obloquy and to life. There were not wanting those who mistook my attitude for compliance, and urged me to a nobler course; ignorant that the joys of a foreign land are sources only of a keener grief.

O Tzŭ-ch'ing, O my friend, I will complete the half-told record of my former tale. His late Majesty commissioned me, with five thousand infantry under my command, to carry on operations ·in a distant country. Five brother generals missed their way: I alone reached the theatre of war. With rations for a long march, leading on my men, I passed beyond the limits of the Celestial Land, and entered the territory of the fierce Huns. With five thousand men I stood opposed to a hundred thousand: mine jaded foot soldiers, theirs horsemen fresh from the stable. Yet we slew their leaders, and captured their standards, and drove them back in confusion towards the north. We obliterated their very traces: we swept them away like dust: we beheaded their general. A martial spirit spread abroad among my men. With them, to die in battle was to return to their homes; while I——I venture to think that I had already accomplished something.

This victory was speedily followed by a general rising of the Huns. New levies were trained to the use of arms,

---

[1] He had taken a Tartar wife.

and at length another hundred thousand barbarians were arrayed against me. The Hun chieftain himself appeared, and with his army surrounded my little band, so unequal in strength,—foot-soldiers opposed to horse. Still my tired veterans fought, each man worth a thousand of the foe, as, covered with wounds, one and all struggled bravely to the fore. The plain was strewed with the dying and the dead: barely a hundred men were left, and these too weak to hold a spear and shield. Yet, when I waved my hand and shouted to them, the sick and wounded arose. Brandishing their blades, and pointing towards the foe, they dismissed the Tartar cavalry like a rabble rout. And even when their arms were gone, their arrows spent, without a foot of steel in their hands, they still rushed, yelling, onward, each eager to lead the way. The very heavens and the earth seemed to gather round me, while my warriors drank tears of blood. Then the Hunnish chieftain, thinking that we should not yield, would have drawn off his forces. But a false traitor told him all: the battle was renewed, and we were lost.

The Emperor Kao Ti, with 300,000 men at his back, was shut up in P'ing-ch'êng. Generals he had, like clouds; counsellors, like drops of rain. Yet he remained seven days without food, and then barely escaped with life. How much more then I, now blamed on all sides that I did not die? This was my crime. But, O Tzŭ-ch'ing, canst thou say that I would live from craven fear of death? Am I one to turn my back on my country and all those dear to me, allured by sordid thoughts of gain? It was not indeed without cause that I did not elect to die. I longed, as explained in my former letter, to prove my loyalty to my prince. Rather than die to no purpose, I chose to live and to establish my good name. It was better to achieve something than to perish. Of old, Fan Li did not slay himself after the battle of Hui-chi; neither did Ts'ao Mo die after the ignominy of three defeats. Revenge came at last; and thus I too had hoped to prevail. Why then was I overtaken with punishment before the plan was matured? Why were my own flesh and blood condemned before the design could be carried out? It is for this that I raise my face to Heaven, and beating my breast, shed tears of blood.

O my friend, thou sayest that the house of Han never fails to reward a deserving servant. But thou art thyself a servant of the house, and it would ill beseem thee to say other words than these. Yet Hsiao and Fan were bound in chains; Han and P'êng were sliced to death. Ch'ao Ts'o was beheaded, Chou Po was disgraced, and Tou Ying paid the penalty with his life. Others too, great in their generation, have also succumbed to the intrigues of base men, and have been overwhelmed beneath a weight of shame from which they were unable to emerge. And now, the misfortunes of Fan Li and Ts'ao Mo command the sympathies of all.

My grandfather filled heaven and earth with the fame of his exploits—the bravest of the brave. Yet, fearing the animosity of an Imperial favourite, he slew himself in a distant land, his death being followed by the secession, in disgust, of many a brother-hero. Can this be the reward of which thou speakest?

Thou too, O my friend, an envoy with a slender equipage, sent on that mission to the robber race, when fortune failed thee even to the last resource of the dagger. Then years of miserable captivity, all but ended by death among the wilds of the far north. Thou left us full of young life, to return a gray-beard; thy old mother dead, thy wife gone from thee to another. Seldom has the like of this been known. Even the savage barbarian respected thy loyal spirit: how much more the lord of all under the canopy of the sky? A many-acred barony should have been thine, the ruler of a thousand-charioted fief! Nevertheless, they tell me 'twas but two paltry millions, and the chancellorship of the Tributary States. Not a foot of soil repaid thee for the past, while some cringing courtier gets the marquisate of ten thousand families, and each greedy parasite of the

Imperial house is gratified by the choicest offices of the State. If then thou farest thus, what could I expect? I have been heavily repaid for that I did not die. Thou hast been meanly rewarded for thy unswerving devotion to thy prince. This is barely that which should attract the absent servant back to his fatherland.

And so it is that I do not now regret the past. Wanting though I may have been in my duty to the State, the State was wanting also in gratitude towards me. It was said of old, "A loyal subject, though not a hero, will rejoice to die for his country." I would die joyfully even now; but the stain of my prince's ingratitude can never be wiped away. Indeed, if the brave man is not to be allowed to achieve a name, but to die like a dog in a barbarian land, who will be found to crook the back and bow the knee before an Imperial throne, where the bitter pens of courtiers tell their lying tales?

O my friend, look for me no more. O Tzŭ-ch'ing, what shall I say? A thousand leagues lie between us, and separate us for ever. I shall live out my life as it were in another sphere: my spirit will find its home among a strange people. Accept my last adieu. Speak for me to my old acquaintances, and bid them serve their sovereign well. O my friend, be happy in the bosom of thy family, and think of me no more. Strive to take all care of thyself; and when time and opportunity are thine, write me once again in reply.

Li Ling salutes thee!

LU WÊN-SHU

1ST CENTURY B.C.

[He taught himself to read and write while working as a shepherd, and soon attracted attention. Graduating as what was in his day the equivalent of B.A., he rose to some distinction in official life. The Memorial given below was presented in 67 B.C.]

ON PUNISHMENTS

MAY it please your Majesty,

Of the ten great follies of our predecessors, one still survives in the maladministration of justice which prevails.[1]

Under the Ch'ins, learning was at a discount: brute force carried everything before it. Those who cultivated a spirit of charity and duty towards their neighbour were despised. Judicial appointments were the prizes coveted by all. He who spoke out the truth was stigmatised as a slanderer, and he who strove to expose abuses was set down as a pestilent fellow. Consequently, all who acted up to the precepts of our ancient code, found themselves out of place in their generation; and loyal words of good advice to the sovereign remained locked up within their bosoms, while hollow notes of obsequious flattery soothed the monarch's ear and lulled his heart with false images, to the exclusion of disagreeable realities. And so the rod of empire fell from their grasp for ever.

At the present moment, the State rests upon the immeasurable bounty and goodness of your Majesty. We are free from the horrors of war, from the calamities of

---

[1] The "ten great follies" which helped to bring about the overthrow of the Ch'in dynasty were—
1. Abolition of the feudal system.
2. Melting down all weapons and casting twelve huge figures from the metal.
3. Building the Great Wall to keep out the Tartars.
4. Building a huge pleasaunce, the central hall of which was over sixty feet in height, and capable of accommodating ten thousand guests. It is described in a poem by Tu Mu, or the younger Tu.
5. The Burning of the Books. See *Li Ssŭ*.
6. The massacre of the Literati.
7. Building a vast mausoleum.
8. Searching for the elixir of life.
9. Appointing the Heir-Apparent to be Commander-in-Chief.
10 Maladministration of justice.

hunger and cold. Father and son, husband and wife, are united in their happy homes. Nothing is wanting to make this a golden age, save only reform in the administration of justice.

Of all trusts, this is the greatest and most sacred. The dead man can never come back to life: that which is once cut off cannot be joined again. " Rather than slay an innocent man, it were better that the guilty escape." Such, however, is not the view of our judicial authorities of to-day. With them, oppression and severity are reckoned to be signs of magisterial acumen, and lead on to fortune; whereas leniency entails naught but trouble. Therefore, their chief aim is to compass the death of their victims; not that they entertain any grudge against humanity in general, but simply that this is the shortest cut to their own personal advantage. Thus, our market-places run with blood, our criminals throng the gaols, and many thousands annually suffer death. These things are injurious to public morals, and hinder the advent of a truly golden age.

Man enjoys life only when his mind is at peace; when he is in distress, his thoughts turn towards death. Beneath the scourge, what is there that cannot be wrung from the lips of the sufferer? His agony is overwhelming, and he seeks to escape by speaking falsely. The officials profit by the opportunity, and cause him to say what will best confirm his guilt. And then, fearing lest the conviction be quashed by higher courts, they dress the victim's deposition so to suit the circumstances of the case, so that, when the record is complete, even were Kao Yao[1] himself to rise from the dead, he would declare that death still left a margin of unexpiated crime. This, because of the refining process adopted to ensure the establishment of guilt.

Our magistrates indeed think of nothing else. They are the bane of the people. They keep in view their own ends, and care not for the welfare of the State. Truly they are

---

[1] A famous Minister of Crime in the third millennium B.C.

the worst criminals of the age.   Hence the saying now runs, " Chalk out a prison on the ground, and no one would remain within.   Set up a gaoler of wood, and he will be found standing there alone." [1]   Imprisonment has become the greatest of all misfortunes; while among those who break the law, who violate family ties, who choke the truth,—there are none to be compared in iniquity with the officers of justice themselves.

Where you let the kite rear its young undisturbed, there will the phœnix come and build its nest.   Do not punish for misguided advice, and by-and-by valuable suggestions will flow in.   The men of old said, " Hills and jungles shelter many noxious things: rivers and marshes receive much filth: even the finest gems are not wholly without flaw.   Surely then the ruler of an empire should put up with a little abuse."   But I would have your majesty exempt from vituperation, and open to the advice of all who have aught to say.   I would have freedom of speech in the advisers of the Throne.   I would sweep away the errors which brought about the downfall of our predecessors.   I would have reverence for the virtues of our ancient kings, and reform in the administration of justice, to the utter confusion of those who now pervert its course.   Then, indeed, would the golden age be renewed over the face of the glad earth, and the people would move ever onwards in peace and happiness boundless as the sky itself.

---

[1] Contrary to what is believed to have been the case during the Golden Age.

SHU KUANG

1ST CENTURY B.C.

[The following is the reply of an aged statesman to his friends and kinsmen, on being urged by them to invest a sum of money, granted to him by the Emperor on his retirement from office, in landed property for his descendants. He began life as a teacher, and his success was so great that pupils flocked to him from a distance. In 67 B.C. he was appointed Tutor to the Heir Apparent.]

THE DISADVANTAGES OF WEALTH

How should I be so infatuated in my old age as to make no provision for my children? There is the family estate. Let them work hard upon it, and that toil will find them in clothes and food, like other people. To add anything, and so create a superfluity, would be to hold up a premium for sloth. The genius of men who possess is stunted by possession. Wealth only aggravates the natural imbecility of fools. Besides, a rich man is an eyesore to all. I may not be able to do much to improve my children; at least, I will not stimulate their vices and cause them to be objects of hate.

Then again, this money was graciously bestowed upon me by His Majesty, as pension for the old age of a servant. Therefore I rejoice to spend it freely among my clansmen and my fellow-villagers, as I pass to my appointed rest. Am I not right?

KU YUNG

1ST CENTURY B.C.

[A distinguished scholar who by 36 B.C. had risen to be a Censor. In 34 B.C. there was an eclipse of the sun, accompanied by a severe earthquake, which he attributed to the favours shown to the Empress and the ladies of the seraglio. For this he suffered no penalty, but ultimately died in high office. The following memorial refers to the reception of a Hun refugee, named Issimoyen, who was seeking to become a naturalised subject of China.]

AGAINST THE NATURALISATION OF HUNS

AT the rise of the Han dynasty, the Huns were a frontier curse. Accordingly, presents and honours were heaped upon them, in the hope that they would be led to join the Empire. And now that the Hun Captain has tendered his allegiance and become an officer of this government, his territory being enrolled among the Tributary States of the north,—he can entertain but one feeling towards us, and it behoves us to treat him in a manner different from that of past years. But if with one hand we receive his tribute, while with the other we welcome his fugitive servant,—is not this to clutch with greedy grasp at a single individual and sacrifice the trust and confidence of a nation; to clasp to our bosom a defaulting officer and cast from us the honourable friendship of a prince?

Possibly the Hun Captain has sent his man here to test our good faith, and the request to be naturalised is but a specious plea. In this case, to receive him would be a breach of duty, and would cause the Hun Captain to separate from us altogether.

Or it may be the Hun Captain's wish to bring about a separation in this way; and then we should but play into his hands, and enable him to quote his own loyalty against our disloyalty.

These are the beginnings of frontier troubles, of recourse to arms, and of military expeditions. Let us rather refuse to receive this man. Let us lay bare the integrity of our own hearts, and prevent the operation of any possible ruse by adhering closely to the principles of honest friendship.

MA YÜAN

DIED A.D. 49.

[Popularly known as the "Wave-quelling General." A famous commander, who crushed a dangerous rebellion in Tonquin, organised by a native Joan of Arc with a view to shake off the suzerainty of China. Was also successfully employed against the Huns and other border tribes.]

AMBITION

MY younger brother used often to find fault with my indomitable ambition. He would say, "The man of letters requires food and clothing only. A modest carriage and a humble hack; some small official post in a quiet place, where he may win golden opinions from the surrounding villagers—that should suffice. Why toil and strive for more?"

Later on, when away in the far barbarian south, before the rebellion was stamped out—a bog beneath my feet, a fog above my head, so that I have even seen kites drop dead in the water, killed by the poisonous vapours of the place—then I used to lie and muse upon the other view of life which my brother had set before my eyes.

And now that, thanks to you my brave comrades, my efforts have been crowned with success, and I have preceded you on the path to glory and honour—I have cause both for joy and for shame.[1]

---

[1] Implying that his success had been due to good luck.

WANG CH'UNG

1ST CENTURY A.D.

[A brilliant exponent of China's "higher school of criticism." Born A.D. 27, in poverty, he managed to pick up a good education and entered official life. After a short spell he retired dissatisfied to his home, and there composed his great work, the *Lun Hêng* or "Animadversions," in which he criticizes freely the teachings of Confucius and Mencius, and tilts generally against the errors and superstitions of his day. His subsequent writings were chiefly of a reforming character. He memorialized the throne on the prevailing vice and extravagance; and in the days of a drunken China, he pleaded for the prohibition of alcohol.]

CONFUCIANISM

THE Confucianists of the present day have great faith in their Master and accept antiquity as the standard of right. They strain every nerve to explain and practise the words which are attributed to their sages and inspired men. The writings, however, of these sages and inspired men, over which much thought and research have been spent, cannot be said to be infallibly true; how much less, then, can their casual utterances be so? But although their utterances are not true, people generally do not know how to convict them; and even if their utterances were true, because of the difficulty of grasping abstruse ideas, people generally would not know how to criticize them. I find that the words of these sages and inspired men are often contradictory, the value of one passage being frequently destroyed by the language of a later passage; but the scholars of our day do not see this. It is invariably said that the seventy disciples of Confucius were superior in talent to the Confucian scholars of to-day; but this is nonsense. According to that view, Confucius was a Master, and the inspired men who preached his doctrines must have been exceptionally gifted, and therefore different (from our scholars). The fact is that there is no difference. Those whom we now call men of genius, the ancients called inspired or divine beings; and therefore it has been said that men like the seventy disciples have rarely been heard of since that time.

VIRTUE ITS OWN REWARD

There are but few good men in the empire, and many bad ones. The good follow right principles, and the bad defy the will of God. Yet the lives of bad men are not therefore shortened, nor the lives of good men prolonged. How is it that God does not arrange that the virtuous shall always enjoy a hundred years of life, and that the wicked shall die young, as punishment for their guilt?

CREATION

Look at the hair and feathers of animals and birds, with their various colourings; can these have all been made? At that rate, animals and birds would never be finished. In spring we see plants growing, and in autumn we see them full-grown. Can God and Mother Earth have done this, or do things grow of themselves? If we say that God and Mother Earth have done it, they must have used hands for the purpose. Do God and Mother Earth possess many thousands or many myriads of hands, so that they can produce many thousands and many myriads of things, all at the same time?

GOD OUR FATHER

All creatures are to God like children, and the kindness and love of father and mother are the same to all their children.

ON SPIRITS

The dead do not become disembodied spirits; neither have they consciousness, nor do they injure anybody. Animals do not become spirits after death; why should man alone undergo this change? That which informs man at his birth is a vital fluid, or soul, and at death this vitality is extinguished, the body decays and becomes dust. How can it become a spirit? Vitality becomes humanity, just as water becomes ice. The ice melts and is water again; man dies and reverts to the condition of the vital fluid. Death is like the extinction of fire. When a fire is extinguished, its light does not shine any more; and when a man dies, his intellect does not perceive any more. The nature of both is the same. If people, nevertheless, pretend that that the dead have knowledge, they are mistaken. The spirits which people see are invariably in the form of human beings, and that very fact is enough of itself to prove that these apparitions cannot be the souls of dead men. If a sack is filled with grain, it will stand up, and is obviously a sack of grain; but if the sack is burst and the grain falls out, then it collapses and disappears from view. Now, man's soul is enfolded in his body as grain in a sack. When the man dies, his body decays and his vitality is dissipated. When the grain is taken away, the sack loses its form; why then, when vitality is gone, should the body obtain a new shape in which to appear again in the world?

The number of persons who have died since the world began, old, middle-aged, and young, must run into thousands of millions, far exceeding the number of persons alive at the present day. If every one of these has become a disembodied spirit, there must be at least one to every yard as we walk along the road; and those who die now must suddenly find themselves face to face with vast crowds of spirits, filling every house and street. If these spirits are the souls of dead men, they should always appear naked; for surely it is not contended that clothes have souls as well as men. It can further be shown not only that dead men never become spirits, but also that they are without consciousness, by the simple fact that before birth they are without consciousness. Before birth man rests in God; when he dies he goes back to God. God is vague and without form, and man's soul is there in a state of unconsciousness. The universe is, indeed, full of disembodied spirits, but these are not the souls of dead men. They are beings only of the mind, conjured up for the most part in sickness, when the patient is especially subject to fear. For sickness induces fear of spirits; fear of spirits causes the mind to dwell upon them; and thus apparitions are produced. Even if disembodied spirits did exist, they could not be either pleased or angry with a sacrifice, for the following reason. We must admit that spirits do not require man for their maintenance; for if they did, they would hardly be spirits. If we believe that spirits only smell the sacrifices, which sacrifices are supposed to bring either happiness or misfortune, how do we picture to ourselves the habitations of these spirits? Have they their own provisions stored up, or must they use the food of man to appease their hunger? Should they possess stores of their own, these would assuredly be other than human, and they would not have to eat human food. If they have no provisions of their own, then we should have to make offerings to them every morning and evening; and according as we sacrificed to them or did not sacrifice, they would be satiated or hungry, pleased or angry, respectively.

MORALS v. SACRIFICE

The people of to-day rely on sacrifice. They do not improve their morals, but multiply their prayers; they do not honour their superiors, but are afraid of spirits. When they die, or when misfortune befalls them, these things are ascribed to noxious influences which have not been properly dealt with. When they have been properly dealt with, and offerings have been prepared, and yet misfortunes continue to be as numerous as before, they attribute it all to the sacrifices, declaring that they have not been performed with sufficient reverence. Exorcism is of no use; sacrifices are of no avail. Wizards and priests have no power, for it is plain that all depends on man, and not on disembodied spirits; on his morality, and not on his sacrifices.

MING TI OF THE HOUSE OF WEI

REIGNED 227–239 A.D.

[An intelligent and kindly monarch, whose beard, when he stood up, is said to have touched the ground. Under his reign women were for the first time admitted into official life, and several actually rose to high office. No women officials however have been known since the eighth century.]

ON AN ECLIPSE.—A RESCRIPT

WE have heard that if a sovereign is remiss in government, God terrifies him by calamities and strange portents. These are divine reprimands sent to recall him to a sense of duty. Thus, partial eclipses of the sun and moon are manifest warnings that the rod of empire is not wielded aright.

Ever since WE ascended the throne, OUR inability to continue the glorious traditions of OUR departed ancestors and carry on the great work of civilisation, has now culminated in a warning message from on high. It therefore behoves US to issue commands for personal reformation, in order to avert the impending calamity.

But the relations of God with Man are those of a father and son; and a father about to chastise his son, would not be deterred were the latter to present him with a dish of meat. WE do not therefore consider it part of OUR duty to act in accordance with certain memorials advising that the Grand Astrologer be instructed to offer up sacrifices on this occasion. Do ye governors of districts and other high officers of State, seek rather to rectify your own hearts; and if any one can devise means to make up for OUR shortcomings, let him submit his proposals to the Throne.

WANG SU

[A very distinguished scholar who wrote and published many volumes of classical commentaries. He is said to have found, in the house of a descendant of the Sage, the text of "The Family Sayings of Confucius," and to have published it in A.D. 240; but the generally received opinion is that he wrote the work himself, based no doubt upon tradition. Specimens are given below.]

JADE

A disciple asked Confucius, saying, "Why, sir, does the superior man value jade much more highly than serpentine? Is it because jade is scarce and serpentine is abundant?" "It is not," replied Confucius; "but it is because the superior men of olden days regarded it as a symbol of the virtues. Its gentle, smooth, glossy appearance suggests *charity of heart;* its fine close texture and hardness suggests *wisdom;* it is firm and yet does not wound, suggesting *duty to one's neighbour;* it hangs down as though sinking, suggesting *ceremony;* struck, it gives a clear note, long drawn out, dying gradually away and suggesting *music;* its flaws do not hide its excellences, nor do its excellences hide its flaws, suggesting *loyalty;* it gains our confidence, suggesting *truth;* its spirituality is like the bright rainbow, suggesting the heavens above; its energy is manifested in hill and stream, suggesting the earth below; as articles of regalia it suggests the exemplification of that than which there is nothing in the world of equal value, and thereby is—TAO itself. We read in the Odes—

> When I think of my husband,[1]
> As gentle as jade,
> In his hutment of planking,
> My heart is afraid . . .

TEMPERANCE

Confucius noticed in the ancestral temple of Duke Huan[2] of the Lu State certain vessels which stood awry,

---

[1] Away at the war.
[2] Reigned 684–642 B.C. A great and wise ruler, who late in life gave way to sensuality, and whose corpse lay unburied while his sons fought for the throne.

and enquired of the verger what these vessels were; to which the verger replied that they were goblets for use at banquets. "I have been told," said Confucius, "that when these goblets are empty they stand awry, that when they are half full they stand up straight, and that when filled up they topple right over. A wise ruler would use them as a warning, and see that such were always placed alongside of his guests." Then turning to his disciples, the Sage said, "Let us try them with water;" and accordingly water was poured in until the goblets were half full, when they stood up straight. They were then filled up, and at once toppled over. "Alas," cried Confucius, heaving a deep sigh, "there are men who are full of wickedness, but they do not topple over."

ENTER NOT INTO TEMPTATION

A man of the Lu State lived alone in a cottage, and a neighbour, who was a widow, lived alone in another. One night, there was a terrific storm of wind and rain; the widow's cottage was destroyed, and she herself ran across to the man and asked to be taken in. The man, however, bolted his door and refused to admit her; whereupon the widow called to him, saying, "Where, sir, is your charity of heart, that you do not let me in?" "I have heard," replied he, "that until a man is sixty, he may not share a house with a woman.[1] Now, you are young, and I too am young; so that I dare not receive you." "Sir," said the widow, "why not play the part of Liu-hsia Hui?[2] Besides, I am an old dame, and not a damsel of doubtful reputation; there would be no scandal talked about us." "Liu-hsia Hui," answered the man, "might act as you say, but I am unable to do so. I will follow my own inability in striving

---

[1] Compare *Mencius*, "Separation of Sexes."

[2] 7th and 6th centuries B.C. His name was Chan Huo; his canonization title was Hui; he was Governor of Liu-hsia; hence the popular term, meaning Hui of Liu-hsia. He was a man of eminent virtue, and is said on one occasion to have held a lady in his lap without the slightest imputation on his moral character.

to imitate the ability of Liu-hsia Hui." When Confucius heard this, he said, " Good indeed! There has never been any one who has better imitated Liu-hsia Hui.[1] Can a desire to be good, without the attempt to succeed, be accounted wisdom? "

CONFUCIUS IN DANGER

The Prince of the Ch'u State having invited Confucius to visit him, the Master proceeded thither to pay his respects. His way lay through Ch'ên and Ts'ai; and the high officials of those States consulted together, saying, " Confucius is an inspired and good man; his counsels will consist of attacks upon the vices of us nobles; and if that should be the case, our States would be in danger." Accordingly, they arranged for a number of armed men to obstruct the Sage's way and to prevent him from continuing his journey. His party were cut off from supplies for seven days, nothing being allowed to reach them. Broth made from leaves was not sufficient, and all fell ill except Confucius himself, whose spirits rose higher than usual, as he lectured, recited, played, and sang without giving way. He called Tzŭ-lu [2] to him and said, " We read in the Odes—

We are neither wild cattle[3] nor tigers,
That we should be kept in these desolate wilds

Has my doctrine of Eternal Right [4] been a failure? How have I come to this pass? " To this, Tzŭ-lu angrily replied, " The superior man can suffer no restrictions. To think that you, Sir, have ever failed in charity of heart is what I cannot believe; to think that you have ever acted unwisely towards others has not come within my experience. Besides, Sir, in other times I have heard you say that God

[1] This of course is a paradox.
[2] See *Tung-fang So.*
[3] This word has always been translated by "rhinoceros." It is quite certain, however, that a kind of buffalo is the real meaning, as witness the Odes (in two places)—"Crumpled is the goblet made from the *ssŭ* horn," in support of which there are many other arguments.
[4] Tao. The Confucian *Tao* and the *Tao* of Lao Tzŭ must be kept strictly apart.

will reward with happiness those who do good,[1] and will punish with misfortunes those who do evil; and now for a long time you have been accumulating a splendid record of virtues and of duty towards your neighbour. How then should you be reduced to this extremity?" "My son," said the Master, "you have not understood me. I will tell you. If all depended on charity of heart, loyalty, and giving good counsel, many great heroes would have escaped suffering and death.[2] But success and failure are matters of opportunity; the worthy and the worthless are distinguished by their talents. Superior men of wide learning and wise schemes, who have failed from want of opportunity, are many indeed; why should I be the only one? The epidendrum grows in the depth of the forest, but it is not wanting in fragrance because there is no one there to smell it; the superior man cultivates the doctrine of Eternal Right and exemplifies it in practice; but he does not give up his principles because he is reduced to extremities. The man acts; the result, whether life or death, belongs to the will of God."

---

[1] These words are not in the spirit of Confucian teaching; those which follow are.
[2] A short list of such personages is here inserted.

LIU LING

3RD CENTURY A.D.

[One of seven hard-drinking poets of the day who formed themselves into a club, known as the Bamboo Grove. He was always accompanied by a servant carrying a wine-flask; and he gave orders that if he fell dead in his cups he should be buried where he lay. In this respect, he was perhaps out-Heroded by another famous tippler, who left instructions that he should be buried in a potter's field, so that, "when time into clay might resolve him again," he would have a chance of re-appearing among men under the form of a wine-jug.]

THE GENIUS OF WINE

AN old gentleman, a friend of mine (*sc.* himself), regards eternity as but a single day, and whole centuries as but an instant of time. The sun and moon are the windows of his house; the cardinal points are the boundaries of his domain. He wanders unrestrained and free; he dwells within no walls. The canopy of Heaven is his roof; his resting-place is the lap of Earth. He follows his fancy in all things. He is never for a moment without a wine-flask in one hand, a goblet in the other. His only thought is wine: he knows of naught beyond.

Two respectable philanthropists, hearing of my friend's weakness, proceeded to tax him on the subject; and with many gestures of disapprobation, fierce scowls, and gnashing of teeth, preached him quite a sermon on the rules of propriety, and sent his faults buzzing round his head like a swarm of bees.

When they began, the old gentleman filled himself another humper; and sitting down, quietly stroked his beard and sipped his wine by turns, until at length he lapsed into a semi-inebriate state of placid enjoyment, varied by intervals of absolute unconsciousness or of partial return to mental lucidity. His ears were beyond the reach of thunder; he could not have seen a mountain. Heat and cold existed for him no more. He knew not even the workings of his own mind. To him, the affairs of this world appeared but as so much duckweed on a river; while the two philanthropists at his side looked like two wasps trying to convert a caterpillar (into a wasp, as the Chinese believe is done).

T'AO YÜAN-MING

365–427 A.D.

[Chiefly remarkable for having thrown up a good official appointment, because as he said his salary did not repay him for being obliged to "crook the pregnant hinges of the knee." In private life, he amused himself with authorship and rearing chrysanthemums. See *The Language of Flowers*, under *Chou Tun-i*.]

HOME AGAIN!

HOMEWARDS I bend my steps. My fields, my gardens, are choked with weeds: should I not go? My soul has led a bondsman's life: why should I remain to pine? But I will waste no grief upon the past: I will devote my energies to the future. I have not wandered far astray. I feel that I am on the right track once again.

Lightly, lightly, speeds my boat along, my garments fluttering to the gentle breeze. I enquire my route as I go. I grudge the slowness of the dawning day. From afar I descry my old home, and joyfully press onwards in my haste. The servants rush forth to meet me: my children cluster at the gate. The place is a wilderness; but there is the old pine-tree and my chrysanthemums. I take the little ones by the hand, and pass in. Wine is brought in full bottles, and I pour out in brimming cups. I gaze out at my favourite branches. I loll against the window in my new-found freedom. I look at the sweet children on my knee.

And now I take my pleasure in my garden. There is a gate, but it is rarely opened. I lean on my staff as I wander about or sit down to rest. I raise my head and contemplate the lovely scene. Clouds rise, unwilling, from the bottom of the hills: the weary bird seeks its nest again. Shadows vanish, but still I linger round my lonely pine. Home once more! I'll have no friendships to distract me hence. The times are out of joint for me; and what have I to seek from men? In the pure enjoyment of the family circle I will pass my days, cheering my idle hours with lute and book. My husbandmen will tell me when spring-time is nigh, and when there will be work in the furrowed fields. Thither I shall repair by cart or by boat, through the deep gorge, over the dizzy cliff, trees bursting merrily into leaf, the streamlet swelling from its tiny source. Glad is this renewal of life in due season: but for me, I rejoice that my journey is over. Ah, how short a time it is that we are here! Why then not set our hearts at rest, ceasing to trouble whether we remain or go? What boots it to wear out the soul with anxious thoughts? I want not wealth: I want not power: heaven is beyond my hopes. Then let me stroll through the bright hours as they pass, in my garden among my flowers; or I will mount the hill and sing my song, or weave my verse beside the limpid brook. Thus will I work out my allotted span, content with the appointments of Fate, my spirit free from care.

THE PEACH-BLOSSOM FOUNTAIN

Towards the close of the fourth century A.D., a certain fisherman of Wu-ling, who had followed up one of the river branches without taking note whither he was going, came suddenly upon a grove of peach-trees in full bloom, extending some distance on each bank, with not a tree of any other kind in sight. The beauty of the scene and the exquisite perfume of the flowers filled the heart of the fisherman with surprise, as he proceeded onwards, anxious to reach the limit of this lovely grove. He found that the peach trees ended where the water began, at the foot of a hill; and there he espied what seemed to be a cave with light issuing from it. So he made fast his boat, and crept in through a narrow entrance, which shortly ushered him into a new world of level country, of fine houses, of rich fields, of fine pools, and of luxuriance of mulberry and bamboo. Highways of traffic ran north and south; sounds of crowing cocks and barking dogs were heard around; the dress of the people who passed along or were at work in the fields was of a strange cut; while young and old alike appeared to be contented and happy.

One of the inhabitants, catching sight of the fisherman, was greatly astonished; but, after learning whence he came, insisted on carrying him home, and killed a chicken and placed some wine before him. Before long, all the people of the place had turned out to see the visitor, and they informed him that their ancestors had sought refuge here, with their wives and families, from the troublous times of the house of Ch‘in, adding that they had thus become finally cut off from the rest of the human race. They then enquired about the politics of the day, ignorant of the establishment of the Han dynasty, and of course of the later dynasties which had succeeded it. And when the fisherman told them the story, they grieved over the vicissitudes of human affairs.

Each in turn invited the fisherman to his home and entertained him hospitably, until at length the latter prepared to take his leave. " It will not be worth while to talk about what you have seen to the outside world," said the people of the place to the fisherman, as he bade them farewell and returned to his boat, making mental notes of his route as he proceeded on his homeward voyage.

When he reached home, he at once went and reported what he had seen to the Governor of the district, and the Governor sent off men with him to seek, by the aid of the fisherman's notes, to discover this unknown region. But he was never able to find it again. Subsequently, another desperate attempt was made by a famous adventurer to pierce the mystery; but he also failed, and died soon afterwards of chagrin, from which time forth no further attempts were made.[1]

---

[1] The whole story is allegorical, and signifies that the fisherman had been strangely permitted to go back once again into the peach-blossom days of his youth.

FA HSIEN

4TH AND 5TH CENTURIES A.D.

[The name in religion of a Chinese Buddhist priest who, in the year A.D. 399, walked from Central China to Central India, then on to Calcutta and Ceylon, and back by sea, finally landing near the modern Kiao-chow. His object was to secure Buddhist texts and images for the purpose of spreading the Law of Buddha in China, and in this he was completely successful. He started with quite a number of companions but came home alone, the others having either turned back or died. In his own words: "I spent six years in travelling from Ch'ang-an to Central India. I stayed there six years, and took three more to reach Kiao-chow. The countries I passed through numbered rather fewer than thirty. Coming home across the sea, I encountered even more difficulties and dangers; but happily I was accorded the awful protection of our holy Trinity,[1] and was thus preserved in the hour of danger. Therefore I wrote down on bamboo slips and silk what I had done, desiring that worthy men should share this information." The result was a small work, known as "Record of the Buddhistic Kingdoms."]

GAYÂ.[2]

FROM this point (Râjagriha) going west four *yôjanas*,[3] the pilgrims arrived at the city of Gayâ, also a complete waste within its walls. Journeying twenty more *li*[4] to the south, they arrived at the place where the Bôdhisatva passed six years in self-mortification;[5] it has forests on all sides. From that point going west three *li*, they arrived at the spot where Buddha entered the water to bathe, and an angel pressed down the branch of a tree to pull him out of the pool. Also, by going two *li* further north, at a place where the two lay-sisters presented Buddha with congee made with milk, and two *li* to the north of this is the place where Buddha, sitting on a large stone and facing the east, ate it. The tree and the stone are both still there, the latter being about six feet in length and breadth by over two feet in height. In Central India the climate is equable; trees will live several thousand, and even so much as ten thousand years. From this point going north-east half a *yôjana*, the pilgrims arrived at a cave where the Bôdhisatva,

---

[1] The doctrine of the Trinity was a Buddhist dogma long before it was adopted by the Christian Church. *See* Chu Hsi, "Taoism and Buddhism."

[2] The scene of General Cunningham's important Buddhist excavations and discoveries.

[3] In popular language, the *yôjana* may mean a day's march; also, from five to nine miles.

[4] The Chinese *li* is about one-third of a mile.

[5] As a preparation for Buddhahood.

having entered, sat down cross-legged with his face to the west, and reflected as follows:—"If I am to attain perfect Wisdom, there should be some divine manifestation." Thereupon, the silhouette of a Buddha appeared upon the stone, over three feet in height; it is plainly visible to this day. Then Heaven and Earth quaked mightily, and the angels in space cried out, saying, "This is not the spot where past and future Buddhas have attained and should attain perfect Wisdom. The proper place is beneath the Bô tree, less than half a *yôjana* to the south-west of this." When the angels had uttered these words, they proceeded to lead the way with singing in order to conduct him thither. The Bôdhisatva got up and followed, and when thirty paces from the tree an angel gave him the *kusa* grass.[1] Having accepted this, he went on fifteen paces further, when five hundred dark-coloured birds came and flew three times round him, and departed. The Bôdhisatva went on to the Bô[2] tree, and laying down his *kusa* grass sat with his face to the east. Then, Mâra, the king of the devils, sent three beautiful girls to approach from the north and tempt him; he himself approaching from the south with the same object. The Bôdhisatva pressed the ground with his toes, whereupon the infernal army retreated in confusion and the three girls became old women.[3]

A STORM AT SEA: A.D. 413.

I remained in Ceylon for two years, and after a prolonged search I obtained copies of several important sacred books, not to be found in China. When I had obtained these in the Pali original, I took passage on board a large merchant-vessel, on which there were over two hundred souls, and astern of which there was a small vessel

---

[1] An odoriferous grass of lucky augury.

[2] The *patra* or palm tree.

[3] The Bôdhisatva, having successfully resisted temptation, became a Buddha, the Buddha of the present day.

in case of accident at sea and the destruction of the big vessel. Catching a fair wind, we proceeded east for two days when we encountered a heavy gale and the ship sprung a leak. The merchants wished to pass on to the small vessel, but the men there, afraid that too many would come, cut the tow-rope. The merchants were very frightened, for death was close at hand; and fearing that the ship would fill, they immediately took what bulky goods there were and threw them into the sea. I also took my pitcher and ewer with whatever else I could spare and threw them into the sea; but I was afraid that the merchants would throw over my books and images, and accordingly I fixed my whole thoughts on the Goddess of Mercy[1] and prayed to our Church in China, saying, "I have journeyed afar in search of the Law. Oh, that by your awful power you would turn back the flow of the leak that we might reach some resting-place!"[2]

[1] Kuan Yin.
[2] Which they shortly afterwards did.

KUMÂRAJÎVA

5TH CENTURY A.D.

[An Indian missionary monk who reached the Chinese capital, in order to preach the gospel of Buddha, in A.D. 401. He translated various *sûtras* into Chinese, from one of which, the so-called "Diamond *Sûtra*," the following passages have been taken. At his death, about 412–417 B.C., his body was cremated, but his tongue remained unhurt in the midst of the fire.]

SUBHÛTI ASKS FOR GUIDANCE

"O rare world-honoured One, O Tathâgata, thou who dost protect and instruct those who are Bôdhisattvas! O world-honoured One! If a good man, or a good woman, should show signs of unexcelled perfect intelligence, upon what should such a one rely, and how should such a one subdue the heart?" Buddha replied, "Good indeed! Good indeed! As you say, I protect and instruct those who are Bôdhisattvas. Listen therefore attentively, and I will tell you." Subhûti promptly answered that he would be glad to hear, and Buddha thereupon told the Bôdhisattvas and Mahâsattvas, as follows: "All living creatures whatsoever, whether born from the egg, or from the womb, or from damp (as wood-lice), or by metamorphosis, whether having form or not, whether possessed of intelligence or not, whether not possessed of intelligence or not not-possessed of intelligence—all such I command to enter into the absolutely non-material state of Nirvâna, and so by extinction (of all sense-values, etc.), to obtain salvation. Thus, all living creatures will be freed from measurement, from number, and from space-limit, though in reality there are no living creatures by such extinction to obtain salvation. Why so? Subhûti, if a Bôdhisattva recognizes such objective existences as self, others, living creatures, or such a concept as old age—he is not a Bôdhisattva . . . A good disciple must accustom himself to think in terms of negation as regards the existence of all living beings, whereafter it will follow that for him there will be no living beings to think about."

FAITH IS THE SUBSTANCE

O Subhûti, if a good man, or a good woman, were to give up in the morning as many of his or her lives (in re-births) as there are sands in the river Ganges, and to do the same at noonday, and again in the evening, and to continue to do this every day for an innumerable number of *kalpas*, each of an innumerable number of years; and if, on the other hand, there should be one who, having heard this *sûtra*, should yield up his heart to implicit belief—then the happiness of this last would exceed the happiness of that other.   And much more would this be so if he were to write out this *sûtra*, hold fast to it himself, and recite and explain it to others.   O Subhûti, let me state its importance.   This *sûtra* has a merit which cannot be conceived of by thought, and cannot be estimated by weight or measurement.

> If any one looks for me through the medium of form,
> Or seeks me through the medium of sound,
> Such a man is walking in a heterodox path,
> And will not be able to see the Lord Buddha.

WANG CHI

6TH AND 7TH CENTURIES A.D.

[Author of many beautiful poems. His official career was marred by his inability to keep sober.]

RECORD OF DRUNK-LAND

DRUNK-LAND lies at I cannot say how many thousand *li* from the Middle Kingdom. Its soil is uncultivated, and has no boundary. It has no hills nor dangerous cliffs. The climate is equable. Nowhere is there either darkness or light, cold or heat. Customs are everywhere the same. There are no towns; the inhabitants live scattered about. They are very refined; they neither love, nor hate, nor rejoice, nor give way to anger. They inhale the breeze, and drink the dew; they do not eat of the five cereals. Happy in their rest, dignified in their movements, they mingle freely with birds, beasts, fishes, and crustaceans. They have no chariots, nor boats, nor weapons of any kind.

Of old, the Yellow Emperor (3rd millennium B.C.) visited the capital of this country; and when he came back, in his confused state he lost his hold on the empire,[1] all through trying to govern by a system of knotted cords.[2] When the throne was handed on to Yao and Shun, there were sacrifices with a thousand goblets and a hundred flagons, the result being that a divine man had to be shot, in order to secure a passage into this territory, on the frontiers of which will be found perfect peace for life. Under the Great Yü (2205 B.C.), laws were instituted, rites were numerous, and music was of varied kinds, so that for many generations there was no communication with Drunk-Land. Then Hsi and Ho threw up their appointments

---

[1] This statement to be based upon imagination only.

[2] Originally used for rudimentary arithmetic, and popularly exaggerated into a method of government.

as astronomers royal and fled,[1] in the hope of reaching this country; but they missed their way and died young, after which there was much unrest in the empire. The last Emperors of the House of Hsia (d. 1763 B.C.) and of the House of Yin (d. 1122 B.C.) toiled violently up the steps of the eight-thousand-feet mountain of Grains;[2] but though long gazing southwards, they never could see Drunk-Land. The Martial King (d. 1116 B.C.) satisfied his ambition in his generation. He ordered his Grand Astrologer to establish a Department of Wine, with its proper officials; and he extended his territory for 7,000 li, until it just reached Drunk-Land. The result was that for forty years punishments were unknown, down to the reigns of king Cruel (878 B.C.) and king Grim (781 B.C.). By the time of the Ch'ins (255 B.C.) and the Hans (206 B.C.), the Middle Kingdom was in a state of confusion and collapse, and communications with Drunk-Land were cut off. However, certain enlightened friends of mine often slipped across on the sly. The poets Yüan Chi, T'ao Ch'ien, and others, to the number of ten or a dozen, went off to Drunk-Land, disappeared there and never came back; they died there and were buried in its earth. They are known in the Middle Kingdom as the Wine Immortals. Ah me! How different are the customs of the people of Drunk-Land from those of the country of the mother of Fu Hsi (3rd millennium B.C.) of old! How pure and peaceful they are! Well, I have been there myself, and therefore I have written this record.

---

[1] "Now here are Hsi and Ho. They have entirely subverted their virtue and are sunk and lost in wine. They have violated the duties of their office, and left their posts. They have been the first to allow the regulations of heaven to get into disorder, putting far from them their proper business. On the first day of the last month, the sun and moon did not meet harmoniously. The blind musicians beat their drums; the inferior officers and common people bustled and ran about." Legge's *Chinese Classics*, vol. III, p. 165.

[2] From which whisky had been distilled.

CHANG YÜEH

667–730 A.D.

[Poet and statesman who rose to high office, and who was one of the first officials appointed to the newly-instituted Han-lin College.]

FIGHTING GOATS

MAY it please your Majesty,

It is on record that the cock's comb and the pheasant's plume were emblems of the bravery of old. This honour might well be extended to goats. Born on the beetling cliff; hardened by a rigorous life; they face all foes without fear, and fight on courageously to the death. Although but brute beasts, their will may not be lightly crossed.

And now that your Majesty is seeking good soldiers in every corner of the empire, even the birds of the air and the beasts of the field should be laid under contribution. Suppose, then, that your Majesty should deign to place the accompanying animals in the Imperial park where they could exhibit to all comers their untiring strength and their unflinching courage, when with impetuous rush they fall blindly upon one another, horns crashing, bones breaking, blood spurting, in the fierce struggle for victory;—then I think that even the bravest of our brave would be thrilled, and yield their unqualified applause. Thus, I too might hope to lend some trifling aid, like him who counselled the purchase of horses' bones, like him who bowed to the intrepid frog.[1]

---

[1] (1) When Chao Wang stood in need of horses for military purposes, he was advised to offer a high price for horses' bones, so that the people, in view of still larger profits, might be induced to bring real horses to the camp for sale.

(2) When the Prince of Ch'u was attacking the Wu State, he one day made obeisance to a frog—a traditionally brave creature—in order that his soldiery might infer how much more he would be likely to honour them for bravery upon the field.

At the same time, could these goats speak they would doubtless say, "If we are to fight on without interference, there will soon be an end of us. We rely on your Majesty's humanity not to exterminate us thus, but to make use of us in the sense required only as far as our strength permits."

I am suffering from gout, and cannot put my foot to the ground. I therefore humbly forward these goats by your Majesty's son-in-law, to be duly laid before the Throne, trembling meanwhile lest I may have incurred the Imperial displeasure.

HAN WÊN-KUNG

768–824 A.D.

[From Mr. Watters' invaluable *Guide to the Tablets in a Confucian Temple*, I learn that we should wash our hands in rose-water before taking up the works of Han Wên-kung, whose official name was Han Yü, Wên-kung being his title by canonisation. Known as the "Prince of Literature," and generally regarded as the most striking figure in the Chinese world of letters, he certainly ranks high as poet, essayist, and philosopher. In official life, he got himself into trouble by his outspoken attacks upon Buddhism, at that time very fashionable at Court, and was banished to the then barbarous south, where he gained great kudos by his wise and incorrupt administration. It was there that he issued his famous manifesto to the crocodile, at which we might well smile if it were not quite clear that to the author superstition was simply, as elsewhere, an instrument of political power. Han Wên-kung was ultimately recalled from his quasi-exile, and died loaded with honours. His tablet has been placed in the Confucian temple, which is otherwise strictly reserved for exponents of the doctrines of Confucius, "because," as Mr. Watters states, "he stood out almost alone against the heresy of Buddhism which had nearly quenched the torch of Confucian truth."]

ON THE TRUE FAITH OF A CONFUCIANIST

UNIVERSAL love is called *charity*: right conduct is called *duty*. The product of these two factors is called the *Method;* and its practice, without external stimulus, is called *Exemplification*.[1]

Charity and Duty are constant terms. Method and Exemplification are variable. Thus, there is the Method of the perfect man, and the Method of the mean man; while Exemplification may be either good or evil.

Lao Tzŭ merely narrowed the scope of charity and duty; he did not attempt to do without them altogether. His view of them was the narrow view of a man sitting at the bottom of a well and inferring the size of the heavens from the small portion visible to himself. He understood Charity and Duty in a limited, individual sense; and narrowness followed as a matter of course. What he called the Method was a Method he had determined was the Method. It was not what I call the Method. What he called Exemplification was different from what I call Exemplification. What I call Method and Exemplification are based upon a combination of Charity and Duty; and this is the opinion of the world at large. What Lao Tzŭ

---

[1] This last term cannot be satisfactorily rendered. It is usually translated by "virtue"; but that, to go no farther, would make nonsense of the next clause. The meaning, however, may be sufficiently gathered from the context. I need hardly add that "method" must be here understood in its philosophical sense.

called Method and Exemplification were based upon a negation of Charity and Duty; but that was the opinion of one man.

Under the Chows, the true Method began to decay; the influence of Confucius to wane. Under the Ch'ins, came the burning of the books.[1] Under the Hans, the doctrines of Lao Tzŭ prevailed, followed by the Buddhism of succeeding dynasties. Those who then occupied themselves with morals, sided either with Yang Chu or with Mo Tzŭ,[2] or embraced the tenets either of Lao Tzŭ or of Buddha. Such a one was necessarily led to denounce the teachings of Confucius. His adopted faith became all in all to him; his former faith, an outcast. He glorified the new; he vilified the old. And now those who would cultivate morality, hesitate between a choice of guides!

The followers of Lao Tzŭ say, "Confucius was a disciple of our Master." The followers of Buddha say, "Confucius was a disciple of our Master."[3] And the followers of Confucius, by dint of repetition, have at length fallen so low as themselves to indulge in such random talk, saying, "Our Master also respected Lao Tzŭ and Buddha." Not only have they uttered this with their tongues, but they have written it down in books; and now, if a man would cultivate morality, from whom should he seek instruction?

Great is the straining of mankind after the supernatural! Great is their neglect of fundamentals in this yearning for the supernatural alone!

Of old, the people were divided into four classes. They are now divided into six.[4] Of old, there was but one faith. Now, there are three. The husbandman tills his field, and six classes eat of its fruits. The artisan plies his craft, and six classes profit by his skill. The trader

---

[1] *See* Li Ssŭ.

[2] Founders of the egoistic and altruistic schools, respectively (*qq.vv.*).

[3] Confucius is reported to have said "There is a prophet in the West," and the Buddhists have explained this to mean Buddha. A few centuries later and the Jesuits would inevitably have appropriated it as a palpable allusion to Christ.

[4] Alluding to the priests of Lao Tzŭ and Buddha.

barters his goods, and six classes are enriched by the exchange. Is it then surprising that beggary and crime are rampant?

In ancient times, man stood face to face with many dangers. Sages arose and taught him the secret of society. They gave him rulers for the people and teachers for the young. They drove away the beasts of the field and the birds of the air, and established him at the centre of the earth.[1] He was cold, and they gave him clothes. He was hungry, and they gave him food. He entrusted his life to the hazard of a branch, or slept himself into sickness on the bare ground; and they built him palaces and houses to live in. They taught him handicrafts that he might furnish himself with useful things; they taught him trade that the deficiency of one region might be supplied from the abundance of another. They taught him medicine that he might battle against premature death; they taught him burial and sacrifice that the memory of the dead might be perpetuated for ever. They taught him ceremonial in order to secure a rule of precedence; they taught him music as a means of dissipating the melancholy of his heart. They taught him government in order to restrain the lax; they taught him punishment in order to weed out the vicious. As a safeguard against fraud, they made for him seals and measures and scales. As a safeguard against robbery, they built walls and organised militia. Thus did they take precautions against whatsoever evils might come upon him.

But now forsooth we are told that "unless our sages are put to death, deeds of violence will not cease;" and that "if we destroy our measures and break our scales, the people will have no further cause for dissension." What thoughtless talk is this![2]

Had there been no sages of old, the race of man would have long since become extinct. Men have not fur and

---

[1] Which the Chinese then believed to be square and flat.

[2] The doctrine elaborated by Chuang Tzŭ, namely, that if good was not defined, evil could not exist.

feathers and scales to adjust the temperature of their bodies; neither have they claws and fangs to aid them in the struggle for food. Hence their organisation, as follows:—The sovereign issues commands. The minister carries out these commands and makes them known to the people. The people produce grain and flax and silk, fashion articles of every-day use, and interchange commodities, in order to fulfil their obligations to their rulers. The sovereign who fails to issue his commands loses his *raison d'être*: the minister who fails to carry out his sovereign's commands and to make them known to the people, loses his *raison d'être*: the people who fail to produce grain and flax and silk, fashion articles of every-day use, and interchange commodities, in order to fulfil their obligations to their rulers,—should lose their heads.

But now the rule runs thus:—"Discard the relationships of sovereign and subject, of father and son." These social obligations are put out of sight in order to secure, as they say, "perfect purity in abstraction from a world of sense." Happily, indeed, these doctrines were not promulgated until after the Three Dynasties, when they were unable to interfere with the already-established landmarks of our great Sages. Unhappily, it might be said, because they have thus escaped demolition at the hands of those mighty teachers of men.

Now the title of emperor is different from that of king; yet the wisdom of each is the same. To slake thirst by drinking and to appease hunger with food; to wear grass-cloth in summer and fur in winter,—these acts cannot be regarded as identical; yet the rationale of each is the same. Those who urge us to revert to the inaction of extreme antiquity, might as well advise us to wear grass-cloth in winter, or to drink when we are hungry. It is written, "He who would manifest his good instincts to all mankind, must first duly order the State. But previous to this he must duly order his Family. And previous to that his own Self. And previous to that his Heart. And previous to that his Thoughts." It will be seen therefore that there was an ulterior motive in thus ordering the heart and the thoughts. What, on the other hand, is the object of the followers of Lao Tzŭ and Buddha? To withdraw themselves from the world, from the State, and from the family! To deny the eternal obligations of society so that sons need no longer submit themselves to their fathers, so that subjects need no longer own allegiance to their sovereigns, so that the people need no longer occupy themselves with their natural duties!

When Confucius wrote his *Spring and Autumn*,[1] he treated as barbarians those of the feudal princes who used a barbarian ceremonial; while those who adopted the ceremonial of the Central State, were treated by him as men of the Central State. It is written in the *Book of Changes*, "A barbarian prince is not the equal of a Chinese peasant." [2] It is written in the *Book of Odes,* "Oppose the hordes of the west and north: punish the tribes of Ching and Shu." But now when they would take the rule of life of barbarians and graft it upon the wisdom of our ancient kings,—is not this the first step on the road to barbarism itself? For what was the wisdom of our ancient kings? It was this:—"Universal love is called charity:

---

[1] The name given to the *Annals* said, but not universally admitted to be, from his pen. *See* p. 1, and Yüan Mei.

[2] As I was leaving China in 1883, I was presented by a literary friend with a complimentary poem, in which the following lines occurred:—
We may easily meet once more: still it is hard to part.
The chrysanthemums will have faded ere I shall see you again.
Deep have been your researches in our Sacred Books;
Shallow, alas! my wit to expound those books to you.
From of old, literature has illumined the nation of nations;
And now its influence has gone forth to regenerate a barbarian official.
The word used for "barbarian" was the character tabooed by Treaty; and yet the writer was undoubtedly conscious only of an effort to please.
Just now, there is a feeling in certain quarters that the term "Chinaman" is offensive to the Chinese people, and recently a young "Chinese" wrote to *The Times* on the subject. Incidentally, he spoke of us as "Britishers," which though harmless is scarcely a term of respect. Britishers, however, are not so foolish as to resent this; nor I think should the Chinese show themselves too sensitive in regard to "Chinaman," which may be too playful but is certainly not meant offensively, considering that they have but lately dropped the less endearing term "foreign devils," and even now may be occasionally detected in the use of *fan* "barbarian." Meanwhile, our American rivals have advised the use of "Chinese" by "Americans who are desirous of improving the relations between the United States and China" (*see* "Commercial Handbook of China," published by the United States Department of Commerce).

right conduct is called duty. The resultant of these two factors is called the Method; and their exemplification, without external stimulus, is called instinct." Their cannon comprised the *Book of Odes*, the *Book of History*, the *Book of Changes*, and the *Spring and Autumn*. Their code embraced Ceremonial, Music, Punishment, and Administration in general. They divided the people into four classes; —Literati, Husbandmen, Artisans, and Traders. Their relationships were those between sovereign and subject, between father and son, with teacher and with friend, between host and guest, between elder and younger brother, and between husband and wife. Their clothes were of cloth or of silk. They dwelt in palaces or in ordinary houses. They ate grain and vegetables and fruit and fish and flesh. Their Method was easy of comprehension: their doctrines were easily carried into practice. Hence their lives passed pleasantly away, a source of satisfaction to themselves, a source of benefit to mankind. At peace within their own hearts, they readily adapted themselves to the necessities of the family and of the State. Happy in life, they were remembered after death. Their sacrifices were grateful to the God of Heaven, and the spirits of the departed rejoiced in the honours of ancestral worship.

And if I am asked what Method is this, I reply that it is what I call *the* Method, and not merely a method like those of Lao Tzǔ and Buddha. The Emperor Yao handed it down to the Emperor Shun; the Emperor Shun handed it down to the Great Yü; and so on until it reached Confucius, and lastly Mencius, who died without transmitting it to any one else. Then followed the heterodox schools of Hsün and Yang, wherein much that was essential was passed over, while the criterion was vaguely formulated. In the days before Chou Kung, the Sages were themselves rulers; hence they were able to secure the reception of their Method. In the days after Chou Kung, the sages were all high officers of State; hence its duration through a long period of time.

And now, it will be asked, what is the remedy? I answer that unless these false doctrines are rooted out, the true faith will not prevail.   Let us insist that the followers of Lao Tzŭ and Buddha behave themselves like ordinary mortals.   Let us burn their books.   Let us turn their temples into dwelling-houses.   Let us make manifest the Method of our ancient kings in order that men may be led to embrace its teachings.   Thus, and thus only, will there be wherewithal to feed the widow and the orphan, to nourish the cripple and the sick;—and the scheme is feasible enough.

ON SLANDER

The perfect men of old were unsparing in censure of their own faults, but gentle in dealing with the short-comings of others.   Thus they kept up the standard of their own conduct, and stimulated others to the practice of virtue.

Among them were Shun and Chou Kung, both models of charity and duty towards one's neighbour.   He who would imitate the lives of these heroes should say to himself, "They were but men after all.   Why cannot I do what they did?"   And then day and night he should ponder over their story; and while holding fast to all in which he might resemble these models, he should put away all in which he might find himself to differ therefrom.   For these were famous sages, whose likes have not appeared in after ages. And if a man were to accuse himself in whatsoever he might be their equal,—would he not be eminently unsparing in censure of his own faults?

And then if, in regard to others, he would say, "Such a one is but a man; we must not expect too much of him: what he has done is very creditable," and so on, taking care to consider only the present, and not rake up past misdeeds, —would not he be eminently gentle in dealing with the shortcomings of others?

The perfect men of the present day, however, are not
constituted thus. They love to be sharp upon the faults of
others and lenient towards their own, the result being that
no advantage accrues thereby to either. In their own
conduct, they are satisfied with a minimum of virtue and
ability, cajoling others as well as themselves into believing
this more than it is. But when it comes to estimating
anybody else's virtue and ability, nothing seems to be good
enough for them. The past is raked up and the present
ignored, in fear lest those should come to the front instead
of themselves. But such men are merely lowering themselves and exalting others thereby, and must necessarily
lose their self-respect.

Remissness and envy are at the bottom of all this.
Men are often too lazy to push forward, and at the same
time horribly jealous of the advance of others. Thus,
whenever I have purposely taken occasion to praise or
censure any one, I have invariably found that all who
agreed or disagreed, respectively, were those whose interests
were closely bound up with the individual praised or blamed;
or those whose interests at any rate did not clash with his;
or those who spoke under the influence of fear. For the
rest, the bolder ones would angrily differ from my praise, or
agree with my censure, in words; the weaker, by their looks.
Hence it is that virtue and merit are sure to be abused.

Alas! the times are evil for him who would seek an
honest fame, and aim at the practice of virtue. Let those
about to enter into official life digest these words, and
benefit to the State may be the result.

THE UNICORN [1]

That the unicorn is a spiritual being is beyond all
doubt. Hymned in the *Odes,* immortalised in *Springs and*

---

[1] This short piece has reference to the sudden appearance of a unicorn not very
long before the death of Confucius, and was written in extenuation of the heterodox
opinion of Shu-sun, who had ventured to regard the creature as an omen, not of good,
but of evil.

Autumns,[1] it has found a place in the writings of all ages. Women and children alike know that it is a portent of good.

Yet it is reared in no farmyard: it is rarely ever seen throughout the empire's breadth. It is classed under no species. It is not of normal growth like a horse, ox, dog, pig, panther, wolf, or deer. Even were one to appear now, it would not be recognised for what it is.

We see horns, and say, "That is an ox." We see a mane, and say, "That is a horse." And by a similar process we know dogs, pigs, panthers, and deer to be what they are. But the unicorn cannot be known. For Shu-sun to regard it as inauspicious, was therefore reasonable enough. On the other hand, for the unicorn to appear, there should be an All-wise[2] in power: it is in token thereof that the unicorn does appear. Then the All-wise recognises the unicorn, and its manifestation comes in due season.

Again, it is said that the unicorn is a unicorn by virtue not of shape, but of the Truth, of which it is the material embodiment. But if the unicorn appears before the All-wise is in power, then, for Shu-sun to regard its manifestation as inauspicious, was once more reasonable enough.[3]

A TAOIST PRIEST

Of the five famous mountains of China, Hêng-shan is farthest off; and of all the myriad great and lofty eminences of the south, Hêng-shan is chief. That its influences are divine, follows therefore as a matter of course.

Three or four hundred miles to the south, the ground rises still higher, the mountains become more precipitous, the streams clearer and of swifter flow. The highest point is on a range running east and west, and about two-thirds

----

[1] These *Annals* (see *K'ung Fu-tzŭ* and *Yüan Mei*) end, so far as Confucius is concerned, with the entry of the unicorn's appearance.

[2] *Sc.*, Confucius, who was then out of power.

[3] Those who can read between the lines will detect the spirit of sceptical irony which pervades this curious essay.

of the way up is situated the town of Pin-chou.   The pure
pellucid atmosphere of China ends here.   And ending
here, in already transcendent purity, it sweeps round, and
doubling back upon itself with tortuous course, enwraps
the mountain in a two-fold coil.

Thus, if Hêng-shan is divine, how much more so must
be Pin-chou, where perfection itself becomes more perfect
still!

And as it cannot be that this wealth of nature, these
heavenly influences, are lavished upon material products,—
upon silver, mercury, cinnabar, crystal, stalactites, the glory
of the orange and the pumelo, the beauty of the straight
bamboo, the lofty growth of fine trees,—one would naturally
conclude that such a spot must be the birthplace of genius,
the home of loyal and honourable and virtuous men.   But I
never saw any; for the people there are sunk, alas! in
superstition, in the worship of Lao Tzŭ and Fo.

However, there is my friend Liao, a priest of the
religion of Tao.[1]   He is a native of these parts, and a man
of infinite learning and goodness of heart.   How can I class
him among those who grovel in superstitious depths?   He
is one who has an eye for talent in others; and thus, though
not available himself, men of action may be looked for in
the ranks of his friends.

I asked him concerning this strange paradox, but he
would not discuss the question, and I must await a more
favourable opportunity.

ON A BONE FROM BUDDHA'S BODY
A Memorial to the Throne

Your Majesty's servant would submit that Buddhism
is but a cult of the barbarians, and that its spread in China
dates only from the later Han dynasty, and that the ancients
knew nothing of it.

---

[1] The superstition which later ages had developed out of the pure philosophy of
Lao Tzŭ.

Of old, Huang Ti sat on the throne one hundred years, dying at the age of one hundred and ten.   Shao Hao sat on the throne eighty years and died at the age of a hundred. Chuan Hsü sat on the throne seventy-nine years and died at the age of ninety-eight.   Ti Ku sat on the throne seventy years and died at the age of a hundred and fifty.   The Emperor Yao sat on the throne ninety-eight years and died at the age of a hundred and eighteen; and the Emperors Shun and Yü both attained the age of one hundred years.   At that epoch the Empire was tranquil, and the people happy in the attainment of old age; and yet no Buddha had yet reached China.   Subsequently, the Emperor T'ang of the Yin dynasty reached the age of a hundred years; his grandson T'ai Mou reigned for seventy-five years; and Wu Ting reigned for fifty-nine years.   Their exact ages are not given in the annals, but at the lowest computation these can hardly have been less than a hundred years.   Wên Wang of the Chou dynasty reached the age of ninety-seven, Wu Wang reached the age of ninety-three; and Mu Wang reigned for one hundred years; and as at that date likewise the Buddhist religion had not reached China, these examples of longevity cannot be attributed to the worship of the Lord Buddha.

The Buddhist religion was in fact introduced during the reign of Ming Ti of the Han dynasty; and that Emperor sat on the throne but eighteen years.   After him came rebellion upon rebellion, with short-lived monarchs.

During the Sung, Ch'i Liang, Ch'ên, Yüan and Wei dynasties, and so on downwards, the Buddhistic religion gradually spread.   The duration of those dynasties was comparatively short, only the Emperor Wu Ti of the Liang dynasty reigning for so long as forty-eight years.   Thrice he devoted himself to the service of Buddha; at the sacrifices in his ancestral shrines no living victims were used; he daily took but one single meal, and that composed of fruits and vegetables; yet he was harassed by the rebel Ho Ching and died of hunger at T'ai-ch'êng, soon after which his dynasty came to an end. He sought happiness in the worship but found misfortune instead; from which it must be clear to all that Buddha himself is after all but an incompetent God.

When Kao Tsu obtained the Empire he contemplated the extermination of this religion; but the officials of that day were men of limited capabilities; they did not understand the way of our rulers of old; they did not understand the exigencies of the past and present; they did not understand how to avail themselves of His Majesty's wisdom, and root out this evil. Therefore, the execution of this design was delayed, to your servant's infinite sorrow.

Now your present Majesty, endowed with wisdom and courage such as are without parallel in the annals of the past thousand years, prohibited on your accession to the throne the practice of receiving candidates, whether male or female, for priestly orders, prohibiting likewise the erection of temples and monasteries; which caused your servant to believe that the mantle of Kao Tsu had descended on Your Majesty's shoulders. And even should prohibition be impossible, patronage would still be out of the question. Yet your servant has now heard that instructions have been issued to the priestly community to proceed to Feng-hsiang and receive a bone of Buddha, and that from a high tower in the palace Your Majesty will view its introduction into the Imperial Palace; also that orders have been sent to the various temples, commanding that the relic be received with the proper ceremonies. Now, foolish though your servant may be, he is well aware that your Majesty does not do this in the vain hope of deriving advantages therefrom; but that in the fulness of our present plenty, and in the joy which reigns in the hearts of all, there is a desire to fall in with the wishes of the people in the celebration at the capital of this delusive mummery. For how could the wisdom of Your Majesty stoop to participation in such ridiculous beliefs? Still the people are slow of perception and easily beguiled; and should they behold Your Majesty thus earnestly worshipping at the feet of Buddha they would cry out, "See! the Son of Heaven, the All-Wise, is a fervent believer; who are we, his people, that we should spare our bodies?" Then would ensue a scorching of heads and burning of fingers; crowds would collect together, and tearing off their clothes and scattering their money, would spend their time from morn to eve in imitation of Your Majesty's example. The result would be that by and by young and old, seized with the same enthusiasm, would totally neglect the business of their lives; and should Your Majesty not prohibit it, they would be found flocking to the temples, ready to cut off an arm or slice their bodies as an offering to the God. Thus would our traditions and customs be seriously injured, and ourselves become a laughing-stock on the face of the earth;—truly, no small matter! For Buddha was a barbarian. His language was not the language of China; his clothes were of an alien cut. He did not utter the maxims of our ancient rulers, nor conform to the customs which they have handed down. He did not appreciate the bond between prince and minister, the tie between father and son. Supposing, indeed, this Buddha had come to our capital in the flesh, under an appointment from his own State, then your Majesty might have received him with a few words of admonition, bestowing on him a banquet and a suit of clothes, previous to sending him out of the country with an escort of soldiers, and thereby have avoided any dangerous influence on the minds of the people. But what are the facts? The bone of a man long since dead and decomposed, is to be admitted, forsooth, within the precincts of the Imperial Palace! Confucius said, "Pay all respect to spiritual beings, but keep them at a distance." And so, when the princes of old paid visits of condolence to one another, it was customary for them to send on a magician in advance, with a peach wand in his hand, whereby to expel all noxious influences previous to the arrival of his master. Yet now Your Majesty is about to causelessly introduce a disgusting object, personally taking part in the proceedings without the intervention either of the magician or of his peach wand. Of the officials, not one has raised his voice against it; of the censors, not one has pointed out the enormity of such an act. Therefore your servant, overwhelmed with shame, implores Your Majesty that this bone may be handed over for destruction by fire or water, whereby the root of this great evil may be exterminated for all time, and the people know how much the wisdom of Your Majesty surpasses that of ordinary men. The glory of such a deed will be beyond all praise. And should the Lord Buddha have power to avenge this insult by the infliction of some misfortune, then let the vials of his wrath be poured out upon the person of your servant who now calls Heaven to witness that he will not repent him of his oath.

In all gratitude and sincerity your Majesty's servant now humbly presents, with fear and trembling, this Memorial for your Majesty's benign consideration.

THE CROCODILE OF CH'AO-CHOU [1]

On a certain date, I, Han Yü, Governor of Ch'ao-chou, gave orders that a goat and a pig should be thrown into the river as prey for the crocodile, together with the following notification:—

"In days of yore, when our ancient rulers first undertook the administration of the empire, they cleared away the jungle by fire, and drove forth with net and spear such denizens of the marsh as were obnoxious to the prosperity of the human race, away beyond the boundaries of the Four Seas. But as years went on, the light of Imperial virtue began to pale; the circle of the empire was narrowed; and lands once subject to the divine sway passed under barbarian rule. Hence, the region of Ch'ao-chou, distant

---

[1] This diatribe has reference to the alleged expulsion of a crocodile which had been devastating the water-courses round Ch'ao-chou, whither Han Wên-kung had been sent in disgrace. The writer's general character and high literary attainments forbid us, indeed, to believe that he believed himself.

many hundred miles from the capital, was then a fitting spot for thee, O crocodile, in which to bask, and breed, and rear thy young. But now again the times are changed. We live under the auspices of an enlightened prince, who seeks to bring within the Imperial fold all, even to the uttermost limits of sea and sky. Moreover, this is soil once trodden by the feet of the Great Yü[1] himself; soil for which I, an officer of the State, am bound to make due return, in order to support the established worship of Heaven and Earth, in order to the maintenance of the Imperial shrines and temples of the Gods of our land.

"O crocodile! thou and I cannot rest together here. The Son of Heaven has confided this district and this people to my charge; and thou, O goggle-eyed, by disturbing the peace of this river and devouring the people and their domestic animals, the bears, the boars, and deer of the neighbourhood, in order to batten thyself and reproduce thy kind,—thou art challenging me to a struggle of life and death. And I, though of weakly frame, am I to bow the knee and yield before a crocodile? No! I am the lawful guardian of this place, and I would scorn to decline thy challenge, even were it to cost me my life.

"Still, in virtue of my commission from the Son of Heaven, I am bound to give fair warning; and thou, O crocodile, if thou art wise, will pay due heed to my words. There before thee lies the broad ocean, the domain alike of the whale and the shrimp. Go thither, and live in peace. It is but the journey of a day.

"And now I bid thee begone, thou and thy foul brood, within the space of three days, from the presence of the servant of the Son of Heaven. If not within three days, then within five; if not within five, then within seven. But if not within seven, then it is that thou wilt not go, but art ready for the fight. Or, may be, that thou hast not wit to seize the purport of my words; though whether it be wilful

---

[1] See *Ch'ao Ts'o*, "On the Value of Agriculture" (note), page 72.

disobedience or stupid misapprehension, the punishment in each case is death.   I will arm some cunning archer with trusty bow and poisoned arrow, and try the issue with thee, until thou and all thy likes have perished.   Repent not then, for it will be too late." [1]

IN MEMORIAM [2]

Seven days had elapsed after the news of thy death ere I could control my grief and collect my thoughts.   I then bade one go and prepare, dear boy, some choice votive offering to thy departed spirit.

Ah, me! betimes an orphan; growing up without a father's care; dependent solely upon an elder brother, thy father, and his wife.   And when, in mid career, that brother died far away in the south, thou and I, mere boys, followed the widow home with the funeral *cortège*.   Then our life together, orphans each, never separated for a day.

My three brothers all early died, leaving only us, a grandson and a son, to carry on the ancestral line.   We were two generations, with but one body, one form, one shadow.   And often when thy mother bore thee in her arms, she would point at me and say, "Of two generations of the house of Han, these are all that remain."   Thou wert too young to remember that now; and I, though I remember the words now, did not understand the sorrow that they expressed.

At sixteen, I went to the capital, returning home after the lapse of four years.   Then four years more, after which I repaired to the family burying-ground, and met thee there, standing by thy mother's grave.   Another two years of official life: a short reunion during thy visit of a year: leave of absence to bring my family to my home.   The next year my chief died, and I quitted my post; but thou didst not

---

[1] The crocodile went.

[2] This exquisite *morceau* tells its own tale, coupled with several interesting details of the writer's own life.

come. In the same year another appointment elsewhere, whence the messenger sent to fetch thee had barely started ere I again had left. Once more thou camest not. Yet I knew that had we gone eastwards together it would have been but for a short time, and that I should do better to make for the west, where we might all gather round the old home.

Alas! why leave me thus and die? To me it seemed that both were young in years, and that although separated for a time, we might still hope to pass our lives together. Therefore we parted, and I went to the capital in search of place; but could I have foreseen what was to happen, the many-charioted territory of a duke should not have tempted me one moment from thy side.

Last year I wrote thee, saying, "Not forty yet: sight dim, hair gray, strength sapped. Father and brothers, lusty men all, died in their prime;—can then this decaying frame last long? I may not go: thou wilt not come. Alas! I fear lest at any moment I may be cut off and leave thee to unutterable grief." Yet who would have thought that the young man was to perish and the old man to live? the strong youth to sink into a premature grave, the sick man to be made whole? Is it reality or a dream? Was it truth they told me? Reality—that the line of my noble-hearted brother should be thus ended in premature death? Reality —that thy pure intelligence shall not survive to continue the traditions of his house? Reality—that the young and strong thus early fade and die, while the old and decaying live on and thrive? Reality indeed it is; and no dream, and no lie. Else why this letter, this notice of death, now lying before me? It is so. The line of my noble-hearted brother has indeed been prematurely cut off. Thy pure intelligence, hope of the family, survives not to continue the traditions of his house. Unfathomable are the appointments of what men call Heaven: inscrutable are the workings of the unseen: unknowable are the mysteries of eternal truth: unrecognisable those who are destined to attain to old age!

Henceforth, my gray hairs will grow white, my strength fail. Physically and mentally hurrying on to decay, how long before I shall follow thee? If there is knowledge after death, this separation will be but for a little while. If there is no knowledge after death, so will this sorrow be but for a little while, and then no more sorrow for ever.

Thy boy is just ten; mine five. But if the young and the strong are to be thus cut off, who shall dare hope that these babes in arms may not share the same unhappy fate?

Thy last year's letters told me of the tender foot and its increasing pains; but I said to myself, "The disease is common in Kiangnan, and need cause no alarm." Was it then this that extinguished thy life, or some other disease that brought thee to the grave?

Thy last letter is dated 17th of the 6th moon. Yet I hear from one that death came on the 2nd, while another sends a letter without date. The messenger never thought to ask; and the family, relying on the letter's date, never thought to tell. I enquired of the messenger, but he replied at random, so that I am still in doubt. I have now sent to sacrifice to thy departed spirit, and to condole with thy orphan and foster-mother, bidding them wait, if possible, until the final rites are paid, but if not, then to come to me, leaving the servants to watch over thy corpse. And when perchance I am able, I will some day see that thy bones are duly laid in our ancestral burying-place.

Alas! of thy sickness I knew not the time; of thy death I knew not the hour. Unable to tend thee in life, I was debarred from weeping over thee in death. I could not touch thy bier: I could not stand by thy grave. I have sinned against Heaven: I have caused thee to be cut off in thy prime. Wretch that I am, separated from thee alike in life and death —thou at one end of the earth, I at the other—thy shadow did not accompany my form, neither shall thy spirit now blend with my dreams. The fault, the blame are mine alone.

O ye blue heavens, when shall my sorrow have end? Henceforth, the world has no charms. I will get me a few acres on the banks of the Ying, and there await the end, teaching my son and thy son, if haply they may grow up,— my daughter and thy daughter, until their day of marriage comes. Alas! though words fail, love endureth. Dost thou hear, or dost thou not hear? Woe is me: Heaven bless thee!

IN MEMORIAM [1]

Alas! Tzŭ-hou, and hast thou come to this pass?—fool that I am! is it not the pass to which mortals have ever come? Man is born into the world like a dream: what need has he to take note of gain or loss? While the dream lasts, he may sorrow or may joy; but when the awakening is at hand, why cling regretfully to the past?

'Twere well for all things an they had no worth. The excellence of its wood is the bane of the tree. And thou, whom God released in mid-career from earthly bonds, weaver of the jewelled words, thou wilt be remembered when the imbeciles of fortune and place are forgot.

The unskilful bungler hacks his hands and streams with sweat, while the expert craftsman looks on with folded arms. O my friend, thy work was not for this age; though I, a bungler, have found employment in the service of the State. Thou didst know thyself above the common herd; but when in shame thou didst depart, never to return, the philistines usurped thy place.

Alas! Tzŭ-hou, now thou art no more. But thy last wish, that I should care for thy little son, is still ringing sadly in my ears. The friendships of the day are those of self-interest alone. How can I feel sure that I shall live to carry out thy behest? I did not arrogate to myself this duty. Thou thyself hast bidden me to the task; and, by the Gods above, I will not betray thy trust.

Thou hast gone to thy eternal home, and wilt not return. With these sacrifices by thy coffin's side, I utter an affectionate farewell.

[1] In memory of his dear friend Liu Tsung-yüan (see p. 134), whose literary name was Tzŭ-hou.

LIU TSUNG-YÜAN

A.D. 773–819.

[A most versatile writer, and one of the intimate friends of Han Wên-kung (*q.v.*), like whom he was banished on political grounds to a distant official post, where he died. His breadth of intelligence allowed him to tolerate Buddhism, in direct opposition to the utterances of Han Wên-kung, who perceived in its growing influence a menacing danger to Confucianism and to the State. He excelled in political satire, and suffered for the sting of his pen. His death called forth the short but beautiful lament, "In Memoriam," by Han Wên-kung.]

REVENGE

IT is on record that during the reign of the Empress Wu, a man named Hsü, whose father had been executed for some misdeed, slew the presiding magistrate and then gave himself up to the authorities. A suggestion was made by one of the Censors of the day that, on the one hand, the son should suffer death for his crime; on the other, that a memorial to him should be erected in his native village. Further, that the case should be entered as a judicial precedent.

I consider this suggestion to be wholly wrong. Honours and rewards originated in a desire to prevent aggression. If therefore a son avenges the death of a guilty father, the former should be slain without mercy. Administration of punishment was also organised with the same object. If, therefore, officers of government put the laws in operation without due cause, they too should be slain without mercy. Though springing from the same source, and with the same object in view, honours and punishments are applicable to different cases and cannot be awarded together. To punish one deserving of reward is to cast a slur upon all punishment: to honour one deserving of punishment is to detract from the value of all honours. And if such a case were to be admitted as a precedent for future generations, then those eager to do their duty, and those anxious to avoid evil, would equally find themselves in a strange dilemma. Is this the stuff that law is made of?

Now, in adjusting reward and punishment, praise and blame, the wise men of old adhered closely to fixed principles, while allowing for such modifications as special circumstances might demand. Their end and aim was a consistent uniformity. And it has ever been the chief object of judicial investigations to distinguish between right and wrong, and to administer justice with impartial hand. Hence the impossibility of applying honour and punishment to the same case.

Let me explain. Suppose that Hsü's father had committed no crime, but had been wrongfully done to death by the magistrate, out of spite or in a rage; and suppose the magistrate and other officials to have treated the matter as of small account, to have rejected all claims, to have turned a deaf ear to all entreaties;—then, if the son, scorning to live under the same heaven, his head pillowed by night upon his sword, his heart brimful of wrong, had struck the murderer to earth, careless of the death to come upon himself,—then I would say that he was a noble fellow who did his duty and deserved the thanks of shame-faced officials for relieving them of their responsibilities of office. Why talk of condemning him?

But if Hsü's father was really guilty, and the magistrate rightly put him to death, in that case it was not the magistrate but the law which took his life; and can a man feel a grudge against the law? Besides, to slay an official in order to be avenged upon the law he administers, is simply open rebellion against properly-constituted authority. Such an offender should indeed suffer death for his crime in accordance with the statutes of the empire; but he should hardly be honoured at the same time with a memorial.

The above-mentioned Censor further went on to say, "Every man has a son, and every son is under the same obligations to his parents. If then it is admissible for sons to slay the murderers of their fathers, the result will of course be an endless chain of slaughter." But here the Censor totally misunderstands the purport of social obligations. The man whom society deems qualified for revenge is one who struggles beneath a terrible load of

136   GEMS OF CHINESE LITERATURE

wrong, with no means of redress. It is not one who, when a guilty father has rightly perished under the knife of the executioner, cries out, "He killed my parent. I will kill him!" oblivious of all questions of right or wrong, and presuming on one's own strength as against another's weakness. This would amount to complete overthrow of all those great principles upon which our system is based.

In the days of the Chou dynasty, the peace officers arranged the *vendette* of the people. If a man was deservedly put to death, they would not allow any revenge to be taken; and disobedience to this order was punished capitally, the State interfering as the aggrieved party, in order to prevent endless reprisals by sons of murdered fathers. Again, in Kung-yang's Commentary to the *Spring and Autumn* the principle is stated thus:—"If a man is wrongfully put to death, his son may avenge him. But if rightly, and yet the son avenges his death, this is to push to extremes the arbitrament of the sword, while the source of all the evil still remains untouched." And in my opinion this principle would be lawfully applied to the present case. Not to neglect vengeance is the duty of a son: to brave death is heroic; and if Hsü, without breaking the social code, proved himself a man of filial piety and heroism, he must necessarily have been a man of lofty virtue; and no man of lofty virtue would ever oppose the operation of his country's laws. His case should not therefore be admitted as a precedent, and I pray that the decree may be rescinded accordingly.

CATCHING SNAKES

In the wilds of Hu-kuang there is an extraordinary kind of snake, having a black body with white rings. Deadly fatal, even to the grass and trees it may chance to touch; in man, its bite is absolutely incurable. Yet if caught and prepared, when dry, in the form of cakes, the flesh of this snake will soothe excitement, heal leprous sores, remove sloughing flesh, and expel evil spirits. And so it came about that the Court physician, acting under Imperial orders, exacted from each family a return of two of these snakes every year; but as few persons were able to comply with the demand, it was subsequently made known that the return of snakes was to be considered in lieu of the usual taxes. Thereupon there ensued a general stampede among the people of those parts.

However, there was one man whose family had lived there for three generations; and from him I obtained the following information:—"My grandfather lost his life in snake-catching. So did my father. And during the twelve years that I have been engaged in the same way, death has several times come very near to me." He was deeply moved during this recital; but when I asked if I should state his sad case to the authorities and apply for him to be allowed to pay taxes in the regular manner, he burst into tears and said, "Alas! sir, you would take away my means of livelihood altogether. The misery of this state is as nothing when compared with the misery of that. Formerly, under the ordinary conditions of life, we suffered greatly; but for the past three generations we have been settled in this district, now some sixty years since. During that period, my fellow-villagers have become more and more impoverished. Their substance has been devoured, and in beggary they have gone weeping and wailing away. Exposed to the inclemency of wind and rain, enduring heat and cold, they have fled from the cruel scourge, in most cases, to die. Of those families which were here in my grandfather's time, there remains not more than one in ten; of those here in my father's time, not more than two or three; and of those still here in my own time, not more than four or five. They are all either dead or gone elsewhere; while we, the snake-catchers, alone survive. Harsh tyrants sweep down upon us, and throw everybody and everything, even to the brute beasts, into paroxysms of terror and disorder. But I,—I get up in the morning and look into the jar where my snakes are kept; and if they are still there, I lie down at night in peace. At the appointed time, I take care that they are fit to be handed in; and when that is done, I retire to enjoy the produce of my farm and complete the allotted span of my existence. Only twice a year have I to risk my life: the rest is peaceful enough and not to be compared with the daily round of annoyance which falls to the share of my fellow-villagers. And even though I were to die now in this employ, I should still have outlived almost all my contemporaries. Can I then complain?

This story gave me food for much sad reflection. I had always doubted the saying of Confucius that "bad government is worse than a tiger,"[1] but now I felt its truth. Alas! who would think that the tax-collector could be more venomous than a snake? I therefore record this for the information of those whom it may concern.

CONGRATULATIONS ON A FIRE

I have received the letter informing me that your house has been attacked by fire, and that you have lost everything. At first, I felt shocked: then doubtful: but now I congratulate you from the bottom of my heart. My sorrow is turned into joy. Still, we are far apart, and you give no particulars. If you mean that you are utterly and irretrievably beggared, then I have further reason to offer you my congratulations.

In the first place, it was only because I knew your happiness to be bound up with the happiness of your parents, and feared that this calamity would disturb the even tenor of their lives, that I felt shocked.

Secondly, the world is never weary of citing the fickleness of fortune and the uncertainty of her favours. And it is an old tradition that the man who is to rise to great things must first be chastened by misfortune and sorrow; and that the evils of flood and fire, and the slanders

---

[1] See under *T'an Kung*, page 41.

of scoundrels, are sent upon him solely that he may shine thereafter with a brighter light. But this doctrine is absurdly far-fetched, and could never command the confidence even of diviner intellects than ours. Therefore I doubted.

My friend, you are widely read in ancient lore. You are an accomplished scholar: a man, in fact, of many gifts. Yet you have failed to rise above the common rank and file. And why? Because you were known to be rich; and men jealous of their reputation refrained from speaking your praises. They kept their knowledge of your virtues to themselves, fearing the calumnious imputations of the world. To speak on your behalf would be to raise a titter, coupled with queries as to the amount transferred.

As for me, it is now some years since I became aware of your literary power; but all that time I selfishly said nothing, disloyal not only to you but to the cause of truth. And even when I became a Censor and a high functionary of State, and rejoiced in my proximity to the Throne and in the liberty of speech which enabled me to bring forth your merits into the blaze of day,—I was only laughed at as one recommending his friends. I have long hated myself for this want of straightforwardness and fear of the world's censure, and with our friend Mêng Chi have often bewailed the impracticability of the position. But now that Heaven has sent this ruin upon you, the suspicions of men vanish with the smoke of the fire, and are refuted by the blackened walls which proclaim your poverty to all. Your talents have now free play, without fear of reproach. Verily the God of Fire is on your side. In one night he has done more to set your praises before men than your own bosom friends have accomplished during the space of ten years. Have patience awhile, and those who have always believed in your genius will be able to open their mouths; and those with whom your advancement lies, will advance you without fear. You must remain in obscurity no longer. I can help you now, and therefore I congratulate you from my heart.

In the olden days, when the capitals of four States were burnt to the ground,[1] the other States, with one exception, sent to condole with the sufferers. The omission on the part of that one State incurred the disapprobation of the superior man. But I have gone even farther. I congratulate where the world condoles; and as for the care of your parents, with the examples of antiquity before you, there need be no cause for fear.

THE BEAUTIES OF BUDDHISM

My learned and estimable friend Han Yü[2] has often reproached my *penchant* for Buddhism and the intercourse that I hold with its priests. And now a letter from him has just reached me, in which he blames me severely for not having denounced the religion in a recent address forwarded to another friend.

In point of fact, there is much in Buddhism which could not well be denounced; *scilicet,* all those tenets which are based on principles common to our own sacred books. And it is precisely to these essentials, at once in perfect harmony with human nature and the teachings of Confucius, that I give in my adhesion.

Han Yü himself could not be a warmer advocate of moral culture (as excluding the supernatural) than was Yang Hsiung; and the works of the latter, as well as those of other heterodox writers, contain a great deal that is valuable. Why then should this be impossible in the case of Buddhism? Han Yü replies, "Buddha was a barbarian." But if this argument is good for anything, we might find ourselves embracing a criminal who happened to be a fellow-countryman, while neglecting a saint whose misfortune it was to be a foreigner! Surely this would be a hollow mockery indeed.

---

[1] Owing, as it was said, to the appearance of a great comet.

[2] Now generally known as Han Wên-kung (*q.v.*).

The lines I admire in Buddhism are those which are coincident with the principles enunciated in our own sacred books. And I do not think that, even were the holy sages of old to revisit the earth, they would fairly be able to denounce these. Now, Han Yü objects to the Buddhist commandments. He objects to the bald pates of the priests, their dark robes, their renunciation of domestic ties, their idleness, and life generally at the expense of others. So do I. But Han Yü misses the kernel while railing at the husk. He sees the lode, but not the ore. I see both; hence my partiality for the faith.

Again, intercourse with men of this religion does not necessarily imply conversion. Even if it did, Buddhism admits no envious rivalry for place or power. The majority of its adherents love only to lead a simple life of contemplation amid the charms of hill and stream. And when I turn my gaze towards the hurry-scurry of the age, in its daily race for the seals and tassels of office, I ask myself if I am to reject those in order to take my place among the ranks of these.

The Buddhist priest, Hao-ch'u, is a man of placid temperament and of passions subdued. He is a fine scholar. His only joy is to muse o'er flood and fell, with occasional indulgence in the delights of composition. His family—for he has one[1]—follow in the same path. He is independent of all men; and no more to be compared with those heterodox sages of whom we make so much, than with the vulgar herd of the greedy, grasping world around us.

IS THERE A GOD?

Over the western hills the road trends away towards the north; and on the further side of the pass, separates into two. The westerly branch leads to nowhere in particular; but if you follow the other, which takes a

[1] Celibacy is now strictly enforced, with only qualified results.

north-easterly turn, for about a quarter of a mile, you will find that the path ends abruptly, while the stream forks to enclose a steep pile of boulders. On the summit of this pile there is what appears to be an elegantly-built look-out tower; below, as it were a battlemented wall, pierced by a city gate, through which one gazes into darkness. A stone thrown in here, falls with a splash suggestive of water; and the reverberations of this sound are audible for some time. There is a way round from behind up to the top, whence nothing is seen far and wide except groves of fine straight trees, which, strange to say, are grouped symmetrically, as if by an artist's hand.

Now, I have always had my doubts about the existence of God; but this scene made me think he really must exist. At the same time, however, I began to wonder why he did not place it in some worthy centre of civilisation, rather than in this out-of-the-way barbarous region, where for centuries there has been no one to enjoy its beauty. And so, on the other hand, such waste of labour and incongruity of position disposed me to think that there could not be a God after all.

A friend suggested that it was designedly placed there to gratify those virtuous men who might be banished in disgrace to that spot (as, for instance, the writer). Another argued that it was simply the nature of the locality, which was unfavourable to the growth of heroes, and fit only for the production of inanimate objects of the kind: as witness the great dearth of men and abundance of boulders in these parts.[1] But I do not accept either explanation.

PAS TROP GOUVERNER

I do not know what Camel-back's real name was. Disease had hunched him up behind, and he walked with his head down, like a camel. Hence, people came to give him

---

[1] A sneer at the inhabitants of Kuang-si, which is rather lost upon the European reader.

the nickname of Camel. "Capital!" cried he, when he first heard of his sobriquet; "the very name for me." And thereafter he entirely left off using his proper name, calling himself "Camel-back."

He lived in the village of Peace-and-Plenty, near the capital, and followed the occupation of a nursery-gardener. All the grand people of the city used to go and see his show; while market-gardeners vied with each other in securing his services, since every tree he either planted or transplanted was sure to thrive and bear fruit, not only early in the season but in abundance. Others in the same line of business, although they closely watched his method, were quite unable to achieve the same success.

One day a customer asked him how this was so; to which he replied, "Old Camel-back cannot make trees live or thrive. He can only let them follow their natural tendencies. Now in planting trees, be careful to set the root straight, to smooth the earth around them, to use good mould, and to ram it down well. Then, don't touch them; don't think about them; don't go and look at them; but leave them alone to take care of themselves, and nature will do the rest. I only avoid trying to make my trees grow. I have no special method of cultivation, no special means for securing luxuriance of growth. I only don't spoil the fruit. I have no way of getting it either early or in abundance. Other gardeners set with bent root, and neglect the mould. They heap up either too much earth or too little. Or if not this, then they become too fond of and too anxious about their trees, and are for ever running backwards and forwards to see how they are growing; sometimes scratching them to make sure they are still alive, or shaking them about to see if they are sufficiently firm in the ground; thus constantly interfering with the natural bias of the tree, and turning their affection and care into an absolute bane and a curse. I only don't do these things. That's all."

"Can these principles you have just now set forth be applied to government?" asked his listener. "Ah!"

replied Camel-back, "I only understand nursery-gardening: government is not my trade. Still, in the village where I live, the officials are for ever issuing all kinds of orders, as if greatly compassionating the people, though really to their utter injury. Morning and night the underlings come round and say, ' His Honour bids us urge on your ploughing, hasten your planting, and superintend your harvest. Do not delay with your spinning and weaving. Take care of your children. Rear poultry and pigs. Come together when the drum beats. Be ready at the sound of the rattle.' Thus are we poor people badgered from morn till eve. We have not a moment to ourselves. How could any one flourish and develop naturally under such conditions? It was this that brought about my illness. And so it is with those who carry on the gardening business."

"Thank you," said the listener. "I simply asked about the management of trees, and I have learnt about the management of men. I will make this known, as a warning to government officials."

LI HUA

9TH CENTURY A.D.

ON AN OLD BATTLE-FIELD

VAST, vast,—a limitless extent of flat sand, without a human being in sight; girdled by a stream and dotted with hills; where in the dismal twilight the wind moans at the setting sun. Shrubs gone: grass withered: all chill as the hoar-frost of early morn. The birds of the air fly past: the beasts of the field shun the spot; for it is, as I was informed by the keeper, the site of an old battle-field. "Many a time and oft," said he, "has an army been overthrown on this spot; and the voices of the dead may frequently be heard weeping and wailing in the darkness of the night."

Oh, sorrow! oh, ye Ch'ins, ye Hans, ye dynasties now passed away! I have heard that when the Ch'is and the Weis gathered at the frontier, and when the Chings and the Hans collected their levies, many were the weary leagues they trod, many were the years of privation and exposure they endured. Grazing their horses by day, fording the river by night, the endless earth beneath, the boundless sky above, they knew not the day of their return; their bodies all the time exposed to the pitiless steel, with many other unspeakable woes.

Again, since the Ch'in and the Han dynasties, countless troubles have occurred within the boundaries of the empire, desolating the Middle Kingdom. No age has been free from these. In the olden days, barbarians and Chinese alike meekly followed their Imperial guide. But the place of right was usurped by might; the rude soldier cast aside the obligations of morality, and the rule of reason lost its sway.

Alas! methinks I see them now, the bitter wind enveloping them in dust, the Tartar warriors in ambuscade. Our general makes light of the foe. He would give battle upon the very threshold of his camp. Banners wave over the plain; the river closes-in the battle array. All is order, though hearts may beat. Discipline is everything: life is of no account.

And now the cruel spear does its work, the startled sand blinds the combatants locked fast in the death-struggle; while hill and vale and stream groan beneath the flash and crash of arms. By-and-by, the chill cold shades of night fall upon them, knee-deep in snow, beards stiff with ice. The hardy vulture seeks its nest: the strength of the war-horse is broken. Clothes are of no avail; hands frost-bitten, flesh cracked. Even nature lends her aid to the Tartars, contributing a deadly blast, the better to complete the work of slaughter begun. Ambulance waggons block the way: our men succumb to flank attacks. Their officers have surrendered: their general is dead. The river is chocked with corpses to its topmost banks: the fosses of the Great Wall are swimming over with blood. All distinctions are obliterated in that heap of rotting bones . . .

Faintly and more faintly beats the drum. Strength exhausted, arrows spent, bow-strings snapped, swords shattered, the two armies fall upon one another in the supreme struggle for life or death. To yield is to become the barbarian's slave: to fight is to mingle our bones with the desert sand . . .

No sound of bird now breaks from the hushed hillside. All is still, save the wind whistling through the long night. Ghosts of the dead wander hither and thither in the gloom: spirits from the nether world collect under the dark clouds. The sun rises and shines coldly over the trampled grass, while the fading moon still twinkles upon the frost-flakes scattered around. What sight more horrible than this!

I have heard that Li Mu led the soldiers of Chao to victory over their Tartar foes, clearing the country for miles, and utterly routing the Huns. The Hans, on the other hand, exhausted in vain the resources of the empire.

They had not the men, and their numbers availed them naught.

The Chows, too, drove back the barbarous hordes of the north; and having garrisoned the country, returned safely home. Then they offered thanks to the Gods, and gave themselves up to the universal enjoyment which peace alone can bring.

The Ch'ins built the Great Wall, stretching far away to the sea. Yet the poison-breath of war decimated the people, and mile upon mile ran with their red blood.

The Hans beat down the Huns, and seized Yin-shan. But their corpses lay pillowed over the plain, and the gain was not equal to the loss.

O high Heaven! which of these but has father and mother, who bore them about in childhood, fearing only lest maturity should never come? Which of these but has brothers, dear to them as themselves? Which of these but has a wife, bound by the closest ties? They owe no thanks for life, for what have they done to deserve death? They may be alive or dead—the family knows it not. And if one brings the news, they listen, half doubting, half believing, while the heart overflows with grief. Sleeping and waking, they seem to see the lost one's form. Sacrifices are made ready and libations poured, with tearful eyes strained towards the far horizon; heaven and earth, nay, the very trees and plants, all seeming to sympathise with their sorrow. And when, in response to prayers and libations, these wanderers return not, where shall their spirits find repose? Verily there shall be a famine over the land,[1] and the people be scattered abroad. Alas! such is life, and such it has ever been. What resource then is left but to keep within our frontier lines?[2]

---

[1] In allusion to some words attributed to Lao Tzŭ.

[2] I doubt if the Peace Society, to whom this essay might well be dedicated, has ever published a more graphic description of the horrors of war.

LIU YÜ-HSI

A.D. 772–842.

[One of the well-known poets of the T'ang dynasty. As an official, he shared the fate of Liu Tsung-yüan, being banished to a distant post in consequence of political intrigue.]

MY HUMBLE HOME

HILLS are not famous for height alone: 'tis the Genius Loci that invests them with their charm. Lakes are not famous for mere depth: 'tis the residing Dragon that imparts to them a spell not their own. And so, too, my hut may be mean; but the fragrance of Virtue is diffused around.

The green lichen creeps up the steps: emerald leaflets peep beneath the bamboo blind. Within, the laugh of cultured wit, where no gross soul intrudes; the notes of the light lute, the words of the *Diamond Book*,[1] marred by no scraping fiddle, no scrannel pipe, no hateful archives of official life.

K'ung-ming had his cottage in the south; Yang Hsiung his cabin in the west. And the Master said, "What foulness can there be where virtue is?"

---

[1] A famous Buddhist *sûtra*, of which there is a handy if not perfect English translation by William Gemmell.

PŎ CHÜ-YI

A.D. 772–846.

[One of China's greatest poets, and a statesman with a varied career. Rising to high rank he was suddenly banished to a distance, with reduced rank, which disgusted him with official life. He then joined with eight congenial companions, and gave himself up to poetry and wine. Later on, he was recalled, and subsequently became President of the Board of War.]

THE LUTE-GIRL'S LAMENT

By night, at the riverside, adieus were spoken: beneath the maple's flower-like leaves, blooming amid autumnal decay. Host had dismounted to speed the parting guest, already on board his boat. Then a stirrup-cup went round, but no flute, no guitar, was heard. And so, ere the heart was warmed with wine, came words of cold farewell, beneath the bright moon glittering over the bosom of the broad stream . . . when suddenly, across the water, a lute broke forth into sound. Host forget to go, guest lingered on, wondering whence the music, and asking who the performer might be. At this, all was hushed, but no answer given. A boat approached, and the musician was invited to join the party. Cups were refilled, lamps trimmed again, and preparations for festivity renewed. At length, after much pressing, she came forth, hiding her face behind her lute; and twice or thrice sweeping the strings, betrayed emotion ere her song was sung. Then every note she struck swelled with pathos deep and strong, as though telling the tale of a wrecked and hopeless life, while with bent head and rapid finger she poured forth her soul in melody. Now softly, now slowly, her plectrum sped to and fro; now this air, now that; loudly, with the crash of falling rain; softly, as the murmur of whispered words; now loud and soft together, like the patter of pearls and pearlets dropping upon a marble dish. Or liquid, like the warbling of the mango-bird in the bush; trickling, like the streamlet on its downward course. And then like the torrent, stilled by the grip of frost, so for a moment was the music lulled, in a passion too deep for sound.[1]   Then, as bursts the water from the broken vase, as clash the arms upon the mailed horseman, so fell the plectrum once more upon the strings with a slash like the rent of silk.

Silence on all sides: not a sound stirred the air.   The autumn moon shone silver athwart the tide, as with a sigh the musician thrust her plectrum beneath the strings and quietly prepared to take leave.   "My childhood," said she, "was spent at the capital, in my home near the hills.   At thirteen, I learnt the guitar, and my name was enrolled among the *primas* of the day.   The *maëstro* himself acknowledged my skill: the most beauteous of women envied my lovely face.   The youths of the neighbourhood vied with each other to do me honour: a single song brought me I know not how many costly bales.   Golden ornaments and silver pins were smashed, blood-red skirts of silk were stained with wine, in oft-times echoing applause.   And so I laughed on from year to year, while the spring breeze and autumn moon swept over my careless head.

"Then my brother went away to the wars: my mother died.   Nights passed and mornings came; and with them my beauty began to fade.   My doors were no longer thronged: but few cavaliers remained.   So I took a husband, and became a trader's wife.   He was all for gain, and little recked of separation from me.   Last month he went off to buy tea, and I remained behind, to wander in my lonely boat on moon-lit nights over the cold wave, thinking of the happy days gone by, my reddened eyes telling of tearful dreams."

The sweet melody of the lute had already moved my soul to pity, and now these words pierced me to the heart again.   "O lady," I cried, "we are companions in misfortune, and need no ceremony to be friends.   Last year I quitted the Imperial city, banished to this fever-stricken

---

[1] "The sure perception of the exact moment when the rest should be silence."

spot, where in its desolation, from year's end to year's end, no flute nor guitar is heard. I live by the marshy river-bank, surrounded by yellow reeds and stunted bamboos. Day and night no sounds reach my ears save the bloodstained note of the goatsucker,[1] the gibbon's mournful wail. Hill songs I have, and village pipes with their harsh discordant twang. But now that I listen to thy lute's discourse, methinks 'tis the music of the Gods. Prithee sit down awhile and sing to us yet again, while I commit thy story to writing."

Grateful to me (for she had been standing long), the lute-girl sat down and quickly broke forth into another song, sad and soft, unlike the song of just now. Then all her hearers melted into tears unrestrained; and none flowed more freely than mine, until my bosom was wet with weeping.

---

[1] Or nightjar (*Caprimulgus europaeus*).

P'EI LIN

9TH CENTURY A.D.

[A statesman who, when the Emperor Hsien Tsung had become very ill from swallowing drugs of immortality, presented the Memorial given below, and was immediately banished to a subordinate post. Under the next Emperor he was recalled and rose to high office.]

THE ELIXIR OF LIFE

MAY it please your Majesty,

I have heard that he who eradicates evil, himself reaps advantage in proportion to his work; and that he who adds to the pleasures of others, himself enjoys happiness. Such was ever the guiding principle of our ancient kings.

Of late years, however, the Court has been overrun by a host of "professors" who profess to have the secret of immortality.

Now supposing that such beings as immortals really did exist—Would they not be likely to hide themselves in deep mountain recesses, far from the ken of man? On the other hand, persons who hang about the vestibules of the rich and great, and brag of their wonderful powers in big words,—what are they more than common adventurers in search of pelf? How should their nonsense be credited and their drugs devoured? Besides, even medicines to cure bodily ailments are not to be swallowed casually, morning, noon, and night. How much less then this poisonous, fiery goldstone, which the viscera of man must be utterly unable to digest?

Of old, when the prince took physic, his prime minister tasted it. I humbly pray that all those who present to your Majesty their concoctions, may be compelled first of all to swallow the same periodically for the space of one year. Thus will truth be effectually separated from falsehood.

WU TSUNG

REIGNED A.D. 838–846.

[A monarch who reached the throne through the murder of a brother, but was not otherwise noteworthy.]

AGAINST BUDDHISM.—A PROCLAMATION

WE have heard that previous to the Three Dynasties (A.D. 221–265) the name of Buddha was unknown. It was from the time of the Hans and the Weis that his images and his doctrines became familiar institutions in the land. The strength of man was lavished over his shrines; the wealth of man diverted to their costly adornment with gold and jewels. Unsurpassed was the injury to public morals: unsurpassed the injury to the welfare of the people!

A man who does not work, suffers bitter consequences in cold and hunger. But these priests and priestesses of Buddha, they consume food and raiment without contributing to the production of either. Their handsome temples reach up to the clouds and vie with the palaces of kings. The vice, the corruption, of those dynasties which followed upon the Three Kingdoms, can be attributed to no other source.

The founders of the House of T'ang put down disorder by *might;* and then proceeded to govern by *right.* With these two engines of power, they succeeded in establishing their rule;—shall, then, some paltry creed from the West be allowed to dispute with Us the sovereign power?

At the beginning of the present dynasty, efforts were made to get rid of this pest; but its extermination was not complete, and the faith became rampant once more. Now WE, having extensively studied the wisdom of the ancients, and guided moreover by public opinion, have no hesitation in saying that this evil can be rooted out. Do you, loyal officers of the State, only aid me in carrying out my great project by enforcing the laws,—and the thing is done. Already, more than 4,600 monasteries have been destroyed; and their inmates, to the number of 265,000 persons of both sexes, have been compelled to return to the world. Of temples and shrines, more than 40,000 have likewise been demolished; while many thousand acres of fat soil have been added to the wealth of the people. The work which my predecessors left undone, I have been able to accomplish. Let us then seize this favourable hour, and from the four quarters of the earth lead back the black-haired people once again into the Imperial fold!

And should there be any to whom OUR action in this matter may not be clear, do you officers of government enlighten them on the subject.

SSŬ-MA KUANG

A.D. 1009–1086.

[A famous historian, second only to Ssŭ-ma Ch'ien (*q.v.*), and a voluminous writer in other directions. He compiled a general history of China from the Chou dynasty down to the end of the T'ang dynasty, popularly known as the "Mirror of History." In political life he was successfully opposed to the great reformer Wang An-Shih (*q.v.*).]

CENSORS

IN ancient times there was no such office as that of Censor. From the highest chamberlain of the Court down to the humblest workman of the people, all were free alike to offer their advice to the Throne.

With the Han dynasty, the functions of Censor became vested in a single individual officer, whose duty it was to advise on all matters involving the welfare of the empire generally. His was a sacred trust; and for this post it was necessary to choose men of resolution and of liberal minds, who could gauge the relative importance of events and entirely subordinate their own interests to those of the commonwealth. Seekers after notoriety or wealth found no place in their ranks.

During the Sung dynasty the number of Censors was increased to six; and later on their names were duly engraved upon wooden boards. But I, fearing lest these should be obliterated by time, caused them to be carved upon stone; so that future generations might point to the record and say, "Such a one was loyal. Such a one was a traitor. Such a one was upright. Such a one was corrupt." Verily this should give good cause for fear!

OU-YANG HSIU

A.D. 1017–1072.

[A leading statesman, historian, poet, and essayist of the Sung dynasty. His tablet is to be found in the Confucian temple; an honour reserved for those alone who have contributed towards the elucidation or dissemination of Confucian truth.]

IMPERIAL EXTRAVAGANCE

MAY it please your Majesty,

I am informed that in consequence of the recent birth of a princess, a demand has been made on the Treasury for no less than 8,000 pieces of silk.

Now the rigour of winter is just at its height, and the wretched workmen of the Dyeing Department, forced to break ice before they can get water, will suffer unspeakable hardships in supplying the amount required. And judging by your Majesty's known sentiments of humanity and thrift, I cannot believe that this wasteful *corvée* is to be imposed, though rumour indeed has it that the dyers are already at work.

I have also noticed that the relatives of the Lady Chang have of late participated too frequently in the Imperial bounty. I am, it is true, but a poor Censor; yet whenever I see anything calculated to impair the *prestige* of the Son of Heaven, it becomes my duty to speak, that the divine wrath may be averted in time.

It is a noticeable fact in our annals that those favoured ladies who modestly and thriftily availed themselves of their connexion with the Throne, always prospered; while those, on the other hand, who gave themselves up to extravagance and nepotism, invariably ended in ruin. I will not cite instances from remote antiquity: I will confine myself to the more recent condition of affairs within the palace. Where, I would ask, are those proud spendthrift ladies who basked but just now in the imperial smiles? In their stead we have the Lady Chang, but yesterday blushing unseen in her quiet home,—to-day, the cynosure of every eye. Report declares her to be of quite another mould, and well qualified to keep the position to which she has been raised. Nevertheless, there seems to be growing up that old tendency to exceed, which sets men's tongues agog; and if your Majesty would save this lady from the fate of her predecessors, it would be well to admonish that a more modest economy prevail. For example: these 8,000 pieces of silk cannot all be for that one lady's use. Doubtless they are for distribution; but in that case their preparation involves waste of money, and gives a handle for public censure, from which even the Throne itself is not exempt.

Only lately the Lady Chang's mother received a District, and four days afterwards a Department; and now it is rumoured that further emoluments are to be bestowed upon distant relatives. That parents should share in the prosperity of their children is perhaps admissible; but propriety has its limits, and these are overstepped in the case of distant relatives. Who were they, forsooth, before the Lady Chang entered the Imperial hareem, that their present rank and riches should yield a subject for conversation injurious to the *prestige* of the Throne?

And were this a question only of the Lady Chang, the principle would still be applicable: how much more so as things are? The fact is that the Imperial bounty is too lavishly bestowed, and that extravagance is rife in the palace. Your Majesty suffers thereby: the State suffers thereby; and it is my duty to speak, trusting that your Majesty will take immediate steps to rectify these abuses.

CLUBS

Your Majesty's servant has heard that associations of friends are of time-honoured antiquity. It only remains for a ruler to distinguish between those of good and those of evil men. In the former case, the bond results from identity of purpose in the cause of truth; in the latter, from identity of personal interest alone. Evil men are, in fact, unable to form friendships; this privilege being reserved for the pure and good. And why? Simply because evil men love wealth and worldly advantage. Hence, as long as their interests are identical, they are friends. But when these begin to clash, first comes rivalry, and then a dissolution of their friendship. Sometimes they turn round and become bitter enemies, even of their own brothers and near relatives. There is therefore no reality about their friendships.

With the virtuous man, it is another thing altogether. His landmarks are duty towards his neighbour and loyalty to his prince: his most precious possession is his good name.

In the golden age, there was one clique of evil men, and two associations of virtuous men. Shun joined the latter, and the empire had peace. And when he came to be emperor himself, he profited by an association of officers who had united for the cultivation of generous principles, —and the empire had peace.

It is written, "The courtiers gathered around Chow Hsin in myriads, but their hearts were distributed in a myriad directions. The officers of Wu Wang were three thousand in number, and the hearts of these three thousand were as *one*." The absence of any real bond, in the first instance, brought about the disruption of the empire; while, in the second, its presence was a safeguard of the national welfare.

Later on, Hsien Ti, the last emperor of the House of Han, seized and threw into prison all the notable men of the day, because of an association they had formed. Then followed the revolt of the Yellow Caps, and his Majesty repented and released the prisoners;—but it was too late.

The question of forming such societies reappeared in the declining years of the T'ang dynasty, when in the reign of Chao Tsung all the best spirits of the day were either beheaded or thrown into the Yellow River, his Majesty exclaiming, "Let these pure ones go and associate with that muddy one!" But the end was at hand.

Of the rulers of old who failed to concentrate the hearts of the people, Chou Hsin is pre-eminent. Of those who put down associations of virtuous men, Hsien Ti stands first. Among those who exterminated honourable friendships, Chao Tsung bears away the palm. The result in each case was the same. The dynasty perished.

Shun, on the other hand, confidently availed himself of the incomparable societies of his day; and no one has ever said that his confidence was misplaced. In point of fact, he is always extolled as an enlightened and discriminating ruler. In Wu Wang's time, three thousand officers of State formed themselves into a society famed ever since for its numbers and power. And Wu Wang availed himself of this association,—and the empire prospered. The society was indeed large; but its members were not one too many.[1]

Your Majesty will doubtless not fail to be instructed by these examples of national prosperity and decay.

RELEASING PRISONERS

Sincerity and a sense of duty,—these are the attributes of the virtuous. Punishment and death,—these are the portion of the depraved. To deserve death in the iniquity of guilt,—this is the climax of crime. To die without regret at the call of duty,—this is the acme of heroism.

When the second Emperor of the late T'ang dynasty had just been six years upon the throne, he released more than 300 condemned criminals, and sent them to their homes on condition that within a certain period they should inflict upon themselves the penalty of death. This was simply to bid those unprincipled wretches play the difficult *rôle* of heroes.

At the expiry of the time, they all returned to the Emperor without one exception. No true hero could have

---

[1] "For the same reason he (Lord Ripon) has begun to consult the popular Associations, hundreds of which have sprung up in recent years, which are springing up day by day, and which reflect educated opinion on such great questions as education, local self-rule, usury laws, agrarian questions and the like."—*Daily News*, 6th Sept., 1883.

acted thus: those men found it easy enough. It was, to say the least of it, unnatural.

A friend has suggested that in spite of their deep-dyed guilt and unqualified want of principle, the Emperor's act of grace might possibly have converted them from their evil ways; such a marvellous and speedy conversion not being without precedent. But I say that his Majesty did this thing solely with a view to gain for himself a good report. We may rest assured that when he released these men he knew full well they would come back in the hope of a pardon; and that therefore he released them. We may rest assured that the return of the prisoners was based upon the certainty of receiving a pardon, and that therefore they came back. And if his Majesty only released them because he felt they would return, he was simply discounting the impulses of his subjects; while if the prisoners only returned because they felt they would be pardoned, they were likewise discounting the mercy of their ruler. As far as I can see, the credit of the whole affair was a product of mutual spoliation. Where indeed was the magnanimity of the one or the heroism of the other?

Let us consider. The Emperor had then been graciously reigning over the land for the space of six years. If during that time he had been unable to prevent evil men from doing evil deeds, it is absurd to suppose that he was suddenly, by a single act of grace, to convert them into heroic and dutiful subjects. What, it may be asked, was the proper course to pursue? I reply that those prisoners who returned should have been put to death; and then, on any future occasion of the kind, it would be fairly established that returning prisoners were influenced by a sincere sense of duty. But under those circumstances, there would of course be no prisoners forthcoming.

To release in that way and to pardon on return, might be all very well in an individual case. But to apply the principle to numbers, would be equivalent to pardoning murderers in general, directly contrary to all laws human and divine. Thus it was that the wise rulers of old based their administration upon the normal workings of the human heart. They sought no extraordinary standard of conduct with a view of exalting themselves; neither did they act in opposition to the natural instincts of man in order to secure the approbation of the public.[1]

FULNESS AND DECAY [2]

Alas for the fulness and decay of human greatness! Though these are called the appointments of Heaven, truly they are the handiwork of man. The rise and fall of Chuan Tsung may be cited as an instance in point.

When the Prince of Chin lay on his death-bed, he took three arrows and handed them to his son, saying, "The Liangs are my foes. The Prince of Yen treats me with ingratitude. The K'i-tan Tartar swore to me as a brother, and then passed over to the Liangs. These three grievances I leave as a legacy of hate to thee. Take these three arrows, and fail not to bear in mind thy father's wishes.

Chuang Tsung accordingly took the arrows and deposited them in a shrine; and by-and-by, when war was declared, he despatched an attendant to sacrifice a goat at the temple and bring out the arrows. He then placed them in an embroidered quiver, and bearing them on his back proceeded to the field of battle.

He returned triumphant, and ascended the Imperial throne. He had captured the Prince of Yen and his son. He had got with him in a box the heads of the ruler and prime minister of the House of Liang. He went to the shrine to replace the arrows and communicate to the spirit of his dead father that the work which had been entrusted

---

[1] A commentator suggests that the act of grace in question was performed merely for the sake of notoriety; just as the same Emperor, during a severe plague of locusts, sought to check the evil by swallowing a locust alive, "which," adds the commentator, "was probably only a paper imitation after all."

[2] "By the law of Nature, too, all manners of Ideals have their fatal limits and lot; their appointed periods of youth, of maturity or perfection, of decline, degradation, and final death and disappearance."—CARLYLE'S *Past and Present.*

to him was accomplished.   Was not this, then, the supreme fulness of glorious achievement?

Vengeance had thus been wreaked, and the empire was his, when suddenly there was a cry in the night,—a rush to arms,—hasty flight,—defection of soldiery,—sovereign and minister blankly gazing in each other's faces,—monastic vows and shaven crowns,—robes drenched with tears,—oh, what a fall was there!   So hard to win: so easy to lose. Surely these were issues that lay in the hand of man.

It is written, "The proud shall suffer; the modest succeed."   And so toil and anxiety may establish a kingdom; dissipation and ease will wreck a life.   At the zenith of his fortune, among all the heroes of the age there could not be found his match.   Yet when the tide turned, a few mummers dragged him to earth; the sceptre fell from his hand, and he perished,—the laughing-stock of all.

Truly misfortunes ofttimes spring from trivial and unexpected causes; and wisdom and courage are often marred by foibles other than a passion for theatrical display.

THE OLD DRUNKARD'S ARBOUR

The district of Ch'u is entirely surrounded by hills, and the peaks to the south-west are clothed with a dense and beautiful growth of trees, over which the eye wanders in rapture away to the confines of Shantung.   A walk of two or three miles on those hills brings one within earshot of the sound of falling water which gushes forth from a ravine, known as the Wine-Fountain; while hard by in a nook at a bend of the road stands a kiosque, commonly spoken of as the *Old Drunkard's Arbour*.   It was built by a Buddhist priest, called Deathless Wisdom, who lived among these hills, and who received the above name from the Governor. The latter used to bring his friends hither to take wine; and as he personally was incapacitated by a very few cups, and was moreover well stricken in years, he gave himself the sobriquet of the Old Drunkard.   But it was not wine that attracted him to this spot. It was the charming scenery which wine enabled him to enjoy.

The sun's rays peeping at dawn through the trees, by-and-by to be obscured behind gathering clouds, leaving naught but gloom around, give to this spot the alternations of morning and night. The wild flowers exhaling their perfume from the darkness of some shady dell; the luxuriant foliage of the dense forest of beautiful trees; the clear frosty wind; and the naked boulders of the lessening torrent;— these are the indications of spring, summer, autumn, and winter. Morning is the time to go thither, returning with the shades of night; and although the place presents a different aspect with the changes of the season, its charms are subject to no interruption, but continue alway. Burden-carriers sing their way along the road, travellers rest awhile under the trees; shouts from one, responses from another; old people hobbling along; children in arms, children dragged along by hand; backwards and forwards all day long without a break;—these are the people of Ch'u. A cast in the stream, and a fine fish taken from some spot where the eddying pools begin to deepen; a draught of cool wine from the fountain; and a few such dishes of meats and fruits as the hills are able to provide;—these, nicely spread out beforehand, constitute the Governor's feast. And in the revelry of the banquet hour there is no thought of toil or trouble. Every archer hits his mark, and every player wins his *partie;* goblets flash from hand to hand, and a buzz of conversation is heard as the guests move unconstrainedly about. Among them is an old man with white hair, bald at the top of his head. This is the drunken Governor, who when the evening sun kisses the tips of the hills, and the falling shadows are drawn out and blurred, bends his steps homewards in company with his friends. Then in the growing darkness are heard sounds above and sounds below: the beasts of the field and the birds of the air are rejoicing at the departure of man. They, too, can rejoice in hills and in trees, but they cannot rejoice as man rejoices. So also the Governor's friends.   They rejoice with him, though they know not at what it is that he rejoices.   Drunk, he can rejoice with them; sober, he can discourse with them;—such is the Governor.   And should you ask who is the Governor, I reply, "Ou-yang Hsiu of Lu-ling." [1]

AN AUTUMN DIRGE

One night, I had just sat down to my books, when suddenly I heard a sound far away towards the south-west. Listening intently, I wondered what it could be.   On it came, at first like the sighing of a gentle zephyr, . . . gradually deepening into the plash of waves upon a surf-beat shore, . . . the roaring of huge breakers in the startled night, amid howling storm-gusts of wind and rain.   It burst upon the hanging bell, and set every one of its pendants tinkling into tune.   It seemed like the muffled march of soldiers, hurriedly advancing bit in mouth to the attack,[2] when no shouted orders rend the air, but only the tramp of men and horses meet the ear.

"Boy," said I; "what noise is that?   Go forth and see." "Sir," replied the boy, on his return, "the moon and stars are brightly shining: the Silver River spans the sky.   No sound of man is heard without: 'tis but the whispering of the trees."

"Alas!" I cried; "autumn is upon us.[3]   And is it thus, O boy, that autumn comes?—autumn the cruel and the cold; autumn the season of rack and mist; autumn the season of cloudless skies; autumn the season of piercing blasts; autumn the season of desolation and blight!   Chill is the sound that heralds its approach; and then it leaps upon us with a shout.   All the rich luxuriance of green is changed;

---

[1] Meaning, of course, himself.
[2] The Chinese have a device by which they can gag their soldiers, and so prevent them from talking in the ranks on the occasion of a night attack.
[3] Any old resident in China will recognise the truth of this description in regard to the change of season here indicated.   In September, 1874, at Hankow, the thermometer fell something like forty degrees in less than forty-eight hours.

all the proud foliage of the forest swept down to earth,—
withered beneath the icy breath of the destroyer. For
autumn is Nature's chief executioner; and its symbol is
darkness. It has the temper of steel; and its symbol is a
sharp sword. It is the avenging angel, riding upon an
atmosphere of death. As spring is the epoch of growth, so
autumn is the epoch of maturity:—

> Its strains decay,
> And melt away,
> In a dying, dying fall.[1]

And sad is the hour when maturity is passed; for that which
passes its prime must die.

"Still what is this to plants and trees, which fade away
in their due season? . . . But stay: there is man, man
the divinest of all things. A hundred cares wreck his
heart: countless anxieties trace their wrinkles on his brow:
until his inmost self is bowed beneath the burden of life.
And swifter still he hurries to decay when vainly striving
to attain the unattainable, or grieving over his ignorance of
that which can never be known. Then comes the whitening
hair;—and why not? Has a man an adamantine frame,
that he should outlast the trees of the field? Yet after all
who is it, save himself, that steals his strength away? Tell
me, O boy, what right has man to accuse his autumn blast?"

My boy made no answer. He was fast asleep. No
sound reached me save that of the cricket chirping its
response to my dirge.

AT A GRAVE

O Man-ch'ing, thy birth gave a hero, thy death a God!
Like the vulgar herd thou wast born and didst die, returning
to the domain of nothingness. But thy earthly form could
not perish like theirs. There was that within which could
not decay: thy bright memory will endure through all

---

[1] A fair rendering of the text.

generations.　For such is the lot of the wise and good: their names are inscribed imperishably, to shine like the stars for ever.

O Man-ch'ing, 'tis long since we met.　Yet methinks I see thee now, as then, lofty of mien, courage upon thy brow.　Ah! when the grave closed over thee, it was not into foul earth, but into the pure essence of gold and gems that thy dear form was changed.[1]　Or haply thou art some towering pine—some rare, some wondrous plant.　What boots it now?　Here in thy loneliness the spreading brambles weave around thy head, while the chill wind blows across thy bed moist with the dew of heaven.　The will-o'-the-wisp and the fire-fly flit by: naught heard but the shepherd and the woodman singing songs on the hill-side; naught seen but the startled bird rising, the affrighted beast scampering from their presence, as they pass to and fro and pour forth their plaintive lays.　Such is thy solitude now.　A thousand, ten thousand years hence, the fox and the badger will burrow into thy tomb, and the weasel make its nest within.　For this also has ever been the lot of the wise and good.　Do not their graves, scattered on every side, bear ample witness of this?

Alas! Man-ch'ing, I know full well that all things are overtaken, sooner or later, by decay.　But musing over days by-gone, my heart grows sad; and standing thus near to thy departed spirit, my tears flow afresh, and I blush for the heartlessness of God.　O Man-ch'ing, rest in peace![1]

---

[1] Of his bones are coral made;
Those are pearls that were his eyes.

[2] At the great spring festival, when every one tries to get away to visit his ancestral burying ground and there perform those harmless rites which time and custom have hallowed, it is not unusual for literary men to indite some such address as the above, and burn it at the grave of the deceased as a means of communication with the spiritual world.　Of this most sacred anniversary, Carlyle has well said, "He (the Emperor) and his three hundred millions visit yearly the Tombs of their Fathers; each man the Tomb of his Father and his Mother; alone there, in silence, with what of *worship* or of other thought there may be, pauses solemnly each man; the divine Skies all silent over him; the divine Graves, and this divinest Grave, all silent under him; the pulsings of his own soul, if he have any soul, alone audible.　Truly it may be a kind of worship!　Truly if a man cannot get some glimpse into the Eternities, looking through this portal,—through what other need he try it?"

SHÊN KUA

A.D. 1030–1093.

[A distinguished scholar who, in accordance with ancient custom, was employed in military expeditions, and who was held responsible for a defeat in which 60,000 Chinese soldiers perished, and was banished to Shensi. He ranks among the highest as an art critic.]

AUREOLES

WHEN painters paint Buddha's aureole, they make it flat and round like a fan. If his body is deflected, then the aureole is also deflected,—a serious blunder. Such a one is only thinking of Buddha as a graven image, and does not know that the roundness of his aureole is everlasting. In like manner, when Buddha is represented as walking, his aureole is made to tail out behind him, and this is called the wind-borne aureole,—also a serious blunder. For Buddha's aureole is a divine aureole which even a universe-wrecking hurricane could not move, still less could our light breezes flutter it.

AERIAL PERSPECTIVE

In painting oxen and tigers, it is always customary to paint the hair, but the hair of horses is not painted. On my asking an artist why this was, he replied that a horse's hair is too fine, and cannot be brought out; but when I suggested that a rat's hair was still finer and yet was always painted, he had nothing to say. Now a horse is never seen in a painting to be more than a foot in size, which is a great proportionate reduction, and therefore the hair would be far too fine to be reproduced; whereas a rat generally has about the same measurement as in real life, and therefore the hair ought to be painted. This principle would seem to apply equally to the ox and to the tiger; the hair however of these animals is long, and a distinction has accordingly to be made. Li Ch'êng,[1] whenever he put kiosques, pagodas, or other buildings, on the mountains of his landscapes, painted them with cocked-up eaves, so that the spectator looked upwards and saw the inner part; because, he said, the point of view was below the object, just as a man

---

[1] A famous painter of landscape. Died A.D. 965 of *delirium tremens*.

standing beneath a pagoda sees above him the rafters of the eaves. This reasoning is faulty. For in landscape there is a method of looking at big things as if they were small (aerial perspective). If people looked at imitation hills in the same way that they look at real hills, that is, looking from the base up to the summit, it would only be possible to see one range at a time, and not range behind range; neither would the ravines and valleys in the mountains be visible. Similarly, you ought not to see the middle court of a house, nor what is going on in the back premises. You cannot lay down the rule that if you have a man on the east side, then the west side of the hill must contain the distant scenery, and *vice versâ;* under such conditions no picture could possibly be painted. Li Ch'êng did not know the method by which big objects are made to look small. By this method effects of height and distance can be more skilfully secured than by simply cocking up the corners of houses.

ESSENTIALS

In calligraphy and painting, soul is more important than form. Most of the good people who look at pictures can point out some slight defect in shape, in position, or in colouring; but that is the extent of their range. As to those who penetrate to deeper principles, they are very hard to find. It has been said that Wang Wei in his pictures paid no attention whatever to the four seasons. With regard to flowers, he would introduce the peach, apricot, hibiscus, and water-lily into one and the same scene. I myself possess a picture of his in which there is a banana-tree covered with snow. The idea flashed through his mind, and was completed by his hand,—an inspiration of genius. But it is difficult to discuss this with the unwashed . . . Does not the poet say

The old masters painted the spirit, they did not paint the form;
Mei Shêng, when singing of things, left no emotion unexpressed.
Those who can ignore the form and seize the spirit are few;
But why not apply to verse what to painting applies so well?

SU TUNG P'O

A.D. 1036–1101.

[An almost universal genius, like Ou-yang Hsiu, this writer is even a greater favourite with the Chinese literary public. Under his hands, the language of which China is so proud may be said to have reached perfection of finish, of art concealed. In subtlety of reasoning, in the lucid expression of abstractions, such as in English too often elude the faculty of the tongue, Su Tung-P'o is an unrivalled master. On behalf of his honoured manes I desire to note my protest against the words of Mr. Baber, recently spoken at a meeting of the Royal Geographical Society, and stating that "the Chinese language is incompetent to express the subtleties of theological reasoning, just as it is inadequate to represent the nomenclature of European science." I am not aware that the nomenclature of European science can be adequately represented even in the English language; at any rate, there can be no comparison between the expression of terms and of ideas, and I take it the doctrine of the Trinity itself is not more difficult of comprehension than the theory of "self abstraction beyond the limits of an external world," so closely reasoned out by Chuang Tzŭ. If Mr. Baber merely means that the gentlemen entrusted with the task have proved themselves so far quite incompetent to express in Chinese the subtleties of theological reasoning, then I am with him to the death.

There is one more point in regard to which I should be glad to cleanse the stuffed bosoms of some from a certain perilous stuff—the belief that Chinese sentences are frequently open to two and even more interpretations. No theory could well be more mischievous than this. It tends to make a student readily satisfied with anything he can get out of an obscure paragraph rather than push on laboriously through the dark passages of thought until the real sense begins to glimmer ahead, and finally to shine brightly upon him. I wish to place it on record, as my opinion, after the arduous task of translation now lying completed before me, that the written language of China is hardly more ambiguous than English; and that an ordinary Chinese sentence, written without malice aforethought, can have but one meaning, though it may often appear at the first blush to have several. There are exceptions, of course; but the rule remains unchanged. I have frequently been trapped myself, and may be again; trapped into satisfaction with a given rendering which I subsequently discovered to be wrong, and which I could then feel to be grammatically wrong though I had previously accepted it as right. The fault in such cases, I venture to suggest, should be sought for outside the text. (*I leave this to stand as it stood in 1884, merely suggesting that it is the extreme difficulty of the book-language which is mistaken for ambiguity.*)

To revert to the subject of this note, Su Tung-P'o shared the fate of most Chinese statesmen of the T'ang and Sung dynasties. He was banished to a distant post. In 1235 he was honoured with a niche in the Confucian temple, but his tablet was removed in 1845. After six hundred years he might well have been left there in peace.]

THE ARBOUR TO JOYFUL RAIN

MY arbour was named after rain, to commemorate joy.

Whenever our forefathers rejoiced greatly, they used the name of whatever caused their joy in order to commemorate the event. Thus, Chou Kung named a book from the auspicious appearance of a double ear of corn. An emperor named a period of his reign from the discovery of an ancient bronze; and a case is on record of one who named his children after prisoners taken captive in war. The joy in each instance was hardly the same; but the principle of commemoration was uniformly applied.

Now the year after I was appointed to rule over Fu-fêng, I began to put my official residence in repair, and arranged for the construction of an arbour at a certain spot, where I let in a stream of water and planted trees, intending to use it as a refuge from the business of life.

In that very year it rained wheat; and the soothsayers predicted in consequence that the ensuing season would be most prosperous. However, for a whole month no rain fell, and the people became alarmed at the prospect. Then rain fell at intervals, but not in sufficient quantities. At length, it poured incessantly for three days. Thereupon, great congratulations were exchanged between officials; tradesmen and traders sang songs of glee in the market-place; while farmers wished each other joy across the furrowed fields. The sorrowful were gladdened: the sick were made whole. And precisely at that moment my arbour was completed.

So I spread a feast there, and invited a number of guests, of whom I enquired, "What would have happened if the rain had held off five days longer?" "There would have been no wheat," was the answer. "And what if it had been ten days?" I continued; to which they replied that then there would have been no crops at all. "And had there been harvest neither of wheat nor of other grain," said I, "a famine must inevitably have ensued. The law courts would have overflowed with litigation. Brigandage and robbery would have been rife. And you and I would have missed the pleasant meeting of to-day beneath this arbour. But God did not leave the people to perish. Drought has been followed by rain; and to rain it is due that we are enjoying ourselves here to-day. Shall we then let its remembrance fade away? I think not; and therefore I have given to this arbour its name, and have added to the record the following verses:—

"Should the sky rain pearls, the cold cannot wear them as clothes;
Should the sky rain jade, the hungry cannot use it as food.
   It has rained without cease for three days—
   Whose was the influence at work?
Should you say it was that of your Governor,
The Governor himself refers it to the Emperor.
But the Emperor says 'No! it was God.'
And God says 'No! it was Nature.'
   And as Nature lies beyond the ken of man,
   I dedicate this arbour instead."

THE BASELESS TOWER

He who lives near hills, in his uprising and in his down-sitting, in his eating and in his drinking, should be in daily communion with the hills.

Of all ranges none is so lofty as Chung-nan. Of all towns situated near hills, none is so close to them as Fu-fêng. Hence it would follow that mountain-peaks were included in the surrounding scenery. Nevertheless, from the Governor's residence there was not a hill to be seen. Although this entailed no consequences either of evil or of good, still it was not in accordance with the eternal fitness of things. And so the Baseless Tower was built.

Before the erection of this Tower, the Governor would frequently stroll about, staff in hand, at the foot of the hills, whence he every now and again caught glimpses of their outlines through the dense groves of trees, much as one sees the top-knots of people who are passing on the other side of a wall. The result was that he ordered workmen to dig a square pond in front of his house, and with the clay taken therefrom to build a tower somewhat higher than the eaves. When this was done, those who mounted to the top lost all sense of the tower's elevation, while the surrounding hills seemed to have started up into view. The Governor therefore named it the Baseless Tower, and bade me commit its record to writing.

To this I replied, "The sequence of fulness and decay lies beyond the limits of our ken. Years ago, when this site was exposed to the hoar-frost and dew of heaven, the home of the adder and of the fox, who could then have forecast the Tower of to-day? And when, obedient to the eternal law, it shall once again by lapse of time become a wilderness and a desert as before,—this is what no man can declare."

"Where now," said I to the Governor, as we mounted the Tower together and gazed over the landscape around us, "where now are the palaces of old, beautiful, spacious buildings, a hundred times more solid than this? They are gone; and not a broken tile, not a crumbling wall remains, to mark the spot. They have passed into the growing grain, into the thorny brake. They have melted into the loamy glebe. Shall not then this Tower in like manner pass away? And if towers cannot last for ever, how much less shall we rely for immortality upon the ever fickle breath of praise? Alas for those who trust by these means to live in the record of their age! For whether the record of their age will endure or perish depends upon something beyond the preservation and decay of towers." [1]

I then retired and committed the above to writing.

THE TOWER OF CONTENTMENT

All things are in some sense worth seeing, and are consequently sources of pleasure: it is not necessary that they should possess either rarity or beauty. Eating grains and swilling lees will make a man drunk: berries and herbs will fill his belly; and it is by parity of reasoning that I am able to enjoy myself wherever I go.

Now those who seek happiness and avoid misery, rejoice or grieve according as they are successful or otherwise. But man's desires are endless, while his means of gratifying them are limited: good and evil strive together for the upper hand, and choice between them is ofttimes a difficult task. It follows therefore that occasions of joy are few, and occasions of grief many. Rather might we say that men pursue misery and eschew happiness. This, however, is contrary to human nature. *Men do so only because they are the slaves of objective existences.* Thus, if existences are considered subjectively (as regards themselves), all idea of their dimension is lost; whereas, if they are considered subjectively (as regards ourselves), then there are none to which the idea of dimension does not apply.

---

[1] A sneer at the Governor for trying to commemorate his prosperous term of office by the erection of a perishable tower.

But when another would refer to me his perceptions of such dimensions then I become troubled in mind, as though I saw a battle through a chink and was asked to decide with which party the victory lay.   And thus it is, alas! that good and evil grow up promiscuously, and sorrow and joy are intertwined together.

On my transfer from Chekiang to Shantung, I exchanged the comfort of boats for the fatigue of horses and carts.   I relinquished the elegance of carved panels for a home among the citron groves of the north.   I turned my back upon hill and lake to wander over acres of mulberry and hemp.   When I reached my post, the year's crops had failed, the country round was alive with banditti, and litigation the order of the day.   I accordingly adopted a diet of lenten fare, living on berries and herbs; from which it was generally inferred that I was unhappy.   But ere a year had passed away, my face filled out, and hair which had grown white became black again.   I learned to love the honest manliness of the people, and my own easy disposition won popularity for my administration.   I set to work upon my garden and my house, hewing down trees to effect the necessary repairs.   On the north, abutting on the city wall, there was an old tower, which had stood there for years. This I to some extent restored; and thither I would often go and give vent to my feelings over the scene below.   Southwards, hills receding, hills looming darkly into view, the home perhaps of some virtuous recluse.   Eastwards, hills: the hill to which Lü Ao retired to hide.   Westwards, the Mu-ling pass in the far distance, like the battlements of a city, hallowed by the memory of many a glorious name. Northwards, the river Wei below; and looking down I would sigh as I remembered him of Huai-yin and his unaccomplished work.

My tower was lofty but solid; and even from its summit a clear view was obtainable.   Cool in summer, it was warm in winter; and on mornings of rain or snow, on windy or moonlit nights, I would be there, always accompanied by friends. Vegetables from the garden, fish from the pool, the small wine of the country, and a dish of millet porridge,—such was our simple fare, over which I would exclaim, "Ho, there! what happiness is this!"

A brother, who lived in Chi-nan, hearing how I passed my time, wrote me some verses on the subject, and named my tower the *Tower of Contentment,* in reference to my knack of enjoying myself under all conditions. This, because I could roam beyond the limits of an external world.

THE CHÂLET OF CRANES

During the autumn of 1078, there was a great flood over a certain district, which nearly submerged the rude dwelling of a recluse named Chang. However, by the following spring the water had fallen, and he was able to occupy a site near his former residence, on a range of hills, in the midst of charming scenery, where he built himself a mountain hut. It was a perfect *cordon* of peaks, except on the west where the line broke; and there, right in the gap, the hermit's cottage stood. Thence, in spring and summer, the eye wandered over a broad expanse of verdure and vegetation: in autumn and winter, over moonlit miles of gleaming snow; while every change of wind and rain, every alternation of darkness and light, brought ever-varying beauties into view.

Chang kept a couple of cranes, which he had carefully trained; and every morning he would release them westwards through the gap, to fly away and alight in the marsh below or soar aloft among the clouds as the birds' own fancy might direct. At nightfall, they would return with the utmost regularity. And so he named his abode the Châlet of Cranes.

When I was Governor in those parts, I went with some friends to call upon Chang, and spent a merry time with him over a stoup of wine. And as I pledged my host, I said, "Are you aware, sir, how perfect is the happiness you enjoy?—happiness that I would not exchange even for the diadem of a prince. Does not the *Book of Changes* speak of the crane's voice sounding in solitude, and the harmony which prevails among its young? Does not the *Book of Poetry* tell us that the crane's note rings through the marsh, and is heard far away in the sky? For the crane is a bird of purity and retirement, taking its pleasure beyond the limits of this dusty world of ours. Therefore it has been made an emblem of the virtuous man and of the lettered recluse; and to cherish such pets in one's home should entail rather profit than harm. Yet the love of cranes once lost a kingdom.[1]

"Then we have had Edicts prohibiting the use of wine,—the greatest curse, as 'twas said, of the curses which afflict mankind. Yet there have been those who attained immortality thereby, and made themselves heroes for ever.

"Ah! 'tis but the prince, who, though pure as the crane itself, dares not indulge a passion for wine. An he do so, it may cost him his throne. But for the lettered recluse of the hill-side, what odds if he perish in his cups? And what harm can his cranes bring to him? Thus, sir, it is that the joys of the prince and the hermit may not be mentioned together."

"True enough!" cried Chang, smiling, as he proceeded to sing the Song of the Cranes:—

> "Away! away! my birds, fly westwards now,
>   To wheel on high and gaze on all below;
>   To swoop together, pinions closed, to earth;
>   To soar aloft once more among the clouds;
>   To wander all day long in sedgy vale;
>   To gather duckweed in the stony marsh.
>   Come back! come back! beneath the lengthening shades,
>   Your serge-clad master stands, guitar in hand.
>   'Tis he that feeds you from his slender store:
>   Come back! come back! nor linger in the west."

---

[1] Alluding to a certain feudal prince who lavished his revenues upon cranes.

INACCURACY

It is stated in the ancient work on *Water-courses* that at a certain place there was a "stone-bell hill." The commentator, Li Yüan, considers the name to have arisen from the fact that the foot of the hill is washed by a deep pool, and that on the slightest agitation of its surface by the wind, waves would splash against the rock and produce a sound like that of a great bell.

This explanation, long regarded with suspicion, was at length exploded by a real bell being placed in the pool, which, no matter how violent the waves, never gave forth a sound. How much less then, it was argued, would stone.

By-and-by, an official, named Li Pŏ, set to work to investigate, and discovered at the pool two stones which when struck emitted ringing sounds of different pitches, the vibration continuing some time after the stroke, and at length dying gradually away. Thus he believed that he had finally settled the point.

Of this settlement, however, I always entertained grave doubts. For many stones will yield a ringing sound when struck; why then should these be more particularly *bell* stones than any others?

Subsequently, I had an opportunity of seeing for myself these so-called stone bells, when accompanying my eldest son on the way to his post as magistrate. The priests of a neighbouring temple bade one of their novices carry an adze, and with this he chipped off several pieces and showed me how they rang when struck. I smiled, but was not convinced; and that same night, the moon shining brightly, I stepped into a boat with my son and we proceeded to the base of the hill where the rock rose almost sheer to a height of near a thousand feet, looking like a fierce beast or huge hobgoblin about to spring upon us. Flocks of birds, startled at our approach, flew out and whirled away into the sky. There were also sounds as of old men coughing and laughing within a chasm of the rock, which one would have said was the noise of herons or cranes.

Much affected by the scene, I was about to leave, when suddenly over the face of the water came clanging and rolling sounds, like the notes of bells and drums. The boatman was horribly alarmed; but on examination we found that the base of the rock was pitted all over with holes, of I know not what depth, and that the sounds were due to the water which had been forced up them rushing noisily out as each wave retired. And steering our boat into a chasm between two rocks, we there found a large boulder of a size to seat a hundred persons, right in mid-channel. This too was full of holes, and when these had been filled with water driven in by the wind, the water would flow out with a noise similar to that we had just heard.

Laughing, I turned to my son and said, "Don't you see? These sounds are identical in timbre with the notes of the two famous bells of old. Ah! the ancients deceive us not. But how should people undertake to decide about what they have neither seen with their eyes nor heard with their ears? Li Yüan was a man of experience equal to my own. Yet his explanation was inaccurate. He doubtless would not be bothered to get into a boat and anchor here at night beneath the cliff. Therefore he could not ascertain the real cause of the phenomenon, while the boatmen and others, who may have known, had no means of publishing the truth. Li Pŏ put his trust in an adze, and thought he had solved the problem thereby."

I accordingly made a note of this adventure, with a sigh for the remissness of Li Yüan, and a smile at the credulity of Li Pŏ.

OLD SQUARE-CAP THE HERMIT

Old Square-Cape was a hermit. In his youth he had been a knight-errant, and the leader of knight-errantry in his hamlet. He was also an enthusiastic student of all kinds of books, hoping by these means to make his mark upon the age.   But he never succeeded, and retired late in life to the hills.   He lived in a hut.   He was a vegetarian. He held no intercourse with the outer world.   He would have neither horse nor carriage.   He destroyed his official uniform.   He walked by himself on the hills.   No one knew who he was; but his tall square hat, apparently a survival of the ancient head-piece of the Han dynasty, earned for him the sobriquet of Old Square-Cap.

When I was banished I lived in the neighbourhood, and one day came suddenly upon him.   "Good gracious!" I cried, "my old friend Ch'ên!   What are you doing here?" Old Square-Cap replied by asking me what I did there; and when I told him, he bent his head in silence and then quickly looked up and smiled.   He took me to sleep at his home, a quiet little place with a mud wall round it, where, nevertheless, his wife and servants all seemed very contented and happy.   I was astonished at what I saw.   For I remembered how, in his wine-bibbing, swash-bucklering youth, he had flung away money like dirt.   Nineteen years before, I had seen him out shooting on the hills with a couple of attendants.   A jay rose in front of them, and he bade one of the attendants shoot, but the man missed; at which he urged his horse forward, drew an arrow, and shot the bird dead.   Then, as he sat there on horseback, he held forth on military matters, and discussed the victories and defeats of ancient and modern times, calling himself the warrior of his age.

And now, after all these years, the old determined look is still to be seen in his face.   How then is he what we mean by a hermit of the hills?   Yet he was of an illustrious house.   He would have had grand opportunities.   He would have made himself famous ere this.   His home was at the capital,—a home of luxury and splendour, like the palace of a prince.   He held an estate which gave him yearly a thousand pieces of silk; so that the pleasures of wealth were in his grasp.   All these things he put aside, and

retired to penury and solitude on the hills. He did not
turn his back upon the world because he had failed to
secure the material blessings of life.

I have heard that there are many weird beings on those
hills, though I never caught a glimpse of one. Doubtless
Old Square-Cap, himself of that clique, has made their
acquaintance long ago.

THOUGHTS SUGGESTED BY THE RED WALL:[1]
SUMMER

In the year 1081, the seventh moon just on the wane,
I went with a friend on a boat excursion to the Red Wall.
A clear breeze was gently blowing, scarce enough to ruffle
the river, as I filled my friend's cup and bade him troll a
lay to the bright moon, singing the song of the *Modest Maid*.

By-and-by, up rose the moon over the eastern hills,
wandering between the Wain and the Goat, shedding forth
her silver beams, and linking the water with the sky. On
a skiff we took our seats, and shot over the liquid plain,
lightly as though travelling through space, riding on the
wind without knowing whither we were bound. We seemed
to be moving in another sphere, sailing through air like the
Gods. So I poured out a bumper for joy, and, beating time
on the skiff's side, sang the following verse:—

> With laughing oars, our joyous prow
>   Shoots swiftly through the glittering wave—
> My heart within grows sadly grave—
> Great heroes dead, where are ye now?

My friend accompanied these words upon his flageolet,
delicately adjusting its notes to express the varied emotions
of pity and regret, without the slightest break in the thread
of sound which seemed to wind around us like a silken skein.
The very monsters of the deep yielded to the influence of

---

[1] Not the spot mentioned in the *San-kuo-chih*, where Chou Yü burnt Ts'ao Ts'ao's
fleet, and where a wall is said to have been reddened by the flames. Su Tung-P'o
seems himself to have mistaken the identity of the place.

his strains, while the boat-woman, who had lost her husband, burst into a flood of tears. Overpowered by my own feelings, I settled myself into a serious mood, and asked my friend for some explanation of his art. To this he replied, "Did not Ts'ao Ts'ao say:—

> The stars are few, the moon is bright,
> The raven southward wings his flight.

"Westwards to Hsia-k'ou, eastwards to Wu-ch'ang, where hill and stream in wild luxuriance blend,—was it not there that Ts'ao Ts'ao was routed by Chou Yü? Ching-chou was at his feet: he was pushing down stream towards the east. His war-vessels stretched stem to stern for a thousand *li*: his banners darkened the sky. He poured out a libation as he neared Chiangling; and sitting in the saddle, armed, *cap-à-pie*, he uttered those words did that hero of his age. Yet where is he to-day?

"Now you and I have fished and gathered fuel together on the river eyots. We have fraternized with the crayfish: we have made friends with the deer. We have embarked together in our frail canoe; we have drawn inspiration together from the wine-flash—a couple of ephemerides, launched on the ocean in a rice-husk! Alas, life is but an instant of Time. I long to be like the Great River which rolls on its way without end. Ah, that I might cling to some angel's wing and roam with him for ever! Ah, that I might clasp the bright moon in my arms and dwell with her for aye! Alas, it only remains to me to enwrap these regrets in the tender melody of sound."

"But do you forsooth comprehend," I enquired, "the mystery of this river and of this moon? The water passes by but is never gone: the moon wanes only to wax once more. Relatively speaking, Time itself is but an instant of time; absolutely speaking, you and I, in common with all matter, shall exist to all eternity. Wherefore then the longing of which you speak?

"The objects we see around us are one and all the property of individuals. If a thing does not belong to me, not a particle of it may be enjoyed by me. But the clear breeze blowing across this stream, the bright moon streaming over yon hills,—these are sounds and sights to be enjoyed without let or hindrance by all. They are the eternal gifts of God to all mankind, and their enjoyment is inexhaustible. Hence it is that you and I are enjoying them now."

My friend smiled as he threw away the dregs from his wine-cup and filled it once more to the brim. And then, when our feast was over, amid the litter of cups and plates, we lay down to rest in the boat: for streaks of light from the east had stolen upon us unawares.

THE RED WALL: AUTUMN

In the same year, when the tenth moon was full, I went again to the Red Wall. Two friends accompanied me; and as we crossed the hill, the landscape glittered white with frost, while the leafless trees cast our shadows upon the ground. The bright moon above inspired our hearts, and many a catch we sang as we strolled along. Then I sighed and said, "Here are the guests gathered together, but where are the cakes and ale? Here in the silver moonlight, here in the clear breeze,—what waste of a night like this!"

Then up spoke a friend and said, "This very eve I netted one of those *gobemouche* small-scaled fishes, for all the world like the famous perch of the Sung. But how about liquor?" However, we went back with our friend to consult his wife, and she at once cried out, "I have a stoup of wine, stored now some time in case of an accident like this." And so with wine and fish we retraced our steps towards the Red Wall.

The river was rushing noisily by, but with narrowed stream; and over the heightened hill-tops the moon was still scarcely visible, while through the shallowing tide

naked boulders stood prominently forth. It was but three
months since, yet I hardly knew the place again.

I picked up my skirts and began to ascend the steep
cliff.   I struggled through bramble-brake.   I sat me
down upon the Tiger rock.   I climbed a gnarled tree, up
to the dizzy hawk's nest, whence I looked down upon the
River God's temple below, and whither my two friends
were unable to follow.

Suddenly there arose a rushing mighty sound.   Trees
and shrubs began to wave, hills to resound, valleys to
re-echo, while wind lashed water into waves.   Fear and
regret entered into my soul; for it was not possible to
remain.   I hurried back and got on board.   We poled the
boat into mid-channel, and letting it take its own course,
our excursion came to an end.

The hour was midnight, and all around was still; when
from the east, across the river, flew a solitary crane,
flapping its huge wings of dusky silk, as, with a long
shrill scream, it whizzed past our boat towards the west.
By-and-by, my friends left me, and I slept and dreamed
that a lame Taoist priest in a feathery robe passed by on
the bank, and, bowing to me, said, "Have you had a pleasant
trip, sir, to the Red Wall?"   I enquired his name, but he
merely bowed again and made no reply.   " Ah! " exclaimed
I, "I know who you are.   Are you not that bird which flew
past me last night and screamed?"   Just then I awakened
with a start.   I opened the door of my boat and looked out,
but no one was to be seen.[1]

A RAT'S CUNNING

I was sitting up one night when suddenly a rat began
to gnaw.   A rap on the couch stopped the noise, which

---

[1] "Alas!" says a commentator, "yesterday was the to-day of yesterday, and
to-morrow will be the to-day of to-morrow."   Compare CARLYLE (*Past and Present*),
"To-day becomes yesterday so fast; all to-morrows become to-days."

however soon began again. Calling a servant to look round with a light, we noticed an empty sack, from the inside of which came a grating sound, and I at once cried out, "Ha! the rat has got shut in here, and can't get out." So we opened the sack, but there was apparently nothing in it, though when we came to throw in the light, there at the bottom lay a dead rat. "Oh!" exclaimed the servant in a fright, "can the animal that was just now gnawing have died so suddenly as this? Or can it have been the rat's ghost that was making the noise?" Meanwhile, he turned the rat out on the ground, when——away it went full speed, escaping before we had time to do anything. " 'Tis passing strange," said I, with a sigh, "the cunning of that rat. Shut up in a sack too hard for it to gnaw its way out, it nevertheless gnawed in order to attract attention by the noise; and then it pretended to be dead in order to save its life under the guise of death. Now I have always understood that in intelligence man stands first. Man can tame the dragon, subdue the mastodon, train the tortoise, and carry captive the unicorn. He makes all things subservient to his will; and yet here he is, trapped by the guile of a rat, which combined the speed of the flying hare with the repose of a blushing girl. Wherein then lies his superior intelligence? "

Thinking over this, with my eyes closed, a voice seemed to say to me, "Your knowledge is the knowledge of books; you gaze towards the truth but see it not. You do not concentrate your mind within yourself, but allow it to be distracted by external influences. Hence it is that you are deceived by the gnawing of a rat. *A man may voluntarily destroy a priceless gem, and yet be unable to restrain his feelings over a broken cooking-pot. Another will bind a fierce tiger, and yet change colour at the sting of a bee.* These words are your own; have you forgotten them? " At this I bent my head and laughed; and then, opening my eyes, I bade a servant bring pen and ink and commit the episode to writing.

THE PRINCE OF LITERATURE

(See page 115)

How has the simple and lowly one become a Teacher for all generations?   Why has a single word of his become law for the whole world?   Because he could place himself in harmony with Nature, and adapt himself to the eternal sequence of fulness and decay.

Life does not come to us without reason: it is not without reason that we lay it down.   Hence, some have descended from the hills to live among us; others have joined the galaxy of the stars above.[1]   The traditions of old lie not.

Mencius said, "I am able to nourish my divine spirit."[2] That spirit may lodge in a specified area; but its volume fills all space.   For him who possesses it, the honours of princes and kings, the wealth of millionaires, the sagacity of counsellors, the courage of heroes, the subtlety of diplomatists,—these are but empty names.   But who plants this spirit within us?   It stands, independent of form; it moves, independent of force; it waits not for life, to exist; it perishes not in the swoon of death.   Above, it assumes the shape of heavenly bodies; on earth, that of hills and streams: in the dark, that of spiritual beings; in the broad light of day, it returns again to man.   But let this pass.

From the age of the Hans, the Truth began to be obscured, and literature to fade.   Supernatural religions sprang up on all sides; and many eminent scholars failed to oppose their advance, until Han Wên-kung, the cotton-clothed, arose, and blasted them with his derisive sneer.[3] Thenceforth, not one but adopted him as their guide, returning into the true path,—now three hundred years ago.   From the dead ashes of the immediate past his genius soared up: his message brought help to many in the hour of their affliction.   His loyalty (to the commonwealth)

---

[1] Two mythological allusions.

[2] Dr. LEGGE, in his translation of Mencius, renders this term by "vast, flowing, passion-nature."   It is, in fact, untranslatable; but what is meant may be easily understood from Wên T'ien-hsiang's splendid poem, headed *Divinæ Particulam Auræ*. See p. 207.

[3] *Cf.* "Sapping a solemn creed with solemn sneer."

called down the wrath of his Imperial master; his bravery eclipsed that of the bravest warrior. Was not this to place himself in harmony with Nature, and adapt himself to the eternal sequence of fulness and decay?

The human, they say, is all-powerful, except as against the divine. What is this distinction between the human and the divine? Cunning may deceive kings and princes, but cannot impose upon pigs and fishes.[1] Brute force may conquer an empire, but cannot win over the hearts of the people. So Han Wên-kung's purity of heart dispersed the clouds at the summit of Mount Hêng,[2] but could not free him from Imperial suspicions. He tamed the fierce monster of the river, but could not shake off the calumnies of his foes. He endeared himself to the inhabitants of the southern shores, where his memory is held sacred after many generations; but he could not secure to himself a day's repose as a courtier about the Throne. His failures were human, his successes divine.

The people of Ch'ao-chou were sunk in ignorance. Han Wên-kung appointed a superintendent of education; and ever since, their city has been a centre of learning, a rival to the classic seats of old. To this day its inhabitants are known for their peace-loving ways; for their faith in the maxim that the "true doctrines inspire lofty natures with love for their fellow-men, inferior natures with respect for the authority of government." And so, when they eat or drink, a portion is always devoted to the memory of their Master. Or if flood, or drought, or pestilence come upon them, it is to him they betake themselves for aid. But his shrine was behind the chief magistrate's *yamên*, and inconvenient of access; and an application to the Throne to build a new shrine had been refused, when a Governor came to rule over the district whose administration was modelled upon that of his great predecessor. This popular official issued a notice that if the people themselves wished

---

[1] Alluding to a passage in the *Book of Changes*.
[2] One of the numerous legendary tales of his supernatural power.

to erect a new shrine, they were at liberty to select a suitable site at a given spot; and within the year the building was completed.

Then some one said, "Han Wên-kung was banished to this spot, a thousand miles from his home, with no hope of return. If knowledge is given to him after death, it will hardly be with feelings of affection that he will look back upon his sojourn at Ch'ao-chou."

"No so," I replied. "Our Master's spirit pervades space as water pervades the earth: there is no place where it is not. The Ch'ao-chou people trusted and loved him more than others, and still venerate his spirit which hovers over their soil. Fancy, if a man boring for water should strike a spring and say, ' Water is *here!*' "

Han Wên-kung's full designation is given in the inscription; and as the inhabitants of Ch'ao-chou desired me to prepare a record to be engraven on stone, I indited the following lines to the memory of this great man:—

> He rode of old on the dragon in the white cloud domain;
> He grasped with his hand the glory of the sky;
> The Weaving Damsel[1] robed him with the effulgence of the stars,
> The wind bore him delicately from the throne of God.
> He swept away the chaff and husks of his generation.
> He roamed over the limits of the earth.
> He clothed all nature with his bright rays,
> The third in the triumvirate of genius.[2]
> His rivals panted after him in vain,
> Dazed by the brilliancy of his light.
> He cursed Buddha: he offended his prince.
> He journeyed far away to the distant south.
> He passed the grave of Shun, and wept over the daughters of Yao.
> The water-god went before him and stilled the waves.
> He drove out the fierce monster as it were a lamb.
> But above, in heaven, there was no music, and God was sad,
> And summoned him to his place beside the Throne.
> And now, with these poor offerings, I salute him;
> With red lichees and yellow plantain fruit.
> Alas, that he did not linger awhile on earth,
> But passed so soon, with streaming hair, into the great unknown.

---

[1] The star α Lyrae.
[2] The other two were Tu Fu and Li T'ai-pŏ (*q.v.*).

A SOUND CRITIC

In Ssŭch'uan there lived a retired scholar, named Tu. He was very fond of calligraphy and painting, and possessed a large and valuable collection. Among the rest was a painting of oxen by Tai Sung, which he regarded as exceptionally precious, and kept in an embroidered case on a jade-mounted roller. One day he put his treasures out to sun, and it chanced that a herdboy saw them. Clapping his hands and laughing loudly, the herdboy shouted out, "Look at the bulls fighting! Bulls trust to their horns, and keep their tails between their legs, but here they are fighting with their tails cocked up in the air; that's wrong!" Mr. Tu smiled, and acknowledged the justice of the criticism. So truly does the old saying run: For ploughing, go to a ploughman; for weaving, to a servant-maid.

WANG AN-SHIH

A.D. 1021–1086.

[A scholar, poet, and statesman, popularly known as "the Reformer," in consequence of certain momentous political reforms he was enabled temporarily to introduce; the most remarkable being a system of compulsory military training for all classes of the people. He denounced the *Tao Tê Ching*, attributed to Lao Tzŭ (*q.v.*), as "akin to nonsense." In 1104, his tablet was placed in the Confucian temple, only, however, to remain there about a hundred and forty years, when it was removed.]

ON THE STUDY OF FALSE DOCTRINES

I HAVE been debarred by illness from writing to you now for some time, though my thoughts have been with you all the while.

In reply to my last letter wherein I expressed a fear that you were not progressing with your study of the Canon, I have received several from you, in all of which you seem to think I meant the Canon of Buddha, and you are astonished at my recommendation of such pernicious works. But how could I possibly have intended any other than the Canon of the sages of China? And for you to have thus missed the point of my letter is a good illustration of what I meant when I said I feared you were not progressing with your study of the Canon.

Now a thorough knowledge of our Canon has not been attained by any one for a very long period. Study of the Canon alone does not suffice for a thorough knowledge of the Canon. Consequently, I have been myself an omnivorous reader of books of all kinds, even, for example, of ancient medical and botanical works. I have moreover dipped into treatises on agriculture and on needlework, all of which I have found very profitable in aiding me to seize the great scheme of the Canon itself. For learning in these days is a totally different pursuit from what it was in the olden times; and it is now impossible otherwise to get at the real meaning of our ancient sages.

There was Yang Hsiung. He hated all books that were not orthodox. Yet he made a wide study of heterodox writers. By force of education he was enabled to take what of good and to reject what of bad he found in each.

Their pernicious influence was altogether lost on him; while on the other hand he was prepared the more effectively to elucidate what we know to be the Truth. Now do you consider that I have been corrupted by these pernicious influences? If so, you know me not.

No! the pernicious influences of the age are not to be sought for in the Canon of Buddha. They are to be found in the corruption and vice of those in high places; in the false and shameless conduct which is now rife among us. Do you not agree with me?

A FALSE ESTIMATE

[The prince of Ch'in held Mêng Ch'ang-chün a prisoner, and intended to slay him. Meanwhile, Mêng Ch'ang-chün sent word to the prince's favourite lady, asking her to intercede for him; to which the latter replied that if he would give her a certain robe of white fox-skin, she would speak on his behalf. Now, it chanced that this very robe had already been presented to the prince; but among Mêng Ch'ang-chün's followers was one who could steal like a dog, and this man introduced himself by night into the palace and transferred the robe from the prince to the lady. The consequence was that Mêng Ch'ang-chün was released and fled at once to the frontier; while the prince soon repented of his clemency, and sent off to recapture his prisoner. When Mêng Ch'ang-chün reached the pass, the great gate was closed, not to be opened until cock-crow; at which he was much alarmed, fearing pursuit, until another of his followers, who possessed the art, began to crow like a cock, and set off all the cocks of the place crowing too. Thereupon, the gate was opened, and they escaped.]

All ages have extolled Mêng Ch'ang-chün as one who possessed the power of attracting men of genius to his side, in consequence of which he was surrounded by such, and availed himself of their skill to escape from the tiger-clutch of the prince of Ch'in.

Dear me! he was but the leader of cock-crowing, cur-stealing swashbucklers—men of genius in no sense were they.

Indeed, had his own powerful State included but one single man of genius, it would have wrested supremacy from the House of Ch'in, and the opportunity for this cock-crowing, cur-stealing skill would never have occurred.

Besides, no true man of genius would condescend to associate with imitators of cocks and dogs.[1]

---

[1] This brief note is considered to be a veritable gem. One commentator says, "Within the space of a hundred words all the conditions of a perfect essay are fulfilled."

CHOU TUN-I

A.D. 1017–1073.

[A distinguished military commander, of whom it was said that he could judge of the number of an enemy by the accompanying cloud of dust. Both he and his son were slain in battle.]

THE LANGUAGE OF FLOWERS

LOVERS of flowering plants and shrubs we have had by scores, but T'ao Yüan-ming (*q.v.*) alone devoted himself to the chrysanthemum. Since the opening days of the T'ang dynasty, it has been fashionable to admire the peony; but my favourite is the water-lily. How stainless it rises from its slimy bed! How modestly it reposes on the clear pool—an emblem of purity and truth! Symmetrically perfect, its subtle perfume is wafted far and wide; while there it rests in spotless state, something to be regarded reverently from a distance, and not to be profaned by familiar approach.

In my opinion, the chrysanthemum is the flower of retirement and culture; the peony, the flower of rank and wealth; the water-lily, the Lady Virtue *sans pareille*.

Alas; few have loved the chrysanthemum since T'ao Yüan-ming; and none now love the water-lily like myself; *whereas the peony is a general favourite with all mankind.*

HUANG T'ING-CHIEN

A.D. 1042–1102.

[Ranks as one of the Four Great Scholars of the empire ; and in consequence of his filial behaviour to his mother, he is placed among the twenty-four examples of filial piety.]

COMMONPLACE

Hsi K'ang's[1] verses are at once vigorous and purely beautiful, without a vestige of commonplace about them. Every student of the poetic art should know them thoroughly, and thus bring the author into his mind's eye.

Those who are sunk in the cares and anxieties of this world's strife, even by a passing glance would gain therefrom enough to clear away some pecks of the cobwebs of mortality. How much more they who penetrate further and seize each hidden meaning and enjoy its flavour to the full! Therefore, my nephew, I send you these poems for family reading, that you may cleanse your heart and solace a weary hour by their perusal.

As I recently observed to my own young people, the true hero should be many-sided, but he must not be commonplace. It is impossible to cure that. Upon which, one of them asked by what characteristics this absence of the commonplace was distinguished. " It is hard to say," I replied. "A man who is not commonplace is, under ordinary circumstances, much like other people. But he who at moments of great trial does not flinch—he is not commonplace."

A hero may exist in his generation, either as a man of action or as a man of retirement; he may be inflexible or he may be of gentler mould. In any case, the above test gives the truest estimate of his value.

---

[1] A famous painter, poet, and philosopher of the third century of our era. As a student of alchemy, he managed to offend one of the Imperial princes and was denounced as a dangerous person. He was ultimately put to death as a magician and a heretic.

LI CHIH

11TH AND 12TH CENTURIES A.D.

[A painter and art-critic who in early life attracted the attention and patronage of Su Tung-P'o, who declared that his style was "like heaving waves, like flying sand, like rolling rocks." Author of the *Hua p'in*, a professedly critical work.]

ON PICTURES

THE colour of old pictures is black, resulting from deposits of dirt over the original thin wash of ink. Sometimes the picture is pleasantly impregnated with some ancient perfume. Faked pictures are mostly made up yellow, but this colour is easily distinguishable from the dark hue caused by dirt.

No more than three or four pictures by eminent artists should ever be hung in one room. After these have been enjoyed for four or five days, others should be substituted. All pictures should occasionally be brought into the open air, and on no account be exposed to smoke or damp. If they are exhibited in turn, they will not collect the dust and dirt, and what is more, you will not get tired of looking at them. Great care must be exercised in unrolling and rolling them up; and when they are brought out, they should be lightly flicked over the surface with a horse-tail or a silk flapper; coir brushes must on no account be used.

If the personages in a picture, when you look at them, seem to speak; if flowers and fruit are swayed by the wind and sparkle with dew; if birds and beasts seem as if they were alive; if hills and streams and forests and fountains are limpid, reposeful, dark, and distant; if buildings have depth; if bridges have movement to and fro; if the base of a hill can be seen below the surface of the clear water at its foot; and if the sources of the water are made obvious and distinct;—then, though his name may not be known, the man who paints such pictures is a great artist.

But if the personages resemble corpses or clay images; if the flowers and fruit look artificial; if the birds and beasts are like, only so far as plumage and fur; if the characteristics of the landscape are blurred and indistinct; if the buildings are out of proportion; if the bridges are out of drawing; if the foot of the hill rests on the top of the water; and if the streams have no apparent source;— pictures with such faults as these may be set aside as of no account.

YŎ FEI

A.D. 1103–1141.

[A famous military commander who was equally successful, at home in suppressing rebellion, and abroad in resisting the encroachments of the Tartars. However, the intrigues of a rival, by whose advice peace with the Tartars was purchased at the price of half the empire, brought him to the sword of the executioner. Posterity has avenged him by adopting the hated name of his betrayer as the common term for a spittoon.]

GOOD HORSES

HIS Majesty asked me one day if I had any good horses; to which I replied that I used to have two excellent animals. "They ate," I added, "large quantities of hay and many pecks of beans, daily; besides drinking each a gallon of spring water. Unless their food was fresh and clean, they would not touch it. On being mounted, they did not immediately break into a gallop; but would gradually warm into eagerness for their work. Between noon and sunset they would cover some sixty and odd miles; and on removing the saddle they would be found neither to have lost wind nor to have turned a hair any more than if they had been doing nothing. Such is the capacity for endurance in those who are well fed and well treated; who are willing, but not over-zealous. Unhappily, they both died; and those I have now do not eat more than a few pints per diem. They are not particular about either their food or their drink. Before you have fairly got hold of the bridle, away they go; and then, ere many miles are passed, they pant and sweat and are like to drop with fatigue. Such is the jaded condition of those who get little and are easily satisfied, who are over-eager and are easily exhausted."

His Majesty praised my reply ("but," as one commentator says, "quite missed the point.")

HU CH'ÜAN

DIED A.D. 1172.

[Statesman and art critic. He first attracted attention in 1129 by his answer to a theme set by the Emperor in an oral examination of scholars. The theme ran thus: "The way of government has its origin in God; the way of God has its origin in the people." We are told that his reply ran to over ten thousand words and that the Emperor was much astonished, but I can find no record of what he said.]

PORTRAITURE

THERE is no branch of painting so difficult as portrait-painting. It is not that reproduction of the features is difficult; the difficulty lies in painting the springs of action hidden in the heart. The face of a great man may resemble that of a mean man, but their hearts will not be alike. Therefore, to paint a likeness which does not exhibit these heart-impulses, leaving it an open question whether the sitter is a great man or a mean man, is to be unskilled in the art of portraiture.

SUNG TZ'Ŭ

MIDDLE OF 13TH CENTURY A.D.

[A scholar who is known for a work entitled "The Washing Away of Wrongs." It is a handbook of instructions to coroners ; and until recent years it was always carried by magistrates to the inquests over which they had to preside. Its opening words may perhaps help to dispel certain false ideas as to the value of human life in China.]

GENERAL REMARKS ON INQUESTS

THERE is nothing more important than human life; there is no punishment greater than death. A murderer gives life for life; the law shows no mercy. If punishment is wrongly inflicted, the mind of the judge cannot be at peace; therefore, confession and sentence are entirely dependent on examination showing the wounds to be genuine,—genuine wounds, with a confession that tallies. Thus, one life given for one death will cause those who know the law to fear the law, crime will be less frequent among the people, and human life will enjoy a more complete protection. If an inquest is not honestly conducted, the wrong of the murdered man will not be washed away, and new wrongs will be raised up among the living. One murder leads on to two murders, or even more; hate and vengeance follow one another, with pitiable results of which no man can foresee the end.

THE DEATH-LIMIT

Murders are rarely the result of premeditation, but can be traced in the majority of cases to a brawl. The statute which treats of wounding in a brawl attaches great weight to the death-limit, which means that the wounded man be handed over to the accused to be taken care of and provided with medical aid, and that a limit of time be fixed, on the expiration of which, punishment be awarded according to circumstances. Now the relatives of a wounded man, unless their ties be of the closest, generally desire his death that they may extort money from his slayer; but the accused wishes him to live that he himself may escape death, and therefore leaves no means untried to restore him to health. This institution of the death-limit is a merciful endeavour to save the lives of both.

LO KUAN-CHUNG

12TH CENTURY A.D.

[The reputed author of the novel based upon the History of the Three Kingdoms, of which specimens are given below. Of all Chinese works of fiction, this one, largely based upon fact, is undoubtedly the prime favourite. It is written in an easy and picturesque style, and therefore appeals to a very large circle of readers. Many of its episodes have been dramatised, and have thus become familiar to audiences drawn from the most unlettered classes.]

EUNUCHS KIDNAP AN EMPEROR

THROUGH fire and smoke, Chang Jang and Tuan Kuei[1] hurried away the Emperor[2] and his brother, the Prince. Day and night they travelled on, until they reached Mt. Mang; then, during the second watch,[3] they heard behind them a great hubbub of voices, with men and horses in pursuit. "Stop! you rascally rebels, stop!" cried out in a stentorian voice an officer who was leading the pursuers; at which, Chang Jang, seeing it was all up, threw himself into the river and was drowned. The Emperor and the Prince, not knowing if it was a real deliverance or not, did not dare to utter a sound but hid themselves in the long grass by the river side. The mounted soldiers scattered on all sides to search for them, but failed to discover their hiding-place. The Emperor and Prince remained concealed until the fourth watch,[4] when drenched with dew and faint with hunger, they embraced one another in tears, at the same time muffling their sobs in the undergrowth lest any one should hear them. At length, the Prince said, "we cannot stay here much longer; let us seek some way of escape." They then tied themselves together by their clothes and climbed up the bank of the river, to find themselves in a tangled mass of brambles, unable for want of light to see which way to go. They were in despair; when suddenly a huge cluster of fireflies, giving forth a brilliant glow, flew round and round the Emperor. "God

---

[1] Eunuchs.
[2] Succeeded A.D. 189, aged 13.
[3] 9 to 11 p.m.
[4] 1 to 3 a.m.

is helping us brothers!" cried the Prince; and by following
the lead of the fireflies, they by-and-by reached a road. It
was now the fifth watch,[1] and their feet were so sore that
they could walk no more. On the hillside they saw a heap
of straw, in the middle of which they lay down; and over
against this heap of straw there was a wooden shanty, the
owner of which had dreamt that very night of two red
suns which had fallen behind his shanty. Waking up
in a fright, he slipped on his clothes and went out to see
if anything had happened. Looking about, he noticed a
bright red glare rising up to the sky from the top of the
heap of straw at the back of his shanty; and on going
hurriedly to find out what it was, he discovered two persons
lying alongside the straw. "And who may you two young
fellows be?" he called out; to which he got no answer from
the Emperor who was afraid to reply; but the Prince
pointed at his brother, saying, "This is his Majesty, the
Emperor; there has been a mutiny of ten of our eunuchs,
and he has taken refuge in flight; I am the Prince, his
younger brother," At this, the farmer was greatly
alarmed; and after twice prostrating himself, he said,
"Your servant is the brother of an official who served
under the last dynasty, but being disgusted with the sale
of office by the ten eunuchs, and their bad treatment of
worthy men, I retired to this spot." He then assisted the
Emperor into the shanty, and on his knees offered wine
and food. Meanwhile, the officer and his men had pursued
and caught Tuan Kuei, and asked him where the Emperor
was; and on being told that the Emperor had disappeared,
without leaving any traces, the officer immediately beheaded
Tuan Kuei and hung the head to his horse's neck, dispersing
his men to search in all directions. He himself rode off
alone, and chance brought him to the farmer's shanty. The
farmer, seeing the decapitated head, enquired whose it
might be; and when the officer had told him the circum-

[1] 3 to 5 a.m.

stances, sovereign and subject met once more, to dissolve
in bitter tears. "The State cannot be for a single day
without its ruler," said the officer; "I beg your Majesty
to return to the capital." The farmer could only produce
one miserable horse, on which the Emperor mounted, while
the Prince rode with the officer on the other.[1]

THE GOD OF WAR[2]

By the loss of two generals, one after the other Ts'ao
Ts'ao[3] was greatly depressed. "Allow me," said one of
his staff, "to recommend the very man you want;" and on
being asked by Ts'ao Ts'ao for the name, he replied, "The
only man for this job is Kuan Yü." Ts'ao Ts'ao was soon
convinced, and gladly dispatched a messenger to summon
him. After taking leave of his two sisters-in-law, who
begged him to enquire for news for their Imperial uncle,
Kuan Yü set out to obey the summons. Seizing his green-
dragon sword, and mounting his hare-brown charger,
accompanied by several followers, he went straight to an
interview with Ts'ao Ts'ao, who told him of the deaths of
the two generals and of the loss of *morale* in the ranks; also,
how Yün Ch'ang had been invited to a consultation with
the enemy.[4] To this, Kuan Yü replied, "Suffer me to see
this business through;" upon which Ts'ao Ts'ao ordered
wine and treated him most cordially. Suddenly, it was

[1] On reaching the capital, the young Emperor was at once deposed by his chief
Minister, and the still more youthful brother, who had shared the above adventure, was
set up in his stead. The former only reigned for five months, and is not included by
Chinese historians as an actual occupant of the throne. The brother resigned the
throne in A.D. 220.

[2] The hero of the above story, Kuan Yü, after long and bloody campaigns was
taken prisoner in A.D. 219 and put to death. Posthumously ennobled in the 12th century,
in 1594 he was made a God; and ever since that date he has been worshipped as the
God of War, and temples in his honour have been built all over the empire.

[3] One of the leading figures in the wars of the Three Kingdoms, whose son became
the first Emperor of the short-lived Wei dynasty. In his last illness, he is said to
have called in the famous physician of the day, who diagnosed wind on the brain and
offered to get rid of this trouble by opening his skull under an anæsthetic. Fearing
treachery, Ts'ao Ts'ao declined the operation.

[4] And was then actually in the enemy's camp.

announced that the enemy, under General Yen, was preparing an attack; and Ts'ao Ts'ao took Kuan Yü to the top of a hill to reconnoitre. They sat down, and the other generals stood round them, while Ts'ao Ts'ao pointed out the position of the enemy, the fresh-looking splendour of his standards, the dense masses of his spears and swords, all drawn up in a formidable array. Then he turned to Kuan Yü and said. " You see this powerful force of men and horses . . ." "I do," answered Kuan Yü; " they remind me of a lot of earthen cocks and pottery dogs." Again Ts'ao Ts'ao pointed and said, " There, under the standard, with the embroidered robe and golden coat of mail, holding a sword and standing still on his horse—is General Yen," Kuan Yü raised his eyes and looked over in the direction indicated; then he said, "To me, General Yen looks as if he had stuck up an advertisement for the sale of his head." " Ah," cried Ts'ao Ts'ao, " you must not underrate him! " At this, Kuan Yü got up and exclaimed, " Although a man of no ability, I am prepared to go into this ten-thousand-man camp and bring you back his head as an offering." " There should be no joking on a battle-field," said one of the staff; " anyhow don't forget that Yün Ch'ang is there." Kuan Yü rushed off at once, and jumping on his horse, with his sword reversed, galloped down the hill. With round, glaring, phœnix-like eyes, and his silkworm-moth eyebrows raised straight up, he dashed right among the enemy whose ranks opened like parting waves, until he reached General Yen himself. The latter, under his standard, seeing Kuan Yü rush forward, was just about to ask what he wanted, when the speed of the brown-as-a-hare charger had already brought Kuan Yü alongside of him. General Yen had no time to lay his hand on his sword before he was knocked off his horse by Yün Ch'ang; whereupon Kuan Yü jumped down, cut off the General's head, hung it round his horse's neck, remounted in a moment, and with sword drawn made his way through the enemy's ranks as though no one was there to stop him. Officers and men were all terrified and a perfect panic ensued. Ts'ao Ts'ao's troops seized the opportunity for attack, and slaughtered the enemy in great numbers, besides capturing many horses and quantities of munitions of war. Kuan Yü rode his horse up the hill, to receive congratulations from the various commanders as he presented the head to Ts'ao Ts'ao, who exclaimed, " General, you are indeed no mortal man! "

CHU HSI

A.D. 1130–1200.

[The most voluminous, and one of the most luminous, of Chinese authors. He successfully introduced interpretations of the Confucian books, either wholly or partly at variance with those which had been put forth by the scholars of the Han dynasty and hitherto received as infallible, thus modifying to a certain extent the prevailing standard of political and social morality. His principle was simply one of consistency. He refused to interpret given words in a given passage in one sense, and the same words, occurring elsewhere, in another sense. Consequently, his are now the only authorised interpretations ; and these, in spite of the hankerings of a few woolly-headed scholars, are never likely to be displaced.

At Chu Hsi's death, his coffin is said to have taken up a suspended position, about three feet from the ground. Whereupon his son-in-law, falling on his knees beside the bier, reminded the departed spirit of the great principles (anti-supernatural) of which it had been such a brilliant exponent in life,—and the coffin descended gently to the ground.]

PORTRAITS

IT has always been considered first-class work in portrait painting, even for the most skilful artist, when the result is a likeness, more or less exact, of the mere features. Such skill is now possessed by Kuo Kung-ch'ên ; but what is still more marvellous, he catches the very expression, and reproduces, as it were, the inmost mind of his model.

I had already heard much of him from a couple of friends ; however, on my sending for him, he did not make his appearance until this year. Thereupon, a number of the gentlemen of the neighbourhood set themselves to test his skill. Sometimes the portrait would be perfect ; sometimes perhaps a little less so ; but in all cases a marked likeness was obtained, and in point of expression of individual character the artist showed powers of a very high order.

I myself sat for two portraits, one large and the other small ; and it was quite a joke to see how accurately he reproduced my coarse ugly face and my vulgar rustic turn of mind, so that even those who had only heard of, but had never seen me, knew at once for whom the portraits were intended.

I was just then about to start on my travels,—eastwards, to the confines of Shantung ; westwards, to the turbid waters of the Tung-t'ing lake ; northwards, to the quiet home of the old recluse, T'ao Yüan-ming ;—after which I contemplated retirement from public life. And I thought how much I should like to bring back with me portraits of the various great and good, but unknown, men I might be fortunate enough to meet with on the way. But Kuo's parents were old, and he could not venture upon such a long journey, for which I felt very sorry. So at parting, I gave him this document.[1]

TAOISM AND BUDDHISM

Taoism was at first confined to purity of life and to inaction. These were associated with long life and immortality, which by-and-by became the sole objects of the cult. Nowadays, they have thought it advisable to adopt a system of magical incantations, and chiefly occupy themselves with exorcism and prayers for blessings. Thus, two radical changes have been made. The Taoists have the writings of Lao Tzǔ and Chuang Tzǔ. They neglected these, and the Buddhists stole them for their own purposes; whereupon the Taoists went off and imitated the *sûtras* of Buddhism. This is just as if the scions of some wealthy house should be robbed of all their valuables, and then go off and gather up the old pots and pans belonging to the thieves. Buddhist books are full of what Buddha said, and Taoist books are similarly full of what *Tao* said. Now

---

[1] The following most interesting note was written for me by my valued friend, Mr. J. B. COUGHTRIE, an artist well-known in Hongkong circles:—

NOTE.

The art of portraiture does not reach a very high standard in China, and its professors meet with limited patronage. The backward condition in which this branch of art remains is probably owing to the fact that the style and taste peculiar to the Chinese combine to render a lifelike resemblance impossible, and the completed picture unattractive. The artist lays upon his paper a flat wash of colour to match the complexion of his sitter, and upon this draws a mere map of the features, making no attempt to obtain roundness or relief by depicting light and shadows, and never by any chance conveying the slightest suggestion of animation or expression. The degree of merit accorded to the production at this stage depends upon the ease and rapidity with which it is seemingly done, a timid highly-wrought face taking rank beneath a facile sketchy production, which latter in many cases is but the affectation of those qualities obtained slowly and with labour. On the drapery the utmost care is bestowed, and the sitter is invariably represented in the finest raiment he is entitled to wear, and equally invariably with fan in one hand and snuff-bottle in the other.

There is a wide-spread belief that the Chinese object to have their portraits taken for superstitious reason; and it is true that artists who have visited the country have always failed to induce picturesque coolies, peasants, and even beggars, to allow themselves to be sketched. The writer, however, has been informed that no such superstition really exists, but merely a proud objection on the part of the native to be depicted in his rags or every-day clothing.

Buddha was a man, but how does *Tao* manage to talk? This belief, however, has prevailed for eight or nine centuries past. Taoism began with Lao Tzŭ. Its Trinity of the Three Pure Ones is copied from the Trinity of the Three Persons as taught by Buddhism. By their trinity the Buddhists mean (1) the spiritual body (of Buddha), (2) his joyful body (showing Buddha rewarded for his virtues), and (3) his fleshly body, under which Buddha appears on earth as a man. The modern schools of Buddhism have divided their Trinity under three images which are placed side by side, thus completely missing the true signification (which is Trinity in Unity); and the adherents of Taoism, wishing to imitate the Buddhists in this particular, worship Lao Tzŭ under (another version of) the Three Pure Ones, namely, (1) as the original revered God, (2) the supreme ruler *Tao*, and (3) the supreme ruler Lao Tzŭ (in the flesh). Almighty God (that is, *T'ien*) is ranked below these three, which is nothing short of an outrageous usurpation. Moreover, the first two do not represent the spiritual and joyful bodies of Lao Tzŭ, and the two images set up cannot form a Unity with him; while the introduction of the third is an aggravated copy of the mistake made by the Buddhists. Chuang Tzŭ has told us in plain language of the death of Lao Tzŭ, who must now be a spirit; how then can he usurp the place of Almighty God? The doctrines of Buddha and Lao Tzŭ should be altogether abolished; but if this is not possible, then only the teachings of Lao Tzŭ should be tolerated, all shrines in honour of him, or of his disciples and various magicians, to be placed under the control of the directors of Public Worship.

TÊNG CH'UN

12TH CENTURY A.D.

[Author of the *Hua Chi* "The Development of Painting."]

PAINTING BUDDHAS

IN India, at the temple of Nalanda, the priests paint many Buddhas, Bôdhisatvas, and Lohans, using the linen of the West. The features of their Buddhas are very different from Chinese features; the eyes are larger and the mouths and ears are curiously shaped; the figures wear girdles and have the right shoulder bare, and are either in sitting or standing attitudes. The artist begins by drawing the heart, liver, stomach, lungs, and kidneys, at the back of the picture; on the other side he paints the figure in colours, using gold or vermilion as a ground. They object to ox-glue as too noticeable, and take the gum from peach-trees mixed with the juice of the willow, which is very strong and clear, but quite unknown in China.

KUO JO-HSÜ

[From the *T'u hua wên chien chih* "Record of Observations on Drawing and Painting." Its author was an art critic and painter, said by Têng Ch'un to be the only artist of his acquaintance who could express the soul, as well as the form, of his subject, human or otherwise.]

KOREAN ART

WHEN the Sung dynasty was at the height of its glory, the roads were thronged with men of foreign nations coming to Court. Of all these the most cultured and refined were the Koreans, who were gradually yielding to the influences of the Flowery Land. In matters of manual skill there was no other people to be compared with them, and they were remarkably proficient in painting. At one house I saw a coloured landscape in four rolls; and at another, two rolls containing pictures of the eight ancient worthies of Korea; while elsewhere I saw a picture on fine calico of the Heavenly Kings, all being works of considerable excellence. In 1074 a Korean envoy arrived, bringing tribute, and also bent upon obtaining specimens of Chinese calligraphy and painting. He bought up a good many of these, with not more than ten to twenty per cent. of inferior works, and paid in some cases as much as 300 ounces of silver. In the winter of 1076 another envoy was sent with tribute; and being about to take back with him several painters, he begged leave to be allowed to copy the frescos in the Hsiang-kuo Temple. This he was permitted to do, and carried away with him copies of all the frescos, the men he employed being fairly skilled in the art. When these envoys came to China they used at their private audiences folding fans made of duck['s egg] blue paper, on which were were painted pictures of their national heroes, men, women, horses, landscape, lotus-flowers, tree-birds and water-fowl, all very cleverly done. Patches of silver were also used for clouds and the moon, with very charming effect. They called the fans their Dwarf fans, because the fans came originally from the Dwarf Nation (Japan).

WÊN T'IEN-HSIANG

A.D. 1236–1282.

[The famous statesman and patriot, who, when finally held captive by Kublai Khan after the complete overthrow of the Sung dynasty, calmly faced death rather than own allegiance to the Mongol conqueror. The following beautiful *morceau* was penned in captivity, and cannot but fill us with admiration for the hero of whom the Chinese may proudly say, "Whatever record leaps to light, he never shall be shamed."]

DIVINÆ PARTICULAM AURÆ

THERE is in the universe an *Aura* which permeates all things, and makes them what they are. Below, it shapes forth land and water; above, the sun and the stars. In man it is called spirit; and there is nowhere where it is not.

In times of national tranquility, this spirit lies *perdu* in the harmony which prevails. Only at some great crisis is it manifested widely abroad. And as to these manifestations, those who run may read. Were there not the fearless and truthful annalists of old?[1] Was there not the disinterested chivalry of Chang Liang?[2] the unswerving devotion of Su Wu?[3] Did not Yen Yen[4] say they had headless generals in his district, but none who surrendered their allegiance? Was not an emperor's robe splashed with blood that might not be washed away?[5] And the teeth of Chang Hsün?[6]—the tongue of Yen Hsi?[6]—the guileless honesty of Kuan Ning,[7] pure as the clearest ice?—the martial genius of K'ung Ming,[8] the admiration of Gods and men?—the oath of Tsu T'i?[9]—the tablet dashed in the rebel's face?[10]

---

[1] In allusion to certain murders which were denounced by the historiographers of the periods in question.

[2] Who, after setting an Emperor upon the throne, refused all reward, and retired into private life. *See* p. 63.

[3] Held prisoner by the Huns for the space of nineteen years. See *Li Ling's Reply,* p. 82. The reference is to his "credentials," from which he never allowed himself to be separated.

[4] In reply to the famous Chang Fei, who took him prisoner, but, in consequence of this bold answer, spared his life.

[5] The blood of Chi Shao, who died to save his Imperial master's life.

[6] Killed for their violent language in the presence of rebels by whom they had been taken prisoners.

[7] Who faithfully repaid all loans made to him while in exile.

[8] The famous general of the *Story of the Three Kingdoms.*

[9] As he was about to cross the Yellow River with troops in pursuit of an enemy— "If I do not succeed in purging the country of these men, may my blood flow away like this river!"

[10] By a virtuous official whose loyalty the said rebel was vainly striving to undermine.

Such is this grand and glorious spirit which endureth for all generations, and which, linked with the sun and moon, knows neither beginning nor end. The foundation of all that is great and good in heaven and earth, it is itself born from the everlasting obligations which are due by man to man.

Alas! the fates were against me: I was without resource. Bound with fetters, hurried away towards the north, death would have been sweet indeed; but that boon was refused.

My dungeon is lighted by the will-o'-the-wisp alone: no breath of spring cheers the murky solitude in which I dwell. The ox and the barb herd together in one stall: the rooster and the phœnix feed together from one dish. Exposed to mist and dew, I had many times thought to die; and yet, through the seasons of two revolving years, disease hovered round me in vain. The dank unhealthy soil to me became Paradise itself. For there was that within me which misfortune could not steal away.[1]   And so I remained firm, gazing at the white clouds floating over my head, and bearing in my heart a sorrow boundless as the sky.

The sun of those dead heroes has long since set; but their record is before me still. And, while the wind whistles under the eaves, I open my books and read; and lo! in their presence my heart glows with a borrowed fire.

---

[1] But there is that within me which shall tire
Torture and Time; and breathe when I expire:
Something unearthly.

LIU YIN

A.D. 1241–1293

[A promising official who was prevented by failing health from rising to eminence.
He lived a retired life in a cottage which he named "Peace with Culture."]

DESIGN

W HEN God made man, he gave him powers to cope
with the exigencies of his environment; and resources
within himself, so that he need not be dependent upon
external circumstances [for good or evil].

Thus, in districts where poisons abound, antidotes
abound also; and in others, where malaria prevails, we find
such correctives as ginger, nutmegs, and dog-wood. Again,
fish, terrapins, and clams, are the most wholesome articles
of diet in excessively damp climates, though themselves
denizens of the water; and musk and deer-horns are
excellent prophylactics in earthy climates, where in fact
they are produced. For, if these things were unable to
prevail against their surroundings, they could not possibly
thrive where they do; while the fact that they do so thrive
is proof positive that they were ordained as specifics against
those surroundings.

Chu Hsi said, "When God is about to send down
calamities upon us, he first raises up the hero whose genius
shall finally prevail against those calamities." From this
point of view, there can be no living man without his
appointed use; nor any state of society which man should
be unable to put right.

T'ANG HOU

13TH CENTURY A.D.

[Art critic and author of the *Hua Lun* "On Painting." The Emperor Hui Tsung, A.D. 1100–1126, mentioned below, was an artist of considerable skill, and a liberal patron of art in general.]

AN IMPERIAL ARTIST

THE old masters always had some deep meaning in their pictures, and never put brush to silk unless dominated by an idea. The Emperor Hui Tsung painted with his own hand a picture entitled "A Dream Journey to the Next World." The inhabitants, several thousands in number, were about half the size of one's little finger. All things in heaven and earth, and most beautifully executed, were to be found therein,—cities with their suburbs, palaces, houses, banners, pennants, bells, drums, beautiful girls, souls of men (*chên tsai*), clouds, red glows, mists, the Milky Way, birds, cattle, dragons, and horses. Gazing at this picture makes one feel a longing to travel away into space and forget the world of men. Verily 'tis a marvellous work.

PICTURE COLLECTING

In forming collections of pictures, Taoist and Buddhist subjects rank first, the reason being that the old masters put a great deal of work into them, wishing to inspire reverence, love, and a fondness for ceremonial. Next come human figures, which may be used as patterns or warnings. Then comes landscape with its inexhaustible delights, followed by flowers, and by horses, which are among divine animals. Portraits of gentlemen and ladies, and pictures of barbarians, though very clever, are scarcely adjuncts to intellectual culture. At the present day collectors of pictures mostly set a high store upon works by old masters, and despise those of modern times.

ANONYMOUS

? 13TH CENTURY.

[From a work entitled *Mên shih hsin yü,* or "Chats while Lice-catching."]

INTERPRETATION

Two lines from a poem of the T'ang dynasty were once set as a test to a company of painters. The lines ran thus:

> Some tender sprays of budding green, with a tiny splash of red,—
> A little goes a long way to put spring thoughts in one's head.

All the painters sought for their interpretations in plants and in hints of the pink blossoms of spring, and all failed alike, with the single exception of one artist, who produced the picture of a kiosque on a cliff, faintly seen in a setting of green willows, with a beautiful girl (dressed according to custom in red) standing up and leaning on the balustrade.[1] The others admitted their defeat, for such a picture may really be said to interpret the thought of the poet.

---

[1] In the Spring a young man's fancy lightly turns to thoughts of love.

ANONYMOUS

? 14TH CENTURY.

[From a work entitled *Mo k'o hui hsi* "The Scholar Waves the Yak's Tail."]

THE CAT AND THE PEONY

OU-YANG HSIU (*q.v.*) picked up an old picture of a cluster of peonies with a cat sitting near by. He was quite at a loss to make out its inner meaning, until a friend who lived next door came in to see it. "Oh," exclaimed the latter, "the subject is Noon;" and he proceeded to explain as follows. "You notice," said he, "that the flowers are wide open and dulled in hue, just as flowers are at midday. Then again, the pupils of the cat's eyes are like a black thread, as they always are at that hour. When flowers have dew on them the calyx is contracted and the hue is fresh; and in the morning and evening the pupils in a cat's eyes are always round. Thus skilfully, is it possible to ferret out the underlying intentions of the men of old."

LIU CHI

A.D. 1311–1375.

[For many years a faithful servant of the quondam Buddhist-novice Emperor, who at length succeeded in overthrowing the dynasty of the Mongols and establishing himself, under the title of Hung Wu, as the first ruler of the House of Ming.]

DIVINATION

WHEN Shao P'ing fell,[1] he repaired to the abode of a famous augur to ask his fate by means of divination.

"What is it you would enquire about?" said the latter.

"He who has lain awhile," replied Shao P'ing, "longs to arise. He who has hidden awhile, longs to come forth. He whose nose is stuffed, longs to sneeze. And I have heard that that which is over-pent breaks out at last; that excessive sorrow finds its own relief; that excessive heat is followed by wind; and that excessive compression makes its own vent. Thus, too, the seasons follow one another with ceaseless change: one rolls away and another comes on. Yet I have my doubts, and would fain receive instruction at your hands."

"Sir," said the augur; "after all you have just now stated, pray tell me what further you would have me divine?"

"The abstruser mysteries," answered Shao P'ing, "I do not pretend to have penetrated; and would beg you to enlighten me thereon."

"Alas!" cried the augur, "what is there that Heaven can bestow save that which virtue can obtain? Where is the efficacy of spiritual beings beyond that with which man has endowed them? The divining-plant is but a dead stalk; the tortoise-shell a dry bone. They are but matter like ourselves. And man, the divinest of all things, why does he not seek wisdom from within, rather than from these grosser stuffs?

"Besides, sir, why not reflect upon the past—that past which gave birth to this present? Your cracked roof and

---

[1] As he did with the Ch'in dynasty (206 B.C.), under which he had been Marquis of Tung-ling.

crumbling walls of to-day are but the complement of yesterday's lofty towers and spacious halls. The straggling bramble is but the complement of the shapely garden tree. The grasshopper and the cicada are but the complement of organs and flutes; the will-o'-the-wisp and firefly, of gilded lamps and painted candles. Your endive and watercresses are but the complement of the elephant-sinews and camel's hump[1] of days by-gone; the maple-leaf and the rush, of your once rich robes and fine attire. Do not repine that those who had not such luxuries then, enjoy them now. Do not be dissatisfied that you who enjoyed them then, have them now no more. In the space of a day and night, the flower blooms and dies. Between spring and autumn things perish and are renewed. Beneath the roaring cascade a deep pool is found: dark valleys lie at the foot of high hills. These things you know: what more can divination teach you?"

OUTSIDES

At Hangchow there lived a costermonger who understood how to keep oranges a whole year without letting them spoil. His fruit was always fresh-looking, firm as jade, and of a beautiful golden hue; but inside—dry as an old cocoon.

One day I asked him, saying, "Are your oranges for altar or sacrificial purposes, or for show at banquets?[2] Or do you make this outside display merely to cheat the foolish? as cheat them, you most outrageously do." "Sir," replied the orangeman, "I have carried on this trade now for many years. It is my source of livelihood. I sell: the world buys. And I have yet to learn that you are the only honest man about, and that I am the only cheat. Perhaps

---

[1] *Sc.*, rich food.

[2] A light touch of nature which seems to prove the kinship of the whole human family.

it never struck you in this light. The bâton-bearers of
to-day, seated on their tiger skins, pose as the martial
guardians of the State; but what are they compared with
the captains of old? The broad-brimmed, long-robed
ministers of to-day, pose as pillars of the constitution; but
have they the wisdom of our ancient counsellors? Evil
doers arise and none can subdue them. The people are in
misery, and none can relieve them. Clerks are corrupt,
and none can restrain them. Laws decay, and none can
renew them. Our officials eat the bread of the State, and
know no shame. They sit in lofty halls, ride fine steeds,
drink themselves drunk with wine, and batten on the richest
fare. Which of them but puts on an awe-inspiring look,
a dignified mien?—all gold and gems without, but dry
cocoons within. You pay, sir, no heed to these things,
while you are very particular about my oranges."

I had no answer to make. I retired to ponder over
this costermonger's wit, which reminded me forcibly of
"The Wag." [1] Was he really out of conceit with the age,
or only quizzing me in defence of his fruit?

---

[1] Tung-fang So. *See* p. 77.

FANG HSIAO-JU

A.D. 1357–1402.

[A Minister of State under Hui Ti, the Emperor who vanished and is supposed to have been recognized forty years afterwards by a mole on his chin. Refusing to serve under the new Emperor, Yung Lo, whose name is connected with the giant encyclopaedia, he was cut to pieces in the market-place and his family was exterminated.]

IT IS ALWAYS THE UNEXPECTED

STATESMEN who forecast the destinies of an empire, oft-times concentrate their genius upon the difficult, and neglect the easy. They provide against likely evils, and disregard combinations which yield no ground for suspicion. Yet calamity often issues from neglected quarters, and sedition springs out of circumstances which have been set aside as trivial. Must this be regarded as due to an absence of care?—No. It results because the things that man can provide against are human, while those that elude his vigilance and overpower his strength are divine.

The Ch'ins obliterated the feudal system and united the empire under one sway. They saw that the Chou dynasty had been overthrown by the turbulence of vassal nobles, and therefore they dispersed these over the land as officers of state responsible to the central government; trusting that thereby appeal to arms would cease, and the empire be theirs for ever. But they could not foresee that the founder of the Hans would arise from the furrowed fields and snatch away the sceptre from their grasp.

The Hans took warning by the Ch'ins, and re-established feudatory princes, choosing them from among the members of the Imperial family, and relying upon their tie of kinship to the throne.[1] Yet the conflict with the Confederate States was at hand, in consequence of which the power of the princes was diminished to prevent similar troubles for the future; when, lo! Wang Mang leaped upon the throne.[2]

---

[1] See *Music*, p. 80.

[2] A famous usurper.

Wang Mang took warning by his predecessors, and others, in like manner, took warning by his fate, each in turn providing against a recurrence of that which had proved fatal before. And in each case calamity came upon them from a quarter whence least expected.

The Emperor T'ai Tsung of the T'angs secretly learned that his issue would be done to death by Wu. He accordingly slew the Wu upon whom his suspicions fell: but the real Wu was all the time at his side.

The Emperor T'ai Tsu of the Sungs persuaded those who had placed him upon the throne to retire into private life. He little foresaw that his descendants would writhe under the barbarian Tartar's yoke.[1]

All the instances above cited include gifted men whose wisdom and genius overshadowed their generation. They took counsel and provided against disruption of their empire with the utmost possible care. Yet misfortune fell upon every one of them, always issuing from some source where its existence was least suspected. This, because human wisdom reaches only to human affairs, and cannot touch the divine. Thus, too, will sickness carry off the children even of the best doctors, and devils play their pranks in the family of an exorcist. How is it that these professors who succeed in grappling with the cases of others, yet fail in treating their own? It is because in those they confine themselves to the human; in these they would meddle with the divine.

The men of old knew that it was impossible to provide infallibly against the convulsions of ages to come. There was no plan, no device, by which they could hope to prevail; and they refrained accordingly from vain scheming. They simply strove by the force of Truth and Virtue to win for themselves the approbation of God; that He, in reward for their virtuous conduct, might watch over them, as a fond mother watches over her babes, for ever. Thus, although fools were not wanting to their posterity,—fools, able to

---

[1] The dynasty of the Mongols, established by Kublai Khan.

drag an empire to the dust,—still, the evil day was deferred. This was indeed foresight of a far-reaching kind.

But he who, regardless of the favour of God, may hope by the light of his own petty understanding to establish that which shall endure through all time,—he shall be confounded indeed.

THE LADY CHANG

16TH CENTURY A.D.

[Wife of the patriot statesman Yang Chi-Shêng.]

FOR HER HUSBAND'S LIFE

M AY it please your Majesty,

My husband was chief minister in the Cavalry Department of the Board of War. Because he advised your Majesty against the establishment of a tradal mart,[1] hoping to prevent Ch'ou Luan from carrying out his design, he was condemned only to a mild punishment; and then when the latter suffered defeat, he was restored to favour and to his former honours.

Thereafter, my husband was for ever seeking to make some return for the Imperial clemency. He would deprive himself of sleep. He would abstain from food. All this I saw with my own eyes. By-and-by, however, he gave ear to some idle rumour of the market-place, and the old habit came strong upon him. He lost his mental balance. He uttered wild statements, and again incurred the displeasure of the Throne. Yet he was not slain forthwith. His punishment was referred to the Board. He was beaten: he was thrown into prison. Several times he nearly died. His flesh was hollowed out beneath the scourge: the sinews of his legs were severed. Blood flowed from him in bowlfuls, splashing him from head to foot. Confined day and night in a cage, he endured the utmost misery.

Then our crops failed, and daily food was wanting in our poverty-stricken home. I strove to earn money by spinning, and worked hard for the space of three years, during which period the Board twice addressed the Throne, receiving on each occasion an Imperial rescript that my husband was to await his fate in gaol. But now, I hear,

---

[1] At the frontier, between China and Tartary, the alleged object of which was to keep China supplied with a fine breed of Tartar horses. Ch'ou Luan was a statesman and general in favour of the project, until complications arose and he was beaten by the Tartars in a pitched battle.

your Majesty has determined that my husband shall die,
in accordance with the statutes of the Empire. Die as he
may, his eyes will close in peace with your Majesty, while
his soul seeks the realms below.

Yet I know that your Majesty has a humane and
kindly heart; and when the creeping things of the earth,—
nay, the very trees and shrubs,—share in the national
tranquillity, it is hard to think that your Majesty would
grudge a pitying glance upon our fallen estate. And
should we be fortunate enough to attract the Imperial
favour to our lowly affairs, that would be joy indeed. But
if my husband's crime is of too deep a dye, I humbly beg
that my head may pay the penalty, and that I be permitted
to die for him. Then, from the far-off land of spirits,
myself brandishing spear and shield, I will lead forth an
army of fierce hobgoblins to do battle in your Majesty's
behalf, and thus make some return for this act of Imperial
grace.[1]

---

[1] Her husband was executed in 1556.

THE LADY CHANG

16TH CENTURY A.D.

[Wife of Shên Shu. Her husband fell a victim to the influence of a powerful rival and was imprisoned for fifteen years, being liberated (1567) on the fall of his rival through the joint petition, given below, by his wife and concubine.]

IN HER HUSBAND'S STEAD

M AY it please your Majesty,

My husband was a Censor attached to the Board of Rites. For his folly in recklessly advising your Majesty, he deserved indeed a thousand deaths; yet, under the Imperial clemency, he was doomed only to await his sentence in prison.

Since then, fourteen years have passed away. His aged parents are still alive, but there are no children in his hall, and the wretched man has none on whom he can rely. I alone remain—a lodger at an inn, working day and night at my needle to provide the necessaries of life; encompassed on all sides by difficulties; to whom every day seems a year.

My father-in-law is eighty-seven years of age. He trembles on the brink of the grave. He is like a candle in the wind. I have naught wherewith to nourish him alive, or to honour him when dead. I am a lone woman. If I tend the one, I lose the other. If I return to my father-in-law, my husband will die of starvation. If I remain to feed him, my father-in-law may die at any hour. My husband is a criminal bound in gaol. He dares give no thought to his home. Yet can it be that when all living things are rejoicing in life under the wise and generous rule of to-day, we alone should taste the cup of poverty and distress, and find ourselves beyond the pale of universal peace?

Oft, as I think of these things, the desire to die comes upon me; but I swallow my grief and live on, trusting in providence for some happy termination, some moistening with the dew of Imperial grace. And now that my father-in-law is face to face with death; now that my husband can hardly expect to live—I venture to offer this body as a hostage, to be bound in prison, while my husband returns to watch over the last hours of his father. Then, when all is over, he will resume his place and await your Majesty's pleasure. Thus, my husband will greet his father once again, and the feelings of father and child will be in some measure relieved. Thus, I shall give to my father-in-law the comfort of his son, and the duty of a wife towards her husband will be fulfilled.[1]

[1] "For every word we read," says a commentator, "we shed a tear of blood." It is at any rate satisfactory to know that the lady's husband was released.

TSUNG CH‘ÊN

16TH CENTURY.

[An official who took the highest degree (*chin shih*) at the age of twenty and rose, with vicissitudes, to high rank. He is noted for his defence of Foochow against the Japanese (*circa* 1560). He opened the west gate, of which he was in charge, as if to admit the enemy by treachery; and then his troops and the populace attacked the invaders from the top of the wall and slaughtered them in great numbers.]

FLUNKEYISM

I WAS very glad at this distance to receive your letter which quite set my mind at rest, together with the present you were so kind as to add. I thank you very much for your good wishes, and especially for your thoughtful allusion to my father.

As to what you are pleased to say in reference to official popularity and fitness for office, I am much obliged by your remarks. Of my unfitness I am only too well aware; while as to popularity with my superiors, I am utterly unqualified to secure that boon.

How indeed does an official find favour in the present day with his chief? Morning and evening he must whip up his horse and go dance attendance at the great man's door.[1] If the porter refuses to admit him, then honied words, a coaxing air, and money drawn from the sleeve, may prevail. The porter takes in his card; but the great man does not come out. So he waits in the stable among grooms, until his clothes are charged with the smell; in spite of hunger, in spite of cold, in spite of a blazing heat. At nightfall, the porter who had pocketed his money comes forth and says his master is tired and begs to be excused, and will he call again next day. So he is forced to come once more as requested. He sits all night in his clothes. At cock-crow he jumps up, performs his toilette, and gallops off and knocks at the entrance gate. "Who's there?" shouts the porter angrily; and when he explains, the porter

---

[1] The reader of JUVENAL will no doubt be reminded of Satire III—

quid das, ut Cossum aliquando salutes?
Ut te respiciat clauso Veiento labello?

gets still more angry and begins to abuse him, saying, "You are in a fine hurry, you are! Do you think my master sees people at this hour?" Then is the visitor shamed, but has to swallow his wrath and try to persuade the porter to let him in. And the porter, another fee to the good, gets up and lets him in; and then he waits again in the stable as before, until perhaps the great man comes out and summons him to an audience.

Now, with many an obeisance, he cringes timidly towards the foot of the dais steps: and when the great man says "Come!" he prostrates himself twice and remains long without rising. At length he goes up to offer his present, which the great man refuses. He entreats acceptance; but in vain. He implores, with many instances; whereupon the great man bids a servant take it. Then two more prostrations, long drawn out; after which he arises, and with five or six salutations he takes his leave.

On going forth, he bows to the porter, saying, "It's all right with your master. Next time I come you need make no delay." The porter returns the bow, well pleased with his share in the business.[1] Meanwhile, our friend springs on his horse, and when he meets an acquaintance flourishes his whip and cries out, " I have just been with His Excellency. He treated me very kindly, very kindly indeed." And then he goes into detail, upon which his friends begin to be more respectful to him as a *protegé* of His Excellency. The great man himself says, "So-and-so is a good fellow, a very good fellow indeed; " upon which the bystanders of course declare that they think so too.[2]

Such is popularity with one's superiors in the present day. Do you think that I could be as one of these? No! Beyond sending in a complimentary card at the summer

---

[1] JUVENAL, Satire III—

> præstare tributa clientes
> Cogimur, et cultis augere peculia servis.

[2] *Ibid.*—

> rides? majore cachinno
> Concutitur: flet, si lachrymas aspexit amici, etc.

and winter festivals, I do not go near the great from one year's end to another. Even when I pass their doors I stuff my ears and cover my eyes and gallop quickly past as if some one was after me. In consequence of this want of breadth, I am of course no favourite with the authorities; but what care I? There is a destiny that shapes our ends and it has shaped mine towards the path of duty alone. For which, no doubt, you think me an ass.

WANG TAO-K'UN

16TH CENTURY.

[Graduated as *chin shih* in 1547, and distinguished himself as a military commander and as a writer.]

HOW TO GET ON

A RETAINER was complaining to Pŏ Tzŭ that no one in the district knew how to get on.

"You gentlemen," said he, "are like square handles which you would thrust into the round sockets of your generation. Consequently, there is not one of you which fits."

"You speak truth," replied Pŏ Tzŭ; "kindly explain how this is so."

"There are five reasons," said the retainer, "why you are at loggerheads with the age, as follows:—

"(1) The path to popularity lies straight before you, but you will not follow it.

"(2) Other men's tongues reach the soft places in the hearts of their superiors, but your tongues are too short.

"(3) Others eschew fur robes, and approach with bentbacks as if their very clothes were too heavy for them; but you remain as stiff-necked as planks.

"(4) Others respond even before they are called, and seek to anticipate the wishes of their superiors; whose enemies, were they the saints above, would not escape abuse; whose friends, were they highwaymen and thieves, would be larded over with praise. But you—you stick at facts, and express opinions adverse to those of your superiors whom it is your special interest to conciliate.[1]

"(5) Others make for gain as though bent upon shooting a pheasant; watching in secret and letting fly with care, so that nothing escapes their aim. But you—you hardly bend your bow, or bend it only to miss the quarry that lies within your reach.

---

[1] *Cf.* the well-known—si dixeris æstuo, sudat.

" One of these five failings is like a tumour hanging to you and impeding your progress in life. How much more all of them ! "

" It is indeed as you state," answered Pŏ Tzŭ. " But would you bid me cut these tumours away? A man may have a tumour and live. To cut it off is to die. And life with a tumour is better than death without. Besides, beauty is a natural gift; and the woman who tried to look like Hsi Shih only succeeded in frightening people out of their wits by her ugliness.[1] Now it is my misfortune to have these tumours, which make me more loathsome even than that woman. Still, I can always so to speak, stick to my needle and my cooking-pots and strive to make my good man happy.[2] There is no occasion for me to proclaim my ugliness in the market-place."

" Ah, sir," said the retainer, "now I know why there are so many ugly people about, and so little beauty in the land."

---

[1] Hsi Shih was a famous beauty who made herself even more lovely by contracting her brows.

[2] *I.e.*, do my duty.

HSÜ HSIEH

16TH AND 17TH CENTURIES.

[Graduated in 1601 as first *Chin shih*, and joined the Han-lin College. He was devoted to study, and vowed that if only he might attain to a good style, he would jump into the ocean to spread it far and wide.]

ANTIQUES

FOR some years I had possessed an old inkstand, left at my house by a friend. It came into ordinary use as such, I being unaware that it was an antique. However, one day a connoisseur told me it was at least a thousand years old, and urged me to preserve it carefully as a valuable relic. This I did, but never took any further trouble to ascertain whether such was actually the case or not. For supposing that this inkstand really dated from the period assigned, its then owner must have regarded it simply as an inkstand. He could not have known that it was destined to survive the wreck of time and come to be cherished as an antique. And while we prize it now, because it has descended to us from a distant past, we forget that then, when antiques were relics of a still earlier period, it could not have been of any value to antiquarians, themselves the moderns of what is antiquity to us!

The surging crowd around us thinks of naught but the acquisition of wealth and material enjoyment, occupied only with the struggle for place and power. Men lift their skirts and hurry through the mire; they suffer indignity and feel no sense of shame. And if from out this mass there arises one spirit purer and simpler than the rest, striving to tread a nobler path than they, and amusing his leisure, for his own gratification, with guitars, and books, and pictures and other relics of olden times,—such a man is indeed a genuine lover of the antique. He can never be one of the common herd, though the common herd always affect to admire whatever is admittedly admirable. In the same way, persons who aim at advancement in their career, will spare no endeavour to collect the choicest rarities, in order, by such gifts, to curry favour with their superiors; who, in their turn, will take pleasure in ostentatious display of their collections of antiquities. Such is but a specious hankering after antiques, arising simply from a desire to eclipse one's neighbours. Such men are not genuine lovers of the antique. Their tastes are those of the common herd after all, though they make a great show and filch the reputation of true antiquarians, in the hope of thus distinguishing themselves from their fellows, ignorant as they are that what they secure is the name alone without the reality. The man whom I call a genuine antiquarian is he who studies the writings of the ancients, and strives to form himself upon their model though unable to greet them in the flesh; who ever and anon, in his wanderings up and down the long avenue of the past, lights upon some choice fragment which brings him in an instant face to face with the immortal dead. Of such enjoyment there is no satiety.[1] Those who truly love antiquity, love not the things, but the men of old; since a relic in the present is much what it was in the past,—a mere thing. And so if it is not to things, but rather to men, that devotion is due, then even I may aspire to be some day an antique. Who shall say that centuries hence an antiquarian of the day may not look up to me as I have looked up to my predecessors? Should I then neglect myself, and foolishly devote my energies to trifling with things?

Such is popular enthusiasm in these matters. It is shadow without substance. But the theme is endless, and I shall therefore content myself with this passing record of my old inkstand.

---

[1] Cf.—

O ye who patiently explore
The wreck of Herculanean lore,
    What rapture could ye seize!—
Some Theban fragment, or unroll
One precious, tender-hearted scroll
    Of pure Simonides.

HUAI TSUNG

DIED A.D. 1644.

[The last Emperor of the Ming dynasty. He made great efforts to rule wisely and to free the country from the curse of eunuch domination. It was, however, too late. Extra taxation, necessary to meet a huge deficit, led to rebellion; a state of anarchy prevailed in the provinces; at the capital all was in confusion; and on April 9, 1644, Peking fell. On the previous night the Emperor, who had refused to flee, tried to kill the eldest princess but only cut off her arm.[1] He commanded the Empress to commit suicide, and sent his three sons into hiding. At dawn, the bell was struck for the Court to assemble, but no one came. His Majesty then ascended the small hill in the palace grounds; and after having written a final Decree upon the lapel of his coat, he hanged himself,[2] as also did one faithful eunuch.]

VALEDICTORY

POOR in virtue and of contemptible personality, I have incurred the wrath of God on high. My Ministers have deceived me. I am ashamed to meet my ancestors; and therefore I myself take off my crown, and with my hair covering my face, await dismemberment at the hands of the rebels. Do not hurt a single one of my people!

---

[1] She was afterwards killed by the rebels.

[2] His body, together with that of the Empress, was reverently encoffined by the Manchus.

THE HUNG LOU-MÊNG

17TH CENTURY A.D.

[Author unknown. Placed in the Chinese *Index Expurgatorius* in consequence of its denunciation of official abuses. As a novel it ranks among the greatest of any nation, for originality of plot and varied delineation of no fewer than 400 characters. The name means " Dream of Red Upper Storeys (*q.d.* of wealth and power) ; " but it is known to foreigners as " The Dream of the Red Chamber."]

A POPULAR PHYSICIAN

JUST then a maid came in to say that the doctor had arrived, and to ask her ladyship to take her seat behind the curtain. "What!" cried her ladyship, "an old woman like me? Why I might easily be the mother of your prodigy! I am not afraid of him. Don't let down the curtain; he must see me as I am." So a small table was brought forward and a pillow placed on it, after which the doctor was called in. He entered with downcast eyes and made a respectful salutation to her ladyship, who at once stretched out her hand to rest upon the pillow, while a stool was arranged for the doctor to sit upon. Holding his head aside,[1] the doctor felt the pulse for a long time, by-and-by doing the same with the other hand.[2] He then bowed and retired.

"Her ladyship," said the doctor to some members of the family, "has nothing the matter with her beyond a slight chill. It is not really necessary for her to take any medicine. Give her light food and keep her warm, and she will soon be all right again. I will, however, write a prescription, and if her ladyship fancies a dose, have it made up and give it to her; but if she would rather not, well—it will be all the same in the end.

---

[1] In order not to look at the patient.

[2] Chinese doctors recognize no fewer than twenty-four varieties of pulse, and always test both wrists.

THE SACRED EDICT

[In 1671, the great Manchu Emperor, K'ang Hsi, published sixteen moral maxims for the guidance of his people, and gave orders for these to be read aloud by certain officials on the 1st and 15th of each month in every city and town in the empire. In 1724, his son and successor, Yung Chêng, caused short amplificatory essays on these maxims to be written by one hundred of the best scholars of the day; and from these were chosen for publication sixteen essays which the Emperor decided to be the best. Below will be found the seventh of K'ang Hsi's maxims, with its amplification by some unknown hand.]

GET RID OF HETERODOXY, IN ORDER TO
GLORIFY THE TRUE DOCTRINE

WE, desiring to improve public morals, must begin by reforming the heart of man; and in order to reform the heart of man, it is necessary first of all to place education upon a sound basis.

When man comes into being between Heaven and Earth, there are certain moral obligations in his daily life, which are for the learned and simple alike; to seek after the mysterious and to practice strange arts is not to follow the example of the wise and the worthy.

The *Canon of Changes* says, "Teach the young in order to bring them up as they should be; such is the function of the sage." The *Canon of History* says, "Without deflection, without unevenness, without perversity, without onesidedness,—such was the WAY of the ancient kings." Both the above have their origin in the true doctrine.

With regard to uninspired books and uncanonical records, such as startle the age and astonish the vulgar herd, bringing confusion in their train and preying upon the substance of the people, all these are heterodox and should be abolished.

You soldiers and people are mostly willing to lead honest lives; but among you there may be some who have been led astray and who fall through ignorance into crime. These WE greatly pity.

From of old three sets of doctrines have come down to us, there being, in addition to Confucianism, the systems of Taoism and Buddhism.

Chu Hsi (*q.v.*) says, "The teaching of Buddha takes no heed of anything between Heaven and Earth and the four points of the compass, beyond cultivation of the heart. The teaching of Lao Tzŭ aims solely at the conservation of vitality." Such was the unbiased judgment of Chu Hsi, and shows what were the original aims of Buddhism and of Taoism.

But ever since penniless and homeless rascals have secretly usurped these names and degraded these cults,—mostly quoting calamities and blessings, evil fortune and happiness, to aid in circulating their visionary and baseless talk, beginning by wheedling money out of people in order to enrich themselves, and ending by bringing men and women together in meetings for burning incense,—ever since then the agriculturist and the artisan have neglected their callings, and on all sides are to be met men whose mouths are full of marvels. What is even worse, traitorous and evil-disposed persons lie concealed in the midst, organizing brotherhoods and swearing oaths, meeting at night and dispersing at dawn, breaking the law and failing in duty, disturbing society and imposing on the people. The day comes when all is discovered. They are seized with their accomplices; they are thrown into prison; and their wives and children are implicated. The head of the sect is punished most severely of all, and their source of happiness yields only misfortune. As in the case of the White-Lily and Smell-Incense sects, all of which may be warnings to you just as is a cart ahead (which gets overset).

So too those Western doctrines which teach the worship of the Lord of Heaven are also uncanonical. However, because the men understood mathematics, the State employed them.[1] It is important for you people to know this.

Now towards heterodoxy which disturbs the minds of the masses, the law shows no mercy; and for wizards and their evil tricks the State provides fixed punishments, the object of OUR Imperial laws being simply to prevent the

---

[1] Adam Schall, Ferdinand, Verbiest, and Matteo Ricci.

people from doing evil and to induce them to be good, to abolish heterodoxy and to glorify the true doctrine, to keep from danger and to court repose.

O ye soldiers and people, to take that body which your parents gave you, born in a peaceful and prosperous age, with clothes to wear and food to eat, and without troubles of any kind, and yet nevertheless to befog its ordinary nature and follow evil tendencies, violating the laws and opposing the authorities of your country,—is not this the height of folly?

OUR sacred ancestor, the Humane Emperor, refined the people by his goodness and improved them by his sense of duty; he cultivated the (Five) Perfections and exhibited the (Five) Virtues. Glorious are the precepts by which he strove to lead men's hearts aright, yea, most profound.

You soldiers and people should respectfully sympathize with these Imperial wishes and reverently obey the Holy Doctrine. Drive out heterodoxy as though it were robbers, fire, or flood. These last indeed harm only the body, whereas heterodoxy harms the heart. And the heart is naturally upright, and with firmness of purpose will not suffer disturbance.

If in the future your behaviour is correct, all these evil influences will fail to turn you from the right path; and if within your homes you are peaceful and obedient, you may meet adversity in such a way as to change it into a blessing.

Those who serve their parents with piety and their sovereign with loyalty, and generally fulfil their duties as men, will assuredly surround themselves with divine favours; while those who seek not what is beyond their lot, and do not that which is improper to be done, are sure to meet with prosperity from the spirits.

Do you people attend to your agriculture, and you soldiers to your military affairs. Rest in the pursuit of cotton and silk and pulse and corn; follow the great and perfect principles (of Confucianism) ; there will then be no need to expel heterodoxy; it will die out of itself!

P'U SUNG-LING

17TH CENTURY A.D.

[After taking his first or bachelor's degree before he was twenty, this now famous writer, popularly known as "Last of the Immortals," failed to secure the second and more important degree which would have brought him into official life; the reason being that he neglected the beaten track of academic study and allowed himself to follow his own fancy. His literary output consists of a large collection of weird fantastic tales, which might well have disappeared but for the extraordinarily beautiful style in which they are written,—a style which has been the envy and admiration of authors for the past two hundred and forty years. They have been translated into English by the present writer under the title of "Strange Stories from a Chinese Studio." All that we really know about him is given in the document translated below.]

AUTHOR'S OWN RECORD

"CLAD in wistaria, girdled with ivy: " thus sang Ch'ü P'ing[1] in his *Falling into Trouble*. Of ox-headed devils and serpent Gods, he of the long nails[2] never wearied to tell. Each interprets in his own way the music of heaven; and whether it be discord or not, depends upon antecedent causes. As for me, I cannot, with my poor autumn fire-fly's light, match myself against the hobgoblins of the age. I am but the dust in the sunbeam, a fit laughing-stock for devils. For my talents are not those of Kan Pao,[3] elegant explorer of the records of the Gods; I am rather animated by the spirit of Su Tung-P'o,[4] who loved to hear men speak of the supernatural. I get people to commit what they tell me to writing, and subsequently I dress it up in the form of a story; thus in the lapse of time my friends from all quarters have supplied me with quantities of material, which, from my habit of collecting, has grown into a vast pile.[5]

Human beings, I would point out, are not beyond the pale of fixed laws, and yet there are more remarkable phenomena in their midst than in the country of those who crop their hair; [6] antiquity is unrolled before us, and many tales are to be found therein stranger than that of the

---

[1] A celebrated statesman and poet, 332–295 B.C.
[2] Li Ho, a poet who lived A.D. 791–817, noted also for his small waist and joined eyebrows.
[3] 4th century A.D.
[4] The famous statesman, poet, and essayist, A.D. 1036–1101.
[5] The plan adopted by Charles Dickens.
[6] Southern savages of early ages.

nation of Flying Heads.[1] "Irrepressible bursts and luxurious ease," [2]—such was always one enthusiastic strain. "For ever indulging in liberal thought," [3]—thus spoke another openly without restraint. Were men like these to open my book, I should be a laughing-stock to them indeed. At the cross-road men will not listen to me, and yet I have some knowledge of the three states of existence spoken of beneath the cliff; [4] neither should the words I utter be set aside because of him that utters them.[5] When the bow was hung at my father's door,[6] he dreamed that a sickly-looking Buddhist priest, but half covered by his stole, entered the chamber. On one of his breasts was a piece of plaster like a *cash;* and my father, waking from sleep, found that I, just born, had a similar black patch on my body. As a child, I was thin and constantly ailing, and unable to hold my own in the battle of life. Our home was chill and desolate as a monastery; and working there for my livelihood with my pen, I was as poor as a priest with his alms-bowl. Often and often I put my hand to my head and exclaimed, "Surely he who sat with his face to the wall[7] was myself in a previous state of existence;" and thus I referred my non-success in this life to the influence of a destiny surviving from the last. I have been tossed hither and thither in the direction of the ruling wind, like a flower falling in filthy places; but the six paths of transmigration[8] are inscrutable indeed, and I have no right to complain. As it is, midnight finds me with an expiring lamp, while the wind whistles mournfully without; and over my cheerless table I piece together my tales,

---

[1] A fabulous race, whose heads leave their bodies at night and fly off in search of food.

[2] From the poet Wang Pieh, A.D. 648–676.

[3] ? The poet Li Po, *d.* A.D. 762.

[4] Referring to the story of an old priest who said that these states, present, past, and future, bore no relation to eternity.

[5] A Confucian maxim.

[6] A small towel announces the birth of a girl.

[7] Bôdhidharma, the Buddhist Patriarch who went as missionary to China and died there *circa* A.D. 535.

[8] Angels, men, demons, hungry devils, brute beasts, and tortured sinners.

vainly hoping to produce a sequel to *The Infernal Regions*.[1]
With a bumper I stimulate my pen, yet I only succeed
thereby in "venting my excited feeling,"[2] and as I thus
commit my thoughts to writing, truly I am an object
worthy of consideration. Alas! I am but the bird that,
dreading the winter frost, finds no shelter in the tree;
the autumn insect that chirps to the moon, and hugs the
door for warmth. For where are they who know me?[3]
They are "in the bosky grove and at the frontier pass,"[4]—
wrapped in an impenetrable gloom!

RAISING THE DEAD

Mr. T'ang P'ing, who took the highest degree in the
year 1661, was suffering from a protracted illness, when
suddenly he felt, as it were, a warm glow rising from his
extremities upwards. By the time it had reached his knees,
his feet were perfectly numb and without sensation; and
before long his knees and the lower part of his body were
similarly affected. Gradually this glow worked its way up
until it attacked his heart, and then some painful moments
ensued. Every single incident of Mr. T'ang's life from
his boyhood upwards, no matter how trivial, seemed to
surge through his mind, borne along on the tide of his
heart's blood. At the revival of any virtuous act of his,
he experienced a delicious feeling of peace and calm; but
when any wicked deed passed before his mind, a painful
disturbance took place within him, like oil boiling and
fretting in a cauldron. He was quite unable to describe
the pangs he suffered; however, he mentioned that he could
recollect having stolen, when only seven or eight years old,
some young birds from their nest, and having killed them;

---

[1] By Lin I-ch'ing.
[2] From the philosopher, *d*. 233 B.C.
[3] Confucius said, "Alas! there is no one who knows me (to be what I am)."
[4] That is, non-existent; like Li Po, whom his brother-poet, Tu Fu, saw coming
to him in a dream.

and for this alone, he said, boiling blood rushed through his heart during the space of an ordinary meal-time. Then when all the acts of his life had passed one after another in panorama before him, the warm glow proceeded up his throat, and entering the brain, issued out at the top of his head like smoke from a chimney. By-and-by Mr. T'ang's soul escaped from his body by the same aperture, and wandered far away, forgetting all about the tenement it had left behind. Just at that moment a huge giant came along, and seizing the soul, thrust it into his sleeve, where it remained cramped and confined, huddled up with a crowd of others, until existence was almost unbearable. Suddenly Mr. T'ang reflected that Buddha alone could save him from this horrible state, and forthwith he began to call on his holy name. At the third or fourth invocation he fell out of the giant's sleeve, whereupon the giant picked him up and put him back; but this happened several times, and at length the giant, wearied of picking him up, let him lie where he was. The soul lay there for some time, not knowing in which direction to proceed; however, it soon recollected that the land of Buddha was in the west, and westwards accordingly it began to shape its course. In a little while the soul came upon a Buddhist priest sitting by the roadside, and hastening forwards, respectfully inquired of him which was the right way. "The Book of Life and Death for scholars," replied the priest, "is in the hands of the God of Literature and Confucius; any application must receive the consent of both." The priest then directed Mr. T'ang on his way, and the latter journeyed along until he reached a Confucian temple, in which the Sage was sitting with his face to the south. On hearing his business, Confucius referred him to the God of Literature; and proceeding onwards in the direction indicated, Mr. T'ang by-and-by arrived at what seemed to be the palace of a king, within which sat the God of Literature precisely as we depict him on earth. "You are an upright man," replied the God, in reply to Mr. T'ang's prayer, "and are certainly entitled to a longer span of life; but by this time your mortal body has become decomposed, and unless you can secure the assistance of a Bôdhisatva, I can give you no aid." So Mr. T'ang set off once more, and hurried along until he came to a magnificent shrine standing in a thick grove of tall bamboos; and entering in, he stood in the presence of the Bôdhisatva,[1] on whose head was the *ushnisha*,[2] whose golden face was round like the full moon, and at whose side was a green willow-branch bending gracefully over the lip of a vase. Humbly Mr. T'ang prostrated himself on the ground, and repeated what Wên Ch'ang had said to him; but the Bôdhisatva seemed to think it would be impossible to grant his request, until one of the Lohans who stood by cried out. "O Bôdhisatva, perform this miracle. Take earth and make his flesh; take a sprig of willow and make his bones." Thereupon the Bôdhisatva broke off a piece from the willow-branch in the vase beside him; and pouring a little water on the ground, he made clay, and casting the whole over Mr. T'ang's soul, he bade an attendant lead the body back to the place where his coffin was. At that instant Mr. T'ang's family heard a groan come from within his coffin; and on rushing to it and helping out the lately deceased man, they found that he had quite recovered. He had then been dead seven days.

A CHINESE JONAH

A man named Sun Pi-chên was crossing the Yang-tze when a great thunder-squall broke upon the boat and caused her to toss about fearfully, to the great terror of all the passengers. Just then, an angel in golden armour appeared standing upon the clouds above them, holding in his hand a scroll inscribed with certain words, also written in gold,

[1] One who has fulfilled all the conditions necessary to the attainment of Buddha-hood and Nirvâna, but from charity of heart continues voluntarily subject to reincorporation for the benefit of mankind.

[2] A fleshy protuberance on the head, which is the distinguishing mark of a Buddha.

which the people on the boat easily made out to be three in number, namely *Sun Pi-chên*. So, turning at once to their fellow-traveller, they said to him, "You have evidently incurred the displeasure of God; get into a boat by yourself and do not involve us in your punishment." And without giving him time to reply whether he would do so or not, they hurried him over the side into a small boat and set him adrift; but when Sun Pi-chên looked back, lo! the vessel itself had disappeared.[1]

CHANG PU-LIANG

A certain trader who was travelling in the province of Chih-li, being overtaken by a storm of rain and hail, took shelter among some standing crops by the wayside. There he heard a voice from the sky, saying, "These are Chang Pu-liang's fields; do not injure his crops!" The trader began to wonder who this Chang Pu-liang could be, and how, if he was *pu liang* (no virtue), he came to be under divine protection; so when the storm was over and he had reached the neighbouring village, he made inquiries on the subject and told the people there what he had heard. The villagers then informed him that Chang Pu-liang was a very wealthy farmer, who was accustomed every spring to make loans of grain to the poor of the district, and who was not too particular about getting back the exact amount he had lent,—taking in fact whatever they brought him without discussion; hence the sobriquet of *pu liang* "no measure" (*i.e.*, the man who doesn't measure the repayments of his loans).[2] After that, they all proceeded in a body to the fields, where it was discovered that vast damage had been done to the crops generally, with the exception of Chang Pu-liang's, which had escaped uninjured.

---

[1] The point of this story is lost in translation. *Pi-chên* may mean to the ear either "must be struck" or "must be saved," through in writing two different characters are used. That the other passengers misread *chên* "to be saved" for *chên* "to be struck"—Sun must be struck—is evident from the catastrophe which overtook their vessel, while Sun's little boat rode safely through the storm.

[2] The two phrases, "no virtue" and "no measure," are pronounced alike.

LAN TING-YÜAN

A.D. 1680–1733.

[Also known as Lan Lu-chou. One of the most attractive writers of the Manchu dynasty, especially of State papers and judicial records, and known in his day as a just and incorrupt judge. He managed however to offend his superiors, and was impeached and thrown into prison. From this he was released by order of the Emperor, who loaded him with honours and appointed him to be Prefect in Canton. He died, however, a month later, of a broken heart.]

ON THE SOUTHERN BARBARIANS

THE barbarians of the south can do no harm to China. The prohibition against trade should be cancelled and the people allowed to do business with them, supplying the deficiencies of the Middle Kingdom from the superabundance of the lands beyond the sea. There should be no delay in this matter.

Recently, a Lieutenant-Governor of Fukien presented a secret memorial to the Throne, stating that he suspected the merchants engaged in foreign trade of selling ships to the barbarians, and that the latter carried rice away to other countries, which practice might ultimately become a great loss to China. He also feared that foreign ships were addicted to piracy, and requested that all native vessels might be prohibited from going abroad and so lessen the risk of such calamities. This was but the shallow, narrow-minded opinion of a book-worm, the limited area of sky which appears to a man sitting at the bottom of a well! He himself regarded it as the far-reaching foresight of a statesman, as an excellent plan laid at the feet of his sovereign;—but he was wrong. His Imperial Majesty K'ang Hsi took it very much to heart, fearing that there was at any rate some chance of what he said turning out to be the case. Accordingly, he made enquiries both among high officials and private individuals; for he had his suspicions about those statements, and wished to get hold of some person who was acquainted with the affairs of these distant peoples, from whom he might learn the actual truth. However, at that time none of the officials had ever been beyond the seas, and it was impossible for private individuals to communicate direct with His Majesty; so that nothing was done and the prohibition came into force, contrary in fact to His Majesty's intentions. Now only those who are versed in the affairs of the maritime nations are competent to give an opinion on the desirability of encouraging their trade. The barbarian countries beyond the sea are thickly scattered about like stars. Of all of them Korea is nearest to the holy city (Peking), and there ceremonies and laws are observed. Of the eastern nations the Japanese are the fiercest and most important. Beyond Japan there are no barbarian nations of any magnitude. Descending a little we come to Lewchow, which consists of a number of islands of different sizes extending over about two thousand *li*. Their watercourses all debouch on the east coast, beyond which there are no other nations. The southern barbarians are many in number. Luzon and Singapore are among the largest; Brunei, Sulu, Malacca, Indragiri, Acheen, Johore, Banjermassin, the Carimon islands, and many others, are all infinitesimally small and not worth mentioning. They have never dared to entertain bad intentions towards China. Annam and Southern Cochin-China are connected together, like Kuang-tung and Kuang-si; and beyond these we have Cambodia, Ligor, Chiya, Patani, and other nations to the south-west, of all of which Siam is the most important. To the extreme west there are the red-haired and western foreigners, a fierce violent lot, quite unlike the other barbarians of the western islands. Among them there are the English, the Islamists, the French, the Dutch, the Spaniards, and the Portuguese. These are all very fierce nations; their ships are strong and do not fear typhoons; and their guns, powder, and munitions of war generally are superior to those of China. Their natures are dark, dangerous, and inscrutable; wherever they go they spy around with a view to seizing other people's lands. Of all the island barbarians under the heaven the red-haired barbarians, the western barbarians and the Japanese are the three most deadly. Singapore originally belonged to the Malays, who were in the habit of trading with these red-haired barbarians. Subsequently, they were ousted by them, and the place became a barbarian harbour and emporium. Luzon also was a Malay colony, but because the Catholic religion was permitted there, it fell similarly into the hands of the western foreigners. During the Ming dynasty Japan rebelled, and many provinces were overrun by them, so that even now the people of those parts cannot mention the name of the robber dwarfs without a shudder. The numerous nations of southern barbarians have never yet given the slightest cause of trouble to China: their only business is trade and the circulation of goods. Now there is no prohibition against trade with Japan or with the red-haired barbarians, and the Catholic religion of the western foreigners is spreading all over the land, Canton and Macao being actually open to them as places of residence; only against these innocent southern barbarians has a prohibition been put forth which stops all intercourse with them. This surely requires some investigation. For the people of Fuhkien and Kuang-tung are very numerous in proportion to the area they inhabit; and as the land is not sufficient to supply their wants, some five or six out of every ten look to the sea for a livelihood. Articles paltry in our estimation acquire the value of jewels when carried across the sea to these barbarians; all the dwellers on the sea-bord send off their trifling embroidery, etc., in the foreign-going ships for sale, and receive annually from the barbarians many hundred thousand taels of silver, all of which comes into China. Thus no small issues depend upon the cancelment of the prohibition. Before trade with these southerners was stopped the people of Fuhkien and Kuang-tung were well-to-do, and the scum and riff raff of their populations went off to try and enrich themselves among the barbarians. Few remained at home either to starve or to steal. But since the arrest of commerce, merchandise cannot circulate and the people daily find it more difficult to support life. The artisans complain that there is no market for their manufactures; the traders sigh that they are unable to carry them to those distant ports. For the four or five thousand taels which it takes to build a foreign-going junk are tied up in vessels which are rotting in a dock or upon the now desolate sea-shore. The occupation of these junks is gone. If put up for sale no purchaser could be found; and breaking them up to make smaller vessels would be like paring down the beam of a house to make a peg, or unpicking embroidered work to get a skein of silk. No one would willingly do that. Besides they hope that some day the clouds will break and the sun shine out, that the prohibition will be repealed and trade go on as before; and the loss of a single one of these large junks would reduce many families to misery and ruin. The present destitute state of the seabord population is entirely due to the stoppage of trade. Those of them who understand marine work and are accustomed to act as sailors are unable to adapt themselves to the duties of weight-carriers and earn their living as ordinary coolies. They prefer the dangers of the sea where piracy supplies them with their daily food. The rowdies and blackguards have still less before them. They go off in large numbers to Formosa, and there rebel against the Imperial Government as they actually did in the year 1721 under the leadership of Ch'en Fu-shou. It is a principle that nothing should be left undone which may turn out of the smallest advantage to the State and to the people; and, similarly, that everything likely to cause the least detriment to either should be incontinently cast away. Now to prohibit trade with the southern foreigners, so far from being advantageous, is very much the contrary. Of the seabord population the rich will be made poor, and the poor, destitute. Their artisans will be changed into loafing vagabonds, their loafing vagabonds into pirates and robbers. Further, Fuhkien has no silver mines and is dependent on the

barbarians for its supply of that metal. But since the
prohibition none has been forthcoming, and the result will
be some such expedient as a paper, cloth, or leather issue,
whereby great mischief will be done. The advantages of
repealing the prohibition would be the circulation of goods
and the absorption of our own bad characters; and thus the
people would have the wherewithal to support their parents
and rear their children. Hence it would follow that a
larger revenue would be yielded by the Customs, and the
country enriched by the wealth of the people. Surely this
is no trifling advantage. As to selling their junks to the
barbarians to carry rice out of the country, or cases of
piracy committed by foreigners, such things have hitherto
been quite unknown. To build a foreign-going junk in
China costs from seven to eight thousand taels for a large
one, from two to three thousand for a small one. How
much could they get for these? A Chinese trader invests
his money in a junk as a means of enriching himself; he
intends to hand it down to his sons and grandsons. In case
he ceases to care about trading abroad himself, he lets his
junks out to somebody else and pockets so much per annum.
He is not likely to wish to sell it. Besides, the barbarian
wood is much stronger than our own; in fact our merchants
buy quantities of it, a mast which costs there only one or two
hundred taels being here worth as much as a thousand.
The barbarians build their vessels much more strongly
than we do, putting a whole tree where we should only use
a plank, and where we use nails of a few inches they use
nails of over a foot in length. Truly I do not think they
would be overjoyed to receive our junks as gifts, to say
nothing of paying a heavy price for them. Fuhkien and
Kuang-tung produce but little rice, least of all Fuhkien.
The people look to T'aiwan for the half of their annual
supply, or are partly furnished from Kiang-si and Cheh-
kiang. Before the prohibition, a considerable quantity of
rice was sent from the Philippines to Amoy. These barbarian countries produce plenty of rice and do not look to

China for their supply. The merchants engaged in the
foreign trade, being all men of means, would be hardly
likely to risk running counter to the law; and under any
circumstances, seeing they can get four or five taels per
picul for conveying other goods, it is hardly likely they
would accept the comparative trifle they would obtain for
carrying rice, and offend against the law into the bargain.
The biggest fool would scarcely be guilty of this. Hitherto
our foreign-going junks have never been plundered on the
high seas. Pirates hang about the coast and dodge in and
out of islands, seldom going farther from land than two or
at most three hundred *li*, for as but few junks go to a
greater distance from the land than that, it would only be
waste of time, to say nothing of their having no anchorage
at hand, if it should chance to come on to blow. The
foreign-going junks on the other hand leave the land
thousands of *li* behind them, and being large vessels have
no fear of the wind and the waves. No pirate junks
could keep up with them. Besides the pirates have a fine
field among the Cheh-kiang and Canton merchant vessels;
there is no need for them to direct their attention to
foreign-going junks. And even if they chanced to fall in
with them, their own junks being so small, they would
require a ladder to get up the sides. Pirate junks carry
from twenty to thirty men; these sea-going junks at the
very least over a hundred men. Neither would they wait
for a hand to hand fight with the pirates, but would get to
windward of them, and then bear right down on them and
sink their junk. Piracy, therefore, is hardly a sufficient
cause of alarm.

That at the present moment, with His Majesty upon
the throne and the empire at peace, and when all the human
race are, as it were, but one family, we should prohibit
trade only with the mild and gentle foreigners of the south,
reflects somewhat upon those officials who know these things
and yet do not speak them. Where is their loyalty, their
patriotism, their care for men from afar and their solicitude

for those who are near, their consideration for the prosperity of the Chinese people? Insignificant I, can only look on and sigh.

AGAINST BUDDHISM

Of all the Eighteen Provinces Cheh-kiang is the one where Buddhist priests and nuns most abound. In the three prefectures of Hang-chow, Chia-hsing, and Hu-chow, there cannot be fewer than several tens of thousands of them, of whom, by the way, not more than one-tenth have willingly taken the vows. The others have been given to the priests when quite little, either because their parents were too poor to keep them, or in return for some act of kindness; and when the children grow up, they are unable to get free. Buddhist nuns are also in most cases bought up when children as a means of making a more extensive show of religion, and are carefully prevented from running away. They are not given in marriage—the desire for which is more or less implanted in every human breast, and exists even amongst prophets and sages. And thus to condemn thousands and ten thousands of human beings to the dull monotony of the cloister, granting that they strictly keep their religious vows, is more than sufficient to seriously interfere with the equilibrium of the universe. Hence floods, famines, and the like catastrophes; to say nothing of the misdeeds of the nuns in question.

When Wên Wang came to the throne (1122 B.C.) his first object was the proper disposition of the sexes, so that there should be no unmarried maids within, no unattached bachelors without. Thus was the good Government of that monarch displayed. And it is the duty of those who occupy high places to see to the due adjustment of the male and female elements; of those whose functions bring them into closer connexion with the people, to give their minds to the improvement of our national manners and customs— duties that should on no account be allowed to fall into

neglect. When I passed through Soochow and Hangchow
I saw many disgraceful advertisements that quite took my
breath away with their barefaced depravity; and the people
there told me that these atrocities were much practised by
the denizens of the cloister, which term is simply another
name for houses of ill-fame. These cloister folk do a great
deal of mischief amongst the populace, wasting the substance of some and robbing others of their good name.
"You, sir," some of the people said to me, "being an official,
and it being your business to look after public morals, will
doubtless refuse to countenance such proceedings. Good
government consists of carrying out the natural wishes of
men and women to mate together. A clever man like you
will necessarily pay attention to this."

A DEAD BEGGAR GETS A WIFE AND SON [1]

The wife of a man, named Chêng, once came before me
to compain that her husband had been driven to commit
suicide. She said that he had been beadle of a certain
village, and that having had some trouble in collecting taxes
from a man, named Hsiao, who withheld his title-deed and
refused to listen to argument, the latter, on the 13th day of
the moon, had collected a number of friends and wrecked
the house, beating her husband so severely that, in despair,
he threw himself into the river and was drowned. She
further indicated the spot at which the body was to be
found; and accordingly, though suspecting in my heart
the truth of her story, I had no alternative but to hold the
usual inquest. Her son got the corpse on board a boat and
brought it along, and I proceeded forthwith to make an
examination. No wounds were visible upon it; the finger-
nails were full of mud and sand—a sure proof of suicide
by drowning—though at the same time I felt confident that
the persons accused, who were all honestly engaged in

---

[1] This is the record of an actual case.

trade, would not thus causelessly set upon and beat another man. Further, deceased had been beadle of the place, and those now arraigned on this charge of murder had frequently complained on previous occasions to my predecessor in office, of the depredations of thieves, with a view to their losses from the beadle; and I, when I took over the seals, had gone so far as to fix a limit of time within which the missing articles were to be restored, but without success. Now, there was this story of attack and suicide; but the flesh on the face of the dead man was too far decomposed to admit of his identification, and I also thought it rather strange that no one should know anything about an affair which had happened eight days previously, and that there should have been such delay in making the charge. At the same time, as the inquest was held only eight days after death, it remained to be shown why the body should be then so far gone in decomposition as if the man had been dead for a fortnight or more. On my putting this last question to the prosecutrix, her son replied that bodies naturally decompose more rapidly in water than otherwise; and as for the accused, they none of them seemed to have a word to say for themselves, while mother and son stood there jabbering away, with their hempen garments and mourning staves, the one bemoaning the loss of her husband, the other of his father, in such affecting tones as would have drawn tears from the bystanders even had they been of iron or of stone. My own conviction was, however, unfavourable to their case, and I bade them go along home and bury the body themselves. At this, there was a general expression of astonishment; and then I called the accused and said to them, "Chêng is not dead; can you not manage to arrest him?" They all declared that they "didn't know;" whereupon I railed at them, saying, "What! you can't find out the affairs of those who live in the same village and draw from the same well as yourselves? This indolent careless behaviour is perfectly amazing. It's all very well to be callous when other people are concerned; but now that you stand charged with this murder and your own necks are in peril, it being my duty to commit you to prison, do you mean to tell me that you are willing to take the consequences?" The accused men then burst into tears, and implored me to save them; to which I replied, " Here is this man Chêng, who was formerly an accomplice of thieves, alarmed by my appointment to office, disappears from the scene. Now, your cities of refuge are confined to some half-dozen or so; and if you separate and go to them in search of the missing man, I have no doubt but that you will find him." Three days passed away, when back came one of them with Chêng, whom he had caught at the city of Hui-lai. They were followed by a large crowd of several thousand persons, who clapped their hands and seemed much amused; among them being the mother and son, overwhelmed with shame, and grovelling in the dust before me. I made the latter tell me the name of the legal adviser who had egged them on to act thus, and I punished all three according to law and to the great delight of the inhabitants of the district. As for the corpse, it was that of a drowned beggar, and no one came forward to claim it. However, as the pretended wife and son had worn sackcloth and carried funeral staves, interring the body with every outward demonstration of respect, the beggar's soul must have had a good laugh over the whole affair down in the realms below.

VISITS TO STRANGE NATIONS

17TH CENTURY A.D.

[The following extracts from the *Ching Hua Yüan* give an imaginary account of some portions of the travels of a party of friends, undertaken in the year A.D. 684 as a protest against the frivolous and aggressive policy of the then reigning Empress, coupled with a strong flavour of commercial enterprise. They are included in this volume not because of any grace of style in the original text, but as specimens of literature akin to such works as "Gulliver's Travels," though lacking the philosophic motive which underlies Swift's work.]

THE COUNTRY OF GENTLEMEN

Imagine that, instead of preferring to buy things at low prices, men habitually preferred to give high prices for them; and imagine that, conversely, sellers rejoiced in getting low prices, instead of high ones.—*Herbert Spencer.*

THEY sailed along for many days until they arrived at the Country of Gentlemen, where they went on shore and proceeded at once to the capital city. There, over the city gate, T'ang and his companions read the following legend:—

Virtue is man's only jewel!

They then entered the city, which they found to be a busy and prosperous mart, the inhabitants all talking the Chinese language. Accordingly, T'ang accosted one of the passers-by and asked him how it was his nation had become so famous for politeness and consideration of others; but to his great astonishment the man did not understand the meaning of his question. T'ang then asked him why this land was called the Country of Gentlemen, to which he likewise replied that he did not know. Several other persons of whom they enquired giving similar answers, the venerable To [1] remarked that the term had undoubtedly been adopted by the inhabitants of adjacent countries, in consequence of the polite manners and considerate behaviour of these people. "For," said he, " the very labourers in the fields and foot-passengers in the streets step aside to make room for one another. High and low, rich and poor, mutually respect each other's feelings without reference to the wealth or social status of either; and this is after all the essence of what constitutes the true gentleman."

---

[1] A *sobriquet* meaning "Much," and referring to the old man's learning.

" In that case," cried T‘ang, "let us not hurry on, but rather improve ourselves by observing the ways and customs of this people."

By-and-by they arrived at the market-place, where they saw an official servant [1] standing at a stall engaged in making purchases. He was holding in his hand the articles he wished to buy and was saying to the owner of the stall, " Just reflect a moment, Sir, how impossible it would be for me to take these excellent goods at the absurdly low price you are asking. If you will oblige me by doubling the amount, I shall do myself the honour of accepting them; otherwise, I cannot but feel that you are unwilling to do business with me to-day."

" How very funny! " whispered T‘ang to his friends. " Here now is quite a different custom from ours, where the buyer invariably tries to beat down the seller, and the seller to run up the price of his goods as high as possible. This certainly looks like the ‘ consideration for others ’ of which we spoke just now."

The man at the stall here replied, " Your wish, Sir, should be law to me, I know; but the fact is I am already overwhelmed with shame at the high price I have ventured to name. Besides I do not profess to adhere rigidly to ‘ marked prices,’ which is a mere trick of the trade; and consequently it should be the aim of every puchaser to make me lower my terms to the very smallest figure. You, on the contrary, are trying to raise the price to an exorbitant figure; and although I fully appreciate your kindness in that respect, I must really ask you to seek what you require at some other establishment. It is quite impossible for me to execute your commands."

T‘ang was again expressing his astonishment at this extraordinary reversal of the platitudes of trade when the would-be purchaser replied, " For you, Sir, to ask such a low sum for these first-class goods and then to turn round

---

[1] A class very much dreaded by shop-keepers in China for their avarice and extortion. Usually called "runners."

and accuse me of over-considering your interests, is indeed a sad breach of etiquette. Trade could not be carried on at all if all the advantages were on one side and the losses on the other; neither am I more devoid of brains than the ordinary run of people that I should fail to understand this principle and let you catch me in a trap."

So they went on wrangling and jangling, the stall-keeper refusing to charge any more and the runner insisting on paying his own price, until the latter made a show of yielding and put down the full sum demanded on the counter, but took only half the amount of goods. Of course the stall-keeper would not consent to this, and they would both have fallen back upon their original positions had not two old gentlemen who happened to be passing stepped aside and arranged the matter for them by deciding that the runner was to pay the full price but to receive only four-fifths of the goods.

T'ang and his companions walked on in silence, meditating upon the strange scene they had just witnessed; but they had not gone many steps when they came across a soldier[1] similarly engaged in buying things at an open shop window. He was saying, " When I asked the price of these goods, you, Sir, begged me to take them at my own valuation; but now that I am willing to do so, you complain of the large sum I offer, whereas the truth is that it is actually very much below their real value. Do not treat me thus unfairly."

" It is not for me, Sir," replied the shopkeeper, " to demand a price for my own goods; my duty is to leave that entirely to you. But the fact is that these goods are old stock and are not even the best of their kind; you would do much better at another shop. However, let us say half what you are good enough to offer; even then I feel I shall

---

[1] If possible a more deadly foe to Chinese tradesmen than the runners above mentioned. These ill-paid, and consequently brutal, vagabonds used to think nothing of snatching pastry or fruit from the costermongers' stalls as they walked along the streets. Hence the delicacy of our author's satire, which is necessarily somewhat lost upon foreign readers.

be taking a great deal too much: I could not think, Sir, of parting with my goods at your price."

"What is that you are saying, Sir?" cried the soldier. "Although not in the trade myself I can tell superior from inferior articles and am not likely to mistake one for the other. And to pay a low price for a good article is simply another way of taking money out of a man's pocket."

"Sir," retorted the shop-keeper, "if you are such a stickler for justice as all that, let us say half the price you first mentioned, and the goods are yours. If you object to that, I must ask you to take your custom elsewhere. You will then find that I am not imposing on you."

The soldier at first stuck to his text, but seeing that the shop-keeper was not inclined to give way, he laid down the sum named and began to take his goods, picking out the very worst he could find. Here, however, the shop-keeper interposed, saying, "Excuse me, Sir, but you are taking all the bad ones. It is doubtless very kind of you to leave the best for me; but if all men were like you, there would be a general collapse of trade."

"Sir," replied the soldier, "As you insist on accepting only half the value of the goods, there is no course open to me but to choose inferior articles. Besides, as a matter of fact the best kind will not answer my purpose so well as the second or third best; and although I fully recognise your good intentions, I must really ask to be allowed to please myself."

"There is no objection, Sir," said the shop-keeper, "to your pleasing yourself; but low-class goods are sold at a low price and do not command the same rates as superior articles."

Thus they went on bandying arguments for a long time without coming to any definite agreement, until at last the soldier picked up the things he had chosen and tried to make off with them. The bystanders, however, all cried shame upon him and said he was a downright cheat, so that he was ultimately obliged to take some of the best kind and some of the inferior kind and put an end to the altercation.

A little farther on our travellers saw a countryman who had just paid the price of some purchases he had succeeded in making, and was hurrying away with them, when the shop-keeper called after him, "Sir! Sir! you have paid me by mistake in finer silver than we are accustomed to use here, and I have to allow you a considerable discount in consequence. Of course this is a mere trifle to a gentleman of your rank and position, but still for my own sake I must ask leave to make it all right with you."

"Pray don't mention such a small matter," replied the countryman, "but oblige me by putting the amount to my credit for use at a future date when I come again to buy some more of your excellent wares."

"No, no," answered the shop-keeper, "you don't catch old birds with chaff. That trick was played upon me last year by another gentleman, and to this day I have never set eyes upon him again, though I have made every endeavour to find out his whereabouts. As it is, I can now only look forward to repaying him in the next life; but if I let you take me in the same way, why, when the next life comes and I am changed, may be into a horse or a donkey, I shall have quite enough to do to find him, and your debt will go dragging on till the life after that. No, no, there is no time like the present; hereafter I might very likely forget what was the exact sum I owed you."

They continued to argue the point until the countryman consented to accept a trifle as a set-off against the fineness of his silver and went away with his goods, the shop-keeper bawling after him as long as he was in sight that he had sold him inferior articles at a high rate and was positively defrauding him of his money. The countryman, however, got clear away, and the shop-keeper returned to his grumbling at the iniquity of the age. Just then a beggar happened to pass, and so in anger at having been compelled to take more than his due he handed him the difference. " Who knows," said he, " but that the present misery of this poor fellow may be retribution for over-charging people in a former life?"

"Ah," said T'ang, when he had witnessed the finale of this little drama, "truly this is the behaviour of gentlemen!"

THE COUNTRY OF GREAT MEN

A voyage of a few days brought them to the Country of Great Men, where they would hardly have landed but for T'ang's curiosity to see a people who he had heard used clouds as a means of locomotion. The omniscient To explained that the city lay at some distance from the shore behind a range of hills, and that it would be absolutely necessary to get as far as that if they wanted to see anything of the manners and customs of the people. So they set off to walk, meeting on the way a few people moving about on clouds of different colours about half a foot from the ground, but they soon lost themselves in a perfect labyrinth of paths and did not know which way to turn. Luckily, they spied out a small temple hidden in a grove of waving bamboos, and were on the point of knocking for admittance, when out came an old man of ordinary appearance, riding on a cloud, with a stoup of wine in one hand and a lump of pork in the other.[1]   On seeing the strangers he turned back and put down the pork and wine, returning at once with a smile on his face to welcome them to his " rush hut." T'ang made him a low bow and enquired what might be the name of the temple. He replied that it was sacred to the goddess of mercy and that he was the officiating priest. The trader Lin opened his eyes at this and said, " But, my venerable Sir, how comes it then that you do not shave your head? And may we presume that there is a lady inside for whom you were about to prepare the pork and wine we saw just now? "

---

[1] Evidencing a gross breach of the rule pasted at the door of every Buddhist temple—

No wine or meat shall enter here!

"There is, indeed, a lady within," replied the priest, "but she is merely the insignificant wife of your humble slave. She and I have lived here ever since we were children, burning incense and candles daily before the shrine. For our countrymen, hearing that China during the Han dynasty had accepted the Law of Buddha and that priests and nuns with shaven heads had become quite common there, determined to adopt the same religion, dispensing however with the usual monastic vows."

The old priest then asked them whence they came, and on learning that they had just arrived from China became anxious to shew them some hospitality; but T'ang prayed him to excuse them, urging that they wished to hurry on to the city. He then added, "May I ask what is the explanation of the clouds I see underneath the feet of the inhabitants of this country? Are you born with them?"

"Sir," answered the old priest, "these clouds are perfectly independent of the will of the individuals to whom they are attached. Their colour varies, and also changes, with the disposition of each particular person. The best clouds to have are striped like a rainbow; yellow is the second best, and black is the worst of all." T'ang then begged him to point out the way to the city, which he did, and our travellers forthwith proceeded on their way thither. At length they arrived, but found nothing very different from what they had previously seen in the Country of Gentlemen, except that all the inhabitants were moving about on clouds of various hues, green, red, yellow, blue, and black. Amongst others they noticed a filthy beggar riding on a striped or rainbow cloud; whereupon T'ang remarked, "Why, the priest told us that the striped cloud was the best of all, and here is a dirty old beggar with one!"

"Don't you recollect," said Lin, "that the wine-bibbing, meat eating, wife-marrying ascetic had a striped cloud himself? You may be pretty sure that neither of them are men of very distinguished virtue."

"When I was here before," explained To, "I heard that the colour of a man's cloud was quite independent of his wishes, being regulated entirely by his natural disposition and actions, so that virtuous people shew good colours and wicked people bad ones whether they like or not; and that nothing short of change of disposition and conduct can possibly alter the hue of any man's cloud. Thus it happens that persons of high rank are sometimes seen on black clouds, while their poorer and humbler neighbours ride about on clouds of the very best colours. As it is, I would have you notice how few—scarcely two in a hundred— are seen on black clouds. For such are held in universal detestation by their fellow-countrymen, who avoid contact with them as much as they can; whereas, on the other hand, nothing gives more pleasure to the inhabitants of this region than the sight of a kindly and benevolent act. Neither are they always striving to get the better of one another, and therefore the people of the adjacent nations have named this the country of great men; not meaning thereby that physically speaking they are greater than the usual run of human beings, but that they are a high-minded and virtuous race."

While they were thus talking, the people in the streets began to fall back to either side, leaving a clear passage in the middle; and by-and-by they saw an official pass in great state with his red unbrella, gongs, tablets, and other instrumental parts of his dignity, besides hosts of attendants on clouds of various hues. They noticed, however, that his own cloud was scrupulously concealed by a valance of red silk so that its colour could not possibly be seen; whereupon T'ang observed, "Of course the high officials of this country have no need for horses or sedan-chairs, provided as they are with these convenient clouds upon which they can move about at their pleasure; but I should like to know why this gentleman keeps his cloud covered up in such a mysterious manner."

"Well," replied To, "the fact is that he, like too many others of his class, has a cloud of a peculiar colour. It is not exactly black but more of an ashen hue, shewing thereby that his hands are not nearly so clean as they ought to be. For although he puts on all the appearance of a virtuous member of society and conceals his misdeeds from the world at large, yet he cannot control his cloud which takes its hue from the real working of his inmost mind. Consequently, he covers it up; but he might as well 'stuff his ears' and 'ring a bell' for all the good that can do him. Other people will hear the bell if he doesn't. Nothing on earth will change the colour of that cloud of his except a conscientious repentance and a thorough reformation of character. Besides there is every danger of the truth becoming bruited abroad, and then he is a lost man. Not only would he be severely punished by the king of the country, but he would further be shunned on all sides as a degraded and dishonourable man."

"Great God!" cried the trader Lin, "how unjust are thy ways."

"Why say you so?" asked T'ang of his uncle, "and to what may you be particularly alluding?"

"I say so," replied Lin, "inasmuch as I see these clouds confined to this nation. How useful it would be in our country to have some such infallible means of distinguishing the good from the bad. For if every wicked man carried about, so to speak, his own shop-sign with him wherever he went, surely this would act as a powerful deterrent from crime."

"My dear friend," said the aged To, "though the wicked in our part of the world carry about with them no tell-tale cloud, there is nevertheless a blackness in their looks by which you may know the colour of their hearts."

"That may be so," answered Lin, "but I for one am unable to perceive whether the blackness is there or not."

"*You* may not detect it," retorted To, "but God does, and deals out rewards and punishments accordingly."

"Sir," said Lin, "I will take your word for it;"— and there the discussion ended.

YÜAN MEI

A.D. 1715–1797.

[An official who got into trouble with his superiors and went into retirement at the early age of 40. Chiefly known as a poet, he wrote prose in a fascinating style, and his witty and amusing letters are widely read. He also composed a famous cookery-book, which amply entitles him to be regarded as the Brillat-Savarin of China.]

THE ART OF DINING

EVERYTHING has its own original constitution, just as each man has certain natural characteristics. If a man's natural abilities are of a low order, Confucius and Mencius themselves would teach him to no purpose. And if an article of food is in itself bad, the greatest *chef* of all ages could not cook a flavour into it.

A ham is a ham; but in point of goodness two hams will be as widely separated as sea and sky. A mackerel is a mackerel; but in point of excellence two mackerel will differ as much as ice and live coals. And other things in the same way. So that the credit of a good dinner should be divided between the cook and the steward,—forty per cent. to the steward, and sixty per cent. to the cook. Cookery is like matrimony. Two things served together should match. Clear should go with clear, thick with thick, hard with hard, and soft with soft. I have known people mix grated lobster with birds'-nest, and mint with chicken or pork! The cooks of to-day think nothing of mixing in one soup the meat of chicken, duck, pig, and goose. But these chickens, ducks, pigs, and geese, have doubtless souls; and these souls will most certainly file plaints in the next world as to the way they have been treated in this.

Let salt food come first, and afterwards food of a more negative flavour. Let the heavy precede the light. Let dry dishes precede those with gravy. No flavour should dominate. If a guest eats his fill of savouries, his stomach will be fatigued. Salt flavours must be relieved by bitter or hot-tasting foods, in order to restore the palate. Too much wine will make the stomach dull. Sour or sweet food will be required to rouse it again into vigour. In winter we should eat beef and mutton; in summer dried and preserved meats. As for condiments, mustard belongs specially to summer; pepper to winter.

Don't eat with your ears! By this I mean do not aim at having extraordinary out-of-the-way foods, just to astonish your guests. For that is to eat with the ears, not with the mouth. Beancurd, if good, is actually nicer than birds'-nest.[1] And better than sea-slugs (*bêche-de-mer*), if not first-rate, is a dish of bamboo shoots. The chicken, the pig, the fish, the duck,—these are the four heroes of the table. Sea-slugs and birds'-nest have no characteristic flavours of their own. They are but usurpers in the house. I once dined with a friend who gave us birds'-nest in bowls more like vats, holding each about four ounces of the plain-boiled article. The other guests applauded vigorously, but I smiled and said, " I came here to eat birds'-nest, not to take delivery of it wholesale."

Don't eat with your eyes! By this I mean do not cover the table with innumerable dishes and multiply courses indefinitely. For this is to eat with the eyes, not with the mouth.

To know right from wrong, a man must be sober. And only a sober man can distinguish good flavours from bad. It has been well said that words are inadequate to describe the various shades of taste. How much less then must a stuttering sot be able to appreciate them!

To make good tea, the water must be poured on at the moment of boiling. If allowed to go on boiling, the water will lose its flavour. If the water is allowed to go off the boil, the tea-leaves will float.

I am not much of a wine-drinker, but this makes me all the more particular. Wine is like scholarship. It ripens with age, and it is best from a fresh-opened jar. " The top of the wine-jar, the bottom of the tea-pot," as the saying has it.

---

[1] Juvenal, too, contends that "magis illa juvant quae pluris emuntur."

DID CONFUCIUS WRITE THE ANNALS OF LU?[1]

I have received a copy of your book, entitled "Some difficult points in the Annals," which I regard as a specimen of accurate scholarship. Based upon the works of Tan Chu and Chao K'uang, it certainly surpasses both of them; and as for the work of Hu An-ting, the less said the better. Nevertheless, my humble opinion, with which I invariably end up, is that the book we know as the Annals of Lu is not the work of Confucius.

Confucius said of himself,[2] "I edited, but did not write,"—the writing of Annals being the business of the official historiographers. Now Confucius was not an official historiographer, and "he who does not hold an office cannot direct its administration."[2] How could he usurp the function of the historiographers, and without authority do their work for them? There is the saying, "By the Annals I shall be known, by the Annals I shall be blamed,"[3] as though Confucius was taking up the attitude of an uncrowned king, which not only the Master himself would not have done, but which the Prince and his Ministers, and the official historiographers, would not have tolerated. Further, Confucius said, "What I have written, I have written; what I have cut out, I have cut out. Tzŭ-yu and Tzŭ-hsia cannot add a single phrase;"[4] yet though he laid down his pen at the capture of the *ch'i lin*,[5] the Annals continued to be written from the 14th to the 16th year of Duke Ai, when Confucius died and the record came to an end. Whose pen was it that provided the Annals of those three years?

---

[1] See under K'ung Fu-tzŭ (Confucius), p. 4. It was Mencius who first attributed these Annals to Confucius, and he makes the Master say, "By these Annals alone will men know me; by these Annals alone will men blame me." They were written at a time when morality was at a low ebb, and their object was, as Ssŭ-ma Ch'ien tells us, to frighten rebellious Ministers and unfilial sons. They are known to the Chinese by the picturesque name of "Springs and Autumns," which means nothing more than "Annals," a more convenient term.

[2] Thus recorded in the "Discourses."

[3] Condensed here in the Chinese to four words, "Know me, blame me," which could only be understood by those familiar with the quotation given above.

[4] The authority is the historian, Ssŭ-ma Ch'ien (*q.v.*).

[5] A fabulous animal, known to collectors of curios as the *kylin*. It was regarded as an evil omen, and Confucius announced that his own end was at hand. Two years later he died (479 B.C.).

Whose were the additions? From this it is clear that the Lu State had its own historiographers, and that the preservation or loss of its Annals had nothing to do with Confucius.

Of all books in which we can put our trust, there is none like the " Discourses." It contains the teaching of the Sage; and taken together with the Canons of History, Poetry, the Book of Rites, and the Canon of Changes,—in regard to which last Confucius said that were his life prolonged for fifty years, he would devote them all to its study,—it may be said that not one of these works makes the slightest reference to the Annals.

When Han Hsüan-tzǔ was invited to the Lu State, he saw the Canon of Changes with its diagrams, and also, the Annals. In the "Records of the Ch'u State" we read of Shên Shu-shih, tutor to the Heir Apparent of King Chuang, teaching his pupils the Annals and in the "Records of the Chin State" we read of Yang-shê Hsi being celebrated for his familiarity with the Annals. That is to say, before the age of Confucius all the various States had for a long period written Annals of their own.

There is a possibility that Confucius, on his return from Wei to Lu, in moments spared from his work on the "Odes," may have read the Annals and perhaps have made some improvements. Whether Kung-yang or Ku-liang[1] quoted from the unimproved text or not, we cannot know; what is certain is that Confucius did no "writing."

---

[1] Two writers of commentaries on the Annals of Lu. Inasmuch as their works were not committed to writing until perhaps two hundred years after the death of Confucius, their value is reduced considerably. Specimens of both have been given.

CHANG KÊNG

18TH CENTURY A.D.

[Author of the *Kuo ch'ao hua ch'êng lu*, published in 1739, a collection of short biographies of one hundred and thirty artists, exclusive of nine Buddhist priests, one Taoist priest, and ten women, followed by a supplement containing lives of seventy-two more artists, exclusive of six Buddhist priests and twelve women. The "Chiao," mentioned below, is Chiao Ping-chên, who painted "according to the method of western foreigners," and reproduced, with improved perspective, the pictures entitled "Agriculture and Weaving," by Liu Sung-nien (A.D. 1195–1224).]

PERSPECTIVE

UNDER the Ming dynasty there was Li Ma-tou (Matteo Ricci), a native of Europe, who, being able to speak Chinese, came to the southern capital (Nanking) and lived in the western camp at the Chêng-yang gate. He painted a picture of the Pope, and depicted a woman holding a little child, declaring that this last was a representation of God. The projection and colouring of these were very fascinating; and the artist himself maintained that the Chinese could only paint flat surfaces, consequently there was no projection or depression (relief) in their pictures. We in our country, he said, paint both the light and the dark, so that the result shows projection and depression. A man's full face is light, and the side parts are dark. If the side parts are coloured dark in a picture, the face will appear in relief. Chiao acquired this art, and modified his style accordingly, but the result was not refined and convincing. Lovers of antiquity would do well not to adopt this method.

LIN TSÊ-HSÜ

A.D. 1785–1850.

[The famous Imperial Commissioner and Viceroy of Hupeh and Hunan, who seized and destroyed some ten million dollars' worth of foreign-owned opium and brought on war with Great Britain. For this he was recalled and disgraced, being subsequently banished to Ili. In 1845 he was restored to office, and once again rose to high rank. He was a fine scholar, a just and merciful official, and a true patriot. As "Commissioner Lin" he appeared for a time in Mme. Tussaud's collection of celebrities.]

A LETTER TO QUEEN VICTORIA

THE ways of God are without partiality; it is not permissible to injure another in order to profit oneself. The feelings of mankind are not diverse; for is there any one who does not hate slaughter and love life? In your honourable nation, which lies 20,000 *li* away, separated by several oceans, these ways of God and feelings of mankind are the same; there is no one who does not understand the distinctions between death, life, profit, and injury. Our divine House reckons as its family all within the Four Seas; and our great Emperor, as though with the goodness of God, offers shelter to all alike, even distant wilds and far off countries sharing with us in life and in the means of nourishment.

Now, ever since the restrictions on sea-borne trade at Canton were relaxed—several decades back—and a free business intercourse followed, the people of the Inner Land and the barbarian ships from outside have been at peace in the enjoyment of their profits. It may be added that rhubarb, tea, silk, etc., are among the most precious products of the Middle Kingdom, and that if the Outside nations were unable to obtain these, they would be deprived of the necessaries of life. That our divine House, regarding all with equal goodness, allows these goods to be sold without stint for export beyond the sea, and extends its favours to sympathy with the foreigner, is solely to model its own feelings upon those of God and Mother Earth. There is, however, a class of treacherous barbarians who manufacture opium, smuggle it in for sale, and deceive our

foolish people, in order to injure their bodies and derive
profit therefrom.   Formerly, smokers were few in number;
but of late the contagion has spread, and its flowing poison
has daily increased.   In China, of those who are thus
involved, a great many are wealthy persons, but there are
also among the foolish masses some who cannot resist a
whiff, and so injure their lives; in all such cases the penalty
is self-inflicted, and there is really no room for pity.   But
ever since the great Ch'ing dynasty united the empire, its
aim has been to regulate manners and customs with the
view of rectifying the heart of man; how then can our
House allow those who live within the girdle of the Seas
to poison themselves at their own sweet will?   Therefore,
all who trade in or smoke opium in the Inner Land will be
most severely punished, and the introduction and circulation
of the drug will be for ever prohibited.

It appears that this particular form of poison is illegally
prepared by scoundrels in the tributary tribes of your
honourable country and in the devil-regions under your
jurisdiction; but of course it is neither prepared nor sold
by your sovereign orders.   Further, that it is not all nations
but only some which prepare this article; and that you do
not allow your own people to smoke, under severe penalties
for disobedience, evidently knowing what a curse it is and
therefore strictly prohibiting the practice.   But better still
than forbidding people to smoke, would it not be to forbid
the sale and also the preparation of opium?   Surely this
would be the method of purifying at the fountain-head.
Not to smoke yourselves, but yet to dare to prepare and
sell to and beguile the foolish masses of the Inner Land—
this is to protect one's own life while leading others to
death, to gather profit for oneself while bringing injury
upon others.   Such behaviour is repugnant to the feelings
of human beings, and is not tolerated by the ways of God.

In view of the dominion exercised by our divine House
over Chinese and barbarian alike, nothing would be easier
than to put the guilty to death; but in respectful sympathy

with the sacred intelligence and great leniency of our Emperor it is only fitting that orders should be issued beforehand. Hitherto, it has not been customary to send written communications to the princes of your honourable nation; and now, if suddenly there came this stringent prohibition, you might try to plead ignorance as an excuse. I now propose that we shall unite to put a final stop to this curse of opium; in the Inner Land by prohibiting its use, and in your dominions by prohibiting its preparation. As to the stocks already prepared, your country must at once issue orders that these shall be searched out and be consigned to the bottom of the sea, and never again allow this poisonous thing to appear between heaven and earth. Not only will the people of the Inner Land benefit thereby, but also the people of your honourable nation—for since they prepare it, who knows but that they smoke it?—if the manufacture is forbidden, will not suffer injury from its use. Will not this plan confer on both parties the blessings of perfect peace, and further manifest the sincerity of the respectful conciliatoriness of your honourable country? Having this clear perception of divine principles, Almighty God will not send down calamities upon you; and being thus in harmony with the feelings of mankind, you will receive the approbation of our Holy Sages.

Further, inasmuch as under strict penalties smoking opium is now forbidden in the Inner Land, even if prepared there will be no opportunity of selling it and therefore no profit to be made, rather than lose capital and toil in vain, why not direct one's energies into another line of business? Also, all opium discovered in the Inner Land will be totally destroyed by fire and burning oil; and if barbarian ships again smuggle in opium, it will only remain to burn them likewise, with the risk that they may have on board other goods, so that jade and pebbles perish alike. Thus, there would be no profit, with evident injury to self; a desire to injure others forestalled by injury to self. Our divine House controls the myriad nations by a spiritual majesty which is unfathomable; do not say that you were not warned in time! And on receipt of this letter, make haste to reply, stating the measures which have been adopted at all sea-ports for cutting off the supply. Do not falsely colour the matter nor procrastinate! Anxiously waiting; anxiously hoping.

2nd moon of the 19th year of Tao Kuang (1839).

TSÊNG KUO-FAN

A.D. 1811–1872.

[The famous statesman and general who was chiefly responsible for the suppression of the T'ai P'ing rebellion, fighting strenuously in the cause of the Manchus from 1853 to the fall of Nanking in 1864. Ennobled as Marquis and raised to the rank of Viceroy, he lived incorruptible, and in spite of all the temptations to which a high Chinese official is exposed, died poor. "When his wardrobe was examined," says the memorial submitted to the Throne, "to find some suitable garments for the last rites, nothing new could be discovered. Every article of dress had been worn many times; and this may be taken as an example of his rigid economy for himself and in all the expenditure of his family." The Chinese government made provision for his family, and for the education of his brilliant son, afterwards popular Minister at the Court of St. James's and known as the Marquis Tsêng.]

A FAMILY LETTER

BROTHER Ch'êng and others,

On former occasions when I sent family letters, they took thirty-five days to reach you. On the last occasion, a special messenger has not reached you, even after forty days. The rebels being just now round about Lo-p'ing and Jao-chou,[1] I fancy that a circuitous route has been taken.

After the recapture of Hsiu-ning[2] on the 12th inst., Tso's[3] army was divided into eight columns, and a small defeat was suffered at Chia-lu, forcing a retreat upon Ching-chên. Luckily, however, the rebels did not follow up their attack, and Tso obtained a few days' grace for reorganization, the result being that the *moral* of the men was not greatly weakened.

Just now, Tso's troops are advancing upon Lo-p'ing and P'o-yang. Pao's[4] troops, because of the critical state of Fu-chou and Chien-ch'ang, were to have been sent to Kiangsi, first of all to secure the general situation, and then to relieve the two cities in question; but recently both P'o-yang and Ying-chên have been considered to be in such

---

[1] In Kiangsi.

[2] In Anhui.

[3] Tso Tsung-t'ang, one of the greatest generals of modern times—in any country.

[4] Pao Ch'ao, who rose to the Commander-in-chief in Hunan.

danger that Pao's troops have been temporarily held back and were not allowed to leave hurriedly for Kiangsi. As for Hu,[1] I fear that the dogs of rebels have come down from Huang-chou[2] to attack An-ch'ing,[3] and brother Yüan's troops have been sent to join Pao's troops in bringing aid to the north bank. On the various ranges in the neighbourhood of Ch'i-mên,[3] the rebels managed, on the 23rd inst. to capture two positions, so that for several months past there has not been much leisure for supporting operations. Dangers have frequently broken out; the foreign devils have been giving trouble in all directions, and there is even talk of their threatening Ch'i-mên. Thus, it seems to me that the present year will be full of difficulties for us to deal with.

Well, ever since the winter of the 3rd year of Hsien Fêng (1853) I have devoted my body to my country's service, and I am willing to die stretched on the battle-field, but not willing to die "beside the window." [4] Such was my original ambition, and of late years, during my career in the army, I have acted always to the best of my ability and to the limit of my strength. I have nothing to be ashamed of, and I shall close my eyes without regret.

It remains for the various members of my family, brothers and their sons and their nephews, to bear in mind the eight words of their grandfather: "Examine, value, early, sweep, books, vegetables, fish, pork." [5] Also, with due reverence, bear in mind the three "Don't believes" of the same grandfather :—

> Don't believe in genii of mountain, river, or tree!
> Don't believe in doctors and their drugs!
> Don't believe in priests of any faith!

---

[1] Hu Lin-i, another general who greatly distinguished himself against the T'ai P'ings.

[2] In Hupeh.

[3] In Anhui.

[4] That is, "in my bed." The allusion is to a visit by Confucius to a disciple who was dying. The Master went to the sick man's house, and grasped his hand through a window, beside which the patient's bed had been placed.

[5] Such is the literal meaning of the Chinese characters employed; their application may perhaps be elucidated by some surviving descendant of the great Viceroy.

In my own diary there are eight other fundamental principles:—

In your studies, make teaching your aim.
In verse or prose, make rhythm your aim.
In serving parents, make their happiness your aim.
In matters of health, make equanimity your aim.
In your career, make restraint of language your aim.
In home life, make getting up in good time your aim.
In official life, make honesty your aim.
In military life, make care for the people your aim.

These eight principles have all been carefully tested by me and found to be suitable for application. My brother, you too should teach your sons and nephews to bear them in mind. For no matter whether the times may be at peace or in rebellion, your family rich or poor, if you can adhere to the eight words of your grandfather and to the eight fundamental principles which I have laid down, you cannot possibly fail to be a man of the highest order. Whenever I write a letter home, it is my duty to impress these points upon you, and also because of the risks of military life, in anticipation of any thing that may happen.

Personally, I am in good health; and although the men's pay is four months in arrear, their *moral* has not seriously weakened. I think we can hold out, but it is impossible to say. The family must not give way to anxiety.

Dated 11th year of Hsien Fêng (1861)

CHANG CHIH-TUNG

A.D. 1835–1909.

[One of the most distinguished officials of modern times, popularly known as the Incorruptible, who raised himself by his learning and ability to the highest posts in the empire. In early life he showed great animosity to the foreigner, and declared that "these outer barbarians are as ravenous as wolves;" yet in the Boxer crisis in 1900, it was he who most materially assisted in saving European and American lives. His literary style was brilliant to a degree surpassed only, perhaps, in these days by Liang Ch'i-ch'ao. His chief work was on education, extracts from which are given below.]

RELIGION

I HAVE heard that those who wish to save us from the upheavals of the present age, arrange their advice under three heads, to wit: (1) Keep safe our State. (2) Keep safe our holy religion. (3) Keep safe our Flowery stock. Now these three points are in reality connected by a single thread, and that is *unanimity*. To keep safe our stock, we must first keep safe our religion; to keep safe our holy religion, we must first keep safe our State. How can the stock be preserved? *Wisdom* will preserve it; wisdom, which is another term for religion. How can religion prevail? *Force* can make it prevail; force, which is another name for militarism. Thus it is that in a State which does not command respect, religion will not obtain; and if the State be not prosperous, the stock will not be held in honour. There is the religion of Islam; it is not based upon right, yet because the Turks are a fierce, cruel, and courageous race, the religion retains its vitality. There is Buddhism; here we find an approximation to right, yet because the Indians are an unwarlike race, Buddhism has lost its hold. There is the "luminous" religion (Nestorianism) of Persia; because the State was weak, the religion was changed. The ancient religion of Greece may exist or it may not; the Roman Catholic and Protestant religions prevail over six-tenths of the earth's surface, a result which is due to powerful militarism. Our holy religion prevails in the Middle Land, where for several thousand years it has undergone no change. The Five Emperors and the Three Kings made clear the Way (*Tao*) and handed down laws, adding the part of teacher to that of ruler.

The conflict of divers religions has been seen among ourselves for over two thousand years. Confucianists and the followers of Mo Tzŭ were in conflict, and so were the followers of Lao Tzŭ and Confucianists. Chuang Tzŭ was a Taoist, yet he was in conflict with other Taoists. Hsün Tzŭ was a Confucianist, yet he was in conflict with other Confucianists. Under the T'ang dynasty (A.D. 618–905), Confucianists and Buddhists were in conflict; and during the next two hundred years Buddhists and the followers of Lao Tzŭ were in conflict. The object of Confucianists in attacking any other faith is to distinguish truth from falsehood; other religions attack one another for the sake of establishing pre-eminence. In our days, the rights and wrongs of these conflicts are clear. Confucius and Mencius have handed down to us a holy religion which is absolutely unvarying and a perfect standard of conduct, glowing brightly like the sun or moon in mid-sky; embodying the pure law of God above with the fullest recognition of human relationships; even in far-off lands, where customs are different, there are none to say a word in its disfavour.

EDUCATION

Students of the present day should begin by making themselves acquainted with the Confucian Canon, in order to understand the aim of the inspired rulers and teachers of old in establishing the religion of the Middle Kingdom. They should examine the dynastic histories, in order to appreciate the various epochs of government and rebellion, as well as the manners and customs of the various parts of the empire. They should hunt through the body of general literature, in order to make themselves acquainted with the best examples of the learning of the Middle Kingdom. After that, they may choose any line in western learning which makes up for deficiencies in ours, and apply the same accordingly; they may also adopt points from the governments of the west which strengthen any weaknesses in our own government. Such action will conduce only to our advantage, and not to our harm.

Western learning should be preceded by Chinese learning. In all schools in foreign countries, there is a daily recitation from the Canon of Jesus, in honour of the religion. In the elementary schools, the study of the Latin language comes first, in honour of antiquity. In geography, students are first familiarized with the maps of their own country, and then proceed to the map of the whole world, thus showing a proper sequence. The books used in these schools mostly set forth the virtuous government of ancient rulers, and the songs sung in public and in private life mostly glorify the strength and prosperity of the nation, thus exhibiting a love of country. A scholar among us who should be unacquainted with our Chinese learning, would be like a man who did not know his own surname, like a horseman without a bridle, or a boat without a rudder. The deeper his knowledge of western learning, the more unfriendly would his attitude become towards China. Even if he were a man of great learning and much ability, of what use would such a man be in the government of his own country?

IN PRAISE OF THE MANCHUS

For the past two hundred and fifty years, the officials and people within the boundaries of the Four Seas, daily marching between high Heaven and Mother Earth, have been nourished in their growth by unremitting care, down to the present day. If we compare the history of China for the past two thousand years with the histories of western countries for the past fifty years, have their governments shown the generosity, the charity of heart, the loyalty, the sincerity of ours? Although China is neither rich nor strong, nevertheless all her people, rich, noble, poor, and humble alike, can pass their days in comfort, and rejoice that they were born into this world. Now although the countries of the west are flourishing, the sorrows of the masses, their sufferings, and the poison of wrongs, which press them on all sides without redress, cause them to watch their opportunity for breaking out and murdering their sovereign or assassinating a Minister, examples of which deeds are recorded every year. Thus we know that their form of government is most certainly not equal to that we have here in China.

YÜAN SHIH-K'AI

1860–1916.

[A statesman with a singular record. He rose to the highest positions under the Manchu dynasty. His attitude towards the Boxers in 1900 was one which foreigners, saved thereby from what would probably have been a terrible massacre, must always remember with gratitude. He subsequently became a great favourite with the Empress Dowager; but in 1909, after attending a meeting of the Grand Council, he received an Edict which informed him that he "was unexpectedly suffering from an affection of the foot" and called upon him to resign. He obeyed at once, the explanation being that he had quarrelled with the Regent; and he remained in retirement until 1911, when he was recalled to deal with the revolutionaries. In 1912 he was elected President of the Republic, taking the oath given below. By 1915 he had engineered a movement in favour of himself as Emperor, which was disclosed and defeated principally by Liang Ch'i-ch'ao (q.v.); and after pretending to refuse, he actually fixed the date of his coronation for 9th February, 1916, and chose the style of his reign. But public opinion was too strong against him—the Chinese will forgive anything sooner than disloyalty—and the project was abandoned. He survived the disgrace only a few months.]

A BROKEN OATH

[FROM A PHOTOGRAPH]

I HEREBY make oath and say:

With reference to the establishment of government by the people and the various administrative measures to be drawn up, I am most anxious to exert my utmost strength in spreading and supporting the republican spirit; to scour out the flaws and filth of autocratic rule; to observe the constitutional laws in accordance with the will of the people; and to associate our State with peaceable and powerful countries, so that the five great members[1] of our nation may one and all derive happiness and profit therefrom. All these aims I swear to follow up without change; and so soon as the National Assembly has been called together and a President[2] has been duly elected for the first term of this office, I will resign my position and will reverently adhere with all sincerity to the oath which I now swear to my countrymen.

(*Signed*) YUAN SHIH-K'AI.

---

[1] Chinese, Manchus, Mongols, Mussulmans, and Tibetans.

[2] He himself was elected, with the consent of Sun Yat-sen, Provisional President in the South.

LIANG CH'I-CH'AO

[Born 1872. One of the most brilliant of the band of reformers who succeeded in establishing the Republic and later on in defeating the treacherous bid for monarchy by Yüan Shih-k'ai. He has written extensively on politics, education, religion, and sociology, in a style which, for beauty and lucidity combined, may well rank with that of China's masterpieces. It has in fact been said that "his style displays so classical a finish that the Chinese often shed tears over his compositions, simply from admiration of their beauty. He has been Minister of Justice, and also of Finance, under the Republic; and in 1919 he attended the Peace Conference at Paris as delegate.]

MY COUNTRY![1]

THE greatest country in the greatest of the five continents of the world,—which is it? My country, the Middle State, the Flowery Land! The people who number one-third of the human race,—who are they? My countrymen of the Middle State, the Flowery Land! Annals which extend back without a break for over four thousand years,—of what country are these? Of my country, the Middle State, the Flowery Land! My country contains four hundred million inhabitants, who all speak what is fundamentally the same language, and use the same script: of no other country can this be said. Her ancient books hand down events which have occurred during more than thirty centuries past: of no other country can this be said.

Of old, there were five States: China, India, Persia, Egypt, and Mexico. Of four of these the territory remains, but as States all four have disappeared. Wandering over the deserted sites, you see only traces of the ruins left by the ironclad horsemen, followers of Mahomet, or the arenas where once warlike Caucasian tribes gloried in the song and dance. But my country, the Middle State, the Flowery Land, stands proudly alone, having survived, in one unbroken line, ever increasing in size and brilliancy, down to the present day. And in the future it will spread into a myriad branches, to be fused together in one furnace.

---

[1] "The biggest thing I have learned in writing the 'Outline' is the importance of Central Asia and China. They have been, and they are now still, the centre of human destiny."

H. G. WELLS.

Ah, beautiful is my country! Ah, great are my countrymen! Now, ere inditing a rough outline of their story,
I must purify myself thrice with perfume and the bath;
then, looking up to heaven, with many prostrations, thank
God that I was born in this lovely land, as one of the sons
of this great people.

THE CIVILIZATION OF JAPAN

The reception of foreign learning by the Chinese people
differs from its reception by the Japanese. Japan is a
small country, and moreover possesses no learning which
is really its own. Therefore, if such learning arrives from
without, the Japanese rush to it as though on galloping
horses, change as rapidly as echo follows sound, and in the
twinkling of an eye the whole nation is transformed.
However, a careful estimate of their capacity shows that
they are really nothing more than mere imitators; they are
in no sense able to add anything of their own or anything
they may have themselves initiated. Now China is not
like that. China is a huge country with a learning of its
own, which has been handed down for several thousand
years and which is so well fortified by defences that foreign
ideas do not easily find their way in. Even if they do get
in, for many—perhaps a hundred years their influence will
not succeed in rumpling the hair of one's head. It is like
throwing ink into water. If the water is in a foot-wide
bowl or in a ten-foot pool, the ink will very rapidly discolour
it all; but if the same ink is thrown into a mighty rushing
river or into the wide and deep ocean, can these be easily
stained in the same way? Again, although China is not
receptive of foreign learning, from what she does receive
she makes a point of extracting all the excellences and
adapting these to her own advantage. She transmutes the
substance and etherializes its use, thus producing a new
factor of civilization which is altogether her own. Her

blue is thus bluer than the original indigo-blue of foreigners; her ice is colder than their water. Ah me! Deep mountains and wide marshes give birth indeed to dragons; but the footprints of our noble representative can never have been familiar to the small-sized gentlemen of the Country of Dwarfs.

CHINA'S NEED

Just now, all China is under the influence of Yang Chu.[1] There are those whose talk is of Confucius but whose deeds are of Yang; there are others whose talk and deeds are both of Yang. The limit is reached by those whose talk is of Mo Ti[2] but whose deeds are of Yang; and there are even some who, recognizing neither Confucius, nor Yang, nor Mo, carry out the principles of Yang amid those of no understanding. Alas! Yang's teachings have been the ruin of China. They have indeed, and the only way to save her is to turn to the teachings of Mo Ti; not to the teachings of any other Mo but to the teachings of the real Mo, Mo the philosopher.

LIBERTY

"Without Liberty, better die." New words these! During the 18th and 19th centuries these words were the foundation on which States were established by the various peoples in Europe and the Americas,—will liberty in the same sense serve the purpose of the modern Chinese nation? I reply that liberty connotes equal rights for all; it is an important factor in human life, and there is no direction in which it will fail to serve such a purpose. At the same time it should be noted that a distinction must be made

[1] Founder of the "selfish" school. *See* p. 19.
[2] Who taught the doctrine of "universal love." *See* p. 14.

between real liberty, false liberty, complete liberty, partial liberty, the liberty of civilization, and the liberty of savages. "Liberty! Liberty!" has gradually become the pious catchword of our callow youth of to-day. But the leaders of our "new people" say, If China would forever enjoy the blessings of a complete civilization and of a genuine liberty, it is necessary to begin by defining exactly that in which liberty consists. Allow me then to discuss this question.

Liberty is diametrically opposed to slavery. If we examine the histories of the development of liberty in Europe and in the Americas, we shall find that the struggle was confined to the four following points: (1) administrative liberty, (2) religious liberty, (3) national liberty, and (4) economic liberty. The object of the first was to protect the people against their own government; of the second, to protect members of a church against the church; of the third, to protect one's own nation against foreign nations; and of the fourth, to protect the people against the operations of Capital and Labour. Administrative liberty may be further divided under three heads, the respective objects being (1) to secure the liberty of the masses in regard to officials, (2) to secure the liberty of the whole nation in regard to the government in power, and (3) to secure the liberty of colonies in regard to the mother country. The principles on which the practice of liberty depends are no more than these.

Liberty means that every man shall be free, except that he may not encroach upon the freedom of others. And since it is forbidden to each individual to encroach upon the freedom of others, it follows that such subjection of the individual is also a point of importance. How can this be regarded as a drag on liberty? Liberty connotes the freedom of the whole community and not the freedom of the individual. In the early ages of savagedom, individual liberty prevailed and the liberty of the community did not exist; whereas in civilized times the liberty of the community has predominated and the liberty of the individual has decreased.   These two statements are indisputable and contain no shade of error.   If the liberty of the individual is to be accounted true liberty, then of the inhabitants of the world who enjoy the blessings of liberty, none can be compared with the people of China at the present day.

The gentry, bullies of the countryside, gobble up their poorer neighbours like fish, and there are no means of resisting them; traders abscond, leaving their debts unpaid, and those who have been swindled have no means of redress. Now, it is open to all men to become gentry or traders; it follows, therefore, that the liberty of the community is also a point of importance.   Is not this so?   In the highest classes there are men and women who make a perfect cesspool of official life;—is this liberty?   In the towns there are young and old who look on opium as a necessary food;—is this liberty?   In a civilized State, there would be, for light offences of the kind, a money fine, and for grave offences, sequestration of property.   Other points in like manner; but so many are they that, were I ten men, I could not reckon then all up.   Viewed in this light, I ask you, "who are they who enjoy liberty,[1]—the people of China, or the people of other nations?"

---

[1] Here, the evils, not the blessings, of too much liberty.

MISCELLANEOUS

[THE proverbial philosophy of the Chinese is on a scale commensurate in every way with other branches of their voluminous literature. Most Western proverbs, maxims, household words, etc., are to be found embedded therein; sometimes expressed in strictly identical terms, at other times differing only in point of local colour. Thus the Chinese say (*e.g.*)—

> One actor does not make a play.
> Out of the wolf's lair into the tiger's mouth.
> Prevention is better than cure.
> Better a living dog than a dead lion.
> As the twig is bent the tree's inclined.
> When the cat's away, the rats play.
> Better be a fowl's beak than a bullock's rump.
> It is the unexpected which always happens.
> Oxen till the fields, and rats eat the corn;
> Bees make honey, and men steal it, etc., etc.

The name of these is legion. A full collection of such proverbs and sayings, gathered from the past four thousand years, would probably embrace all that is contained in Western literatures in this sense, and leave a margin to the credit of China. The specimens which are given below have been taken at random and brought together without classification. In the majority of cases, the flavour of these will, I think, be found to be peculiarly Chinese.]

DEAL with the faults of others as gently as with your own.

Three men's strength cannot prevail against Truth.

If you bow at all, bow low.

Pay attention to what a man is, not to what he has been.

A man thinks he knows, but a woman knows better.

If Fortune smiles,—who doesn't? If Fortune doesn't, —who does?

The host is happy when the guest has gone.

No medicine is as good as a middling doctor.

Great truths cannot penetrate rustic ears.

Better to jilt than be jilted: better to sin than to be sinned against.[1]

A bottle-nosed man may be a teetotaler, but no one will think so.

Like climbing a tree to catch a fish [*Mencius*].

"Forbearance" is a rule of life in a word.

With money you can move the Gods; without it, you can't move a man.

Oblige, and you will be obliged.

---

[1] [This was a *mot* of the great and unscrupulous general, Ts'ao Ts'ao. It is in no sense a Chinese household word.]

Armies are maintained for years, to be used on a single day.

More trees are upright, than men.

Only imbeciles want credit for the achievements of their ancestors.

Long visits bring short compliments.

Deep people don't say shallow things.

A thousand pictures are not equal to one book.

You can't talk of the ocean to a well-frog.

If you owe a man money, there is nothing like seeing him often.

A quack will kill a man without a knife.

Let the sovereign be thin so long as his subjects are fat.

Some study shows the need for more.

Better eighty per cent. ready money than cent. per cent. on trust.

The highest towers begin from the ground.

Medicine cures the man who is fated not to die.

If a man has money, he will find plenty who have scales.

Even the best artificial flowers have no smell.

A thousand soldiers are easier to be got than one general.

A thousand prescriptions are more readily forthcoming than a single cure.

No needle is sharp at both ends.

Straight trees are felled first.

No image-maker worships the Gods. He knows what they are made of.

Half an orange tastes as sweet as a whole one.

Even the Yellow River is sometimes clear.

We love our own compositions, but other men's wives.

Don't pull up your shoe in a melon-field, nor adjust your hat under a plum-tree (*i.e.*, avoid the appearance of evil).

Free-sitters at the play always grumble most.

Laugh and keep young.

Happiness stands beside the ugly.

A good memory is not equal to bad ink.

With money—a dragon; without it—a worm.

He who has his back to a draught has his face to the grave.

Be quick over your work, but not over your food.

He who will only mount a unicorn will never ride a horse.

If you suspect a man, don't employ him; if you employ him, don't suspect him [*Confucius*].

Men grow old and pearls yellow. There is no cure for age.

When a man is at peace, he is silent; as level water does not flow.

It is not the wine which makes a man drunk: it is the man himself.

Whispered words are heard afar.

Ripe melons drop without plucking.

Better a dog in peace than a man in war.

The faults which a man condemns when out of office, he commits when in.

Losing money is begotten of winning.

One needn't devour a whole chicken to know the flavour of the bird.

There's sure to be fuel near a big tree.

Man combs his hair every morning. Why not his heart?

There is no thief like a family of five daughters.

There is something to be learnt from every book.

The sky covers no man in particular.

Dogs do not object to poor masters.

Have no friends not equal to yourself.

The tusks of the elephant are its own undoing.

The tongue is a sharp sword which slays though it draws no blood.

One man makes a road and another walks on it.

Don't break a vase for a shy at a rat.

Every one gives a shove to the tumbling wall.

Sweep the snow from your own doorstep.

You can't chop a thing as round as you can pare it.

One jibbing horse throws out the troop.

All language is not in books, nor all thoughts in language.

The men of old see not the moon of to-day; yet the moon of to-day is the moon that shone on them.

He who rides a tiger, cannot dismount.

A stupid son is better than a clever daughter.

Politeness before force.

Life feeds upon adversity and sorrow. Death comes amid pleasure and repose [*Mencius*].

If you can't draw a tiger, draw a dog.

One dog barks at something, and the rest bark at him.

You can't clap hands with one palm.

Cleanse your heart as you would cleanse a dish.

All that a man needs in this transitory life is a splint hat and a rice-bowl.

A pretty woman entering a family has the ugly ones for her foes.

He who has seen little is astonished at much.

Shoes for the same foot must be worn by different people.

Draw your bow, but don't shoot.

One more good man on earth is better than an extra angel in heaven.

Don't take a pole-axe to kill a fowl [*Confucius*].

Don't make dumplings in a teapot.

Good or bad, 'tis the wine of my country.

> The virtuous man is his own arbitrator:
> The foolish man carries his suit into court.
> Man's heart is like iron:
> The law like a smelting-furnace.

In the market-place, money; in solitude, peace.

One man spreads a false report and a hundred report it as truth.

Gold is tested by fire; man, by gold.

The influence of good is all too little. The influence of bad is all too much.

Man dies and leaves a name. The tiger dies and leaves a skin.

Those who have not tasted the bitterest of life's bitters, can never appreciate the sweetest of life's sweets.

An angry fist cannot strike a smiling face.

It takes a rat to know a rat.

Extraordinary men are ordinary to God.

Man dreads fame as a pig dreads fat.

Wine can both make and mar.

You can't get ivory out of a dog's mouth.

He who is first is prince. He who comes after is minister only.

New-born calves don't fear tigers.

Money makes a blind man see.

For every man that Heaven creates, Earth provides a grave.

Man is God upon a small scale. God is man upon a large scale.

A near neighbour is better than a distant relation.

Women share adversity better than prosperity.

If a man keeps his mouth shut, his words become proverbial.

You can't wrap fire in a paper parcel.

Intimate talks leave us few friends.

Without Error, there could be no such thing as Truth.

NOTE.—Sir E. J. Reed, in his work on Japan, quietly includes as specimens of Japanese proverbs, etc., well-known quotations from Mencius and other Chinese authors, the truth being, of course, that all the high-class literature of Japan, its art, and its civilization, are essentially of Chinese origin.

[Since writing the above paragraph in 1883, I have met with similar instances in overwhelming number. *See* "The XIX Century and After," February, 1905.]

GEMS OF CHINESE
LITERATURE

EDITED BY

HERBERT A. GILES

Late Professor of Chinese in the University of Cambridge

Volume II — Verse

PREFACE

In translating Chinese poetry, so soon as the meaning has been secured, there is always open for its reproduction a choice between rhymed verse and prose. Personally, I am on the side of the former. It is a much more difficult feat to achieve than a prose rendering, further involving, as it does, considerable "labour of the file"; that is, if the *meaning*, which is essential in both cases, is to be retained in approximately all its fullness —a consummation unfortunately denied to the *spirit*, whether the vehicle be verse or prose.

All Chinese poetry is lyrical, in the sense that it was originally intended to be set to music and sung; and the great bulk of it is also lyrical in the later senses of the term, as well as in rhyme. Swinburne, in his *Essays and Studies*, 1875, says "Rhyme is the native condition of lyric verse in English; a rhymeless lyric is a maimed thing." Mr. George Moore in *The Observer* of 9th June, 1918, declares that "verse cannot be translated into verse," and that all such attempts are "an amateurish adventure." It will surprise many to hear that Conington, Fitzgerald, Rossetti, Burton, and other notable translators of verse into verse were mere amateurs; all the same, Mr. Moore is entitled to his own opinion. Keats, on the other hand, tells us that never did he breathe the pure serene of Homer until he heard Chapman speak out loud and bold in his rhymed versions of the *Iliad* and the *Odyssey*; but there is no record of any one into whose ken the accurate prose version of Butcher and Lang has ever swum like a new planet.

Herewith a word-for-word translation of "The Chaste Wife's Reply" (p. 369), with which the general reader may compare my rhymed version, and may be able to judge how far I have drifted from the meaning of the original.

> Sir know handmaid have husband
> Offer handmaid pair bright pearls
> Sympathize sir entangle floss purpose
> Wrap stop red silk vest
> Handmaid home lofty storey connect park rise

> Good man hold halberd bright glory inside
> Know sir use mind like sun moon
> Serve husband swear intend together live die
> Return sir bright pearls pair tears drop
> Hate not mutual meet not marry time

The above is written with five words to each of the first four lines, and with seven words to the remaining six. It must not be supposed that each Chinese monosyllable presents to the reader the same bald front as the English equivalent which I have set down. That is where style and spirit come in; neither of them communicable in an alien tongue.

Chinese poetry may be written with any number of words from one to eleven, or even more, to each line; and it is hoped that the above example will show how it is possible to extract sense from a congeries of monosyllables unconnected by most of the parts of speech which guide, or fail to guide, the reader of an English poem. This feature, constant in Chinese poetry, can be produced as a *tour de force* in other languages. A verse, consisting of only one monosyllabic word to the line, which yields immediate sense, and one sense only, can easily be constructed in English. With apologies for its triviality, I hasten to add—

> Boy
>   Jam
> Joy
>   Cram

> Ill
>   Bed
> Pill
>   Dead

The first edition of this work was published in 1898, and has long been out of print. The present edition, considerably enlarged, is a companion volume to *Gems of Chinese Literature*, also in its second and enlarged edition, which contains specimens from the great prose writers of all ages down to the present day. My best thanks are due to my son, Mr. Lancelot Giles, H.B.M. Consul at Ch'ang-sha, who has carried out for me the troublesome task of proof-reading.

HERBERT A. GILES.

Cambridge, 1922.

Dear Land of Flowers, forgive me!—that I took
  These snatches from thy glittering wealth of song,
And twisted to the uses of a book
  Strains that to alien harps can ne'er belong.

Thy gems shine purer in their native bed
  Concealed, beyond the pry of vulgar eyes;
Until, through labyrinths of language led,
  The patient student grasps the glowing prize.

Yet many, in their race toward other goals,
  May joy to feel, albeit at second-hand,
Some far faint heart-throb of poetic souls
  Whose breath makes incense in the Flowery Land.

                              H. A. G.

THE ODES

[These are some 300 of the old national ballads of China, collected and edited by Confucius, 551–479 B.C. On one occasion, the Master said to his son, "Have you studied the *Odes*?" And on receiving an answer in the negative, Confucius warned him, saying, "If you do not study the *Odes*, you will have no command of language."]

1. TO A YOUNG GENTLEMAN

Don't come in, sir, please!
Don't break my willow-trees!
Not that *that* would very much grieve me;
But alack-a-day! what would my parents say?
    And love you as I may,
I cannot bear to think what that would be.

Don't cross my wall, sir, please!
Don't spoil my mulberry-trees!
Not that *that* would very much grieve me;
But alack-a-day! what would my brothers say?
    And love you as I may,
I cannot bear to think what that would be.

Keep outside, sir, please!
    Don't spoil my sandal-trees!
Not that *that* would very much grieve me;
But alack-a-day! what the world would say!
And love you as I may,
I cannot bear to think what that would be.*

---

* Set to music by Cyril Scott and J. A. Carpenter.

2. A MALE LIGHT-OF-LOVE

Away I must run;
There is work to be done,
Though I'm thinking to-day
Of the eldest Miss K.
In the mulberry-grove
I shall pour out my love;
For she's promised to meet me
And as lover to greet me—
　　The eldest Miss K.

Away I must run;
There is work to be done.
But to-day I shall be
With the eldest Miss E.
In the mulberry-grove
I shall pour out my love;
For she's promised to meet me
And as lover to greet me—
　　The eldest Miss E.

Away I must run;
There is work to be done.
But to-day I shall sigh
For the eldest Miss Y.
In the mulberry-grove
I shall pour out my love;
For she's promised to meet me
And as lover to greet me—
　　The eldest Miss Y.

3. "AT BEST A CONTRADICTION"

A clever man will build a town,
A clever woman pull it down.
Though woman's wit is sometimes heard,

She's really an ill-omened bird;
Her long tongue's like a flight of stairs
Which leads to miserable cares.
It is not God who mars our lives,
The fault is rather with our wives.
Of all we cannot teach or train,
Women and eunuchs are our bane.

4. DESPERATE!

The ripe plums are falling,—
　One-third of them gone;
To my lovers I'm calling,
　" 'Tis time to come on!"

The ripe plums are dropping,—
　Two-thirds are away;
" 'Tis time to be popping!"
　To my lovers I say.

Down has dropt every plum;
　In baskets they lie.
What, will no lover come?
　"Now or never!" say I.

5. TO A MAN

You seemed a guileless youth enough,
Offering for silk your woven stuff;*
But silk was not required by you:
I was the silk you had in view.

---

* Pieces of stamped linen, used as a circulating medium before the introduction of the bank-note.

With you I crossed the ford, and while
We wandered on for many a mile
I said, "I do not wish delay,
But friends must fix our wedding-day. . . .
Oh, do not let my words give pain,
But with the autumn come again."

And then I used to watch and wait
To see you passing through the gate;
And sometimes when I watched in vain,
My tears would flow like falling rain;
But when I saw my darling boy,
I laughed and cried aloud for joy.
The fortune-tellers, you declared,
Had all pronounced us duly paired;
"Then bring a carriage," I replied,
"And I'll away to be your bride."

The mulberry-leaf, not yet undone
By autumn chill, shines in the sun.
O tender dove, I would advise,
Beware the fruit that tempts thy eyes!*
O maiden fair, not yet a spouse,
List lightly not to lovers' vows!
A man may do this wrong, and time
Will fling its shadow o'er his crime;
A woman who has lost her name
Is doomed to everlasting shame.

The mulberry-tree upon the ground
Now sheds its yellow leaves around.
Three years have slipped away from me,
Since first I shared your poverty;
And now again, alas the day!
Back through the ford I take my way.
My heart is still unchanged, but you

* The dove is very fond of mulberries, and is said to become intoxicated by them.

Have uttered words now proved untrue;
And you have left me to deplore
A love that can be mine no more.

For three long years I was your wife,
And led in truth a toilsome life;
Early to rise and late to bed,
Each day alike passed o'er my head.
I honestly fulfilled my part;
And you,—well, you have broke my heart.
The truth my brothers will not know,
So all the more their gibes will flow.
I grieve in silence and repine
That such a wretched fate is mine.

Ah, hand in hand to face old age!—
Instead, I turn a bitter page.
Oh for the river-banks of yore;
Oh for the much-loved marshy shore;
The hours of girlhood, with my hair
Ungathered, as we lingered there.
The words we spoke, that seemed so true,
I little thought that I should rue;
I little thought the vows we swore
Would some day bind us two no more.

6. THE CRICKET

The cricket chirrups in the hall,
    The year is dying fast;
Now let us hold high festival
    Ere the days and months be past.
Yet push not revels to excess
    That our fair fame be marred;
Lest pleasures verge to wickedness
    Let each be on his guard.

ANONYMOUS ANCIENT POETRY

1. THE HUSBANDMAN'S SONG

Work, work,—from the rising sun
Till sunset comes and the day is done
    I plough the sod
    And harrow the clod,
And meat and drink both come to me,
So what care I for the powers that be?

2. YAO'S ADVICE*

With trembling heart and cautious steps
    Walk daily in fear of God. . . .
Though you never trip over a mountain,
    You may often trip over a clod.

3. INSCRIPTION ON A WASH-BASIN

Oh, rather than sink in the world's foul tide
I would sink in the bottomless main;
For he who sinks in the world's foul tide
    In noisome depths shall for ever abide,
But he who sinks in the bottomless main
    May hope to float to the surface again.

---

* An Emperor of the 3rd millennium B.C., formerly regarded as legendary.

CH'Ü YÜAN or CH'Ü P'ING

332–295 B.C.

[The typical loyal statesman of China. Unable to prevail against the evil policy of his sovereign, he committed suicide by drowning. The modern Dragon-Boat festival is supposed to be a search for his body. See p. 33.]

1. THE BATTLE

We take our trusty spears in hand,
  We don our coats of mail;*
When chariot-wheels are interlocked,
  With daggers we assail.
Standards obscure the light of day,
  Like rushing clouds their brunt;
Arrows on both sides fall around;
  All struggle to the front.
Our line at last is broken through,
  Beneath the foeman's heels;
My own near horse is killed outright,
  The off horse wounded reels,
The team becomes a useless mass,
  Entangled in the wheels.
With stick of jade I strike the drum,†
  And beat to hurry on,
For though by God's decree I fell,
  My ardour was not gone.
Our best men were all done to death,
  Their corpses strewed the plain;
They went out but did not come in,
  Not to return again,
And now upon the battle-field,
  Far from their homes they lie,

---

* Of buffalo-hide; not of rhinoceros-hide, as has been wrongly supposed.
† The drum is the signal for advance, the gong for retreat.

Their long swords still within their grasp,
   And their stout bows near by.
A head is here, a body there,
   And yet they never quailed,
Being so brave and soldiers too,
   Nor in their duty failed.
But now, though lifeless clay, their souls
   Are with the heavenly hosts,
To lead once more an army corps
   Of disembodied ghosts.

2. COMMEMORATION SERVICE AND AFTER

The funeral rites are over;
   Now let us beat the drum. . . . .
The priest gives up his plantain-wand,*
   And now the dancers come.
In unison fair maidens sing,
   "Asters for autumn, orchids for spring"—
Thus it always is,
   And thus it has always been.†

---

* Passing it on to the next dancer after his own performance.

† Life must go on again as usual, with dance and song and flowers.

SUNG YÜ

4TH CENTURY B.C.

[Nephew of Ch'ü Yüan, and like his uncle a statesman and a poet.]

UNPOPULARITY

Among birds the phœnix, among fishes the leviathan
    holds the chiefest place;
Cleaving the crimson clouds
    the phœnix soars apace,
With only the blue sky above,
    far into the realms of space;
But the grandeur of heaven and earth
    is as naught to the hedge-sparrow race.
And the leviathan rises in one ocean
    to go to rest in a second,
While the depth of a puddle by a humble minnow
    as the depth of the sea is reckoned.
And just as with birds and fishes,
    so too it is with man;
Here soars a phœnix,
    there swims a leviathan.
Behold the philosopher, full of nervous thought,
    with a fame that never grows dim,
Dwelling complacently alone,—say,
    what can the vulgar herd know of him?

MEI SHÊNG

2ND CENTURY B.C.

[Statesman and poet, of whose writings only nine short poems remain.]

1. NEGLECTED

Green grows the grass upon the bank,
The willow-shoots are long and lank;
A lady in a glistening gown
Opens the casement and looks down.
The roses on her cheek blush bright,
Her rounded arm is dazzling white;
A singing-girl in early life,
And now a careless roué's wife......
Ah, if he does not mind his own,
He'll find some day the bird has flown!

2. PARTED

The red hibiscus and the reed,
The fragrant flowers of marsh and mead,—
All these I gather as I stray,
As though for one now far away.
I strive to pierce with straining eyes
The distance that between us lies.
Alas that hearts which beat as one
Should thus be parted and undone!

T'AI TSUNG (LIU HÊNG)

DIED 156 B.C.

[Fourth Emperor of the Han dynasty, and a wise ruler. He is one of the 24 examples of filial piety, having waited on his sick mother for three years without changing his clothes.]

ON THE DEATH OF HIS FATHER

I look up, the curtains are there as of yore;
I look down, and there is the mat on the floor;
These things I behold, but the man is no more.

To the infinite azure his spirit has flown,
And I am left friendless, uncared-for, alone,
Of solace bereft, save to weep and to moan.

The deer on the hillside caressingly bleat,
And offer the grass for their young ones to eat,
While birds of the air to their nestlings bring meat.

But I a poor orphan must ever remain,
My heart, still so young, overburdened with pain
For him I shall never set eyes on again.

'Tis a well-worn old saying, which all men allow,
That grief stamps the deepest of lines on the brow:
Alas for my hair, it is silvery now!

Alas for my father, cut off in his pride!
Alas that no more I may stand by his side!
Oh where were the gods when that great hero died?

SHIH TSUNG (LIU CH'Ê)

156–87 B.C.

[Sixth Emperor of the Han dynasty. During his reign copper coins were cast, academical degrees were instituted, Greek music took the place of the old native art, and the calendar was scientifically reformed. Personally, he was a Taoist and made efforts to obtain an elixir of immortality.]

1. AMARI ALIQUID

The autumn blast drives the white scud in the sky,
Leaves fade, and wild geese sweeping south meet the eye;
The scent of late flowers fills the soft air above,
My heart full of thoughts of the lady I love.
In the river the barges for revel-carouse
Are lined by white waves which break over their bows;
Their oarsmen keep time to the piping and drumming. . . .
        Yet joy is as naught
        Alloyed by the thought
That youth slips away and that old age is coming.

2. GONE*

The sound of rustling silk is stilled,
With dust the marble courtyard filled;
No footfalls echo on the floor,
Fallen leaves in heaps block up the door . . .
For she, my pride, my lovely one is lost,
And I am left, in hopeless anguish tossed.

---

* Referring to the loss of a favourite concubine.

PAN CHIEH-YÜ

1st Century b.c.

[For a long time chief favourite of the Emperor Ch'êng Ti. "Chieh-yü" was a title conferred upon the concubine most distinguished for literary ability.]

THE AUTUMN FAN*

O fair white silk, fresh from the weaver's loom,
Clear as the frost, bright as the winter snow—
See! friendship fashions out of thee a fan,
Round as the round moon shines in heaven above;
At home, abroad, a close companion thou,
Stirring at every move the grateful gale;
And yet I fear, ah me! that autumn chills,
Cooling the dying summer's torrid rage,
Will see thee laid neglected on the shelf,
All thought of by-gone days, like them by-gone.

ANONYMOUS

1st Century b.c.

1. CARPE DIEM

Man reaches scarce a hundred, yet his tears
Would fill a lifetime of a thousand years.
When days are short and night's long hours move slow,
Why not with lamp in search of pleasure go?
This day alone gives sure enjoyment—this!
Why then await to-morrow's doubtful bliss?

---

* This term is now used of a deserted wife.

Fools grudge to spend their wealth while life abides,
And then posterity their thrift derides.
We cannot hope, like Wang Tzŭ-ch'iao,* to rise
And find a paradise beyond the skies.

2. THE ELIXIR OF LIFE

Forth from the eastern gate my steeds I drive,
   And lo! a cemetery meets my view;
Aspens around in wild luxuriance thrive,
   The road is fringed with fir and pine and yew.
Beneath my feet lie the forgotten dead,
   Wrapped in a twilight of eternal gloom;
Down by the Yellow Springs† their earthy bed,
   And everlasting silence is their doom.
How fast the lights and shadows come and go!
   Like morning dew our fleeting life has passed;
Man, a poor traveller on earth below,
   Is gone, while brass and stone can still outlast.
Time is inexorable, and in vain
   Against his might the holiest mortal strives;
Can *we* then hope this precious boon to gain,
   By strange elixirs to prolong our lives? . . .
Oh, rather quaff good liquor while we may,
   And dress in silk and satin every day!

---

*A prince of the 6th century B.C., who rode up to heaven on the back of a crane. See Ts'ui Hao, p. 327.

† The Chinese Hades.

FÊNG YEN

1st Century a.d.

[A precocious boy—at 9 he could repeat the *Odes*—who entered official life under Wang Mang, the Usurper, and later on served under the first two Emperors of the E. Han dynasty. He left behind him a large collection of miscellaneous writings.]

"A BOLD PEASANTRY"

When you ride in a cart,
        let the wheels be your care;
In governing States,
        look well after the masses.
For just as a cart
        without wheels cannot fare,
So a State comes to grief
        if reduced to the classes.

ANONYMOUS

1st or 2nd Century a.d.

[From the *Yo fu* collection.]

1. TO A DEPARTING HUSBAND

Drawn by brave steeds thy chariot
        out on its way has set;
My heart will always follow thee
        and never can forget.
Upon thy western journey now
        I wish thee all repose. . . . .
Ah, would I were thy shadow, dear,
        that I might follow close!

But a gloom has closed around thee,
        and thy shadow is not near.
Oh, pass into the light of day
        and once again appear!

2. A WAITING WIFE

Boom!—Boom!—the thunder peals;
A sense of happening o'er me steals.
I turn my ear to catch the sound—
'Tis not thy chariot-wheels!

3. "WHAT IS FRIENDSHIP BUT A NAME?"

I had a friend, a school-boy chum,
    And hand in hand we took our way;
But he to higher things has come,
    And I am left alone to-day.

4. A TRYST

In the snow on the mountain
        a hero is sitting. . . .
Through the forest by moonlight
        a maiden is flitting. . . .

5. LOVE'S SWAY

When Love has carried off the heart
        ten thousand miles away,
The glittering starlit sky above
        seems reft of every ray.

K'UNG JUNG

DIED A.D. 208.

[A descendant from Confucius in the 20th Generation, and an anti-prohibitionist. "If my halls are full of guests," he said, "and my jars are full of wine, I am happy." He was put to death by Ts'ao Ts'ao. See p. 199.]

A FIRST-BORN

The wanderer reaches home with joy
   From absence of a year and more;
His eye seeks a beloved boy—
   His wife lies weeping on the floor.

They whisper he is gone. The glooms
   Of evening fall; beyond the gate
A lonely grave in outline looms
   To greet the sire who came too late.

Forth to the little mound he flings,
   Where wild-flowers bloom on every side . . .
His bones are in the Yellow Springs,
   His flesh like dust is scattered wide.

"O child who never knew thy sire,
   For ever now to be unknown,
Ere long thy wandering ghost shall tire
   Of flitting friendless and alone.

"O son, man's greatest earthly boon,
   With thee I bury hopes and fears."
He bowed his head in grief and soon
   His breast was wet with rolling tears.

Life's dread uncertainty he knows,
But oh for this untimely close!

HSÜ KAN

2ND AND 3RD CENTURIES A.D.

[An official and poet who was ranked as one of the Seven Scholars of his day.]

AN ABSENT HUSBAND

O floating clouds that swim in heaven above
Bear on your wings these words to him I love. . . .
Alas, you float along nor heed my pain,
And leave me here to love and long in vain!
I see other dear ones to their homes return,
And for his coming shall not I too yearn?

Since my lord left—ah me, unhappy day!—
My mirror's dust has not been brushed away;
My heart, like running water, knows no peace,
But bleeds and bleeds forever without cease.*

FU YÜAN

3RD CENTURY A.D.

[A scholar and statesman who rose by the year 268 to be Censor and Imperial Chamberlain. He was of such an eager disposition that whenever he had any Memorial to submit to the Emperor he would proceed at once to the palace, at no matter what hour of the day or night, and sit there until audience at the following dawn. Thus he caught the chill of which he died. Seven only of his poems are still extant.]

LOVE IMPETUOUS

The lover and maiden are fair to be seen;
Though close are their homes, there are mountains
between
With a cloud for a car and the wind for a horse,
The lover and maiden might meet in due course,

---

* See Chang Chiu-ling, p. 324.

But clouds are uncertain, and breezes may drop,
While love is impatient and suffers no stop.

TS'AO CHIH

A.D. 192–232.

[Son of the great Ts'ao Ts'ao, and like Hsü Kan one of the Seven Scholars of his day.   He is said to have composed an impromptu stanza while walking only seven steps; reminding us of Lucilius, who threw off two hundred lines *stans pede in uno*.]

THE BROTHERS

A fine dish of beans had been placed in the pot
With a view to a good mess of pottage, all hot.
The beanstalks, aflame, a fierce heat were begetting,
The beans in the pot were all fuming and fretting.
Yet the beans and the stalks were not born to be foes;
Oh why should these hurry to finish off those ?

LIU KUN

DIED A.D. 317.

[A distinguished military commander.   While defending the city of Chin-yang against the Tartars, with no prospect of holding out, he mounted a tower by moon-light and played on the Tartar pipe.   The besiegers were so overcome by their emotions and thoughts of home that next morning they raised the siege.]

A BARMAID

A rainbow at morning was bridging the sky,
And fragrant a stream full of lilies hard by,
When lo! I beheld a young maid of fifteen,
Who stood, sweetly smiling, behind the canteen.

She outshone the flowers which blossomed around;
Men grudged that her shadow should fall on the
                                    ground;
So peerless her beauty and youth,—in a trice
I found I had paid for my wine double price!

FU MI

3RD AND 4TH CENTURIES A.D.

1. LOVERS PARTED

In the Kingdom of Yen
                    a young gallant resides,
In the Kingdom of Chao
                    a fair damsel abides;
No long leagues of wearisome
                    road intervene,
But a chain of steep mountains
                    is set in between.
Ye clouds, on your broad bosoms
                    bear me afar,
The winds for my horses
                    made fast to my car!
Ah, jade lies deep hid
                    in the bowels of earth;
To the fair epidendrum
                    the prairie gives birth;
And the clouds in the sky,
                    they come not at call;
And the fickle breeze rises,
                    alas, but to fall.
And so I am left
                    with my thoughts to repine,
And think of that loved one
                    who ne'er can be mine.

2. AFTER PARTING

Thy chariot and horses
        have gone, and I fret
And long for the lover
        I ne'er can forget.

O wanderer, bound
        in far countries to dwell,
Would I were thy shadow!—
        I'd follow thee well.

And though clouds and though darkness
        my presence should hide,
In the bright light of day
        I would stand by thy side!

ANONYMOUS

TRUE PLEASURES

The bright moon shining overhead,
  The stream beneath the breeze's touch,
Are pure and perfect joys indeed,—
  But few are they who think them such.

T'AO CH'IEN (T'AO YÜAN-MING)

A.D. 365–427.

[A magistrate who held office for only 83 days, resigning on the ground that he could not "crook the hinges of his back for five pecks of rice a day," his official salary. In private life he occupied himself with writing beautiful poetry, with music and flowers. He even composed his own funeral oration.]

1. A PORTRAIT*

A scholar lives on yonder hill,
   His clothes are rarely whole to view,
Nine times a month he eats his fill,
   Once in ten years his hat is new.
A wretched lot!—and yet the while
He ever wears a sunny smile.

Longing to know what like was he,
   At dawn my steps a path unclosed
Where dark firs left the passage free
   And on the eaves the white clouds dozed.

But he, when spying my intent,
    Seized his guitar and swept the strings;
Up flew a crane towards heaven bent,
   And now a startled pheasant springs. . . .

Oh, I would live beside my friend—
   But not beyond the summer's end.

2. A PRAYER

Ye fluttering birds in plumage gay
   That to and fro direct your flight,—

---

* This poem is meant as a description of the writer.

The Western Mother's* court by day,
  The far-off mountain-peaks at night,—
Oh, be my messengers and go
  And bear to her these words of mine:
I ask for nothing here below
  Save length of years and depth of wine!

3. SIC TRANSIT

A tower a hundred feet erect
  Looks round upon the scene which girds;
'Tis here at eve the clouds collect,
  At dawn a trysting-place for birds.

Here hills and streams the observer hold,
  Or boundless prairie mocks the eyes:
Some famous warriors of old
  Made this their bloody battle-prize.

The centuries of time roll on,
  And I, a traveller, passing there,
Mark firs and cypresses all gone,
  And grave-mounds, high and low, laid bare.

The ruined tombs uncared-for stand—
  Where do their wandering spirits hide?—
Oh, glory makes us great and grand,
  And yet it has its seamy side.

---

* Now known to be Hera (Juno). See *Adversaria Sinica*, 1st Series, p. 1 and p. 298.

PAO CHAO

Died a.d. 466.

[An official and well-known poet.   He was killed in a rebellion.]

ALONE

What do these halls of jasper mean,
                    and shining floor,
Where tapestries of satin screen
                    window and door?
A lady on a lonely seat,
                    embroidering
Fair flowers which seem to smell as sweet
                    as buds in spring.
Swallows flit past, a zephyr shakes
                    the plum-blooms down;
She draws the blind, a goblet takes
                    her thoughts to drown.
And now she sits in tears, or hums,
                    nursing her grief
That in her life joy rarely comes
                    to bring relief. . . . . . .
Oh for the humble turtle's flight,
                    my mate and I;
Not the lone crane far out of sight
                    beyond the sky!

CHIANG YEN

A.D. 443–504.

[A statesman and voluminous writer.　He is responsible for the first biography of a woman ever published in China.]

FORGOTTEN

To learn the art of fencing, forth
I wandered, with my master, north.
I saw an ancient battle-plain
Engirt by hills which still remain;
And while I gazed upon the scene,
A wide expanse of sky and green,
I thought how like a summer's day
Each warrior's name has passed away.

WU TI (HSIAO YEN)

A.D. 464–549.

[Founder in 502 of the Liang dynasty.　A devout Buddhist, he interpreted the commandment "Thou shalt not kill!" in its strictest sense, and caused the sacrificial victims to be made of dough.　Under stress of rebellion, he took refuge in a monastery and died there of want and mortification.]

1. "IN THE SPRING......"

At the steps I am met
　　　　by a scent-laden breeze;
The flowers in the court-yard
　　　　are smiling their best.
When the mind is affected
　　　　by spring thoughts like these,
Do you wonder that passion
　　　　flames up in my breast?

2. ULTIMATE CAUSES

Trees grow, not alike,
                    by the mound and the moat;
Birds sing in the forest
                    with varying note;
Of the fish in the river
                    some dive and some float;
The mountains rise high
                    and the waters sink low,
But the why and the wherefore
                    we never can know.

LIU HSIAO-WEI

6TH CENTURY A.D.

[An official in the service of the Prince of Chin-an.   He died of disease during the campaign against the rebel, Hou Ching, A.D. 552.]

AT FIRST SIGHT

A couple of love-birds philandering nigh;
The moon intermittently seen in the sky . . .
Stay, who is the beauty with flowers in her hand,
Whose eyes and whose eyebrows my senses command?
Rich blues and bright greens shine behind the glass door,
And a casket of jade contains raiment galore;
The maiden herself is quite young, I believe,
For she blushes and smiles as the wind flirts her sleeve.

.   .   .   .

The bolt to the crossbow can never return,
And how quench the passion with which I now burn?

HSIEH TAO-HÊNG

6TH AND 7TH CENTURIES A.D.

[A statesman noted for his brilliant scholarship. He was called the Confucius of the West, a title which had already been given to a greater scholar of the 2nd Century A.D. He managed to offend the Emperor, and was put to death.]

ANTICIPATION

A week in the spring to the exile appears
Like an absence from home of a couple of years.
If home, with the wild geese of autumn, we're going,
Our hearts will be off ere the spring flowers are blowing.

WANG CHI

6TH AND 7TH CENTURIES A.D.

[A strange, unconventional philosopher and poet; author, among other works, of a skit entitled "Drunk-Land." His career was marred by drunkenness, for which the disturbed and dangerous times may be pleaded as some excuse.]

1. TO A KILL-JOY

Indulgence in the flowing bowl
Impedes the culture of the soul;
And yet, when all around me swill,
Shall I alone be sober still?

2. IN ABSENCE

At eve, I stand upon the bank and gaze;
  Restless, I know not where my bark may rest;
I see the forest through the autumn haze;
  I see the hills of radiance all divest;

I see the herdsman homing o'er the lea;
  I see the huntsman's laden horse return. . . . . .
Alas, no loved one comes to beckon me!—
  I sit and croon the thoughts that in me burn.

WANG PIEH

A.D. 648–676.

[A precocious scholar, who began to compose at the age of six and took his degree at sixteen. Employed on the dynastic annals, he offended by denouncing the Emperor's fondness for cockfighting and was dismissed. Thereafter he occupied himself with getting drunk and writing poetry—in that order. He was drowned on his way to Cochin China to see his banished father.]

ICHABOD

Near the islands a palace was built by a prince,
But its music and song have departed long since;
The hill-mists of morning sweep down on the halls,
At night the red curtains lie furled on the walls.
The clouds o'er the water their shadows still cast,
Things change like the stars: how few autumns have
                passed
And yet where is that prince?   Where is he?—No reply,
Save the plash of the stream rolling ceaselessly by.

CH'ÊN TZŬ-ANG

A.D. 656–698.

[After a youth spent in hunting and gambling, he became an intimate adviser of
the famous Empress Wu who appeared in the Council Chamber wearing a false beard
and subsequently took the title of "God Almighty." Arrested on a trumped-up
charge, he died in prison.]

1. REGRETS

My eyes saw not the men of old;
And now their age away has rolled
I weep—to think I shall not see
The heroes of posterity!

2. AGAINST IDOLS

On Self the Prophet* never rests his eye,
    His to relieve the doom of humankind;
No fairy palaces beyond the sky,
    Rewards to come, are present to his mind.

And I have heard the faith by Buddha taught
    Lauded as pure and free from earthly taint;
Why then these carved and graven idols, fraught
    With gold and silver, gems, and jade, and paint?

The heavens that roof this earth, mountain and dale,
    All that is great and grand shall pass away;
And if the art of gods may not prevail,
    Shall man's poor handiwork escape decay?

Fools that ye are! In this ignoble light
The true faith fades and passes out of sight.

* This term includes the rulers under the Golden Age, Confucius, Mencius, and
any other divinely-inspired teacher of the cardinal virtues.

HO CHIH-CHANG

Born a.d. 659.

[Poet and official who rose to be Director of the Imperial Library. He was one of the Eight Immortals of the Wine-cup, and the Emperor called him Devil Ho. Once, when drunk, he fell into a dry well and was found snoring at the bottom.]

THE RETURN

Bowed down with age I seek my native place,
Unchanged my speech, my hair is silvered now;
My very children do not know my face,
But smiling ask, "O stranger, whence art thou?"

SUNG CHIH-WÊN

Died a.d. 710.

[A brilliant poet who had a disreputable career as an official. He was ultimately forced to commit suicide.]

1. A VISION

The dust of the morn had been laid by a shower,
And the trees by the bridge were all covered with flower,
When a white palfrey passed with a saddle of gold,
And a damsel as fair as the fairest of old.

But she veiled so discreetly her charms from my eyes
That the boy who was with her quite felt for my sighs;
And although not a light-o'-love reckoned, I deem,
It was hard that this vision should pass like a dream.*

---

* Set to music by Cyril Scott.

2. "THIS GENTLEMAN"*

There, on the banks of a verdant pool,
    with leaves of selfsame hue
And all its slender grace of form,
    he reared the tall bamboo.

But time sped on; no phœnix came
    the precious fruit to taste;
For far from haunts of man they soar
    across the mountain's waste.†

And so, still young, with eager heart
    he fled the vulgar crowd,
Back to the hills true joys to find
    in every fleecy cloud.

And then, while silently he sat
    and nursed his conscious pride,
Not for a day "this gentleman"
    was absent from his side.

CHANG CHIU-LING

A.D. 673–740.

[Statesman and poet; one of the first officials of the newly-instituted Han-lin College. On an Imperial birthday, when others presented costly articles, he offered only a collection of wise precepts.]

1. BY MOONLIGHT

Over the sea the round moon rises bright,
And floods the horizon with its silver light.
In absence lovers grieve that nights should be,
But all the livelong night I think of thee.

---

* A name given to the bamboo by Wang Hui-chih (died A.D. 388), in whose memory this poem was written.

† Suggesting that Wang was unequal to official life.

I blow my lamp out to enjoy this rest,
And shake the gathering dewdrop from my vest.
Alas! I cannot share with thee these beams,
So lay me down to seek thee in my dreams.

2. AN ABSENT HUSBAND*

Since my lord left—ah me, unhappy hour!—
The half-spun web hangs idly in my bower;
My heart is like the full moon, full of pains,
Save that 'tis always full and never wanes.

MÊNG HAO-JAN

A.D. 689–740.

[After failing at the public Examinations, he retired to the mountains and led the life of a hermit, producing poetry of the first order.]

1. WAITING

The sun has sunk behind the western hill,
   And darkness glides across the vale below;
Between the firs the moon shines cold and chill,
   No breezes whisper to the streamlet's flow.
Belated woodsmen homeward hurry past,
   Birds seek their evening refuge in the tree:
O my beloved, wilt thou come at last?
   With lute, among the flowers, I wait for thee.†

---

* See Hsü Kan, p. 310.
† Set to music by Cyril Scott.

2. IN DREAMLAND

The sun has set behind the western slope,
  The eastern moon lies mirrored in the pool;
With streaming hair my balcony I ope,
  And stretch my limbs out to enjoy the cool.
Loaded with lotus-scent the breeze sweeps by,
  Clear dripping drops from tall bamboos I hear,
I gaze upon my idle lute and sigh:
  Alas no sympathetic soul is near!
And so I doze, the while before mine eyes
Dear friends of other days in dream-clad forms arise.

3. AT ANCHOR

I steer my boat to anchor
                    by the mist-clad river eyot,
And mourn the dying day that brings me
                    nearer to my fate.
Across the woodland wild I see
                    the sky lean on the trees,
While close to hand the mirrored moon
                    floats on the shining seas.

LI SHIH-CHIH

DIED A.D. 747.

[A Minister of State and one of the Eight Immortals of the Wine-cup.　Falling into disfavour, he committed suicide by poison.]

OUT OF OFFICE

For my betters—my office resigned—I make way,
And seek with the wine-cup to shorten the day.
You ask for the friends who once thronged in my hall:
Alas! with my place they have gone, one and all.

WANG WEI

A.D. 699–759.

[Famous as a poet and a painter; also, as a physician.　His poems (like Livy's pages) were said to contain pictures, and his pictures to contain poems.　After a brief official career, he went into seclusion.]

1. OVERLOOKED

Beneath the bamboo grove, alone,
　I seize my lute and sit and croon;
No ear to hear me, save mine own;
　No eye to see me, save the moon.

2. GOODBYE

We parted at the gorge and cried "Good cheer!"
The sun was setting as I closed my door;
Methought, the spring will come again next year,
　But he may come no more.

3. A RENCONTRE

Sir, from my dear old home you come,
    And all its glories you can name;
Oh tell me,—has the winter-plum
    Yet blossomed o'er the window-frame?

4. GOODBYE TO MÊNG HAO-JAN

Dismounted, o'er wine we had said our last say;
Then I whisper, "Dear friend, tell me whither away."
"Alas!" he replied, "I am sick of life's ills
"And I long for repose on the slumbering hills.
"But oh seek not to pierce where my footsteps may stray:
"The white clouds will soothe me for ever and ay."

TS‘UI HAO

8TH CENTURY A.D.

[A poet, a wine-bibber, and a gambler.]

HOME LONGINGS

Here a mortal once sailed up to heaven on a crane,*
And the Yellow-Crane Kiosque will for ever remain;†
But the bird flew away and will come back no more,
Though the white clouds are there as the white clouds of
        yore.
Away to the east lie fair forests of trees,
From the flowers on the west comes a scent-laden breeze,

---

* See "Carpe Diem," p. 305.

† It was standing until quite recently, though probably several times restored.

Yet my eyes daily turn to their far-away home,
Beyond the broad River, its waves, and its foam.

LI PO

A.D. 705–762.

[Regarded by many as China's greatest poet, and popularly known as "The Banished Angel." He flourished at a dissolute Court, himself one of its most dissolute members. He was a founder of the drunken club called the Six Idlers of the Bamboo Brook, and also belonged to the Eight Immortals of the Wine-cup. He is said to have been drowned by leaning over the gunwale of a boat in a drunken effort to embrace the reflection of the moon.]

1. TO A FIREFLY*

Rain cannot quench thy lantern's light,
Wind makes it shine more brightly bright;
Oh why not fly to heaven afar,
And twinkle near the moon—a star?

2. AT PARTING

The river rolls crystal as clear as the sky,
To blend far away with the blue waves of ocean;
Man alone, when the hour of departure is nigh,
With the wine cup can soothe his emotion.
The birds of the valley sing loud in the sun,
Where the gibbons their vigils will shortly be keeping;
I thought that with tears I had long ago done,
But now I shall never cease weeping.

---

* An impromptu, at the age of ten.

3. NIGHT THOUGHTS

I wake, and moonbeams play around my bed,
Glittering like hoar-frost to my wondering eyes;
Up towards the glorious moon I raise my head,
Then lay me down—and thoughts of home arise.

4. COMPANIONS

The birds have all flown to their roost in the tree,
    The last cloud has just floated lazily by;
But we never tire of each other, not we,
    As we sit there together—the mountains and I.

5. FROM A BELVEDERE

With yellow leaves the hill is strown,
    A young wife gazes o'er the scene,
The sky with grey clouds overthrown,
    While autumn swoops upon the green.

See, Tartar troops mass on the plain;
    Homeward our envoy hurries on;
When will her lord come back again? . . . .
    To find her youth and beauty gone!

6. FOR HER HUSBAND

Homeward, at dusk, the clanging rookery wings its eager flight;
Then, chattering on the branches, all are pairing for the night.
Plying her busy loom, a high-born dame is sitting near,
And through the silken window-screen their voices strike her
        ear.

She stops, and thinks of the absent spouse she may never see
        again;
And late in the lonely hours of night her tears flow down like
        rain.

7. "THE BEST OF LIFE IS BUT ..."

What is life after all but a dream?
    And why should such pother be made?
Better far to be tipsy, I deem,
    And doze all day long in the shade.

When I wake and look out on the lawn,
    I hear midst the flowers a bird sing;
I ask, "Is it evening or dawn?"
    The mango-bird whistles, "'Tis spring."

Overpower'd with the beautiful sight,
    Another full goblet I pour,
And would sing till the moon rises bright—
    But soon I'm as drunk as before.

8. FAREWELL BY THE RIVER

The breeze blows the willow-scent in from the dell,
    While Phyllis with bumpers would fain cheer us up;
Dear friends press around me to bid me farewell:
    Goodbye! and goodbye!—and yet just one more
        cup. . . .
I whisper, Thou'lt see this great stream flow away
Ere I cease to love as I love thee to-day!

9. GONE

At the Yellow-Crane pagoda,* where we stopped to bid adieu,
The mists and flowers of April seemed to wish good speed to you.
At the Emerald Isle, your lessening sail had vanished from my
      eye,
And left me with the River, rolling onward to the sky.

10. NO INSPIRATION

The autumn breeze is blowing,
The autumn moon is glowing,
  The falling leaves collect but to disperse.
The parson-crow flies here and there
    with ever restless feet;
I think of you and wonder much
    when you and I shall meet......
  Alas to-night I cannot pour my feelings
    forth in verse!

11. GENERAL HSIEH AN

I anchor at the Newchew hill,
The autumn sky serene and still,
And watch the moon her crescent fill,
And vainly think on him by whom
    this shore was made renowned.†
Though mine is no ungraceful lay,
He cannot hear the words I say,
And I must sail at break of day......
And all this while the maple leaves
    are fluttering to the ground.

* See Ts'ui Hao, p. 327.

† Referring to the meeting at this spot of the General (A.D. 320–385) with Yüan Hung, a distinguished scholar and statesman.

12. A SNAP-SHOT

A tortoise I see on a lotus-flower resting;
A bird 'mid the reeds and the rushes is nesting;
A light skiff propelled by some boatman's fair daughter,
Whose song dies away o'er the fast-flowing water.*

13. A FAREWELL

Where blue hills cross the northern sky,
   Beyond the moat which girds the town,
'Twas there we stopped to say Goodbye!
   And one white sail alone dropped down.
Your heart was full of wandering thought;
   For me,—my sun had set indeed;
To wave a last adieu we sought,
   Voiced for us by each whinnying steed!

14. BOYHOOD FANCIES†

In days gone by the moon appeared
   to my still boyish eyes
Some bright jade plate or mirror from
   the palace of the skies.
I used to see the Old Man's legs
   and Cassias fair as god can make them,
I saw the White Hare pounding drugs,
   and wondered who was there to take them.
Ah, how I watched the eclipsing Toad,
   and marked the ravages it made,

---

* Set to music by J. Alden Carpenter.

† Chinese fable says that the moon is inhabited by a huge toad which occasionally swallows it; hence eclipses. Also, that there are groves of cassia, and a hare visible to the naked eye, engaged in preparing the drug of immortality.

And longed for him who slew the suns
    and all the angels' fears allayed.*
Then when the days of waning came,
    and scarce a silver streak remained,
I wept to lose my favourite thus,
    and cruel grief my eyelids stained.

15. FROM THE PALACE

Cold dews of night the terrace crown,
And soak my stockings and my gown;
    I'll step behind
    The crystal blind,
And watch the autumn moon sink down.

16. THE POET

You ask what my soul does away in the sky,
I inwardly smile but I cannot reply;
Like the peach-blossom carried away by the stream,
I soar to a world of which you cannot dream.

17. TEARS

A fair girl draws the blind aside
    And sadly sits with drooping head;
I see her burning tear-drops glide
    But know not why those tears are shed.

---

* The legendary archer, Hou I, who, when a number of false suns appeared in the sky, to the great detriment of the crops, shot at and destroyed them with his arrows.

18. A FAVOURITE*

Oh the joy of youth spent in a gold-fretted hall,
In the Crape-flower Pavilion, the fairest of all,
My tresses for headdress with gay garlands girt,
Carnations arranged o'er my jacket and skirt!
Then to wander away in the soft-scented air,
And return by the side of his Majesty's chair. . . .
But the dance and the song will be o'er by and by,
And we shall dislimn like the rack in the sky.

19. IN EXILE

I drink deep draughts of Lan-ling wine
                fragrant with borage made,
The liquid amber mantling up
                in cups of costly jade.
My host insists on making me
                as drunk as any sot,
Until I'm quite oblivious
                of the exile's wretched lot.

20. ANTI-PUSSYFOOT

If God does not love wine,
    Why shine the wine-star† in the sky?
If Earth does not love wine,
    Her flowing wine-spring‡ should be dry.
And since unharmed these Powers combine
    To love the wine-cup, so will I.

---

* One of ten stanzas thrown off by the poet when tipsy and concealed behind a pink silk screen held up by two ladies of the seraglio.

† First mentioned in the 2nd Century A.D. A poet of the 8th Century said:
    You cannot pour the wine-star's wine,
    Nor eat the cassia of the moon.

‡ Mentioned several centuries B.C., and placed by Yen Shih-ku (died A.D. 645) in the province of Kansuh.

21. IN A MIRROR

My whitening hair would make a long long rope,
  Yet could not fathom all my depth of woe;
Though how it comes within a mirror's scope
  To sprinkle autumn frosts, I do not know.

22. LAST WORDS

An arbour of flowers
             and a kettle of wine:
Alas! in the bowers
             no companion is mine.

Then the moon sheds her rays
             on my goblet and me,
And my shadow betrays
             we're a party of three!

Though the moon cannot swallow
             her share of the grog,
And my shadow must follow
             wherever I jog,

Yet their friendship I'll borrow
             and gaily carouse,
And laugh away sorrow
             while spring-time allows.

See the moon—how she glances
             response to my song;
See my shadow—it dances
             so lightly along!

While sober I feel,
             you are both my good friends;
When drunken I reel,
             our companionship ends,

But we'll soon have a greeting
              without a goodbye,
At our next merry meeting
              away in the sky.

TU FU

A.D. 712–770.

[A poet whose fame rivalled—many say eclipsed—that of the great Li Po. He had indeed such a high opinion of his own poetry that he prescribed it for malarial fever. After serving without success as Censor, and secretary in the Board of Works, he resigned and took up a wandering life, finally dying from the effects of starvation during a flood, followed by over-indulgence in roast beef and white wine.]

1. IN ABSENCE

White gleam the gulls across the darkling tide,
   On the green hills the red flowers seem to burn;
Alas! I see another spring has died . . .
   When will it come—the day of my return?

2. WINE

The setting sun shines low upon my door
   Ere dusk enwraps the river fringed with spring;
Sweet perfumes rise from gardens by the shore,
   And smoke, where crews their boats to anchor bring.
Now twittering birds are roosting in the bower,
   And flying insects fill the air around . . .
O wine, who gave to thee thy subtle power?—
   A thousand cares in one small goblet drowned!

3. TO HIS BROTHER

The evening drum has emptied every street,
One autumn goose screams on its frontier flight,
The crystal dew is glittering at my feet,
The moon sheds, as of old, her silvery light.

The brothers,—ah, where are they? Scattered each;
No home whence one might learn the other's harms.
Letters have oft miscarried: shall they reach
Now when the land rings with the clash of arms?

4. A LANDSCAPE

Two orioles sit in the green willows singing;
See egrets in flight to the blue sky are winging!
From my window the snow-peaks eternal I spy,
And an ocean-bound vessel is anchored hard by.

5. HOME JOYS

My home is girdled by a limpid stream,
    And there in summer days life's movements pause,
Save where some swallow flits from beam to beam,
    And the wild sea-gull near and nearer draws.

The goodwife rules a paper board for chess;
    The children beat a fish-hook out of wire;
My ailments call for physic more or less,
    What else should this poor frame of mine require?

6. SSU-MA HSIANG-JU*

'Twas here, from sickness sore oppressed,
He found relief on Wên-chün's breast;
'Twas here the vulgar tavern lay
On mountain cloud-capped night and day.
And still mid flowers and leaves I trace
Her fluttering robe, her tender face;
But ah! the phœnix calls in vain,
Such mate shall not be seen again.

7. THE HERMIT

Alone I wandered o'er the hills
        to seek the hermit's den,
While sounds of chopping rang around
        the forest's leafy glen.
I passed on ice across the brook
        which had not ceased to freeze,
As the slanting rays of afternoon
        shot sparkling through the trees.

I found he did not joy to gloat
        o'er fetid wealth by night,
But far from taint, to watch the deer
        in the golden morning light. . . .
My mind was clear at coming;
        but now I've lost my guide,
And rudderless my little bark
        is drifting with the tide!†

---

* A poet of the 2nd Century B.C. who eloped with a beautiful young widow and was driven to keep a tavern until the father-in-law relented.

† Hinting that he is now contemplating a hermit's life himself.

8. SUPERSEDED

Alas for the lonely plant that grows
              beside the river bed,
While the mango-bird screams loud and long
              from the tall tree overhead!
Full with the freshets of the spring,
              the torrent rushes on;
The ferry-boat swings idly, for
              the ferryman is gone.*

9. SOLO CHI SEGUE CIÒ CHE PIACE E SAGGIO

A petal falls!—the spring begins to fail,
And my heart saddens with the growing gale.
Come then, ere autumn spoils bestrew the ground,
Do not forget to pass the wine-cup round.
Kingfishers build where man once laughed elate,
And now stone dragons guard his graveyard gate!
Who follows pleasure, he alone is wise;
Why waste our life in deeds of high emprise?

10. DUM RES ET AETAS

From the court every eve to the pawnshop I pass,
    To come back from the river the drunkest of men;
As often as not I'm in debt for my glass;—
    Well, few of us live to be threescore and ten.
The butterfly flutters from flower to flower,
    The dragon-fly sips and springs lightly away,

---

* A specimen of political allegory. The "lonely plant" refers to a virtuous statesman for whom the time is out of joint, like Lord Rosebery and his "lonely furrow." The "mango-bird" is a worthless politician in power. The "ferry-boat" is our ship of State.

Each creature is merry its brief little hour,
  So let us enjoy our short life while we may.

11. A PICNIC

The sun is setting as we loose the boat,
And lightly o'er the breeze-swept waters float.
We seek a corner where the bamboo grows,
And fragrant lilies offer cool repose.
Here well-iced draughts of wine the men prepare,
With lotus shredded fine by fingers fair. . . .
But now a black cloud gathering in the sky
Warns me to finish off my verse and fly.*

12. THE PRESSGANG

There, where at eve I sought a bed,
  A pressgang came, recruits to hunt;
Over the wall the goodman sped,
  And left his wife to bear the brunt.

Ah me! the cruel serjeant's rage!
  Ah me! how sadly she anon
Told all her story's mournful page,—
  How three sons to the war had gone;

How one had sent a line to say
  That two had been in battle slain:
He, from the fight had run away,
  But they could ne'er come back again.

She swore 'twas all the family—
  Except a grandson at the breast;
His mother too was there, but she
  Was all in rags and tatters drest.

* Set to music by Cyril Scott.

The crone with age was troubled sore,
　　But for herself she'd not think twice
To journey to the seat of war
　　And help to cook the soldiers' rice.

The night wore on and stopped her talk;
　　Then sobs upon my hearing fell. . . .
At dawn when I set forth to walk,
　　Only the goodman cried Farewell!

CH'ANG CHIEN

8TH CENTURY A.D.

[A poet who in 727 took the highest degree and entered into official life, but ultimately retired to the mountains as a hermit.]

DHYANA*

The clear dawn creeps into the convent old,
The rising sun tips its tall trees with gold,—
As, darkly, by a winding path I reach
Dhyâna's hall, hidden midst fir and beech.
Around these hills sweet birds their pleasure take,
Man's heart as free from shadows as this lake;
Here worldly sounds are hushed, as by a spell,
Save for the booming of the altar bell.

---

* A state of mental abstraction, by recourse to which the Buddhist gradually shakes off all desire for sublunary existence. In every monastery there is a hall in which priests may be seen sitting for hours together with their eyes closed.

HSÜ HSÜAN-P'ING

8TH CENTURY A.D.

[A singular being, who in 708 retired to the mountains and tried to live without eating, but not without drinking, as the following verse of which he himself was the woodman-hero will show. The poet, Li Po, tried to find him, but without success.]

"BACCHE, PLENUM TUI"

In the morning my woodman will sell his load,
And he'll buy his wine on his homeward road.
You ask where the home of my pedlar lies. . . .
The home of that man is in Paradise!

CHIA CHIH

A.D. 718–772.

[Poet and statesman with a chequered career.]

SPRING SORROWS

The willow sprays are yellow fringed,
        the grass is gaily green;
Peach-blooms in wild confusion with
        the perfumed plum are seen;
The eastern breeze sweeps past me, yet
        my sorrows never go,
And the lengthening days of spring to me
        mean lengthening days of woe.

WEI YING-WU

8TH CENTURY A.D.

[In early life a soldier; later, after a course of study, he entered upon a civil career. His poetry has been described as "simple in expression, pregnant with meaning."]

1. AN ABSENT HUSBAND

The oriole trills its little lay,
Orchids around in wild array,
What time the wife, immured behind,
Sees sunlight pierce the muslin blind.
Her lovely eyebrows, mothlike made,
Her parted lips, her teeth of jade. . . .
She sighs to think that peach and plum
Bloom while her hero may not come;
Since parting, time has sadly fled:
Is he indeed alive or dead?

2. SPRING JOYS

When freshets cease in early spring
      and the river dwindles low,
I take my staff and wander
      by the banks where wild flowers grow.
I watch the willow-catkins
      wildly whirled on every side;
I watch the falling peach-bloom
      lightly floating down the tide.

3. REMEMBRANCES

In autumn, when the nights are chill,
    I stroll, and croon, and think of thee.

When dropping pine-cones strew the hill,
Say, hast thou waking dreams of me?

4. A PROMISE

Sweet flowers were blooming all around
        when your last farewell you said,
And now the opening buds proclaim
        another year has fled.
'Tis difficult to prophesy
        beyond the present day,
And the remedy for trouble
        is to sleep it all away.
I suffer much in body,
        and I long for the old spot,
But cannot bring myself in pensioned
        idleness to rot.
You say that you will visit me,
        that you are coming soon:
'Twixt now and then how often
        shall I see the full-orbed moon?

HSÜ AN-CHÊN

8TH CENTURY A.D.

[An official who took the highest degree and was on intimate terms with the famous Emperor Ming Huang, whose literary draughts were always examined by him.]

MY NEIGHBOUR

When the Bear athwart was lying
And the night was just on dying,
And the moon was all but gone,
How my thoughts did ramble on!

Then a sound of music breaks
From a lute that some one wakes,
And I know that it is she,
The sweet maid next door to me.

And as the strains steal o'er me
Her moth-eyebrows* rise before me,
And I feel a gentle thrill
That her fingers must be chill.

But doors and locks between us
So effectually screen us
That I hasten from the street
And in dreamland pray to meet.

TS'ÊN TS'AN

8TH CENTURY A.D.

[Took the highest degree about the year 750, and rose to be a Censor.]

IN PRAISE OF BUDDHISM

A shrine, whose eaves in far-off cloudland hide:
I mount, and with the sun stand side by side.

The air is clear; I see wide forests spread
And mist-crowned heights where Kings of old lie dead.

Scarce o'er my threshold peeps the Southern Hill;
The Wei shrinks through my window to a rill. . . .

O thou Pure Faith, had I but known thy scope,
The Golden God had long since been my hope!

---

* Referring to the delicately curved eye-markings of the silkworm moth.

KÊNG WEI

8TH CENTURY A.D.

[An official and poet who took the highest degree in 762, and was one of the Ten Men of Genius of his day.   Two of his lines have become proverbial:
Hireling respect with loss of fortune ends,
And loss of influence means loss of friends.]

LONELY

The evening sun slants o'er the village street;
   My griefs alas! in solitude are borne;
Along the road no wayfarers I meet,—
   Naught but the autumn breeze across the corn.

LIU CH'ANG-CH'ING

8TH CENTURY A.D.

[Took the highest degree in the year 757, and rose to be a Censor and Judge.]

THE WASHERWOMAN'S GRAVE*

The hero ne'er forgot the meal she gave,—
   My tale is of a thousand years ago,—
And every woodsman knows the time-worn grave,
   Though naught remains of dynasties save the river's ceaseless
      flow.

With votive flower the traveller is seen,
   The while the grief-bird† trills his mournful lays;
Around, the grass of spring grows wildly green
   Where footprints of the "nobleman"‡ were left in bygone
      days.

---

* The great General of the 2nd Century B.C., Han Hsin, was saved from starving by a kindly washerwoman.   Later on he remembered and provided for his benefactress.

† The goatsucker or nightjar.

‡ As the washerwoman called Han Hsin, by a presentiment of his future greatness.

KA CHIA-YÜN

8TH CENTURY A.D.

[A Commissioner of Revenue about A.D. 725, who presented to the Emperor the stanza given below, though apparently not claiming it as his own composition.]

AT DAWN

Drive the young orioles away,
Nor let them on the branches play;
Their chirping breaks my slumber through
And keeps me from my dreams of you.

CHANG WEI

8TH CENTURY A.D.

[A poet who took the highest degree in 743 and rose to be President of the Board of Rites.]

NOSTALGIA

'Tis autumn, and I watch the streams
  Which towards my dear home flow;
I span the distance in my dreams,
  And wake to deeper woe.

I cannot read to ease my care,
  But solace seek in wine,
And think of friends all gathered there—
  When will that lot be mine?

WANG CH'ANG-LING

8TH CENTURY A.D.

[A poet who took the highest degree and entered official life.   He was killed in a rebellion.]

1. AT THE WARS

See the young wife whose bosom ne'er
        has ached with cruel pain!—
In gay array she mounts the tower
        when spring comes round again.
Sudden she sees the willow-trees
        their newest green put on,
And sighs for her husband far away
        in search of glory gone.

2. A MESSAGE

Onwards tonight my storm-beat course I steer,
  At dawn these mountains will for ever fade;
Should those I leave behind enquire my cheer,
  Tell them, "an icy heart in vase of jade."

HUANG-FU JÊN

8TH CENTURY A.D.

[Took the highest degree about the year 750 and entered official life. His poetry, which he began to write at the age of ten, was much admired by Chang Chiu-ling.]

SPRETÆ INJURIA FORMÆ

See! fair girls are flocking through corridors bright,
  With music and mirth borne along on the breeze......
Come, tell me if she who is favoured tonight
  Has eyebrows much longer than these?

TSU YUNG

8TH CENTURY A.D.

[An official who took the highest degree about the year 730, and rose to be a Secretary in the Board of Rites. His poetry is much admired.]

A GROTTO

Deep in a darksome grove their Grotto lies,
And deep the thoughts that now within me rise.
Fronting the door the South Hill looming near,
The forest mirrored in the river clear,
The bamboo bends beneath last winter's snow,
The court-yard darkens ere the day sinks low.
I seem to pass beyond this world of clay,
And sit and listen to the spring-bird's lay.

TS'UI HU

8TH OR 9TH CENTURY A.D.

[A poet of whom I can find no record.]

A RETROSPECT

Oh this day last year what a party were we
Pink cheeks and pink peach-blossoms smiled upon me;
But alas the pink cheeks are now far far away,
Though the peach-blossoms smile as they smiled on that day.

LIU T'ING-CHIH

CIRCA A.D. 800.

[A poet of whom I can find no record.]

"YOUTH AT THE PROW"

Beneath the bridge spring freshets hurry by;
Above, there passes many a cavalier;
The sound of trampling horses fills the sky,
And mirrored forms are dancing on the mere.

Beneath green waves the mud-banks turn to jade,
The setting sun paints the blue clouds with gold;
Alas, ye willow trees, for sorrow made!*
Alas, ye peach and plum, for grief enrolled!†

---

* Referring to the custom of giving a spray of willow at parting.

† There is a very old belief in China that the decay of a plum-tree is due to maggots from a peach-tree growing alongside.

Now is the time to seek the blooming fair,
Now is the hour to join the dance and song;
See how the lovely girls flit here and there,
Among the noble youths in lordly throng!

The pearl-sewn blind glints in the sunshine clear,
Pink cheeks make contrast with complexion blond;
Among the flowers two butterflies career,
I see two love-birds paddling in the pond.

I think of her whose glance could wreck a State,*
Of her whose lover came in mist and rain.†
Ah! beauty as of yore makes man elate,
And I to-day feel the old thrill again.

Oh, could I be the zone that clasps thy waist!—
Thy mirror, that thy beauty I might share!
Together always, by thy presence graced,
A single being, a united pair.

Oh, could we be some pure, some long-lived pine,
Unconscious of the life each spring renewed,
Each eve to watch the westering sun incline,
For ever happy in our solitude!

---

* "One glance from her would overthrow a city, a second a State,"—so beautiful was she—was said by the brother of Lady Li, concubine to the Emperor Wu Ti. 140–86 B.C.

† This refers to a dream by a Prince of Ch'u of the Goddess of Clouds and Rain who received him on Mt. Wu in Ssŭch'uan.

CH'ÜAN TÊ-YÜ

A.D. 759–818.

[Scholar and statesman.   It is recorded that he began to write verse at four years of age.]

HOPE

Last eve thou wert a bride,
　　This morn thy dream is o'er. . . . .
Cast not thy rouge aside,
　　He may be thine once more.

HAN YÜ (HAN WÊN-KUNG)

A.D. 768–824.

[One of China's greatest statesmen, who also occupies a foremost place as a writer and is popularly known as the Prince of Literature.   For his prose works, including his attack upon Buddhism, see p. 115.]

1. THE WOUNDED FALCON

Within a ditch beyond my wall
I saw a falcon headlong fall.
Bedaubed with mud and racked with pain,
It beat its wings to rise, in vain;
While little boys threw tiles and stones,
Eager to break the wretch's bones.
　O bird, methinks thy life of late
Hath amply justified this fate!
Thy sole delight to kill and steal,
And then exultingly to wheel,
Now sailing in the clear blue sky,
Now on the wild gale sweeping by.

Scorning thy kind of less degree
As all unfit to mate with thee.
　　But mark how fortune's wheel goes round;
A pellet lays thee on the ground,
Sore stricken at some vital part,—
And where is then thy pride of heart?
　　What's this to me?—I could not bear
To see the fallen one lying there.
I begged its life, and from the brook
Water to wash its wounds I took.
Fed it with bits of fish by day,
At night from foxes kept away.
My care I knew would naught avail
For gratitude, that empty tale.
And so this bird would crouch and hide
Till want its stimulus applied;
And I, with no reward to hope,
Allowed its callousness full scope.
　　Last eve the bird showed signs of rage,
With health renewed, and beat its cage.
Today it forced a passage through,
And took its leave, without adieu.
　　Good luck hath saved thee, not desert;
Beware, O bird, of further hurt;
Beware the archer's deadly tools!—
'Tis hard to scape the shafts of fools—
Nor e'er forget the chastening ditch
That found thee poor, and left thee rich.*

2. HOURS OF IDLENESS

A little lake of mine I know,
Where waving weeds and rushes grow,

---

* In experience of the vicissitudes of life.

And in its depths by day and night
The water-monsters swarm and fight.
Ah, how I loved to idle there!. . . .
But now I can no longer bear
To pass my days in that sweet spot,
And lost in meditation rot.
A sense of duty gives me pause,
Obedient to my Master's* laws;
Our span of life is all too short
To waste its hours in empty sport.

3. IN CAMP

Across the steppes the bitter north winds roam,
   At dawn the Tartar moon shines cold and bright;
My soul relapses into dreams of home,
   Till the loud rappel summons to the fight.

4. MEDITATIONS

The leaves fall fluttering from the trees,
And now, responsive to the breeze,
Rustling with weird uncanny sound,
Are dancing merrily around.
On my lone hall the dusk has come
And there I sit in silence dumb.
My servant glides into the room
And with a lamp dispels the gloom.
He speaks; I give him no reply.
He proffers food; in vain.   Then I
Move to escape his wondering looks
And seek a refuge in my books.

---

* Confucius, in whose Temple the tablet of Han Yü was placed in the year 1084.

Alas, the men who charm me so
Perished a thousand years ago!
And while I muse o'er human fate
My heart grows less and less elate . . .
"O boy, whose eyes stare from your head,
"Put up those books and get to bed,
"And leave me to the dreary naught
"Of endless, overwhelming thought."

5. DISCONTENT

To stand upon the river-bank
           and snare the purple fish,
My net well cast across the stream,
            was all that I could wish.
Or lie concealed and shoot the geese
            that scream and pass apace,
And pay my rent and taxes with
           the profits of the chase.
Then home to peace and happiness,
           with wife and children gay,
Though clothes be coarse and fare be hard,
           and earned from day to day.
But now I read and read, scarce knowing
           what 'tis all about,
And eager to improve my mind
           I wear my body out.
I draw a snake and give it legs,
           to find I've wasted skill,
And my hair grows daily whiter
           as I hurry towards the hill.*
I sit amid the sorrows
           I have brought on my own head,

---

* The Chinese prefer hillsides for their burying-grounds.

And find myself estranged from all,
        among the living dead.
I seek to drown my consciousness
        in wine, alas! in vain:
Oblivion passes quickly
        and my griefs begin again.
Old age comes on and yet withholds
        the summons to depart. . . .
So I'll take another bumper
        just to ease my aching heart.

6. HUMANITY

Oh spare the busy morning fly!
  Spare the mosquitoes of the night!
And if their wicked trade they ply
  Let a partition stop their flight.

Their span is brief from birth to death;
  Like you they bite their little day;
And then, with autumn's earliest breath,
Like you too they are swept away.

LI HO

A.D. 791–817.

[A poet and military official who was noted for his small waist, joined eyebrows, long finger-nails, and for the speed at which he could write. He began to compose poems at the age of seven.]

NEAERA'S TANGLES

With flowers on the ground like embroidery spread,
At twenty, the soft glow of wine in my head,
My white courser's bit-tassels motionless gleam
While the gold-threaded willow scent sweeps o'er the
        stream.
Yet until *she* has smiled all these flowers yield no ray;
When her tresses fall down, the whole landscape is gay;
My hand on her sleeve as I gaze in her eyes,
A kingfisher hairpin* will soon be my prize.

LIU YÜ-HSI

A.D. 772–842.

[A statesman with a chequered career of banishment and success, and also a poet who was such a purist that he left a beautiful piece unfinished because it was necessary to use the word *dumplings*, which was not to be found in the Confucian Canon. Po Chü-i called him a Hero of Song.]

1. SUMMER DYING

Whence comes the autumn's whistling blast,
With flocks of wild geese hurrying past? . . .
Alas, when wintry breezes burst,
The lonely traveller hears them first!

---

* Inlaid with kingfisher feathers, and much affected by the *demi-mondaine*.

2. THE ODALISQUE

A gaily dressed damsel steps forth from her bower,
    Bewailing the fate that forbids her to roam;
In the courtyard she counts up the buds on each flower,*
    While a dragon-fly flutters and sits on her comb.†

MU TSUNG (LI HÊNG)

A.D. 795–824.

[Written by the twelfth Emperor of the T'ang dynasty, while still Heir Apparent.
To the end of his life, which he brought to a premature close by a fatal dose of the
elixir of immortality, he remained always a puppet in the hands of his eunuchs.]

EUNUCH DOMINATION

Autumnal weeds sprout on my royal way‡
Though summer blossoms still the branches
        sway.
My crowding thoughts I hold within my
        breast,
Safe from the prying eyes of eunuch quest.

---

   * Having nothing better to do. The dragon-fly on the comb strikes a note of
loneliness.

   † Set to music by J. A. Carpenter.

   ‡ So long is it since the prince has cared to drive out in his chariot.

PO CHÜ-I

A.D. 772–846.

[One of China's greatest and most voluminous poets, and a successful statesman, with the usual ups and downs. He was a very precocious child, and took the highest degree at the early age of seventeen.]

1. "THE GAY LICENTIOUS CROWD"

With haughty mien they fill the ways,
And gorgeous gleam their saddletrees;
I ask, who are they?   Someone says,
            The Court officials these.

Scarlet-sashed ministers are there,
Red-tasselled generals in crowds;
Their minds are bent on sumptuous fare;
            Their steeds pass by like clouds.

Wine of the rarest brands they take;
Rich meats are set before their eyes,—
An orange from the Tung-t'ing lake,
            And fish from Paradise.

Serenely full, their greed assuaged,
Half-drunken, and still happier then. . . .
That year a cruel famine raged,
            And men were eating men.

2. THE TAO TÊ CHING

"Who know, speak not; who speak, know
           naught"
Are words from Lao Tzŭ's lore.
If Lao Tzŭ knew, why did he speak
    "Five thousand words and more?"*

---

* The number of characters in the *Tao Tê Ching*, from which line 1 is quoted. See Lao Tzŭ, p. 2.

3.

"Elle était du monde où les plus belles choses Ont le pire destin"

'Tis of a gentle maiden I would speak;
Her eyes like willow-leaves, and pink her cheek.
Two years ago, her glass first played its part;
One year ago, she learned the 'broidering art.
Then, at thirteen accomplishments complete,
Ready was she her destiny to meet.
Like flowers her jewelled tresses crowned her head,
A wind-borne fragrance from her person shed;
Her face, her form, alike beyond compare,
Glowing at every turn with radiance rare.
But frosts, that peach and plum untimely blight,
Touched, and she fell, her wedding day in sight.

. . . . . .

Father and mother, lay your grief aside;
She was not fashioned for a mortal's bride—
An angel, banished from her place of birth,
Condemned to spend a few short years on earth.
The loveliest things are of the frailest make;
Like clouds they vanish, and like glass they break.

4. "I CAN'T GET OUT!"

To me, from distant climes, a parrot came;
And as time passed his beak grew all aflame.
I clipped his wings, dreading a homesick
        mood,
And oped the cage but slightly for his food.

We grew to love him for his clever jeers;
But birds have other aims in other spheres;
And without freedom, this poor bird would
        seem,
Like a caged beauty in some rich hareem.

5. "VINA LIQUES"

Come bring me a bumper
                    and fill it up fair,
Ere the flowers have all fallen
                    and the trees are all bare;
Nor imagine that thirty
                    still leaves a long run;
If you live to a hundred,
                    one-third of it's done.

6. TO A LOST CRANE

With snow the inner court was white;
The sea-breeze aided in thy flight.
Hast met some sky-borne pal of thine?—
Away three nights without a sign.

Faint from the clouds thy voice was heard;
Thy shadow in the moonbeams blurred.
My home is bare! Ah, if not thou,
Who'll be the old man's comrade now?

7. SIC VOS NON VOBIS

My taste for the banquet is long ago o'er;
The guitar and the winecup delight me no more;
But my friends and my servants all have a good
                    time. . . .
'Twould appear 'tis for them that to fortune I climb.

8.

I. A BIRTH

At last, at fifty-eight I have a boy;
But sighs are mingled with my notes of joy.
We blame the single pearl the oyster grows;
Yet no one wants a quiverful of crows.

Late autumn sees the cassia's fruitful bough;
Spring winds the purple orchids stir—and now
I raise my glass and breathe my heart's
        desire,—
Oh, be not such a fool as was thy sire!

II. A DEATH

O precious pearl, O much-loved little boy,
Of me, thy graybeard sire, sole hope and joy,
A shade thou art, ere life has yet begun,
And I remain to mourn a hapless son.

My heart is cut in twain, but not with steel;
My eyes are swollen, but not with dust;—I feel
My arms are empty: God has willed it so;
A childless man I linger here below.

9. "MULTA DECEDENTES ADIMUNT"

Alas! I'm sixty-six to-day;
  How short life is doth now appear.
I grieve to see men pass away,
  But joy to think I still am here.

We cannot always boast black heads,
    Nor eyes with fiery youth alive;
Tall trees surround my friends' last beds,*
    My grooms will see my grandsons thrive.

I'm thin, my back with stiffness bound;
    I'm weak, the snows my locks have
        caught;
What cure for growing old is found,
    Save refuge in the Halls of Naught?†

10. "SWEET AUBURN"

Far from the ken of worldly eyes,
Nestling in trees, a village lies.
There, mid the loom's incessant sound,
Oxen and asses tramp around;
Young girls draw water from the rills;
Young men bring fuel from the hills.
Foul litigation never sears
The pure life of these mountaineers;
Their wealth is not by commerce earned;
To war their youths have never turned;
Each works out his appointed task;
Old age is left at home to bask.
In life, mere peasants they remain;
In death, to village dust again.
The youths and elders you may see
Meet in the fields with joyous glee;
One village 'tis, with but two clans;
Enough indeed for marriage banns.
Their forbears boast the selfsame stock;
They roam afield, a single flock.

---

* So long have they been buried.
† In Buddhism.

Fat capons and good wine appear
On festive days throughout the year.
No cruel partings blight their lives;
From neighbours near they seek their
                    wives.
No distance parts them when they die;
Around the hamlet's side they lie;
And thus in life and death at peace,
Their health and spirits never cease;
Old age is theirs; they live to see
Their great great grandson's progeny!

.   .   .   .   .

Born in a cultured family,
An orphan soon, in poverty,
The Right I sought by midnight oil,
With no result save bitter toil.
The world, in name, towards goodness
                    strives,
But what men want is "place" and wives,
Thus forging fetters for their necks,
And ending miserable wrecks.
At ten, the Books I read and learned;
At fifteen, prose and verses turned;
At twenty, baccalaureate;
At thirty, joined the Censorate.
At home, the thrall of wife and child;
At Court, although the Emperor smiled,
The statesman's toil, domestic care,
O'erwhelmed me, more than I could bear.
I think of all my journeys done,
While fifteen years away have run;
Whether by boat I steered my course,
Or ambled on a weary horse.
Hunger was oft my lot by day;
The livelong night I restless lay;

Now east, now west, no stop allowed;
Hither and thither, like a cloud.
Rebellion came, my home was lost;
My relatives, all tempest-tost,
Scattered, some north, some south, were seen,
And the Great River flowed between.
Of some, I never heard again;
Of others, in a year or twain.
From morn to eve I sat in grief;
From eve to morn, still no relief.
Scorched with these fires my heart is dead;
Sorrow has blanched my troubled head;
And now, amid this stress and strife,
My spirit longs for village life.

11. DESERTED

Soaked is her kerchief through with tears,
　　　　　　yet slumber will not come;
In the deep dead of night she hears
　　　　　　the song and beat of drum.*

Alas, although his love has gone,
　　　　　　her beauty lingers yet;
Sadly she sits till early dawn,
　　　　　　but never can forget.

---

* The revels in which she once played the leading part.

YÜAN CHÊN

A.D. 779–831.

[An official who rose through a chequered career to the highest posts of State. His poems were great favourites with the ladies of the Imperial seraglio.]

1. AT AN OLD PALACE

Deserted now the Imperial bowers
Save by some few poor lonely flowers . . .
One white-haired dame,
An Emperor's flame,
Sits down and tells of bygone hours.

2. TAKING ORDERS

Talk not of hills and streams to him
who once has seen the sea;
The clouds that mantle Wu's peak are
the only clouds for me.

Though convent walls must always be
my lot until the end,
And half my heart must be with God,
the rest is with my friend.

LI I

DIED CIRCA A.D. 827.

[An official and poet whose poems were at one time sung all over the empire.]

A CAST-OFF FAVOURITE

The dewdrops gleam on bright spring flowers
    whose scent is borne along;
Beneath the moon the palace rings
    with sounds of lute and song.
It seems that the clepsydra*
    has been filled up with the sea,
To make the long long night appear
    an endless night to me!

SSŬ-K'UNG SHU

9TH CENTURY A.D.

[Poet and official. One of the Ten Men of Genius of his day.]

OH STAY!

We shall meet, I believe you, again;
    Yet to part!—such a beautiful night. . . .
Shall friendship and wine ask in vain
    What a head-wind would take as its right?

---

* Water-clocks were known to the Chinese at a very early date, and are still to be found in China.

CHU CH'ING-YÜ

9TH CENTURY A.D.

[Took the highest degree in 827, but failed as an official and retired.]

IN THE HAREM

It was the time of flowers, the gate was closed;
Within an arbour's shade fair girls reposed.
But though their hearts were full, they nothing said,
Fearing the tell-tale parrot overhead.

KU K'UANG

8TH AND 9TH CENTURIES A.D.

[A distinguished poet of the day, who finally went into retirement as a hermit.]

AT A GRAVE

An old man lays to rest a much-loved son . . .
By day and night his tears of blood will run,
Albeit when threescore years and ten have fled,
'Tis not a long farewell that he has said.*

---

* The authorities of the Infernal Regions were so touched by the above that they allowed his son to be born again into the family.

CHANG CHI

8TH AND 9TH CENTURIES A.D.

[A scholar and poet who rose to be a Secretary in the Board of Works.   He was a
vigorous opponent of Buddhism and Taoism, both of which he held in contempt.]

THE CHASTE WIFE'S REPLY

Knowing, fair sir, my matrimonial thrall,
Two pearls thou sentest me, costly withal.
And I, seeing that Love thy heart possessed,
I wrapped them coldly in my silken vest.

For mine is a household of high degree,
My husband captain in the King's army;
And one with wit like thine should say,
"The troth of wives is for ever and ay."

With thy two pearls I send thee back two years:
Tears——that we did not meet in earlier years!

YANG CHÜ-YÜAN

8TH AND 9TH CENTURIES A.D.

[A poet who took the highest degree about the year 790, and rose to be a Director
of Education in 830.]

1. TASTE

The landscape which the poet loves
            is that of early May,
When budding greenness half concealed
            enwraps each willow spray.
That beautiful embroidery
            the days of summer yield,

Appeals to every bumpkin
        who may take his walks afield.*

2. A GLIMPSE

The buds of the peach were just blossoming out,
And swallows in couples were skimming about,
When a beautiful damsel, of ravishing mien,
Diffusing the odour of spring-time is seen.

She toys with the mirror which lies by her side,
Then blushes to note that the casement is wide;
For she knows that the traveller passing that way
Will joy in the fragrance he carries away.

TU MU

A.D. 803–852.

[A poet and painter.   He took the highest degree in 830 and rose to be a Secretary in the Grand Council.   Often spoken of as the Younger Tu, to distinguish him from Tu Fu.]

1. A LOST LOVE†

Too late, alas!. . . . I came to find
                the lovely spring had fled.
Yet must I not regret the days
                of youth that now are dead;

---

* Set to music by Cyril Scott.

† When ordered to a distant post, he said to his *fiancée*, "Within ten years I shall be Governor.   If I do not return by then, marry whomsoever you please."   He came back after fourteen years to find her married and the mother of three children.

For though the rosy buds of spring
                  the cruel winds have laid,
Behold the clustering fruit that hangs
                  beneath the leafy shade!*

2. THE OLD PLACE

A wilderness alone remains,
                  all garden glories gone;
The river runs unheeded by,
                  weeds grow unheeded on.
Dusk comes, the east wind blows, and birds
                  pipe forth a mournful sound;
Petals, like nymphs from balconies,
                  come tumbling to the ground.

3. THE LAST NIGHT

Old love would seem as though not love to-day;
Spell-bound by thee, my laughter dies away.
The very wax sheds sympathetic tears
And gutters sadly down till dawn appears.

4. LOVERS PARTED

Across the screen the autumn moon
                  stares coldly from the sky;
With silken fan I sit and flick
                  the fireflies sailing by.
The night grows colder every hour,—
                  it chills me to the heart

---

* Set to music by Cyril Scott.

To watch the Spinning Damsel
             from the Herdboy far apart.*

LI SHANG-YIN

A.D. 813–858.

[A scholar and poet who took the highest degree in 837, and rose to be an officer in the Han-lin College.]

1. THE NIGHT COMES

'Tis evening, and in restless vein
At the old mount I slacken rein:
      The glorious day
      Fades fast away
And naught but twilight glooms remain!

2. SOUVENIRS

You ask when I'm coming; alas, not just yet. . . . . .
How the rain filled the pools on that night
         when we met!
Ah, when shall we ever snuff candles again,
And recall the glad hours of that evening of rain?

---

* Referring to the stars α Lyræ and α, β, γ Aquilæ, respectively, which are separated by the Milky Way except on the 7th night of the 7th moon, when magpies form a bridge for the Damsel to pass over to her lover.

SHAO YEH

9TH CENTURY A.D.

[A scholar of whom nothing in particular is recorded, except that the threat by a Magistrate of bambooing caused him to turn his attention to books.]

TIME'S HAVOC

I take a glance, and shake my head;
Another look; my beauty's fled.
My suns and moons like water run;
A moment, and my day is done.

But yesterday my cheeks were red,
And now white locks hang round my head.
Red cheeks, white locks,—see how time flies—
What little space between them lies!

LIU CHIA

9TH CENTURY A.D.

[Of whom I can find no record.]

WITH WINE AND FLOWERS

One day while I tipsily snoozed in my bower,
   The sun disappearing had darkened the land;
My guests had all left me for many an hour;
   The cup and the wine-jar lay strewn on
        the sand. . . .
I could not recall I had picked me a flower,
   Yet I woke up to find I had one in my hand.

LIU SHANG

9TH CENTURY A.D.

[A painter of landscape and portraits who wrote the following lines in despair at the banishment of his master. The latter, in addition to being a very distinguished artist, could paint, as Sir Edwin Landseer after him, two pictures at once with two separate brushes.]

A LAMENT

The lichen grows thick on the stones in the brook,
　　And the breeze stirs the boughs of the pines by the
　　　　shore. . . .
Ah, Chang Tsao alone could interpret this book,
　　But now he is gone and we see him no more.

CHANG YEN

9TH CENTURY A.D.

[A scholar who took the highest degree in the year 872.]

1. A SPRING FEAST

The paddy crops are waxing rich
　　　　　　upon the Goose-Lake hill;
The fowls have just now gone to roost,
　　　　　　the grunting pigs are still;
The mulberry casts a lengthening shade—
　　　　　　the festival is o'er,
And tipsy revellers are helped
　　　　　　each to his cottage door.

2. "FILL THE BUMPER FAIR"

All joys are poor to sober glance,
 True joys to wine belong—
When every step we take is dance,
 And every word is song.

LI SHÊ

9TH CENTURY A.D.

[A poet noted for having fallen into the hands of brigands who were great admirers of his verse, and who bade him at once compose a poem for them.   Hence the lines below, on seeing which the brigands laughed and set him free.]

1. ON HIGHWAYMEN

The rainy mist sweeps gently
     o'er the village by the stream,
When from the leafy forest glades
     the brigand daggers gleam. . . .
And yet there is no need to fear
     or step from out their way,
For more than half the world consists
     of bigger rogues than they!*

2. SPRING PASSES

Waking from mingled dreams and fumes
    of a long-drawn drunken bout,
I heard that spring was dying fast
    and forthwith hied me out.

---

* Set to music by J. A. Carpenter.

I passed the Bamboo Garden
                    where the old priest hailed me stay
And then with "All is vanity"
                    we whiled the hours away.

WANG CHIA

9TH AND 10TH CENTURIES A.D.

[A poet and official who took the highest degree in 890 and rose to be a Secretary in the Board of Rites.   He gave himself the sobriquet of Simplicitarian.]

A STORM

No rain, and lovely flowers bloom around;
Rain falls, and battered petals strew the ground.
The bees and butterflies flit, one and all,
To seek the spring beyond my neighbour's wall.

CHU SHU-CHÊN

9TH CENTURY A.D.

[A poetess, and a descendant of Han Yü. See p. 115.]

1. SUMMER BEGINS

What time the bamboo casts a deeper shade,
When birds fill up the afternoon with song,
When catkins vanish, and when pear-blooms fade,—
Then man is weary and the day is long.

2. "ROUGH WINDS DO SHAKE THE DARLING BUDS OF MAY"

The lattice-like sprays had scarce burst into bloom,
Ere the storm in its envy accomplished their doom. . . .
Ah, would that the Spring-God might evermore reign,
No dotting the sward with these petals again.

CHAO CHIA

9TH CENTURY A.D.

[An official who took the highest degree in 842, and whose poems gained praise from Tu Mu.]

WHERE ARE THEY?

Alone I mount to the kiosque which stands
　　　　on the river-bank, and sigh,
While the moonbeams dance on the tops of the waves
　　　　where the waters touch the sky;
For the lovely scene is to last year's scene
　　　　as like as like can be,
All but the friends, the much-loved friends,
　　　　who gazed at the moon with me.*

---

* Set to music by Cyril Scott.

TAI SHU-LUN

9TH CENTURY A.D.

[Distinguished as a poet and an official.   Under his rule the gaols were empty, as "in Alfred's golden reign."]

NEW YEAR'S EVE AT AN INN

Here in this inn no friend is nigh;
We sit alone, my lamp and I,
    A thousand miles from love and smiles,
To see another year pass by.

Ah me, that ever I was born!
Is life worth living, thus forlorn?
    Youth, beauty, pass; and yet alas
It will be spring tomorrow morn.

HSIEH JUNG

9TH CENTURY A.D.

[No record to be found.]

MUSING

At eve, along the river bank,
    The mist-crowned wavelets lure me on
To think how all antiquity
    Has floated down the stream and gone!

MA TZŬ-JAN

Died a.d. 880.

[A man who possessed a wide knowledge of simples and was in great request as a doctor.   He is said to have been taken up to the Taoist heaven alive.]

UT MELIUS

In youth I went to study Tao*
    at its living fountain-head,
And then lay tipsy half the day
    upon a gilded bed.
"What oaf is this," the Master cried,
    "content with human lot?"
And bade me to the world get back
    and call myself a Sot.
But wherefore seek immortal life
    by means of wondrous pills?
Noise is not in the market-place,†
    nor quiet on the hills.
The secret of perpetual youth
    is already known to me:
Accept with philosophic calm
    whatever fate may be.

---

* Here the Way of Lao Tzŭ.

† "Who carry music in their heart
 Through dusky lane and wrangling mart."—*Keble.*

CH'IN T'AO-YÜ

9TH CENTURY A.D.

[No record that I can find.]

THE SEMPSTRESS

In silk and satin ne'er arrayed,
My fate to be a lone old maid;
No handsome bridegroom comes for me
Dressed in the garb of poverty.
I learned to sew with skill and grace,
Though not to paint my brows and face,
Yet I must ply my golden thread
For other maids about to wed.

TS'UI T'U

9TH CENTURY A.D.

[No record that I can find.]

THE TRAVELLER

The stream glides by, the flower fades,
      and neither feels a sting
That thus they pass and bear away
      the glory of the spring.
I dream myself once more at home,
      a thousand miles away;
The night-jar wakes me with its cry
      ere yet 'tis early day.
Long months have passed and no word comes
      to tell me of my own;

With each New Year my scattered locks
        have white and whiter grown,
Ah, my dear home, if once within
        thy threshold I could be,
The Five Lakes and their lovely scenes
        might all go hang for me.

TU CH'IU-NIANG

9TH CENTURY A.D.

[A poetess, who when fifteen years old became concubine to an official, and afterwards passed into the Palace where she was appointed by the Emperor in 820 to be Instructress to the Heir Apparent. When the Heir Apparent was deposed, she was allowed to return home.]

GOLDEN SANDS

I would not have thee grudge those robes
        which gleam in rich array,
But I would have thee grudge the hours
        of youth which glide away.
Go pluck the blooming flower betimes,
        lest when thou com'st again
Alas, upon the withered stem
        no blooming flowers remain!

LI CH'ANG-FU

9TH CENTURY A.D.

[No record that I can find.]

WANDERJAHRE

Roused from the fumes of wine, I hear the drum,
  Midst thoughts of home, roll from the distant tower,
While through the trees faint streaks of daylight come,
  And the spring passes in a pattering shower.

The tired bird homeward wings its way at last;
  Flowers fade and die beneath wild winds oppressed.
What have my wanderings earned these ten years past? . . . .
  My wayworn horse is sick of east and west.

LI TUAN

9TH CENTURY A.D.

[No record that I can find.]

MUSIC HATH CHARMS

Hark to the rapturous melody!
    Her white arm o'er the lute she flings. . . .
To break her lover's reverie
  She strikes a discord on the strings.

LI CHIA-YU

9TH CENTURY A.D.

[No record that I can find.]

IN RETIREMENT

He envies none, the pure and proud
          ex-Minister of State;
On the Western Lake he shuts himself
          within his bamboo gate.
He needs no fan to cool his brow, for
          the south wind never lulls,
While idly his official hat lies
          staring at the gulls.

LIU FANG-P'ING

9TH CENTURY A.D.

[No record that I can find.]

THE SPINSTER

Dim twilight throws a deeper shade
          across the window-screen;
Alone within a gilded hall
          her tear-drops flow unseen.
No sound the lonely court-yard stirs;
          the spring is all but through;
Around the pear-blooms fade and fall. . . .
          and no one comes to woo.

CHI P'O

9TH CENTURY A.D.

[No record that I can find.]

THOUGHTS BY MOONLIGHT

Bright in the void the mirror moon* appears,
To the hushed music of the heavenly spheres,
Full orbed, while autumn wealth beneath her lies,
On her eternal journey through the skies.
Oh may we ever walk within the light
Nor lose the true path in the eclipse of night!
Oh let us mount where rays of glory beam
And purge our grossness in the Silver Stream!†

HAN WU

9TH CENTURY A.D.

[An official who took the highest degree and served under the Emperor Chao Tsung.   He disappeared from the scene after the *coup d'état* of 904.]

CONTEMPLATION

When my court-yard by the placid moon is lit,
    When around me leaves come dropping
            from the trees,
On the terrace steps, contemplative, I sit,
    The swing-ropes swaying idly in the breeze.

---

* Referring to the polished discs of metal anciently used as mirrors by the Chinese.
† The Milky Way.

ANONYMOUS

9TH CENTURY A.D.

VIEW FROM AN OLD TOWER

The story of a thousand years
    In one brief morning lies unrolled;
Though other voices greet the ears,
    'Tis still the moonlit tower of old.

The heroes of those thousand years?
    Alas! like running water, gone;
Yet still the fever-blast one hears,
    And still the plum-rain patters on.

'Twas here ambition marched sublime—
    An empty fame scarce marks the spot;
Away! . . . . for I will never climb
    To see flowers bloom and man forgot.

LI PIN

9TH CENTURY A.D.

[An official who took the highest degree in 853 and held various posts through very troubled times.]

HOMEWARD

No letters to the frontier come,
    The winter softens into spring. . . . .
I tremble as I draw near home,
    And dare not ask what news you bring.

CH'ÊN T'AO

9TH AND 10TH CENTURIES A.D.

[A poet and astronomer, who lived in retirement on the hills with his wife, also a scholar, and grew oranges for a livelihood.]

AN OATH

They swore the Huns should perish:
   they would die if needs they must. . . .
And now five thousand, sable-clad,
   have bit the Tartar dust.

Along the river-bank their bones
   lie scattered where they may,
But still their forms in dreams arise
   to fair ones far away.

WANG HAN

10TH CENTURY A.D.

[Noted for having taken out his right eye to replace one of his mother's eyes, in both of which she had gone blind.   The operation is said to have been successful.]

A REASON FAIR

'Tis night: the grape-juice mantles high
   in cups of gold galore;
We set to drink,——but now the bugle
   sounds to horse once more.
Oh marvel not if drunken we
   lie strewed about the plain;
How few of all who seek the fight
   shall e'er come back again!

CH'ÊN PO

10TH CENTURY A.D.

[A strange being who, when four or five years old, was suckled by a lady wearing dark clothes, whom he met when playing by the riverside; after which he became extraordinarily enlightened. His enlightenment took the form of devotion to Taoism, research for the elixir of life, for transmutation of metals, etc., but it did not help him to take the highest degree, for which he was a candidate in 932.]

DISILLUSIONED

For ten long years I plodded through
        the vale of lust and strife,
Then through my dreams there flashed a ray
        of the old sweet peaceful life. . . .
No scarlet-tasselled hat of state
        can vie with soft repose;
Grand mansions do not taste the joys
        that the poor man's cabin knows.
I hate the threatening clash of arms
        when fierce retainers throng,
I loathe the drunkard's revels and
        the sound of fife and song;
But I love to seek a quiet nook, and
        some old volume bring
Where I can see the wild flowers bloom
        and hear the birds in spring.

CHANG PI

11TH CENTURY A.D.

[An official who took the highest degree about 1045 and rose to be President of the Board of Punishments.]

TO AN ABSENT FAIR ONE

After parting, dreams possessed me
　　　　and I wandered you know where,
And we sat in the verandah
　　　　and you sang the sweet old air.
Then I woke, with no one near me
　　　　save the moon still shining on,
And lighting up dead petals
　　　　which like you have passed and gone.

YANG I

A.D. 974–1030.

[Author and statesman, who at birth was covered with hair a foot long, which however disappeared within a month.　He took the highest degree, and was employed upon the dynastic annals.　For some years he could not speak; at length, being carried one day to the top of a pagoda, he burst out with the lines given below.]

'TWIXT HEAVEN AND EARTH

Upon this tall pagoda's peak
　　My hands can nigh the stars enclose;
I dare not raise my voice to speak,
　　For fear of startling God's repose.

OU-YANG HSIU

A.D. 1007–1072.

[Historian, statesman, and voluminous writer on many subjects (see p. 156), he came out first at the examination for the highest degree and rose to be President of the Board of War.]

CONSOLATION

The balmy breath of spring must fail
    to reach that distant spot
Where early wild-flowers do not bloom
    to cheer my exile's lot.
See how the oranges still hang
    amid the clinging snow,
And shoots and buds, benumbed by cold,
    around reluctant grow!
At night your heart is with your home
    when you hear the wild goose cry,
And your sadness ever deepens
    as the smiling months go by.
Yet when you think of happy hours
    at Loyang in the past,
Grieve not that spring is late, but joy
    that spring is yours at last.

SHAO YUNG

A.D. 1011–1077.

[One of the most famous of the classical scholars of China, whose tablet stands in
the Confucian Temple.   For many years he denied himself a stove in winter and a fan
in summer, travelling far and wide in China to increase his knowledge by contact with
men of learning.   Always poor, he was made comfortable towards the end of his life
by the generosity of friends.]

1. "THE KINGDOM OF GOD IS WITHIN YOU"

The heavens are still: no sound.
Where then shall God be found?
Search not in distant skies;
In man's own heart He lies.

2. A STRUGGLE

Fair flowers from above in my goblet are shining,
And add by reflection an infinite zest;
Through two generations I've lived, unrepining,
While four mighty rulers have sunk to their rest.
My body in health has done nothing to spite me,
And sweet are the moments which pass o'er my head;
But now, with this wine and these flowers to
            delight me,
How shall I keep sober and get home to bed?

SSŬ-MA KUANG

A.D. 1019–1086.

[A statesman who took the highest degree and rose to be a Minister of State.   He resigned, however, in order to devote himself to his famous work, known as the "Mirror of History," which covered a period from the 5th Century B.C. to the 10th Century A.D.]

WAITING

'Tis the festival of Yellow Plums!
   the rain unceasing pours,
And croaking bullfrogs hoarsely wake
   the echoes out of doors.
I sit and wait for him in vain,
   while midnight hours go by,
And push about the chessmen
   till the lamp-wick sinks to die.

HUANG T'ING-CHIEN

A.D. 1042–1102.

[An official who took the highest degree and rose to be a Grand Secretary.   He is one of the twenty-four examples of Filial Piety and was ranked as one of the Four Great Scholars of the empire.]

ANNUAL WORSHIP AT TOMBS

The peach and plum trees smile with flowers
   this famous day of spring,
And country graveyards round about
   with lamentations ring.
Thunder has startled insect life
   and roused the gnats and bees,
A gentle rain has urged the crops
   and soothed the flowers and trees. . . .

Perhaps on this side lie the bones
        of a wretch whom no one knows;
On that, the sacred ashes
        of a patriot repose.
But who across the centuries
        can hope to mark each spot
Where fool or hero, joined in death,
        beneath the brambles rot?

WANG AN-SHIH

A.D. 1021–1086.

[A famous statesman who introduced a number of reforms into the economic, military, and educational systems of China. The reactionaries were, however, too strong for him, and he lived to see all his policy reversed.]

1. A WHITE NIGHT

The incense-stick is burnt to ash,
        the water-clock is stilled,
The midnight breeze blows sharply by
        and all around is chilled.

Yet I am kept from slumber
        by the beauty of the spring:
Sweet shapes of flowers across the blind
        the quivering moonbeams fling!

2. WHY LATE?

I stayed indeed too long——
        to count the fallen flowers
And search for fragrant blooms——
        I took no note of hours.*

---

* Too late I stayed; forgive the crime,
  Unheeded flew the hours;
How noiseless falls the foot of time
  That only treads on flowers!—*W. R. Spencer.*

CH'ÊNG HAO

A.D. 1032–1085.

[One of two famous brothers, both of whom took the highest degree and whose tablets were admitted in 1241, as representing orthodox scholars, into the Confucian Temple.]

1. INSOUCIANCE

I wander north, I wander south,
                          I rest me where I please. . . .
See how the river-banks are nipped
                          beneath the autumn breeze!
Yet what care I if autumn blasts
                          the river-banks lay bare?
The loss of hue to river-banks
                          is the river-banks' affair.*

2. SPRING FANCIES

When clouds are thin, and the wind is light,
                          about the noontide hour,
I cross the stream, through willow paths
                          with all around in flower.
The world knows not my inmost thoughts
                          which make me seem a fool;
I'm taken for a truant boy
                          escaped from tedious school.

---

* Set to music by Cyril Scott.

KUO HSIANG-CHÊNG

11TH CENTURY A.D.

[A poet whose mother, before his birth, had dreamed of the great Li Po (see p. 328), and of whom, for his poetical skill, he was afterwards declared to be a re-incarnation.]

"SPLENDIDIOR VITRO"

Men come and go, but thou art there;
　Men hurry by, there thou art still;
No fish nor thirsty bird to break
　The image of yon verdant hill.

TS'AI CH'O

11TH CENTURY A.D.

[A statesman who rose to high rank but was banished in 1087. His son, P'i-pa, who accompanied him, and whose name had become familiar to a favourite parrot, soon died; upon which the father seized a pen and wrote the lines given below.]

1. A DEAD BOY

The parrot calls him as of yore,
Though P'i-pa's earthly days are o'er.
Together to this distant shore
We crossed—but shall return no more.

2. MUSIC

Paper screen, bamboo couch, and a stone for my
　　　　pillow;—
　I doze, and the book from my dreamy grasp slips;
Then the note of a fisherman's flute o'er the billow
　Awakes me from sleep with a smile on my lips.

SU SHIH (SU TUNG-P'O)

A.D. 1036–1101.

[Statesman who suffered banishment more than once. In 1057 he took the highest degree, coming out second on the list. As a *littérateur* he is in the very first rank. See p. 168.]

1. SPRING NIGHTS

One half-hour of a night in spring
        is worth a thousand taels,
When the clear sweet scent of flowers is felt
        and the moon her lustre pales;
When mellowed sounds of song and flute
        are borne along the breeze,
And through the stilly scene the swing
        sounds swishing from the trees.

2. WHIGS AND TORIES

Thickly o'er the jasper terrace
        flower-shadows play;
In vain I call my garden boy
        to sweep them all away.
They vanish when the sun sets
        in the west, but very soon
They spring to giddy life again
        beneath the rising moon!*

---

* The "flower-shadows" stand for evil politicians who held their own against the brooms of virtuous statesmen, but disappeared at the death of a misguided Emperor, to re-appear at the death of his successor.

HUNG CHÜEH-FAN

11TH AND 12TH CENTURIES A.D.

[Distinguished as a poet and a calligraphist.   He finally took orders as a Buddhist priest, and produced several well-known works.]

SWINGING*

Two green silk ropes, with painted stand,
        from heights aerial swing,
And there outside the house a maid
        disports herself in spring.
Along the ground her blood-red skirts
        all swiftly swishing fly,
As though to bear her off to be
        an angel in the sky.

Strewed thick with fluttering almond-blooms
        the painted stand is seen;
The embroidered ropes flit to and fro
        amid the willow green.
Then when she stops and out she springs
        to stand with downcast eyes,
You think she *is* some angel
        just now banished from the skies.

---

* Chinese girls swing standing up on the seat.

TAI FU-KU

12TH AND 13TH CENTURIES A.D.

[A poet, without further occupation, who spent twenty years in travelling about
to places of interest.]

SUMMER

When ducklings seek the puddles, mostly dry,
In the hot plum-time, with its changeful sky,
'Tis then in shady arbour we carouse,
And strip the golden loquat from the boughs.

YEH SHIH

A.D. 1150–1223.

[A statesman who came out second on the list for the highest degree, and in 1206
began a series of important military operations against the Golden Tartars.]

AT A PARK GATE

'Tis closed!—lest trampling footsteps mar
    the glory of the green.
Time after time we knock and knock;
    no janitor is seen.
Yet bolts and bars can't quite shut in
    the spring-time's beauteous pall:
A pink-flowered almond-spray peeps out
    athwart the envious wall!

WANG FÊNG-YÜAN

12TH CENTURY A.D.

[No record that I can find.]

THE THIRD MOON

In May flowers fade, and others come
   to bloom among the leaves,
While all day long the nesting swallow
   flits around the eaves.
The night-jar cries half through the night
   until the blood flows fast,
Ah vainly hoping to recall the
   spring that now is past!

LU YU

A.D. 1125–1209.

[A statesman with a varied career, and a skilled *littérateur*. He was employed upon the dynastic history, and his poetry was much admired. He spoke of himself as "Old *Laisser-Aller*."]

TO WINE

Soft as the spring-time, as the autumn sweet,
 One stoup of thee, at night, all joys will yield;
Demons of care fall harmless at my feet,
 Therefore I say, Be thou my spear and shield!

LIU CHI-SUN

CIRCA A.D. 1200.

[A poor scholar, who left behind him at death a library of 30,000 volumes and a collection of many hundred pictures.   This is his only known poem; it was picked up and carried off by a visitor to his mountain refuge, who failed to find him at home.]

A HERMIT

Ye swallows twittering among the beams,
Why thus intrusive break upon my dreams?
Dreams vague with fancies that I cannot plain. . . .
With staff and flask I seek the hills again.

KAO CHÜ-NIEN

12TH CENTURY A.D.

[No record that I can find.]

WORSHIP, AND AFTER*

The northern and the southern hills
        are one large burying-ground,
And all is life and bustle there
        when the sacred day comes round.
Burnt paper *cash*, like butterflies,
        fly fluttering far and wide,
While mourners' robes with tears of blood
        a crimson hue are dyed.
The sun sets, and the red fox crouches
        down beside the tomb;

---

* Referring to the annual spring worship at the tombs of ancestors.

Night comes, and youths and maidens laugh
　　　　where lamps light up the gloom.
Let him, whose fortune brings him wine,
　　　　get tipsy while he may;
For no man, when the long night comes,
　　　　can take one drop away!

YANG CHIEN

12TH AND 13TH CENTURIES A.D.

[A poet and official who gained such a reputation as a Magistrate that the people called him Father Yang.]

TOO LATE AGAIN

This year I swore I would enjoy the sweets of spring enow:
Alas! spring breezes died away ere yet I quite knew how.
'Tis hard to note the beauties of the landscape slipping by,
When sorrow and when fell disease, alternate, dim the eye.

TS'AO PIN

13TH CENTURY A.D.

[A distinguished scholar and statesman, who rose to high office and was known as one of the Four Censors of the Chia Hsi period, A.D. 1237–1241.]

A SPRING EVENING

Now no one takes heed of the flowers that have dropped,
　　And dark is the landscape's predominant note;
The oriole's song in the forest has stopped,
　　And the only sound heard is the frog in the moat.

HSIEH FANG-TÊ

A.D. 1226–1289.

[An official who took the highest degree about 1253.   He got into trouble when holding the post of Examiner by setting an unpopular theme and was degraded.   He then became an itinerant fortune-teller, and finally starved himself to death.]

AT HIS CLUB

Long past midnight the wife hears
                  the goatsucker's cry,
And rises to see that the
                  silkworms are fed;
Alas! there's the moon shining
                  low in the sky,
But her husband has not yet
                  come back to his bed.

YEH LI

A.D. 1241–1292.

[A statesman who played an important part in the later years of transition from Chinese to Mongol rule.]

AT HIS BOOKS

Shadows of pairing sparrows cross his book,
    Of poplar catkins, dropping overhead . . .
The weary student from his window-nook
    Looks up to find that spring has long since fled.

LIU CHI

A.D. 1311–1375.

[A poet and official who helped the first Emperor of the Ming dynasty to expel the Mongols, but later on fell into disfavour and was poisoned.]

1. AT A MOUNTAIN MONASTERY

I mounted when the cock had just begun,
And reached the convent ere the bells were done.
A gentle zephyr whispered o'er the lawn;
Behind the wood the moon gave way to dawn.
And in this pure sweet solitude I lay,
Stretching my limbs out to await the day,
No sound along the willow pathway dim
Save the soft echo of the bonzes' hymn.

2. OMNES EODEM

A centenarian 'mongst men
Is rare; and if one comes, what then?
The mightiest heroes of the past
Upon the hillside sleep at last.

HSIEH CHIN

A.D. 1369–1415.

[A scholar and statesman who was on very intimate terms with the first two Emperors of the Ming dynasty, and under whose presidency the enormous encyclopaedia, mostly destroyed during the Boxer trouble, was ultimately produced. Falling into disfavour, he was thrown into prison and four years later was made drunk and was buried under a heap of snow.

1. AN EMPEROR IN A SNOWSTORM

The snowflakes fall thickly on every side,
   And unstained by the mud they lie lightly about.
God knows that his Majesty's gone for a ride,
   So a carpet of flowers* for his steed is laid out.

2. A SNOW PRIEST

   This priest is not of woman born,
      But straight from heaven descended;
   And back he'll go tomorrow morn,
      When his short stay is ended.

3. APOLOGIA

In vain hands bent on sacrifice
         or clasped in prayer we see;
The ways of God are not exactly
         what those ways should be.
The swindler and the ruffian
         lead pleasant lives enough,
While judgments overtake the good
         and many a sharp rebuff.

---

* "Flowers" takes the place of "flakes" in Chinese.

The swaggering bully stalks along
                as blithely as you please,
While those who never miss their prayers
                are martyrs to disease.
And if great God Almighty fails
                to keep the balance true,
What can we hope that paltry mortal
                magistrates will do?

LIN HUNG-CHUNG

15TH CENTURY A.D.

[A poet who declined office on the ground that he could not leave his aged mother. He was killed by rebels because he refused to kneel to them.]

A MOUNTAIN BROOK

One draught for my poetic soul I take,
Unconscious river, ere thou glid'st away
To serve the orgies of the Western Lake,
And be no more the pure stream of to-day.

CHAO TS'AI-CHI

15TH CENTURY A.D.

[A courtesan-poetess.]

TO HER LOVER

The tide in the river beginning to rise,
Near the sad hour of parting, brings tears to our
     eyes;
Alas that these furlongs of willow-strings gay
Cannot hold fast the boat that will soon be away!

ANONYMOUS

15TH CENTURY A.D.

Do not forget your cotton days
  When robed in cloth of gold;
Among new friends who crowd around,
  Do not forget the old!

A BROKEN TRYST

"Meet me," said I, "at the rise of the moon."
  The moon duly rose, but in vain did I wait;
For I live on the plain, where the moon rises soon,
  And he among hills, where the moon rises late.

SHIH TSUNG (CHU HOU-TSUNG)

A.D. 1507–1566.

[Eleventh Emperor of the Ming dynasty, and a worthless ruler. His north-west frontiers were raided, the Japanese harried the coast provinces, and a Portuguese envoy, who had reached Peking in 1520, was sent back to Canton where he died in prison. Meanwhile, his Majesty was engaged in searching for an elixir of life.]

TO GENERAL MAO*

Southward, in all the panoply
　　　　of cruel war arrayed,
See, Our heroic general points
　　　　and waves his glittering blade!
Across the hills and streams
　　　　the lizard-drums† terrific roll,
While glint of myriad banners
　　　　flashes high from pole to pole. . . .
Go, scion of the Unicorn,
　　　　and prove thy heavenly birth,
And crush to all eternity
　　　　these insects of the earth;
And when thou com'st, a conqueror,
　　　　from those wild barbarian lands,
We will unhitch thy war-cloak
　　　　with Our own Imperial hands!

---

* He crushed a serious revolt in Annam, 1539–1541.
† Covered with lizard-skin.

CHAO LI-HUA

16TH CENTURY A.D.

[A courtesan-poetess.]

TO AN ABSENT LOVER

Your notes on paper rare to see,
Two flying joy-birds bear;
Be like the birds and fly to me,
Not like the paper——rare.*

SSŬ-K'UNG SHAN

(?) 16TH CENTURY A.D.

[The following lines are from the *Chih yüeh lu*, published in A.D. 1602 by Ch'u Ju-chi.]

TO A BUDDHIST PRIEST

Seeing the Way,† a follower I would be;
How can I follow what I do not see?
The Way itself is unsubstantial air;
How can I follow that which is not there?
Those who to walk along the Way aspire,
Are seeking water-bubbles in a fire.
'Tis just like "Punch and Judy"‡ and its fun;
If the strings break, the little play is done.

---

* Chinese note-paper is prettily covered with pictures of various design, mostly symbolical.

† Here, of course, the Buddhist Way, Mârga; not to be confused with the Way (*Tao*) either of Lao Tzŭ or of Confucius.

‡ A favourite diversion of the Chinese for many centuries past.

HSÜ WEI

16TH CENTURY A.D.

[A very brilliant young man who had an unfortunate career.   His patron being thrown into prison, he went mad and attempted to commit suicide, and killed his second wife.   He was distinguished as a calligraphist, a writer of prose and verse, and as an artist.]

ON A WINE-JAR IN AN OLD GRAVE

My thoughts are with the owner, far away,
Who had a goblet, but who could not quaff;
A hare-shaped* piece of common yellow clay,
Sole friend for a millennium and a half.

But here beside him rests a legal deed†
For ground where now in winding-sheet he lies;
'Tis clear that long ere death his soul had freed
He had no lack of fortune's choice supplies——

Vessels of jade, all exquisitely wrought,
And silken robes with these upon a par——
By what spell were his dainty fingers taught
To raise to lips refined this earthen jar?

'Twixt quick and dead a grave-mound—a mere
                    thing;
Yet joy and silence seem so far apart.
A living rat's more worth than a dead king:
A fact we'll all do well to lay to heart.

---

* The hare is an auspicious animal.   There is one in the moon, pounding drugs for the elixir of immortality.

† The amount mentioned is 4,000,000 *cash*, whatever that might mean at such a remote date.

P'U SUNG-LING

Born a.d. 1622.

[A scholar who failed disastrously at the public examinations, but who ultimately produced one of the greatest masterpieces in style to be found in the Chinese language. See p. 235.]

INWARD LIGHT

With wine and flowers we chase the hours,
    In one eternal spring;
No moon, no light, to cheer the night,
    Thyself that ray must bring.

FANG SHU-SHAO

Died a.d. 1642.

[A poet and calligraphist, who led a very harum-scarum life until 1642, when he had "something wrong with his teeth" (probably *pyorrhoea*). He got into his coffin, wrote the valedictory below, and died.]

TO HIS COFFIN

An eternal home awaits me,
    shall I hesitate to go?
Or struggle for a few more hours
    of fleeting life below?
A home, wherein the clash of arms
    I can never hear again!
And shall I strive to linger
    in this thorny world of pain?
The breeze will soon blow cool o'er me,
    and the bright moon shine o'erhead
When blended with the gems of earth
    I lie in my last bed.

My pen and ink shall go with me
            inside my funeral hearse,
So that if I've leisure "over there"
            I may soothe my soul with verse.

ANONYMOUS

18TH CENTURY A.D.

AN AGNOSTIC

You ask me why I greet the priest
        But not his God;
The God sits mute, the man at least
        Returns my nod.

CHANG WÊN-T'AO

18TH CENTURY A.D.

[A poetess who wrote the following lines after reading the work on the duties of women by Pan Chao, the female historian of the 1st Century A.D.]

ADVICE TO GIRLS

Trust not spring clouds, trust not to flowers:
        The butterfly is caught;
Oh snatch no passing joy in hours
        Of pleasure wrongly sought!
A mien severe and eyes that freeze
        Become the future bride;

No whispering underneath the trees
  Ere yet the knot be tied.
'Tis heaven on earth when woman wed
  Leans on her husband's arm;
Beauty, like flowers, is quickly shed:
  Oh envy not its charm!

ANONYMOUS

18TH CENTURY A.D.

INTEGER VITÆ

Riches and rank—a morning dream in spring;
Fame—but an unsubstantial cloud above;
Thy very body is not thine for ay;
  Hate is the end of love.

Fix not a golden collar on thy neck;
Be not with chain of jade in service bound;
Pure heart and few desires: earth's dust shake off—
  And happiness is found.

YÜAN MEI

A.D. 1715–1797.

[Poet, essayist, letter-writer, and for a few years an official.   Among other works, he produced a famous cookery-book, which is as well known in China as *La Physiologie du Goût* in Europe.   See p. 260.]

A SCOFFER

I've ever thought it passing odd
How all men reverence some God,
And wear their lives out for his sake
And bow their heads until they ache.
'Tis clear to me the Gods are made
Of the same stuff as wind or shade. . . .
Ah, if they came to every caller,
I'd be the very loudest bawler!

LU CHU-CH'I

18TH CENTURY A.D.

[A poet who, when found lying drunk in the road, made the following reply to the Prefect; adding that his condition was his own business and not the Prefect's.]

AN IMPROMPTU

Though the torrent be swift, it can ne'er carry off
        the moonbeam that lights up its bed;
Though the mountain be high, yet it cannot arrest
        the fast-flying cloud overhead.

THE EMPEROR CH'IEN LUNG

A.D. 1710–1799.

[One of the two great literary rulers of the Manchu dynasty, for whose achievements, see p. vi. He was an ardent writer of verse, and produced about 34,000 short
poems, after Wordsworth in his lowliest moods. In 1793 he received Lord Macartney.]

1. BEST OF ALL THINGS IS WATER

Searching among the mountain streams,
        against this spring we ran;
Pure as a saint and placid too,
        as any Perfect Man.*
The Hangchow hyson,† world renowned,
        is good as good can be. . . .
We gather pine-sticks for a fire
        and brew a cup of tea.

2. UP NORTH

The season was a month behind
        in this land of northern breeze,
When first I heard the harsh cicadæ
        shrieking through the trees.
I looked but could not mark its form
        amid the foliage fair;
Naught but a flash of shadow which
        went flitting here and there.

---

* The Confucian ideal.

† A kind of green tea. The name is a corruption of two Chinese words meaning
"glorious spring"—the season, not the fountain.

CHAO I

A.D. 1727–1814.

[A poet, historian, and official, who came out first at the examination for the second degree but was placed second by the Emperor in order to encourage candidates from another province. In 1810 he attended his Jubilee (60th year) banquet as graduate.]

THE DIVINEST OF ALL THINGS

Man is indeed of heavenly birth,
Though seeming earthy of the earth;
The sky is but a denser pall
Of the thin air that covers all.
Just as this air, so is that sky;
Why call this low, and call that high?

The dewdrop sparkles in the cup—
Note how the eager flowers spring up;
Confine and crib them in a room,
They fade and find an early doom.
So 'tis that at our very feet
The earth and the empyrean meet.

The babe at birth points heavenward too,
Enveloped by the eternal blue;
As fishes in the water bide,
So heaven surrounds on every side;
Yet men sin on, because they say
Great God in heaven is far away.

FANG WEI-I

19TH CENTURY A.D.

[A young and disconsolate widow who, after the death of her young husband,
shaved her head and became a Buddhist nun.]

PARTINGS

'Tis common talk how partings sadden life:
　　There are no partings for us after death.
But let that pass; I, now no more a wife,
　　Will face Fate's issues to my latest breath.*

The north wind whistles through the mulberry-grove,
　　Daily and nightly making moan for me;
I look up to the shifting sky above,
　　No little prattler smiling on my knee.

Life's sweetest boon is after all to die. . . .
　　My weeping parents still are loth to yield;
Yet east and west the callow fledglings fly,
　　And autumn's herbage wanders far afield.

What will life bring to me an I should stay?
　　What will death bring to me an I should go?
These thoughts surge through me in the light of day,
　　And make me conscious that at last I know.

---

* Rejecting the alternative of suicide, regarded formerly as an honourable exit for
a youthful widow.

CH'IU CHIN

Died a.d. 1907.

[A young married woman who in 1904 left her husband, and after a period of study in Japan, devoted herself to forwarding the revolutionary movement against the Manchu dynasty. She was arrested and executed, leaving behind her a small volume of verse and the honorific title, "Woman-knight of the Mirror Lake."]

ENLIGHTENMENT

When through my casement dawn appears
        And early breezes stroke my cheek,
'Mid endless crowding hopes and fears
        I bow my head, I cannot speak.
I long to mount the wind and fly——
        The far horizon seems too near;
But why seek God in distant sky?
        Knock, and His doors are opened here!

HSIEH WEI-NUNG

Present Day.

[From Nanking, at the close of the T'ai-p'ing rebellion, all the golden glories of the Southern Dynasties—4th, 5th, and 6th Centuries a.d.—had been completely wiped out. When Tsêng Kuo-fan had recovered the city (in 1864), he set to work to replant flowers and trees. Then once more it became possible to pass through a splendour of peach-blossoms, and to enjoy the beauty of the river, with its bevies of pink-cheeked damsels as of old, and the music of flute and guitar. *Reprinted by permission from* The Times *of 4th September, 1918.*]

RETURN OF THE *GENIUS LOCI*

Towards the White Gate I am bent,
Led by love of flowers and scent. . . .
Now I linger at the door
Where we quaffed our wine of yore. . . .

Now I see old scenes arise,
Taking shape before my eyes,
And with brush I limn the blaze
Of gay flowers amid the haze. . . .
Now a friend or two I bring,
And we're off to seek the spring. . . .
Once again I cross the ridge
Of the famous Red Rail bridge;
But alack-a-day, alas!
All the willows which we pass,
Lately set, have sprung to life
Since those days of bloody strife. . . .
Now we haste to get afloat,
Tea and wine aboard the boat. . . .
Then we hear a grumbler say
"But the elves are all away!"
Little knowing spirits all
Are responsive to the call
Of a sympathetic heart,
And incontinently start
And their hidden forms arouse
From the music-making boughs
Where their lurking-place they made
Safe beneath some leaf's sweet shade.

LIU PO-TUAN

PRESENT DAY.

ODE TO SHAKESPEARE

Hearken! low wails through heaven's vault resound,
And angels' tears drip, pearl-like, to the ground*. . . .
That day the influence of spring was stilled,†
And even now by thee mankind is thrilled.‡

Master of language, eager to reform,
Showing the heart surcharged with bitter storm,——
Three hundred years have passed 'twixt then and
        now,
Yet all the world looks to that mountain's brow!

ANONYMOUS

1. OPPORTUNITY

The cup's in the hand,
        seize the hour ere 'tis fled;
How seldom in life
        is the moon overhead!

2. HIGH THINKING

Do not ask upon what
        is the anchorite fed—
A stream past his window,
        a book by his bed.

---

* Supposed to change into pearls or jade as they fall.

† Nature's operations were checked.

‡ This line is not translation; it is a guess at the meaning which is concealed in a charade-like interpretation of a famous inscription on a tombstone.

3. CHANCE

You may set with all care,
        but the flow'ret will fade,
While the chance-planted willow-twig
        grows into shade.

4. DRINKING-SONG

Day by day we grow old
        and have nothing to show;
Year by year we behold
        the new spring coming on;
In the winecup is found
        our chief joy here below;
Why grieve over flowers
        too soon faded and gone?

5. A LAMENT

O ruthless Fate!
  O cruel boon!
To meet so late
  And part so soon.

6. A LULLABY

The poplars are whispering, la-la-la,
And baby must sleep with his ma-ma-ma.
Bye-bye, baby, go sleep I say;
If Bogy comes near us, I'll drive him away.

ENGLISH–CHINESE INDEX OF PROSE AUTHORS

(ALPHABETICALLY ARRANGED)

INDEX TO PROSE SELECTIONS

INDEX TO POETS

CATALOGUE OF DOVER BOOKS

Books Explaining Science and Mathematics

WHAT IS SCIENCE?, N. Campbell. The role of experiment and measurement, the function of mathematics, the nature of scientific laws, the difference between laws and theories, the limitations of science, and many similarly provocative topics are treated clearly and without technicalities by an eminent scientist. "Still an excellent introduction to scientific philosophy," H. Margenau in PHYSICS TODAY. "A first-rate primer . . . deserves a wide audience," SCIENTIFIC AMERICAN. 192pp. 5⅜ x 8.   S43 Paperbound **$1.25**

THE NATURE OF PHYSICAL THEORY, P. W. Bridgman. A Nobel Laureate's clear, non-technical lectures on difficulties and paradoxes connected with frontier research on the physical sciences. Concerned with such central concepts as thought, logic, mathematics, relativity, probability, wave mechanics, etc. he analyzes the contributions of such men as Newton, Einstein, Bohr, Heisenberg, and many others. "Lucid and entertaining . . . recommended to anyone who wants to get some insight into current philosophies of science," THE NEW PHILOSOPHY. Index. xi + 138pp. 5⅜ x 8.   S33 Paperbound **$1.25**

EXPERIMENT AND THEORY IN PHYSICS, Max Born. A Nobel Laureate examines the nature of experiment and theory in theoretical physics and analyzes the advances made by the great physicists of our day: Heisenberg, Einstein, Bohr, Planck, Dirac, and others. The actual process of creation is detailed step-by-step by one who participated. A fine examination of the scientific method at work. 44pp. 5⅜ x 8.   S308 Paperbound **75¢**

THE PSYCHOLOGY OF INVENTION IN THE MATHEMATICAL FIELD, J. Hadamard. The reports of such men as Descartes, Pascal, Einstein, Poincaré, and others are considered in this investigation of the method of idea-creation in mathematics and other sciences and the thinking process in general. How do ideas originate? What is the role of the unconscious? What is Poincaré's forgetting hypothesis? are some of the fascinating questions treated. A penetrating analysis of Einstein's thought processes concludes the book. xiii + 145pp. 5⅜ x 8.   T107 Paperbound **$1.25**

THE NATURE OF LIGHT AND COLOUR IN THE OPEN AIR, M. Minnaert. Why are shadows sometimes blue, sometimes green, or other colors depending on the light and surroundings? What causes mirages? Why do multiple suns and moons appear in the sky? Professor Minnaert explains these unusual phenomena and hundreds of others in simple, easy-to-understand terms based on optical laws and the properties of light and color. No mathematics is required but artists, scientists, students, and everyone fascinated by these "tricks" of nature will find thousands of useful and amazing pieces of information. Hundreds of observational experiments are suggested which require no special equipment. 200 illustrations; 42 photos. xvi + 362pp. 5⅜ x 8.   T196 Paperbound **$2.00**

THE UNIVERSE OF LIGHT, W. Bragg. Sir William Bragg, Nobel Laureate and great modern physicist, is also well known for his powers of clear exposition. Here he analyzes all aspects of light for the layman: lenses, reflection, refraction, the optics of vision, x-rays, the photoelectric effect, etc. He tells you what causes the color of spectra, rainbows, and soap bubbles, how magic mirrors work, and much more. Dozens of simple experiments are described. Preface. Index. 199 line drawings and photographs, including 2 full-page color plates. x + 283pp. 5⅜ x 8.   T538 Paperbound **$1.85**

SOAP-BUBBLES: THEIR COLOURS AND THE FORCES THAT MOULD THEM, C. V. Boys. For continuing popularity and validity as scientific primer, few books can match this volume of easily-followed experiments, explanations. Lucid exposition of complexities of liquid films, surface tension and related phenomena, bubbles' reaction to heat, motion, music, magnetic fields. Experiments with capillary attraction, soap bubbles on frames, composite bubbles, liquid cylinders and jets, bubbles other than soap, etc. Wonderful introduction to scientific method, natural laws that have many ramifications in areas of modern physics. Only complete edition in print. New Introduction by S. Z. Lewin, New York University. 83 illustrations; 1 full-page color plate. xii + 190pp. 5⅜ x 8½.   T542 Paperbound **95¢**

CATALOGUE OF DOVER BOOKS

THE STORY OF X-RAYS FROM RONTGEN TO ISOTOPES, A. R. Bleich, M.D. This book, by a member of the American College of Radiology, gives the scientific explanation of x-rays, their applications in medicine, industry and art, and their danger (and that of atmospheric radiation) to the individual and the species. You learn how radiation therapy is applied against cancer, how x-rays diagnose heart disease and other ailments, how they are used to examine mummies for information on diseases of early societies, and industrial materials for hidden weaknesses. 54 illustrations show x-rays of flowers, bones, stomach, gears with flaws, etc. 1st publication. Index. xix + 186pp. 5⅜ x 8. T622 Paperbound **$1.50**

SPINNING TOPS AND GYROSCOPIC MOTION, John Perry. A classic elementary text of the dynamics of rotation — the behavior and use of rotating bodies such as gyroscopes and tops. In simple, everyday English you are shown how quasi-rigidity is induced in discs of paper, smoke rings, chains, etc., by rapid motions; why a gyrostat falls and why a top rises; precession; how the earth's motion affects climate; and many other phenomena. Appendix on practical use of gyroscopes. 62 figures. 128pp. 5⅜ x 8. T416 Paperbound **$1.25**

SNOW CRYSTALS, W. A. Bentley, M. J. Humphreys. For almost 50 years W. A. Bentley photographed snow flakes in his laboratory in Jericho, Vermont; in 1931 the American Meteorological Society gathered together the best of his work, some 2400 photographs of snow flakes, plus a few ice flowers, windowpane frosts, dew, frozen rain, and other ice formations. Pictures were selected for beauty and scientific value. A very valuable work to anyone in meteorology, cryology; most interesting to layman; extremely useful for artist who wants beautiful, crystalline designs. All copyright free. Unabridged reprint of 1931 edition. 2453 illustrations. 227pp. 8 x 10½. T287 Paperbound **$3.00**

A DOVER SCIENCE SAMPLER, edited by George Barkin. A collection of brief, non-technical passages from 44 Dover Books Explaining Science for the enjoyment of the science-minded browser. Includes work of Bertrand Russell, Poincaré, Laplace, Max Born, Galileo, Newton; material on physics, mathematics, metallurgy, anatomy, astronomy, chemistry, etc. You will be fascinated by Martin Gardner's analysis of the sincere pseudo-scientist, Moritz's account of Newton's absentmindedness, Bernard's examples of human vivisection, etc. Illustrations from the Diderot Pictorial Encyclopedia and De Re Metallica. 64 pages. **FREE**

THE STORY OF ATOMIC THEORY AND ATOMIC ENERGY, J. G. Feinberg. A broader approach to subject of nuclear energy and its cultural implications than any other similar source. Very readable, informal, completely non-technical text. Begins with first atomic theory, 600 B.C. and carries you through the work of Mendelejeff, Röntgen, Madame Curie, to Einstein's equation and the A-bomb. New chapter goes through thermonuclear fission, binding energy, other events up to 1959. Radioactive decay and radiation hazards, future benefits, work of Bohr, moderns, hundreds more topics. "Deserves special mention . . . not only authoritative but thoroughly popular in the best sense of the word," Saturday Review. Formerly, "The Atom Story." Expanded with new chapter. Three appendixes. Index. 34 illustrations. vii + 243pp. 5⅜ x 8. T625 Paperbound **$1.60**

THE STRANGE STORY OF THE QUANTUM, AN ACCOUNT FOR THE GENERAL READER OF THE GROWTH OF IDEAS UNDERLYING OUR PRESENT ATOMIC KNOWLEDGE, B. Hoffmann. Presents lucidly and expertly, with barest amount of mathematics, the problems and theories which led to modern quantum physics. Dr. Hoffmann begins with the closing years of the 19th century, when certain trifling discrepancies were noticed, and with illuminating analogies and examples takes you through the brilliant concepts of Planck, Einstein, Pauli, Broglie, Bohr, Schroedinger, Heisenberg, Dirac, Sommerfeld, Feynman, etc. This edition includes a new, long postscript carrying the story through 1958. "Of the books attempting an account of the history and contents of our modern atomic physics which have come to my attention, this is the best," H. Margenau, Yale University, in "American Journal of Physics." 32 tables and line illustrations. Index. 275pp. 5⅜ x 8. T518 Paperbound **$1.50**

SPACE AND TIME, E. Borel. Written by a versatile mathematician of world renown with his customary lucidity and precision, this introduction to relativity for the layman presents scores of examples, analogies, and illustrations that open up new ways of thinking about space and time. It covers abstract geometry and geographical maps, continuity and topology, the propagation of light, the special theory of relativity, the general theory of relativity, theoretical researches, and much more. Mathematical notes. 2 Indexes. 4 Appendices. 15 figures. xvi + 243pp. 5⅜ x 8. T592 Paperbound **$1.75**

FROM EUCLID TO EDDINGTON: A STUDY OF THE CONCEPTIONS OF THE EXTERNAL WORLD, Sir Edmund Whittaker. A foremost British scientist traces the development of theories of natural philosophy from the western rediscovery of Euclid to Eddington, Einstein, Dirac, etc. The inadequacy of classical physics is contrasted with present day attempts to understand the physical world through relativity, non-Euclidean geometry, space curvature, wave mechanics, etc. 5 major divisions of examination: Space; Time and Movement; the Concepts of Classical Physics; the Concepts of Quantum Mechanics; the Eddington Universe 212pp. 5⅜ x 8. T491 Paperbound **$1.35**

Nature, Biology,

NATURE RECREATION: Group Guidance for the Out-of-doors, William Gould Vinal. Intended for both the uninitiated nature instructor and the education student on the college level, this complete "how-to" program surveys the entire area of nature education for the young. Philosophy of nature recreation; requirements, responsibilities, important information for group leaders; nature games; suggested group projects; conducting meetings and getting discussions started; etc. Scores of immediately applicable teaching aids, plus completely updated sources of information, pamphlets, field guides, recordings, etc. Bibliography. 74 photographs. + 310pp. 5⅜ x 8½.   T1015 Paperbound **$1.75**

HOW TO KNOW THE WILD FLOWERS, Mrs. William Starr Dana. Classic nature book that has introduced thousands to wonders of American wild flowers. Color-season principle of organization is easy to use, even by those with no botanical training, and the genial, refreshing discussions of history, folklore, uses of over 1,000 native and escape flowers, foliage plants are informative as well as fun to read. Over 170 full-page plates, collected from several editions, may be colored in to make permanent records of finds. Revised to conform with 1950 edition of Gray's Manual of Botany. xlii + 438pp. 5⅜ x 8½.   T332 Paperbound **$2.00**

HOW TO KNOW THE FERNS, F. T. Parsons. Ferns, among our most lovely native plants, are all too little known. This classic of nature lore will enable the layman to identify almost any American fern he may come across. After an introduction on the structure and life of ferns, the 57 most important ferns are fully pictured and described (arranged upon a simple identification key). Index of Latin and English names. 61 illustrations and 42 full-page plates. xiv + 215pp. 5⅜ x 8.   T740 Paperbound **$1.35**

MANUAL OF THE TREES OF NORTH AMERICA, Charles Sprague Sargent. Still unsurpassed as most comprehensive, reliable study of North American tree characteristics, precise locations and distribution. By dean of American dendrologists. Every tree native to U.S., Canada, Alaska, 185 genera, 717 species, described in detail—leaves, flowers, fruit, winterbuds, bark, wood, growth habits etc. plus discussion of varieties and local variants, immaturity variations. Over 100 keys, including unusual 11-page analytical key to genera, aid in identification. 783 clear illustrations of flowers, fruit, leaves. An unmatched permanent reference work for all nature lovers. Second enlarged (1926) edition. Synopsis of families. Analytical key to genera. Glossary of technical terms. Index. 783 illustrations, 1 map. Two volumes. Total of 982pp. 5⅜ x 8.   T277 Vol. I Paperbound **$2.25**
                                                       T278 Vol. II Paperbound **$2.25**
                                                                      The set **$4.50**

TREES OF THE EASTERN AND CENTRAL UNITED STATES AND CANADA, W. M. Harlow. A revised edition of a standard middle-level guide to native trees and important escapes. More than 140 trees are described in detail, and illustrated with more than 600 drawings and photographs. Supplementary keys will enable the careful reader to identify almost any tree he might encounter. xiii + 288pp. 5⅜ x 8.   T395 Paperbound **$1.35**

GUIDE TO SOUTHERN TREES, Ellwood S. Harrar and J. George Harrar. All the essential information about trees indigenous to the South, in an extremely handy format. Introductory essay on methods of tree classification and study, nomenclature, chief divisions of Southern trees, etc. Approximately 100 keys and synopses allow for swift, accurate identification of trees. Numerous excellent illustrations, non-technical text make this a useful book for teachers of biology or natural science, nature lovers, amateur naturalists. Revised 1962 edition. Index. Bibliography. Glossary of technical terms. 920 illustrations; 201 full-page plates. ix + 709pp. 4⅝ x 6⅜.   T945 Paperbound **$2.35**

FRUIT KEY AND TWIG KEY TO TREES AND SHRUBS, W. M. Harlow. Bound together in one volume for the first time, these handy and accurate keys to fruit and twig identification are the only guides of their sort with photographs (up to 3 times natural size). "Fruit Key": Key to over 120 different deciduous and evergreen fruits. 139 photographs and 11 line drawings. Synoptic summary of fruit types. Bibliography. 2 Indexes (common and scientific names). "Twig Key": Key to over 160 different twigs and buds. 173 photographs. Glossary of technical terms. Bibliography. 2 Indexes (common and scientific names). Two volumes bound as one. Total of xvii + 126pp. 5⅝ x 8⅜.   T511 Paperbound **$1.25**

INSECT LIFE AND INSECT NATURAL HISTORY, S. W. Frost. A work emphasizing habits, social life, and ecological relations of insects, rather than more academic aspects of classification and morphology. Prof. Frost's enthusiasm and knowledge are everywhere evident as he discusses insect associations and specialized habits like leaf-rolling, leaf-mining, and case-making, the gall insects, the boring insects, aquatic insects, etc. He examines all sorts of matters not usually covered in general works, such as: insects as human food, insect music and musicians, insect response to electric and radio waves, use of insects in art and literature. The admirably executed purpose of this book, which covers the middle ground between elementary treatment and scholarly monographs, is to excite the reader to observe for himself. Over 700 illustrations. Extensive bibliography. x + 524pp. 5⅜ x 8.   T517 Paperbound **$2.50**

COMMON SPIDERS OF THE UNITED STATES, J. H. Emerton. Here is a nature hobby you can pursue right in your own cellar! Only non-technical, but thorough, reliable guide to spiders for the layman. Over 200 spiders from all parts of the country, arranged by scientific classification, are identified by shape and color, number of eyes, habitat and range, habits, etc. Full text, 501 line drawings and photographs, and valuable introduction explain webs, poisons, threads, capturing and preserving spiders, etc. Index. New synoptic key by S. W. Frost. xxiv + 225pp. 5⅜ x 8.   T223 Paperbound **$1.45**

THE LIFE STORY OF THE FISH: HIS MANNERS AND MORALS, Brian Curtis. A comprehensive, non-technical survey of just about everything worth knowing about fish. Written for the aquarist, the angler, and the layman with an inquisitive mind, the text covers such topics as evolution, external covering and protective coloration, physics and physiology of vision, maintenance of equilibrium, function of the lateral line canal for auditory and temperature senses, nervous system, function of the air bladder, reproductive system and methods—courtship, mating, spawning, care of young—and many more. Also sections on game fish, the problems of conservation and a fascinating chapter on fish curiosities. "Clear, simple language . . . excellent judgment in choice of subjects . . . delightful sense of humor," New York Times. Revised (1949) edition. Index. Bibliography of 72 items. 6 full-page photographic plates. xii + 284pp. 5⅜ x 8.   T929 Paperbound **$1.65**

BATS, Glover Morrill Allen. The most comprehensive study of bats as a life-form by the world's foremost authority. A thorough summary of just about everything known about this fascinating and mysterious flying mammal, including its unique location sense, hibernation and cycles, its habitats and distribution, its wing structure and flying habits, and its relationship to man in the long history of folklore and superstition. Written on a middle-level, the book can be profitably studied by a trained zoologist and thoroughly enjoyed by the layman. "An absorbing text with excellent illustrations. Bats should have more friends and fewer thoughtless detractors as a result of the publication of this volume," William Beebe, Books. Extensive bibliography. 57 photographs and illustrations. x + 368pp. 5⅜ x 8½.
T984 Paperbound **$2.00**

BIRDS AND THEIR ATTRIBUTES, Glover Morrill Allen. A fine general introduction to birds as living organisms, especially valuable because of emphasis on structure, physiology, habits, behavior. Discusses relationship of bird to man, early attempts at scientific ornithology, feathers and coloration, skeletal structure including bills, legs and feet, wings. Also food habits, evolution and present distribution, feeding and nest-building, still unsolved questions of migrations and location sense, many more similar topics. Final chapter on classification, nomenclature. A good popular-level summary for the biologist; a first-rate introduction for the layman. Reprint of 1925 edition. References and index. 51 illustrations. viii + 338pp. 5⅜ x 8½.   T957 Paperbound **$1.85**

LIFE HISTORIES OF NORTH AMERICAN BIRDS, Arthur Cleveland Bent. Bent's monumental series of books on North American birds, prepared and published under auspices of Smithsonian Institute, is the definitive coverage of the subject, the most-used single source of information. Now the entire set is to be made available by Dover in inexpensive editions. This encyclopedic collection of detailed, specific observations utilizes reports of hundreds of contemporary observers, writings of such naturalists as Audubon, Burroughs, William Brewster, as well as author's own extensive investigations. Contains literally everything known about life history of each bird considered: nesting, eggs, plumage, distribution and migration, voice, enemies, courtship, etc. These not over-technical works are musts for ornithologists, conservationists, amateur naturalists, anyone seriously interested in American birds.

BIRDS OF PREY. More than 100 subspecies of hawks, falcons, eagles, buzzards, condors and owls, from the common barn owl to the extinct caracara of Guadaloupe Island. 400 photographs. Two volume set. Index for each volume. Bibliographies of 403, 520 items. 197 full-page plates. Total of 907pp. 5⅜ x 8½.   Vol. I T931 Paperbound **$2.50**
                                                 Vol. II T932 Paperbound **$2.50**

WILD FOWL. Ducks, geese, swans, and tree ducks—73 different subspecies. Two volume set. Index for each volume. Bibliographies of 124, 144 items. 106 full-page plates. Total of 685pp. 5⅜ x 8½.   Vol. I T285 Paperbound **$2.50**
                                                 Vol. II T286 Paperbound **$2.50**

SHORE BIRDS. 81 varieties (sandpipers, woodcocks, plovers, snipes, phalaropes, curlews, oyster catchers, etc.). More than 200 photographs of eggs, nesting sites, adult and young of important species. Two volume set. Index for each volume. Bibliographies of 261, 188 items. 121 full-page plates. Total of 860pp. 5⅜ x 8½.   Vol. I T933 Paperbound **$2.35**
                                                 Vol. II T934 Paperbound **$2.35**

THE LIFE OF PASTEUR, R. Vallery-Radot. 13th edition of this definitive biography, cited in Encyclopaedia Britannica. Authoritative, scholarly, well-documented with contemporary quotes, observations; gives complete picture of Pasteur's personal life; especially thorough presentation of scientific activities with silkworms, fermentation, hydrophobia, inoculation, etc. Introduction by Sir William Osler. Index. 505pp. 5⅜ x 8.   T632 Paperbound **$2.00**

Puzzles, Mathematical Recreations

SYMBOLIC LOGIC and THE GAME OF LOGIC, Lewis Carroll. "Symbolic Logic" is not concerned with modern symbolic logic, but is instead a collection of over 380 problems posed with charm and imagination, using the syllogism, and a fascinating diagrammatic method of drawing conclusions. In "The Game of Logic" Carroll's whimsical imagination devises a logical game played with 2 diagrams and counters (included) to manipulate hundreds of tricky syllogisms. The final section, "Hit or Miss" is a lagniappe of 101 additional puzzles in the delightful Carroll manner. Until this reprint edition, both of these books were rarities costing up to $15 each. Symbolic Logic: Index. xxxi + 199pp. The Game of Logic: 96pp. 2 vols. bound as one. 5⅜ x 8.   T492 Paperbound **$1.75**

PILLOW PROBLEMS and A TANGLED TALE, Lewis Carroll. One of the rarest of all Carroll's works, "Pillow Problems" contains 72 original math puzzles, all typically ingenious. Particularly fascinating are Carroll's answers which remain exactly as he thought them out, reflecting his actual mental process. The problems in "A Tangled Tale" are in story form, originally appearing as a monthly magazine serial. Carroll not only gives the solutions, but uses answers sent in by readers to discuss wrong approaches and misleading paths, and grades them for insight. Both of these books were rarities until this edition, "Pillow Problems" costing up to $25, and "A Tangled Tale" $15. Pillow Problems: Preface and Introduction by Lewis Carroll. xx + 109pp. A Tangled Tale: 6 illustrations. 152pp. Two vols. bound as one. 5⅜ x 8.   T493 Paperbound **$1.50**

AMUSEMENTS IN MATHEMATICS, Henry Ernest Dudeney. The foremost British originator of mathematical puzzles is always intriguing, witty, and paradoxical in this classic, one of the largest collections of mathematical amusements. More than 430 puzzles, problems, and paradoxes. Mazes and games, problems on number manipulation, unicursal and other route problems, puzzles on measuring, weighing, packing, age, kinship, chessboards, joiners', crossing river, plane figure dissection, and many others. Solutions. More than 450 illustrations. vii +. 258pp. 5⅜ x 8.   T473 Paperbound **$1.25**

THE CANTERBURY PUZZLES, Henry Dudeney. Chaucer's pilgrims set one another problems in story form. Also Adventures of the Puzzle Club, the Strange Escape of the King's Jester, the Monks of Riddlewell, the Squire's Christmas Puzzle Party, and others. All puzzles are original, based on dissecting plane figures, arithmetic, algebra, elementary calculus and other branches of mathematics, and purely logical ingenuity. "The limit of ingenuity and intricacy," The Observer. Over 110 puzzles. Full Solutions. 150 illustrations. vii + 225pp. 5⅜ x 8.
T474 Paperbound **$1.25**

MATHEMATICAL EXCURSIONS, H. A. Merrill. Even if you hardly remember your high school math, you'll enjoy the 90 stimulating problems contained in this book and you will come to understand a great many mathematical principles with surprisingly little effort. Many useful shortcuts and diversions not generally known are included: division by inspection, Russian peasant multiplication, memory systems for pi, building odd and even magic squares, square roots by geometry, dyadic systems, and many more. Solutions to difficult problems. 50 illustrations. 145pp. 5⅜ x 8.   T350 Paperbound **$1.00**

MAGIC SQUARES AND CUBES, W. S. Andrews. Only book-length treatment in English, a thorough non-technical description and analysis. Here are nasik, overlapping, pandiagonal, serrated squares; magic circles, cubes, spheres, rhombuses. Try your hand at 4-dimensional magical figures! Much unusual folklore and tradition included. High school algebra is sufficient. 754 diagrams and illustrations. viii + 419pp. 5⅜ x 8.   T658 Paperbound **$1.85**

CALIBAN'S PROBLEM BOOK: MATHEMATICAL, INFERENTIAL AND CRYPTOGRAPHIC PUZZLES, H. Phillips (Caliban), S. T. Shovelton, G. S. Marshall. 105 ingenious problems by the greatest living creator of puzzles based on logic and inference. Rigorous, modern, piquant; reflecting their author's unusual personality, these intermediate and advanced puzzles all involve the ability to reason clearly through complex situations; some call for mathematical knowledge, ranging from algebra to number theory. Solutions. xi + 180pp. 5⅜ x 8.
T736 Paperbound **$1.25**

MATHEMATICAL PUZZLES FOR BEGINNERS AND ENTHUSIASTS, G. Mott-Smith. 188 mathematical puzzles based on algebra, dissection of plane figures, permutations, and probability, that will test and improve your powers of inference and interpretation. The Odic Force, The Spider's Cousin, Ellipse Drawing, theory and strategy of card and board games like tit-tat-toe, go moku, salvo, and many others. 100 pages of detailed mathematical explanations. Appendix of primes, square roots, etc. 135 illustrations. 2nd revised edition. 248pp. 5⅜ x 8.
T198 Paperbound **$1.00**

MATHEMAGIC, MAGIC PUZZLES, AND GAMES WITH NUMBERS, R. V. Heath. More than 60 new puzzles and stunts based on the properties of numbers. Easy techniques for multiplying large numbers mentally, revealing hidden numbers magically, finding the date of any day in any year, and dozens more. Over 30 pages devoted to magic squares, triangles, cubes, circles, etc. Edited by J. S. Meyer. 76 illustrations. 128pp. 5⅜ x 8.   T110 Paperbound **$1.00**

THE BOOK OF MODERN PUZZLES, G. L. Kaufman. A completely new series of puzzles as fascinating as crossword and deduction puzzles but based upon different principles and techniques. Simple 2-minute teasers, word labyrinths, design and pattern puzzles, logic and observation puzzles — over 150 braincrackers. Answers to all problems. 116 illustrations. 192pp. 5⅜ x 8.

T143 Paperbound **$1.00**

NEW WORD PUZZLES, G. L. Kaufman. 100 ENTIRELY NEW puzzles based on words and their combinations that will delight crossword puzzle, Scrabble and Jotto fans. Chess words, based on the moves of the chess king; design-onyms, symmetrical designs made of synonyms; rhymed double-crostics; syllable sentences; addle letter anagrams; alphagrams; linkograms; and many others all brand new. Full solutions. Space to work problems. 196 figures. vi + 122pp. 5⅜ x 8.

T344 Paperbound **$1.00**

MAZES AND LABYRINTHS: A BOOK OF PUZZLES, W. Shepherd. Mazes, formerly associated with mystery and ritual, are still among the most intriguing of intellectual puzzles. This is a novel and different collection of 50 amusements that embody the principle of the maze: mazes in the classical tradition; 3-dimensional, ribbon, and Möbius-strip mazes; hidden messages; spatial arrangements; etc.—almost all built on amusing story situations. 84 illustrations. Essay on maze psychology. Solutions. xv + 122pp. 5⅜ x 8.

T731 Paperbound **$1.00**

MAGIC TRICKS & CARD TRICKS, W. Jonson. Two books bound as one. 52 tricks with cards, 37 tricks with coins, bills, eggs, smoke, ribbons, slates, etc. Details on presentation, misdirection, and routining will help you master such famous tricks as the Changing Card, Card in the Pocket, Four Aces, Coin Through the Hand, Bill in the Egg, Afghan Bands, and over 75 others. If you follow the lucid exposition and key diagrams carefully, you will finish these two books with an astonishing mastery of magic. 106 figures. 224pp. 5⅜ x 8. T909 Paperbound **$1.00**

PANORAMA OF MAGIC, Milbourne Christopher. A profusely illustrated history of stage magic, a unique selection of prints and engravings from the author's private collection of magic memorabilia, the largest of its kind. Apparatus, stage settings and costumes; ingenious ads distributed by the performers and satiric broadsides passed around in the streets ridiculing pompous showmen; programs; decorative souvenirs. The lively text, by one of America's foremost professional magicians, is full of anecdotes about almost legendary wizards: Dede, the Egyptian; Philadelphia, the wonder-worker; Robert-Houdin, "the father of modern magic;" Harry Houdini; scores more. Altogether a pleasure package for anyone interested in magic, stage setting and design, ethnology, psychology, or simply in unusual people. A Dover original. 295 illustrations; 8 in full color. Index. viii + 216pp. 8⅜ x 11¼.

T774 Paperbound **$2.25**

HOUDINI ON MAGIC, Harry Houdini. One of the greatest magicians of modern times explains his most prized secrets. How locks are picked, with illustrated picks and skeleton keys; how a girl is sawed into twins; how to walk through a brick wall — Houdini's explanations of 44 stage tricks with many diagrams. Also included is a fascinating discussion of great magicians of the past and the story of his fight against fraudulent mediums and spiritualists. Edited by W.B. Gibson and M.N. Young. Bibliography. 155 figures, photos. xv + 280pp. 5⅜ x 8.

T384 Paperbound **$1.35**

MATHEMATICS, MAGIC AND MYSTERY, Martin Gardner. Why do card tricks work? How do magicians perform astonishing mathematical feats? How is stage mind-reading possible? This is the first book length study explaining the application of probability, set theory, theory of numbers, topology, etc., to achieve many startling tricks. Non-technical, accurate, detailed! 115 sections discuss tricks with cards, dice, coins, knots, geometrical vanishing illusions, how a Curry square "demonstrates" that the sum of the parts may be greater than the whole, and dozens of others. No sleight of hand necessary! 135 illustrations. xii + 174pp. 5⅜ x 8.

T335 Paperbound **$1.00**

EASY-TO-DO ENTERTAINMENTS AND DIVERSIONS WITH COINS, CARDS, STRING, PAPER AND MATCHES, R. M. Abraham. Over 300 tricks, games and puzzles will provide young readers with absorbing fun. Sections on card games; paper-folding; tricks with coins, matches and pieces of string; games for the agile; toy-making from common household objects; mathematical recreations; and 50 miscellaneous pastimes. Anyone in charge of groups of youngsters, including hard-pressed parents, and in need of suggestions on how to keep children sensibly amused and quietly content will find this book indispensable. Clear, simple text, copious number of delightful line drawings and illustrative diagrams. Originally titled "Winter Nights Entertainments." Introduction by Lord Baden Powell. 329 illustrations. v + 186pp. 5⅜ x 8½.

T921 Paperbound **$1.00**

STRING FIGURES AND HOW TO MAKE THEM, Caroline Furness Jayne. 107 string figures plus variations selected from the best primitive and modern examples developed by Navajo, Apache, pygmies of Africa, Eskimo, in Europe, Australia, China, etc. The most readily understandable, easy-to-follow book in English on perennially popular recreation. Crystal-clear exposition; step-by-step diagrams. Everyone from kindergarten children to adults looking for unusual diversion will be endlessly amused. Index. Bibliography. Introduction by A. C. Haddon. 17 full-page plates. 960 illustrations. xxiii + 401pp. 5⅜ x 8½.

T152 Paperbound **$2.00**

Entertainments, Humor

ODDITIES AND CURIOSITIES OF WORDS AND LITERATURE, C. Bombaugh, edited by M. Gardner. The largest collection of idiosyncratic prose and poetry techniques in English, a legendary work in the curious and amusing bypaths of literary recreations and the play technique in literature—so important in modern works. Contains alphabetic poetry, acrostics, palindromes, scissors verse, centos, emblematic poetry, famous literary puns, hoaxes, notorious slips of the press, hilarious mistranslations, and much more. Revised and enlarged with modern material by Martin Gardner. 368pp. 5⅜ x 8. T759 Paperbound **$1.75**

A NONSENSE ANTHOLOGY, collected by Carolyn Wells. 245 of the best nonsense verses ever written, including nonsense puns, absurd arguments, mock epics and sagas, nonsense ballads, odes, "sick" verses, dog-Latin verses, French nonsense verses, songs. By Edward Lear, Lewis Carroll, Gelett Burgess, W. S. Gilbert, Hilaire Belloc, Peter Newell, Oliver Herford, etc., 83 writers in all plus over four score anonymous nonsense verses. A special section of limericks, plus famous nonsense such as Carroll's "Jabberwocky" and Lear's "The Jumblies" and much excellent verse virtually impossible to locate elsewhere. For 50 years considered the best anthology available. Index of first lines specially prepared for this edition. Introduction by Carolyn Wells. 3 indexes: Title, Author, First lines. xxxiii + 279pp. T499 Paperbound **$1.35**

THE BAD CHILD'S BOOK OF BEASTS, MORE BEASTS FOR WORSE CHILDREN, and A MORAL ALPHABET, H. Belloc. Hardly an anthology of humorous verse has appeared in the last 50 years without at least a couple of these famous nonsense verses. But one must see the entire volumes—with all the delightful original illustrations by Sir Basil Blackwood—to appreciate fully Belloc's charming and witty verses that play so subacidly on the platitudes of life and morals that beset his day—and ours. A great humor classic. Three books in one. Total of 157pp. 5⅜ x 8. T749 Paperbound **$1.00**

THE DEVIL'S DICTIONARY, Ambrose Bierce. Sardonic and irreverent barbs puncturing the pomposities and absurdities of American politics, business, religion, literature, and arts, by the country's greatest satirist in the classic tradition. Epigrammatic as Shaw, piercing as Swift, American as Mark Twain, Will Rogers, and Fred Allen, Bierce will always remain the favorite of a small coterie of enthusiasts, and of writers and speakers whom he supplies with "some of the most gorgeous witticisms of the English language" (H. L. Mencken). Over 1000 entries in alphabetical order. 144pp. 5⅜ x 8. T487 Paperbound **$1.00**

THE PURPLE COW AND OTHER NONSENSE, Gelett Burgess. The best of Burgess's early nonsense, selected from the first edition of the "Burgess Nonsense Book." Contains many of his most unusual and truly awe-inspiring pieces: 36 nonsense quatrains, the Poems of Patagonia, Alphabet of Famous Goops, and the other hilarious (and rare) adult nonsense that place him in the forefront of American humorists. All pieces are accompanied by the original Burgess illustrations. 123 illustrations. xiii + 113pp. 5⅜ x 8. T772 Paperbound **$1.00**

MY PIOUS FRIENDS AND DRUNKEN COMPANIONS and MORE PIOUS FRIENDS AND DRUNKEN COMPANIONS, Frank Shay. Folksingers, amateur and professional, and everyone who loves singing: here, available for the first time in 30 years, is this valued collection of 132 ballads, blues, vaudeville numbers, drinking songs, sea chanties, comedy songs. Songs of pre-Beatnik Bohemia; songs from all over America, England, France, Australia; the great songs of the Naughty Nineties and early twentieth-century America. Over a third with music. Woodcuts by John Held, Jr. convey perfectly the brash insouciance of an era of rollicking unabashed song. 12 illustrations by John Held, Jr. Two indexes (Titles and First lines and Choruses). Introductions by the author. Two volumes bound as one. Total of xvi + 235pp. 5⅜ x 8½. T946 Paperbound **$1.25**

HOW TO TELL THE BIRDS FROM THE FLOWERS, R. W. Wood. How not to confuse a carrot with a parrot, a grape with an ape, a puffin with nuffin. Delightful drawings, clever puns, absurd little poems point out far-fetched resemblances in nature. The author was a leading physicist. Introduction by Margaret Wood White. 106 illus. 60pp. 5⅜ x 8. T523 Paperbound **75¢**

PECK'S BAD BOY AND HIS PA, George W. Peck. The complete edition, containing both volumes, of one of the most widely read American humor books. The endless ingenious pranks played by bad boy "Hennery" on his pa and the grocery man, the outraged pomposity of Pa, the perpetual ridiculing of middle class institutions, are as entertaining today as they were in 1883. No pale sophistications or subtleties, but rather humor vigorous, raw, earthy, imaginative, and, as folk humor often is, sadistic. This peculiarly fascinating book is also valuable to historians and students of American culture as a portrait of an age. 100 original illustrations by True Williams. Introduction by E. F. Bleiler. 347pp. 5⅜ x 8. T497 Paperbound **$1.50**

THE HUMOROUS VERSE OF LEWIS CARROLL. Almost every poem Carroll ever wrote, the largest collection ever published, including much never published elsewhere: 150 parodies, burlesques, riddles, ballads, acrostics, etc., with 130 original illustrations by Tenniel, Carroll, and others. "Addicts will be grateful . . . there is nothing for the faithful to do but sit down and fall to the banquet," N. Y. Times. Index to first lines. xiv + 446pp. 5⅜ x 8.
T654 Paperbound **$2.00**

DIVERSIONS AND DIGRESSIONS OF LEWIS CARROLL. A major new treasure for Carroll fans! Rare privately published humor, fantasy, puzzles, and games by Carroll at his whimsical best, with a new vein of frank satire. Includes many new mathematical amusements and recreations, among them the fragmentary Part III of "Curiosa Mathematica." Contains "The Rectory Umbrella," "The New Belfry," "The Vision of the Three T's," and much more. New 32-page supplement of rare photographs taken by Carroll. x + 375pp. 5⅜ x 8.
T732 Paperbound **$2.00**

THE COMPLETE NONSENSE OF EDWARD LEAR. This is the only complete edition of this master of gentle madness available at a popular price. A BOOK OF NONSENSE, NONSENSE SONGS, MORE NONSENSE SONGS AND STORIES in their entirety with all the old favorites that have delighted children and adults for years. The Dong With A Luminous Nose, The Jumblies, The Owl and the Pussycat, and hundreds of other bits of wonderful nonsense. 214 limericks, 3 sets of Nonsense Botany, 5 Nonsense Alphabets, 546 drawings by Lear himself, and much more. 320pp. 5⅜ x 8.
T167 Paperbound **$1.00**

THE MELANCHOLY LUTE, The Humorous Verse of Franklin P. Adams ("FPA"). The author's own selection of light verse, drawn from thirty years of FPA's column, "The Conning Tower," syndicated all over the English-speaking world. Witty, perceptive, literate, these ninety-six poems range from parodies of other poets, Millay, Longfellow, Edgar Guest, Kipling, Masefield, etc., and free and hilarious translations of Horace and other Latin poets, to satiric comments on fabled American institutions—the New York Subways, preposterous ads, suburbanites, sensational journalism, etc. They reveal with vigor and clarity the humor, integrity and restraint of a wise and gentle American satirist. Introduction by Robert Hutchinson. vi + 122pp. 5⅜ x 8½.
T108 Paperbound **$1.00**

SINGULAR TRAVELS, CAMPAIGNS, AND ADVENTURES OF BARON MUNCHAUSEN, R. E. Raspe, with 90 illustrations by Gustave Doré. The first edition in over 150 years to reestablish the deeds of the Prince of Liars exactly as Raspe first recorded them in 1785—the genuine Baron Munchausen, one of the most popular personalities in English literature. Included also are the best of the many sequels, written by other hands. Introduction on Raspe by J. Carswell. Bibliography of early editions. xliv + 192pp. 5⅜ x 8.
T698 Paperbound **$1.00**

THE WIT AND HUMOR OF OSCAR WILDE, ed. by Alvin Redman. Wilde at his most brilliant, in 1000 epigrams exposing weaknesses and hypocrisies of "civilized" society. Divided into 49 categories—sin, wealth, women, America, etc.—to aid writers, speakers. Includes excerpts from his trials, books, plays, criticism. Formerly "The Epigrams of Oscar Wilde." Introduction by Vyvyan Holland, Wilde's only living son. Introductory essay by editor. 260pp. 5⅜ x 8.
T602 Paperbound **$1.00**

MAX AND MORITZ, Wilhelm Busch. Busch is one of the great humorists of all time, as well as the father of the modern comic strip. This volume, translated by H. A. Klein and other hands, contains the perennial favorite "Max and Moritz" (translated by C. T. Brooks), Plisch and Plum, Das Rabennest, Eispeter, and seven other whimsical, sardonic, jovial, diabolical cartoon and verse stories. Lively English translations parallel the original German. This work has delighted millions since it first appeared in the 19th century, and is guaranteed to please almost anyone. Edited by H. A. Klein, with an afterword. x + 205pp. 5⅝ x 8½.
T181 Paperbound **$1.15**

HYPOCRITICAL HELENA, Wilhelm Busch. A companion volume to "Max and Moritz," with the title piece (Die Fromme Helena) and 10 other highly amusing cartoon and verse stories, all newly translated by H. A. Klein and M. C. Klein: Adventure on New Year's Eve (Abenteuer in der Neujahrsnacht), Hangover on the Morning after New Year's Eve (Der Katzenjammer am Neujahrsmorgen), etc. English and German in parallel columns. Hours of pleasure, also a fine language aid. x + 205pp. 5⅝ x 8½.
T184 Paperbound **$1.00**

THE BEAR THAT WASN'T, Frank Tashlin. What does it mean? Is it simply delightful wry humor, or a charming story of a bear who wakes up in the midst of a factory, or a satire on Big Business, or an existential cartoon-story of the human condition, or a symbolization of the struggle between conformity and the individual? New York Herald Tribune said of the first edition: ". . . a fable for grownups that will be fun for children. Sit down with the book and get your own bearings." Long an underground favorite with readers of all ages and opinions. v + 51pp. Illustrated. 5⅜ x 8½.
T939 Paperbound **75¢**

RUTHLESS RHYMES FOR HEARTLESS HOMES and MORE RUTHLESS RHYMES FOR HEARTLESS HOMES, Harry Graham ("Col. D. Streamer"). Two volumes of Little Willy and 48 other poetic disasters. A bright, new reprint of oft-quoted, never forgotten, devastating humor by a precursor of today's "sick" joke school. For connoisseurs of wicked, wacky humor and all who delight in the comedy of manners. Original drawings are a perfect complement. 61 illustrations. Index. vi + 69pp. Two vols. bound as one. 5⅜ x 8½.
T930 Paperbound **75¢**

Say It language phrase books

These handy phrase books (128 to 196 pages each) make grammatical drills unnecessary for an elementary knowledge of a spoken foreign language. Covering most matters of travel and everyday life each volume contains:

Over 1000 phrases and sentences in immediately useful forms — foreign language plus English.

Modern usage designed for Americans. Specific phrases like, "Give me small change," and "Please call a taxi."

Simplified phonetic transcription you will be able to read at sight.

The only completely indexed phrase books on the market.

Covers scores of important situations: — Greetings, restaurants, sightseeing, useful expressions, etc.

These books are prepared by native linguists who are professors at Columbia, N.Y.U., Fordham and other great universities. Use them independently or with any other book or record course. They provide a supplementary living element that most other courses lack. Individual volumes in:

Russian 75¢	Italian 75¢	Spanish 75¢	German 75¢
Hebrew 75¢	Danish 75¢	Japanese 75¢	Swedish 75¢
Dutch 75¢	Esperanto 75¢	Modern Greek 75¢	Portuguese 75¢
Norwegian 75¢	Polish 75¢	French 75¢	Yiddish 75¢
Turkish 75¢		English for German-speaking people 75¢	
English for Italian-speaking people 75¢		English for Spanish-speaking people 75¢	

Large clear type. 128-196 pages each. 3½ x 5¼. Sturdy paper binding.

Listen and Learn language records

LISTEN & LEARN is the only language record course designed especially to meet your travel and everyday needs. It is available in separate sets for FRENCH, SPANISH, GERMAN, JAPANESE, RUSSIAN, MODERN GREEK, PORTUGUESE, ITALIAN and HEBREW, and each set contains three 33⅓ rpm long-playing records—1½ hours of recorded speech by eminent native speakers who are professors at Columbia, New York University, Queens College.

Check the following special features found only in LISTEN & LEARN:

- **Dual-language recording. 812 selected phrases and sentences, over 3200 words,** spoken first in English, then in their foreign language equivalents. A suitable pause follows each foreign phrase, allowing you time to repeat the expression. You learn by unconscious assimilation.

- **128 to 206-page manual** contains everything on the records, plus a simple phonetic pronunciation guide.

- **Indexed for convenience. The only set on the market** that is completely indexed. No more puzzling over where to find the phrase you need. Just look in the rear of the manual.

- **Practical.** No time wasted on material you can find in any grammar. LISTEN & LEARN covers central core material with phrase approach. Ideal for the person with limited learning time.

- **Living, modern expressions,** not found in other courses. Hygienic products, modern equipment, shopping—expressions used every day, like "nylon" and "air-conditioned."

- **Limited objective.** Everything you learn, no matter where you stop, is immediately useful. You have to finish other courses, wade through grammar and vocabulary drill, before they help you.

- **High-fidelity recording.** LISTEN & LEARN records equal in clarity and surface-silence any record on the market costing up to $6.

"Excellent . . . the spoken records . . . impress me as being among the very best on the market," **Prof. Mario Pei,** Dept. of Romance Languages, Columbia University. "Inexpensive and well-done . . . it would make an ideal present," CHICAGO SUNDAY TRIBUNE. "More genuinely helpful than anything of its kind which I have previously encountered," **Sidney Clark,** well-known author of "ALL THE BEST" travel books.

UNCONDITIONAL GUARANTEE. Try LISTEN & LEARN, then return it within 10 days for full refund if you are not satisfied.

Each set contains three twelve-inch 33⅓ records, manual, and album.

SPANISH	the set $5.95	GERMAN	the set $5.95
FRENCH	the set $5.95	ITALIAN	the set $5.95
RUSSIAN	the set $5.95	JAPANESE	the set $6.95
PORTUGUESE	the set $5.95	MODERN GREEK	the set $5.95
MODERN HEBREW	the set $5.95		

Americana

THE EYES OF DISCOVERY, J. Bakeless. A vivid reconstruction of how unspoiled America appeared to the first white men. Authentic and enlightening accounts of Hudson's landing in New York, Coronado's trek through the Southwest; scores of explorers, settlers, trappers, soldiers. America's pristine flora, fauna, and Indians in every region and state in fresh and unusual new aspects. "A fascinating view of what the land was like before the first highway went through," Time. 68 contemporary illustrations, 39 newly added in this edition. Index. Bibliography. x + 500pp. 5⅜ x 8.   T761 Paperbound **$2.25**

AUDUBON AND HIS JOURNALS, J. J. Audubon. A collection of fascinating accounts of Europe and America in the early 1800's through Audubon's own eyes. Includes the Missouri River Journals —an eventful trip through America's untouched heartland, the Labrador Journals, the European Journals, the famous "Episodes", and other rare Audubon material, including the descriptive chapters from the original letterpress edition of the "Ornithological Studies", omitted in all later editions. Indispensable for ornithologists, naturalists, and all lovers of Americana and adventure. 70-page biography by Audubon's granddaughter. 38 illustrations. Total of 1106pp. 5⅜ x 8.   T675 Vol I Paperbound **$2.25**
T676 Vol II Paperbound **$2.25**
The set **$4.50**

TRAVELS OF WILLIAM BARTRAM, edited by Mark Van Doren. The first inexpensive illustrated edition of one of the 18th century's most delightful books is an excellent source of first-hand material on American geography, anthropology, and natural history. Many descriptions of early Indian tribes are our only source of information on them prior to the infiltration of the white man. "The mind of a scientist with the soul of a poet," John Livingston Lowes. 13 original illustrations and maps. Edited with an introduction by Mark Van Doren. 448pp. 5⅜ x 8.
T13 Paperbound **$2.00**

GARRETS AND PRETENDERS: A HISTORY OF BOHEMIANISM IN AMERICA, A. Parry. The colorful and fantastic history of American Bohemianism from Poe to Kerouac. This is the only complete record of hoboes, cranks, starving poets, and suicides. Here are Pfaff, Whitman, Crane, Bierce, Pound, and many others. New chapters by the author and by H. T. Moore bring this thorough and well-documented history down to the Beatniks. "An excellent account," N. Y. Times. Scores of cartoons, drawings, and caricatures. Bibliography. Index. xxviii + 421pp. 5⅝ x 8⅜.   T708 Paperbound **$1.95**

THE EXPLORATION OF THE COLORADO RIVER AND ITS CANYONS, J. W. Powell. The thrilling first-hand account of the expedition that filled in the last white space on the map of the United States. Rapids, famine, hostile Indians, and mutiny are among the perils encountered as the unknown Colorado Valley reveals its secrets. This is the only uncut version of Major Powell's classic of exploration that has been printed in the last 60 years. Includes later reflections and subsequent expedition. 250 illustrations, new map. 400pp. 5⅝ x 8⅜.
T94 Paperbound **$2.25**

THE JOURNAL OF HENRY D. THOREAU, Edited by Bradford Torrey and Francis H. Allen. Henry Thoreau is not only one of the most important figures in American literature and social thought; his voluminous journals (from which his books emerged as selections and crystallizations) constitute both the longest, most sensitive record of personal internal development and a most penetrating description of a historical moment in American culture. This present set, which was first issued in fourteen volumes, contains Thoreau's entire journals from 1837 to 1862, with the exception of the lost years which were found only recently. We are reissuing it, complete and unabridged, with a new introduction by Walter Harding, Secretary of the Thoreau Society. Fourteen volumes reissued in two volumes. Foreword by Henry Seidel Canby. Total of 1888pp. 8⅜ x 12¼.   T312-3 Two volume set, Clothbound **$20.00**

GAMES AND SONGS OF AMERICAN CHILDREN, collected by William Wells Newell. A remarkable collection of 190 games with songs that accompany many of them; cross references to show similarities, differences among them; variations; musical notation for 38 songs. Textual discussions show relations with folk-drama and other aspects of folk tradition. Grouped into categories for ready comparative study: Love-games, histories, playing at work, human life, bird and beast, mythology, guessing-games, etc. New introduction covers relations of songs and dances to timeless heritage of folklore, biographical sketch of Newell, other pertinent data. A good source of inspiration for those in charge of groups of children and a valuable reference for anthropologists, sociologists, psychiatrists. Introduction by Carl Withers. New indexes of first lines, games. 5⅜ x 8½. xii + 242pp.   T354 Paperbound **$1.75**

Art, History of Art, Antiques, Graphic Arts, Handcrafts

ART STUDENTS' ANATOMY, E. J. Farris. Outstanding art anatomy that uses chiefly living objects for its illustrations. 71 photos of undraped men, women, children are accompanied by carefully labeled matching sketches to illustrate the skeletal system, articulations and movements, bony landmarks, the muscular system, skin, fasciae, fat, etc. 9 x-ray photos show movement of joints. Undraped models are shown in such actions as serving in tennis, drawing a bow in archery, playing football, dancing, preparing to spring and to dive. Also discussed and illustrated are proportions, age and sex differences, the anatomy of the smile, etc. 8 plates by the great early 18th century anatomic illustrator Siegfried Albinus are also included. Glossary. 158 figures, 7 in color. x + 159pp. 5⅝ x 8⅜.   T744 Paperbound **$1.50**

AN ATLAS OF ANATOMY FOR ARTISTS, F Schider. A new 3rd edition of this standard text enlarged by 52 new illustrations of hands, anatomical studies by Cloquet, and expressive life studies of the body by Barcsay. 189 clear, detailed plates offer you precise information of impeccable accuracy. 29 plates show all aspects of the skeleton, with closeups of special areas, while 54 full-page plates, mostly in two colors, give human musculature as seen from four different points of view, with cutaways for important portions of the body. 14 full-page plates provide photographs of hand forms, eyelids, female breasts, and indicate the location of muscles upon models. 59 additional plates show how great artists of the past utilized human anatomy. They reproduce sketches and finished work by such artists as Michelangelo, Leonardo da Vinci, Goya, and 15 others. This is a lifetime reference work which will be one of the most important books in any artist's library. "The standard reference tool," AMERICAN LIBRARY ASSOCIATION. "Excellent," AMERICAN ARTIST. Third enlarged edition. 189 plates, 647 illustrations. xxvi + 192pp. 7⅞ x 10⅝.   T241 Clothbound **$6.00**

AN ATLAS OF ANIMAL ANATOMY FOR ARTISTS, W. Ellenberger, H. Baum, H. Dittrich. The largest, richest animal anatomy for artists available in English. 99 detailed anatomical plates of such animals as the horse, dog, cat, lion, deer, seal, kangaroo, flying squirrel, cow, bull, goat, monkey, hare, and bat. Surface features are clearly indicated, while progressive beneath-the-skin pictures show musculature, tendons, and bone structure. Rest and action are exhibited in terms of musculature and skeletal structure and detailed cross-sections are given for heads and important features. The animals chosen are representative of specific families so that a study of these anatomies will provide knowledge of hundreds of related species. "Highly recommended as one of the very few books on the subject worthy of being used as an authoritative guide," DESIGN. "Gives a fundamental knowledge," AMERICAN ARTIST. Second revised, enlarged edition with new plates from Cuvier, Stubbs, etc. 288 illustrations. 153pp. 11⅜ x 9.   T82 Clothbound **$6.00**

THE HUMAN FIGURE IN MOTION, Eadweard Muybridge. The largest selection in print of Muybridge's famous high-speed action photos of the human figure in motion. 4789 photographs illustrate 162 different actions: men, women, children—mostly undraped—are shown walking, running, carrying various objects, sitting, lying down, climbing, throwing, arising, and performing over 150 other actions. Some actions are shown in as many as 150 photographs each. All in all there are more than 500 action strips in this enormous volume, series shots taken at shutter speeds of as high as 1/6000th of a second! These are not posed shots, but true stopped motion. They show bone and muscle in situations that the human eye is not fast enough to capture. Earlier, smaller editions of these prints have brought $40 and more on the out-of-print market. "A must for artists," ART IN FOCUS. "An unparalleled dictionary of action for all artists," AMERICAN ARTIST. 390 full-page plates, with 4789 photographs. Printed on heavy glossy stock. Reinforced binding with headbands. xxi + 390pp. 7⅞ x 10⅝.
T204 Clothbound **$10.00**

ANIMALS IN MOTION, Eadweard Muybridge. This is the largest collection of animal action photos in print. 34 different animals (horses, mules, oxen, goats, camels, pigs, cats, guanacos, lions, gnus, deer, monkeys, eagles—and 21 others) in 132 characteristic actions. The horse alone is shown in more than 40 different actions. All 3919 photographs are taken in series at speeds up to 1/6000th of a second. The secrets of leg motion, spinal patterns, head movements, strains and contortions shown nowhere else are captured. You will see exactly how a lion sets his foot down; how an elephant's knees are like a human's—and how they differ; the position of a kangaroo's legs in mid-leap; how an ostrich's head bobs; details of the flight of birds—and thousands of facets of motion only the fastest cameras can catch. Photographed from domestic animals and animals in the Philadelphia zoo, it contains neither semiposed artificial shots nor distorted telephoto shots taken under adverse conditions. Artists, biologists, decorators, cartoonists, will find this book indispensable for photographing animals in motion. "A really marvelous series of plates," NATURE (London). "The dry plate's most spectacular early use was by Eadweard Muybridge," LIFE. 3919 photographs; 380 full pages of plates. 440pp. Printed on heavy glossy paper. Deluxe binding with headbands. 7⅞ x 10⅝.   T203 Clothbound **$10.00**

CATALOGUE OF DOVER BOOKS

THE AUTOBIOGRAPHY OF AN IDEA, Louis Sullivan. The pioneer architect whom Frank Lloyd Wright called "the master" reveals an acute sensitivity to social forces and values in this passionately honest account. He records the crystallization of his opinions and theories, the growth of his organic theory of architecture that still influences American designers and architects, contemporary ideas, etc. This volume contains the first appearance of 34 full-page plates of his finest architecture. Unabridged reissue of 1924 edition. New introduction by R. M. Line. Index. xiv + 335pp. 5⅜ x 8. T281 Paperbound **$2.00**

THE DRAWINGS OF HEINRICH KLEY. The first uncut republication of both of Kley's devastating sketchbooks, which first appeared in pre-World War I Germany. One of the greatest cartoonists and social satirists of modern times, his exuberant and iconoclastic fantasy and his extraordinary technique place him in the great tradition of Bosch, Breughel, and Goya, while his subject matter has all the immediacy and tension of our century. 200 drawings. viii + 128pp. 7¾ x 10¾. T24 Paperbound **$1.85**

MORE DRAWINGS BY HEINRICH KLEY. All the sketches from Leut' Und Viecher (1912) and Sammel-Album (1923) not included in the previous Dover edition of Drawings. More of the bizarre, mercilessly iconoclastic sketches that shocked and amused on their original publication. Nothing was too sacred, no one too eminent for satirization by this imaginative, individual and accomplished master cartoonist. A total of 158 illustrations. lv + 104pp. 7¾ x 10¾. T41 Paperbound **$1.85**

PINE FURNITURE OF EARLY NEW ENGLAND, R. H. Kettell. A rich understanding of one of America's most original folk arts that collectors of antiques, interior decorators, craftsmen, woodworkers, and everyone interested in American history and art will find fascinating and immensely useful. 413 illustrations of more than 300 chairs, benches, racks, beds, cupboards, mirrors, shelves, tables, and other furniture will show all the simple beauty and character of early New England furniture. 55 detailed drawings carefully analyze outstanding pieces. "With its rich store of illustrations, this book emphasizes the individuality and varied design of early American pine furniture. It should be welcomed," ANTIQUES. 413 illustrations and 55 working drawings. 475. 8 x 10¾. T145 Clothbound **$10.00**

THE HUMAN FIGURE, J. H. Vanderpoel. Every important artistic element of the human figure is pointed out in minutely detailed word descriptions in this classic text and illustrated as well in 430 pencil and charcoal drawings. Thus the text of this book directs your attention to all the characteristic features and subtle differences of the male and female (adults, children, and aged persons), as though a master artist were telling you what to look for at each stage. 2nd edition, revised and enlarged by George Bridgman. Foreword. 430 illustrations. 143pp. 6⅛ x 9¼. T432 Paperbound **$1.50**

LETTERING AND ALPHABETS, J. A. Cavanagh. This unabridged reissue of LETTERING offers a full discussion, analysis, illustration of 89 basic hand lettering styles — styles derived from Caslons, Bodonis, Garamonds, Gothic, Black Letter, Oriental, and many others. Upper and lower cases, numerals and common signs pictured. Hundreds of technical hints on make-up, construction, artistic validity, strokes, pens, brushes, white areas, etc. May be reproduced without permission! 89 complete alphabets; 72 lettered specimens. 121pp. 9⅜ x 8. T53 Paperbound **$1.35**

STICKS AND STONES, Lewis Mumford. A survey of the forces that have conditioned American architecture and altered its forms. The author discusses the medieval tradition in early New England villages; the Renaissance influence which developed with the rise of the merchant class; the classical influence of Jefferson's time; the "Mechanicsvilles" of Poe's generation; the Brown Decades; the philosophy of the Imperial facade; and finally the modern machine age. "A truly remarkable book," SAT. REV. OF LITERATURE. 2nd revised edition. 21 illustrations. xvii + 228pp. 5⅜ x 8. T202 Paperbound **$1.75**

THE STANDARD BOOK OF QUILT MAKING AND COLLECTING, Marguerite Ickis. A complete easy-to-follow guide with all the information you need to make beautiful, useful quilts. How to plan, design, cut, sew, appliqué, avoid sewing problems, use rag bag, make borders, tuft, every other aspect. Over 100 traditional quilts shown, including over 40 full-size patterns. At-home hobby for fun, profit. Index. 483 illus. 1 color plate. 287pp. 6¾ x 9½. T582 Paperbound **$2.00**

THE BOOK OF SIGNS, Rudolf Koch. Formerly $20 to $25 on the out-of-print market, now only $1.00 in this unabridged new edition! 493 symbols from ancient manuscripts, medieval cathedrals, coins, catacombs, pottery, etc. Crosses, monograms of Roman emperors, astrological, chemical, botanical, runes, housemarks, and 7 other categories. Invaluable for handicraft workers, illustrators, scholars, etc., this material may be reproduced without permission. 493 illustrations by Fritz Kredel. 104pp. 6½ x 9¼. T162 Paperbound **$1.00**

PRIMITIVE ART, Franz Boas. This authoritative and exhaustive work by a great American anthropologist covers the entire gamut of primitive art. Pottery, leatherwork, metal work, stone work, wood, basketry, are treated in detail. Theories of primitive art, historical depth in art history, technical virtuosity, unconscious levels of patterning, symbolism, styles, literature, music, dance, etc. A must book for the interested layman, the anthropologist, artist, handicrafter (hundreds of unusual motifs), and the historian. Over 900 illustrations (50 ceramic vessels, 12 totem poles, etc.). 376pp. 5⅜ x 8. T25 Paperbound **$2.25**

Fiction

FLATLAND, E. A. Abbott. A science-fiction classic of life in a 2-dimensional world that is also a first-rate introduction to such aspects of modern science as relativity and hyperspace. Political, moral, satirical, and humorous overtones have made FLATLAND fascinating reading for thousands. 7th edition. New introduction by Banesh Hoffmann. 16 illustrations. 128pp. 5⅜ x 8.   T1 Paperbound **$1.00**

THE WONDERFUL WIZARD OF OZ, L. F. Baum. Only edition in print with all the original W. W. Denslow illustrations in full color—as much a part of "The Wizard" as Tenniel's drawings are of "Alice in Wonderland." "The Wizard" is still America's best-loved fairy tale, in which, as the author expresses it, "The wonderment and joy are retained and the heartaches and nightmares left out." Now today's young readers can enjoy every word and wonderful picture of the original book. New introduction by Martin Gardner. A Baum bibliography. 23 full-page color plates. viii + 268pp. 5⅜ x 8.   T691 Paperbound **$1.50**

THE MARVELOUS LAND OF OZ, L. F. Baum. This is the equally enchanting sequel to the "Wizard," continuing the adventures of the Scarecrow and the Tin Woodman. The hero this time is a little boy named Tip, and all the delightful Oz magic is still present. This is the Oz book with the Animated Saw-Horse, the Woggle-Bug, and Jack Pumpkinhead. All the original John R. Neill illustrations, 10 in full color. 287 pp. 5⅜ x 8.   T692 Paperbound **$1.50**

28 SCIENCE FICTION STORIES OF H. G. WELLS. Two full unabridged novels, MEN LIKE GODS and STAR BEGOTTEN, plus 26 short stories by the master science-fiction writer of all time! Stories of space, time, invention, exploration, future adventure—an indispensable part of the library of everyone interested in science and adventure. PARTIAL CONTENTS: Men Like Gods, The Country of the Blind, In the Abyss, The Crystal Egg, The Man Who Could Work Miracles, A Story of the Days to Come, The Valley of Spiders, and 21 more! 928pp. 5⅜ x 8.
T265 Clothbound **$4.50**

THREE MARTIAN NOVELS, Edgar Rice Burroughs. Contains: Thuvia, Maid of Mars; The Chessmen of Mars; and The Master Mind of Mars. High adventure set in an imaginative and intricate conception of the Red Planet. Mars is peopled with an intelligent, heroic human race which lives in densely populated cities and with fierce barbarians who inhabit dead sea bottoms. Other exciting creatures abound amidst an inventive framework of Martian history and geography. Complete unabridged reprintings of the first edition. 16 illustrations by J. Allen St. John. vi + 499pp. 5⅜ x 8½.   T39 Paperbound **$1.85**

SEVEN SCIENCE FICTION NOVELS, H. G. Wells. Full unabridged texts of 7 science-fiction novels of the master. Ranging from biology, physics, chemistry, astronomy to sociology and other studies, Mr. Wells extrapolates whole worlds of strange and intriguing character. "One will have to go far to match this for entertainment, excitement, and sheer pleasure . . . ," NEW YORK TIMES. Contents: The Time Machine, The Island of Dr. Moreau, First Men in the Moon, The Invisible Man, The War of the Worlds, The Food of the Gods, In the Days of the Comet. 1015pp. 5⅜ x 8.   T264 Clothbound **$4.50**

THE LAND THAT TIME FORGOT and THE MOON MAID, Edgar Rice Burroughs. In the opinion of many, Burroughs' best work. The first concerns a strange island where evolution is individual rather than phylogenetic. Speechless anthropoids develop into intelligent human beings within a single generation. The second projects the reader far into the future and describes the first voyage to the Moon (in the year 2025), the conquest of the Earth by the Moon, and years of violence and adventure as the enslaved Earthmen try to regain possession of their planet. "An imaginative tour de force that keeps the reader keyed up and expectant," NEW YORK TIMES. Complete, unabridged text of the original two novels (three parts in each). 5 illustrations by J. Allen St. John. vi + 552pp. 5⅜ x 8½.
T1020 Clothbound **$3.75**
T358 Paperbound **$2.00**

3 ADVENTURE NOVELS by H. Rider Haggard. Complete texts of "She," "King Solomon's Mines," "Allan Quatermain." Qualities of discovery; desire for immortality; search for primitive, for what is unadorned by civilization, have kept these novels of African adventure exciting, alive to readers from R. L. Stevenson to George Orwell. 636pp. 5⅜ x 8.
T584 Paperbound **$2.00**

A PRINCESS OF MARS and A FIGHTING MAN OF MARS: TWO MARTIAN NOVELS BY EDGAR RICE BURROUGHS. "Princess of Mars" is the very first of the great Martian novels written by Burroughs, and it is probably the best of them all; it set the pattern for all of his later fantasy novels and contains a thrilling cast of strange peoples and creatures and the formula of Olympian heroism amidst ever-fluctuating fortunes which Burroughs carries off so successfully. "Fighting Man" returns to the same scenes and cities—many years later. A mad scientist, a degenerate dictator, and an indomitable defender of the right clash—with the fate of the Red Planet at stake! Complete, unabridged reprinting of original editions. Illustrations by F. E. Schoonover and Hugh Hutton. v + 356pp. 5⅜ x 8½.
T1140 Paperbound **$1.75**

Music

A GENERAL HISTORY OF MUSIC, Charles Burney. A detailed coverage of music from the Greeks up to 1789, with full information on all types of music: sacred and secular, vocal and instrumental, operatic and symphonic. Theory, notation, forms, instruments, innovators, composers, performers, typical and important works, and much more in an easy, entertaining style. Burney covered much of Europe and spoke with hundreds of authorities and composers so that this work is more than a compilation of records . . . it is a living work of careful and first-hand scholarship. Its account of thoroughbass (18th century) Italian music is probably still the best introduction on the subject. A recent NEW YORK TIMES review said, "Surprisingly few of Burney's statements have been invalidated by modern research . . . still of great value." Edited and corrected by Frank Mercer. 35 figures. Indices. 1915pp. 5⅜ x 8. 2 volumes. **T36 The Set, Clothbound $12.50**

A DICTIONARY OF HYMNOLOGY, John Julian. This exhaustive and scholarly work has become known as an invaluable source of hundreds of thousands of important and often difficult to obtain facts on the history and use of hymns in the western world. Everyone interested in hymns will be fascinated by the accounts of famous hymns and hymn writers and amazed by the amount of practical information he will find. More than 30,000 entries on individual hymns, giving authorship, date and circumstances of composition, publication, textual variations, translations, denominational and ritual usage, etc. Biographies of more than 9,000 hymn writers, and essays on important topics such as Christmas carols and children's hymns, and much other unusual and valuable information. A 200 page double-columned index of first lines — the largest in print. Total of 1786 pages in two reinforced clothbound volumes. 6¼ x 9¼. **The set, T333 Clothbound $17.50**

MUSIC IN MEDIEVAL BRITAIN, F. Ll. Harrison. The most thorough, up-to-date, and accurate treatment of the subject ever published, beautifully illustrated. Complete account of institutions and choirs; carols, masses, and motets; liturgy and plainsong; and polyphonic music from the Norman Conquest to the Reformation. Discusses the various schools of music and their reciprocal influences; the origin and development of new ritual forms; development and use of instruments; and new evidence on many problems of the period. Reproductions of scores, over 200 excerpts from medieval melodies. Rules of harmony and dissonance; influence of Continental styles; great composers (Dunstable, Cornysh, Fairfax, etc.); and much more. Register and index of more than 400 musicians. Index of titles. General Index. 225-item bibliography. 6 Appendices. xix + 491pp. 5⅝ x 8¾. **T705 Clothbound $10.00**

THE MUSIC OF SPAIN, Gilbert Chase. Only book in English to give concise, comprehensive account of Iberian music; new Chapter covers music since 1941. Victoria, Albéniz, Cabezón, Pedrell, Turina, hundreds of other composers; popular and folk music; the Gypsies; the guitar; dance, theatre, opera, with only extensive discussion in English of the Zarzuela; virtuosi such as Casals; much more. "Distinguished . . . readable," Saturday Review. 400-item bibliography. Index. 27 photos. 383pp. 5⅜ x 8. **T549 Paperbound $2.25**

ON STUDYING SINGING, Sergius Kagen. An intelligent method of voice-training, which leads you around pitfalls that waste your time, money, and effort. Exposes rigid, mechanical systems, baseless theories, deleterious exercises. "Logical, clear, convincing . . . dead right," Virgil Thomson, N.Y. Herald Tribune. "I recommend this volume highly," Maggie Teyte, Saturday Review. 119pp. 5⅜ x 8. **T622 Paperbound $1.35**

Prices subject to change without notice.

Dover publishes books on art, music, philosophy, literature, languages, history, social sciences, psychology, handcrafts, orientalia, puzzles and entertainments, chess, pets and gardens, books explaining science, intermediate and higher mathematics, mathematical physics, engineering, biological sciences, earth sciences, classics of science, etc. Write to:

Dept. catrr.
Dover Publications, Inc.
180 Varick Street, N.Y. 14, N.Y.